CW01214764

BIAFRA'S WAR 1967-1970

A Tribal Conflict in Nigeria That Left a Million Dead

Books by the same author

Underwater Africa
Under the Indian Ocean
Report on Portugal's War in Guiné-Bissau
Africa at War
The Zambezi Salient
Underwater Seychelles
Coloured: A Profile of Two Million South Africans
Africa Today
South African Handbook for Divers
The Second South African Handbook for Divers
Challenge: South Africa in the African Revolutionary Context
Underwater Mauritius
The Ultimate Handbook on Diving in South Africa
Where to Dive: In Southern Africa and off the Indian Ocean Islands
War in Angola
The Iraqi War Debrief: Why Saddam Hussein was Toppled
Iran's Nuclear Option
War Dog: Fighting Other People's Wars
Allah's Bomb: The Islamic Quest for Nuclear Weapons
Cops: Cheating Death: How One Man Saved the Lives of 3,000 Americans
How South Africa Built Six Atom Bombs
Dive South Africa
African Stories by Al Venter and Friends
Barrel of a Gun: A War Correspondent's Misspent Moments in Combat
War Stories by Al J. Venter and Friends
Gunship Ace – The Wars of Neall Ellis, Helicopter Pilot and Mercenary
Shark Stories by Al J. Venter and Friends
Portugal's Guerrilla Wars in Africa
Shipwreck Stories by Al Venter and Friends
South Africa's Border War (Photographs, with Willem Steenkamp)
The Chopper Boys: Helicopter Warfare in Africa (New, revised and enlarged edition due out in 2016 through Helion & Company Limited)
Battle for Angola (Scheduled for publication through Helion & Company Limited in 2016)

BIAFRA'S WAR 1967-1970

A Tribal Conflict in Nigeria That Left a Million Dead

Al J. Venter

Helion & Company

Helion & Company Limited
26 Willow Road
Solihull
West Midlands
B91 1UE
England
Tel. 0121 705 3393
Fax 0121 711 4075
Email: info@helion.co.uk
Website: www.helion.co.uk
Twitter: @helionbooks
Visit our blog http://blog.helion.co.uk/

Published by Helion & Company 2015
Designed and typeset by Bookcraft Ltd, Stroud, Gloucestershire
Cover designed by Euan Carter, Leicester (www.euancarter.com)
Printed by Gutenberg Press Limited, Tarxien, Malta

Text © Al J. Venter 2015
Photographs © Al J. Venter unless noted otherwise

Front cover photo by Peter Obe; rear cover photo open source.

ISBN 978-1-910294-69-7

British Library Cataloguing-in-Publication Data.
A catalogue record for this book is available from the British Library.

All rights reserved. No part of this publication may be reproduced, stored in a retrieval system, or transmitted, in any form, or by any means, electronic, mechanical, photocopying, recording or otherwise, without the express written consent of Helion & Company Limited.

For details of other military history titles published by Helion & Company Limited contact the above address, or visit our website: http://www.helion.co.uk.

We always welcome receiving book proposals from prospective authors.

For Freddie, with grateful thanks…

Contents

Foreword		viii
Acknowledgements		xiv
1	Lagos and a Nigerian Army Mutiny	19
2	A Day Later: Back in the Firing Line	29
3	Biafra: The Build-up	38
4	Hostilities Take Shape	52
5	Air Attack in Warri Harbour	64
6	The Conflict Escalates	76
7	Frederick Forsyth's Biafra	87
8	A Broader View of Hostilities	96
9	The Conflict That Created *Médecins Sans Frontières*	109
10	Flying Soviet MiG Fighters in the Biafran War	118
11	Biafra's Aerial War of Attrition	134
12	The Rebel State and its Bombers	147
13	Gibson and Son: Into Biafra on Supply Runs	158
14	Nigeria's Enigmatic Leader: General Yakubu Gowon	173
15	How Washington Assessed Nigeria's Civil War	180
16	The Media and Biafra	190
17	A Retrospective Nigerian Military View of the War	204
18	Biafra's Mercenaries: A Diverse Bunch of Professionals	212
19	Colonel Jan Breytenbach Takes On the Biafran War	223
20	Keeping Biafra Alive: From the Air	236
21	A Portuguese Mercenary Aviator tells his Story	247
22	Notes from the Diary of a Mercenary Fighter Pilot in Biafra	255
23	The Air Attacks Continue	265
24	Fault Lines: Nature of the War	274
25	The Next Great African War – Christian against Muslim – and the Role of Boko Haram	286
Bibliography		306
Index		309

Foreword

Every war has its cathartic moments for those involved – and Biafra was no exception. It was also very different from all the other conflicts I've witnessed from up close – sometimes too close, which is why I am almost deaf. In my case, this West African conflict was a life-changing experience that I never quite got over – and for several reasons…

I'd arrived in Lagos only a week or two after the first army mutiny had taken place, when on 14 January 1966 a dissident group of junior officers – mostly of Ibo extraction and led by Major Chukwuma Kaduna Nzeogwu – violently overthrew the Nigerian Government.

Having been recruited as a shipping specialist by the British company John Holt, my job was largely transport-related and I was posted to Lagos' Ikeja Airport – the country's international air transport hub. Only six months later was I to discover that it was at Ikeja where the second army mutiny had started to gel. The only difference this time was that it was mainly soldiers from Nigeria's Islamic north who were in the driving seat. As the phrase suggests, it was 'payback time'.

In the second – retaliatory – coup, the first place targeted was Ikeja Airport, followed by the headquarters of the Nigerian Police, State House, the naval headquarters at Apapa, and the offices of the national radio station. Other government civilian and military agencies and installations were taken over soon afterwards.

My first chapter details that bloody battle on the outskirts of Ikeja Airport – a singular event which set off a chain of more drama that resulted in the civil war. I was on my way to work, and inadvertently I stumbled into the aftermath of that bloody early-morning fire-fight that involved dissident army units and armour. The Battle for Ikeja lasted less than an hour and was the brainchild of Lieutenant-Colonel Murtala Muhammed – after whom the airport was subsequently renamed.

It is worth mentioning that prior to the second army mutiny, my job entailed a considerable amount of travel throughout Nigeria. During the course of these duties, I met a lot of people both in civilian and government roles – including quite a few military types in the various hotels and bars along the way.

In those days, everybody could freely express their opinions; the all-encompassing security apparatus for which Nigeria became notorious in subsequent military governments only came afterwards. British author Frederick Forsyth told me when we got together in Washington 30 years later that he still didn't dare visit the country: 'I'm pretty sure they would kill me if I did,' were his words.

In the early days following the revolution, it didn't take much gumption to appreciate that there were some serious things taking place, both in Lagos and in Northern Nigeria. You could actually sense that another army coup was imminent. I even predicted as much in several magazines for which I was writing at the time – including the now-defunct *News Check*, as well as the mass-circulation *Huisgenoot* (both published in South Africa). It is all on file for those interested in looking back on those almost forgotten chapters of Africa's post-independence history.

I was also doing the odd story for United Press International in London at the time, but their editors scoffed at the premise that more Nigerian violence might follow – so, apparently, did Britain's intelligence agencies. Like Washington, they were (as the saying goes) caught with their pants around their ankles.

FOREWORD ix

Nigeria's first Prime Minister, Alhaji Sir Abubakar Tafawa Balewa, assassinated in Northern Nigeria during the Ibo-led army *coup d'état* in January 1966. (*New Nigerian*, Kano)

When I started reporting these sentiments back to my bosses at John Holt, they were appalled. It took no time at all for the order to come down from the top: 'instead of meddling in political matters, you should concentrate on your work' was the gist of it – but then, when it happened at midnight on 29 July 1966, even the British High Commission in Lagos was found wanting. Effectively, the first shots of the Biafran War had been fired…

Looking back at those events, and my subsequently going into Biafra itself – my first real experience of a war – it might be trite to say that I was severely affected by the plight of thousands of emaciated and starving children encountered at every turn. I was – rather severely so – and I don't believe I ever got over it.

Three decades later, while covering the civil war in Sierra Leone, I spent a bit of time at the Murraytown amputee camp on the outskirts of Freetown and that horrific experience haunted me for months – something I go into in some detail in one of my earlier books about that country's insurrection.[1]

Biafra had the immediate effect of changing my entire approach to what was going on in Africa at the time – South Africa included. I went back to my home in Cape Town and saw it as a challenge to prevent the same kind of thing happening in South Africa. It also meant that I spent the next two years working on what I still regard as one of the most important projects on which I have been involved: the effects of South Africa's apartheid racial laws on the people traditionally referred to as 'coloured'. This society, today about three million strong – perhaps more – did not happen by accident. The majority of mixed blood emanated from three centuries of social intermingling at the southern tip of Africa.

I suppose I could have tackled the apartheid problem in its entirety, but South Africa's so-called 'coloureds' – *Mestiço* or *Mulatto* in Portuguese, or *Kleurlinge* in Afrikaans – were all around me and my family where I lived in Cape Town. The maid who looked after my infant son was 'coloured'; so

---

1 Venter, Al J., *War Dog; Fighting Other People's Wars* (USA and UK: Casemate, 2005).

A Biafran 'parking lot' at Owerri later in the war, with rather futile efforts at trying to screen the vehicles from strafing Soviet- supplied MiG-17s flown by South African and former RAF mercenary pilots. (Author's photo)

A Biafran mortar team. (Author's photo)

A Biafran soldier with one of the metal-improvised Claymore devices which proved extremely effective in ambushes and were dubbed 'Ojukwu Buckets'. (Author's photo)

was the crew that cleared our garbage and the man who helped me at the local filling station – as well as the majority of those folk who served my meals in that city's restaurants (very much as it still is today).

The book *Coloured: A Profile of Two Million South Africans*[2] that came off the presses in 1973 made almost no impact at all – in part because until then, very few South Africans had the temerity to suggest the unthinkable: that their forefathers might have had carnal links with these people. In the eyes of the elders of the Dutch Reformed Church, that was simply impossible – and they said so. I was castigated in Parliament and though I subsequently spent a lot of time with the army and air force in the Border War, I'm aware that they appointed someone quite senior to look into the book in a bid to establish whether or not I was a closet communist. I wasn't, though it didn't help that my mother's dearest friend (with whom she had gone to school in Potchefstroom) was Dolly Sachs – sister of Violet Weinberg, who (with her husband, Eli) served on the Central Committee of the South African Communist Party. Sheila Weinberg, their daughter, went on to play a significant role in Nelson Mandela's African National Congress until her death in November 2004 – as did their nephew, the eminent Dr Albie Sachs.

What I did discover in Biafra was unsettling in the extreme: the majority of kids – by then mostly orphaned – were gathered together in camps by the various aid groups and given whatever

---

2 Venter, Al J., *Coloured: A Profile of Two Million South Africans* (Cape Town: Human and Rousseau, 1973).

assistance was available, but it was clear to just about all of us that the 'Air Bridge' from São Tomé, Fernando Pó, Libreville and elsewhere was simply not bringing in enough food to feed several million people.

Most of the million souls who died in that war either starved to death, or were so debilitated that their frail bodies were unable to counter infection or disease. After the death camps of Hitler's War, it was a severe case of *déjà vu*...

It is also true that conditions in the rebel enclave were exacerbated by the constantly changing fortunes of war: the front line would regularly bulge or contract – sometimes quite dramatically and overnight. With time, areas dominated by Colonel Chukwuemeka Odumegwu Ojukwu's rebel command steadily diminished until all the big towns were lost; then it was only a matter of time…

I stayed on until the last few weeks and by then, it was pretty obvious to us all that when it came, the collapse would be quick. It was – and Ojukwu got out on the second-to-last flight. Forsyth also cut it fine, because when I departed, he had been hospitalised with malaria. I'd intended to bid my farewells, but travelling on the roads by then – with the skies dominated by Nigerian fighter aircraft that regarded anything that moved on the roads as fair game – I accepted the offer of a flight to Libreville. That meant I didn't dither when I was told to get myself to Uli Airport as soon as possible.

At that stage, if you had a seat, you took it because the planes were on the ground for perhaps 30 minutes before they took off again; the air crews did not wait on the ground to be bombed by the Nigerian Air Force's foreign-crewed DC-3 'Marauder' – all of which begs the question: why tackle a project as painful and as controversial as the Biafran War, long forgotten by all but a tiny minority of people?

Some may recall many of the dramatic images from local broadcasts and from extremely unsettling news reports – quite a few of which made headlines in newspapers not toeing the emphatic line of Mr Wilson's government. His spokespeople regularly made utterances about casualties: that they were hugely exaggerated and that there were very few people (and almost no children) dying as a consequence of hostilities. Clearly, none of them had been anywhere near *Kilometre Onze* in Gabon – the camp for starving Biafran children run by Caritas.

There is another, more pertinent, reason for this book: during the many years that I wrote for what was then Jane's Information Group in Coulsdon, Surrey I kept my finger firmly on Africa's pulse. I covered many of the conflicts that subsequently emerged, but one issue kept on cropping up: ongoing violence between Christian and Muslim people in Nigeria. Although fairly low-key today (following the entrance of Boko Haram, which tends to focus all attention on insurrection in the Islamic north), conflict between southern Christians and folk of Islamic persuasion in the north of that country was an almost weekly event. Muslim militants would attack Christian churches one weekend, and a week later, Christian militants would retaliate in force. It was an agonisingly brutal business in which tens of thousands of people have died over many years – and it started even before the Biafran War ended.

Western newspapers and reports rarely make mention of this violence – even though it continues unabated. It got so bad at one stage that before he died in 2011 the former Biafran military leader Colonel Ojukwu – having returned from exile – warned in a radio broadcast that if the bloodletting continued (and seemingly with tacit government support from Abuja),[3] serious consideration would have to be given to his people taking up arms again 'if only to protect us from this savagery'.

---

3   After the Biafran War, the capital of Nigeria was relocated from Lagos to Abuja.

Biafran troops preparing local versions of a primitive, locally-built version of a Claymore mine that proved enormously successful in the war – particularly when deployed in convoy ambushes in the jungle. They were rather appropriately called 'Ojukwu Buckets'. (Author's photo)

The possibility of another full-scale war between Nigeria's Christian (and animist) south and the Islamic north is a reality of which the international community needs to take cognisance. There have already been several religious-based conflicts in Africa in recent years – almost all of them pitting followers of the Koran against those who believe in the Bible. These include civil wars in the Ivory Coast; the recent violence in the Central African Republic; ongoing struggles in the Sudan; and, more recently, a familiar pattern of similar developments in Kenya. For this reason, I end this book with a chapter entitled: 'The Next Great African War – Christian against Muslim – and the Role of Boko Haram'.

This is no idle conjecture; Nigeria sits on enormous deposits of oil. Because of developments east of Suez, the United States today buys much more of its fuel supplies from countries like Nigeria, Angola, the Cameroons, Equatorial Guinea and others than it did in the past. Nigeria supplies America with about 20 percent of its raw crude. If these supplies are threatened – as they have been vocally and consistently by Al-Qaeda and its Boko Haram and AQIM[4] offshoots – both the United States, as well as its European allies, are not going to sit on their thumbs. Over decades, these nations have invested billions into the African oil industry – and they will almost certainly react with force.

That is only one aspect of an equation that, sadly, holds innumerable imponderables – including the possibility that Africa might became a huge ideological battlefront that will almost certainly involve western forces fighting in another foreign war.

The French Army and Air Force are already doing exactly that in Africa's Sahel – that giant region half the size of Western Europe that fringes the Sahara Desert and includes several countries. Among them are Mali, Chad and the Niger Republic – as well as Burkina Faso.

---

4   AQIM: Al-Qaeda in the Islamic Maghreb.

Acknowledgements

I dedicate this book to Frederick Forsyth because he has been of enormous assistance to me over quite a few years – not only in providing background to the time he spent covering the war in Biafra, but also helping me relocate to the UK from the United States. As the Americans would say, Freddie has been a good buddy.

I also have 20-something pages of interviews that I had with him and from which I quote. All were done when we spent a bit of time together at my house at the mouth of the Columbia River in Washington State. He'd asked me to arrange meetings for him with the local wildlife people for a novel on which he was working at the time. That was *The Afghan* and everything seems to have worked out well.

Another good friend is Akhil Kadidal – these days in a senior editorial position on one of India's major newspapers. Though his colleagues might not be aware of it, Akhil wears several hats: he is a talented artist and has written quite a few historical books – including the one on which he is currently working – dealing with the air war over Malta during World War II. Some of Akhil's sketches of RAF fighters being prepared for sorties against the *Luftwaffe* and still more of Malta itself – in wartime – are splendid. His classic, full-colour illustration of Uli Airstrip is certainly among the best to emerge from that African conflict.

Ares Klootwyk – another old pal from Constantia – flew Nigerian Air Force Soviet MiG-17s against the rebel colony for a year and he provided quite a few photos to be seen between these covers. He couldn't really refuse because I suspect I came into his sights a couple of times while moving about the rebel enclave; Nigerian MiGs hit everything on the ground that moved.

Trained on Harvard T-6s and Vampire jets in the SAAF, Ares went on to join the RAF as a flying officer, where he earned a magnificent £90 a month. During this time, he was posted operational in the Gulf (including Oman, during the troubles there) and then Aden before returning to the UK to fly helicopters. Not long thereafter – having been offered a job as a mercenary pilot in the Congo, where he flew combat for three years – he resigned his commission. I suspect there is a book in there somewhere…

Another stalwart who gave solid support was the illustrious Jan Breytenbach, who served briefly in Biafra (unofficially, of course, because he was still a serving member of the South African Army). I visited Jan and his lovely wife, Rosalind, at their home at Sedgefield near Knysna and he gave me as much as he could on his Biafran exploits (it appears in Chapter 19).

Paul Els, too, was a member of the South African Special Forces group involved in the South African military contingent that operated in Biafra. It was Paul's job to set up a forward communications centre in one of Libreville's more affluent suburbs.

Tom Cooper – the Austrian artist and author – deserves special mention. Several illustrations used in this book are his – and there would be more but for space limitations. British aviation enthusiast Michael Robson also helped with photos of the struggle.

I originally communicated with Ian Draper more than a decade ago when he first published his seminal volume on Biafra's air war – titled *Shadows: Airlift and Airwar in Biafra and Nigeria 1967-1970*. This is arguably one of the best books to emerge from that conflict – and more is the pity that it's out of print. Interestingly, Frederick Forsyth wrote the Foreword – underscoring its unique approach to the subject, which could be one of the reasons why (the last time I looked) a copy was selling on www.amazon.com for £500.

ACKNOWLEDGEMENTS

While living in Nigeria, I spent a lot of time with two of my John Holt colleagues: Tony Cusack and Ian Hunter. They feature briefly – as does (proudly) Ibo Silas Anusiam, who accompanied me on some of my trips around this vast country; then slipping irrevocably into one of the most horrific civil wars the African continent has experienced in the past century.

On the civilian airlift of supplies into the enclave, Mike Gibson came to the fore – though he was only 21 the first time he served as co-pilot to his father, John, on board a DC-6 freighter. Their plane came within a whisker of being downed, which was when Mike's mother determined that from then on, father and son would not fly into Biafra on the same plane. Some of the pictures in his chapter came from him.

I must also acknowledge using excerpts from Gunnar Haglund's experiences as a Minicon pilot in Biafra (Chapters 11 and 22). This was originally published in Swedish under the title *Gerillapilot i Biafra* (*Guerrilla Pilot in Biafra*) by the Stockholm publishing house Bokus AB. Leif Hellström, one of my old compadres and a leading aviation authority in Scandinavia, translated the book into English. Sadly, it was never published. Thanks go to Mattias Stenbom of Allt om Hobby for permission to use these excerpts.

Laura Atkins, who handles Permissions at *The Spectator* in London, was kind enough to allow me to use some of Auberon's Waugh's insightful material on his own experiences inside the rebel territory. It was published under the heading 'Hail Biafra' on 1 August 1968. Auberon was actually the last person you would have expected to have become a war correspondent, but his observations were incisive and quite moving.

No history of this war would be complete without at least one photo from that great Italian lensman, Romano Cagnoni. My caravan was parked adjacent to his in the jungle – and he must have been blessed, because we were never hit by enemy jets. Thanks must also go to Romano for keeping me alive, because I took no food with me when I went in, and he came up trumps with a meal on several occasions. Don McCullin very briefly features in these pages, and though our paths didn't cross while there, his reputation as one of the best combat photographers in the business had already preceded him.

Other photographers who I'd like to acknowledge include Leif Hellström, Philip Effiong Jnr, 'Monster' Wilkins and Steve Darke (of Air-Britain Photographic Images Collection) – as well as material from the *New Nigerian* newspaper, for whom I was stringing while I worked in Lagos. There are also photos from Peter Williams and Björn Larsson-Ask.

If I left anybody out, my sincerest apologies; memory does tend to play tricks after almost half a century.

On books about this war, there are many: Frederick Forsyth's *The Biafra Story: The Making of an African Legend* leads the pack, followed by John de St Jorre's *The Brothers War* (though he was accused by some of his colleagues of playing down the number of people who died during the course of the war).

There is also the outstanding *Half of a Yellow Sun* by the young Nigerian author Chimamanda Ngozi Adichie, who captures the atmosphere of this terrible bloodletting like few other contemporary writers. The Nigerian director Biyi Bandele has since produced a film under the same title.

From the perspective of a Biafran survivor, anybody interested should read Chinua Achebe's *There was a Country*, which looks back on his very personal experiences in Nigeria. Nobel Prize winner Nadine Gordimer tells us the book 'is a meditation on the condition of freedom'.

She goes on: 'It has the tense narrative grip of the best fiction. It is also a revelatory entry into the intimate character of the writer's brilliant mind and bold spirit'. That said, it would be well worth the effort to get hold of a copy of Achebe's earlier work, *Biafra: The Darkness in Africa*. Being Biafran, he may be damned by some for being partisan, but he certainly elucidates like few others are able to…

From a military point of view, *The Caged Bird Sang No More: My Biafra Odyssey, 1966-1970* by Major-General Philip Effiong is hugely instructive. I got to know him briefly while I was there and he always struck me as somebody who knew exactly what he wanted, though sadly deprived of all because of circumstances. Notably, he served with the British Army on the Rhine, and thereafter, on a peacekeeping mission in the Congo – all of which he put to good use in the Biafran War.

Look also at *War Stories: A Memoir of Nigeria and Biafra* by John Sherman – a former American Peace Corps volunteer who served with a food/medical team operated by the International Committee of the Red Cross during the civil war.

Another interesting work came from a book by Portuguese mercenary Artur Alves. Titled *My Escapades as a Biafran Wartime Pilot*, he was subsequently interviewed by Kenechukwu Okeke – an enterprising Nigerian journalist with the Lagos *Sunday Sun* – whom I quote.

From the start of this war, Washington kept close tabs on these African developments – especially since it was already clear that even if the war were to end sooner, there was bitter animosity between Christian and Muslim Nigerians. Those powerful sentiments are still integral to what is going on in West Africa today – and I deal with those issues in the last chapter.

In 1992 – almost a quarter-century after the Biafran conflict ended – Major Abubakar A. Atofarati, a Northern Nigerian officer attending the United States Marines Command and Staff College, wrote a thesis titled 'The Nigerian Civil War, Causes, Strategies and Lessons Learnt'. It appears *in toto*, as Chapter 17.

I also have to give thanks to Obi Nwakanma, who published his thoughts about Colonel Ojukwu in Nigeria's *Vanguard* magazine in 2003 – and for those looking for the nitty-gritty about Biafra's unconventional and highly irregular system of air support (it went on for almost three years), there is David L. Koren's *Far Away in the Sky: A Memoir of the Biafran Airlift*. As www.amazon.com declares: 'Some were paid. Some felt compelled by a duty to God. Some volunteered. Some died doing it. All flew on rickety old aircraft into a nighttime [*sic*], wartime patch of African forest called Biafra…'

Read it, because this book is outstanding and gives a very good idea of what the airlift was all about.

Others involved on the periphery were Bruce Gonneau, who handled many of the photos that he keeps on file for me, as well as Neall Ellis, for giving me a solid insight into the Nigerian fighting man. 'Nellis' was able to view the average Nigerian soldier from up close while he flew helicopter gunships in the civil war in Sierra Leone – the subject of *Gunship Ace: The Wars of Neall Ellis, Helicopter Pilot and Mercenary* (one of my earlier books). I quote him in some detail in the final chapter.

Finally, there is the production team at Helion & Company Limited, who brought this work to fruition. Headed by Duncan Rogers, he is not only an outstanding literary judge, but with time, has become a good friend. When I first mentioned Biafra as the possibility of a book, he prevaricated for about a minute-and-a-half before deciding that this was something he wanted.

My editor (and also a Helion publisher) is Christian Ewen, who has not only done a very professional job in putting all the bits and pieces together, but in the process, has also become a good friend – as has the delightful Kim McSweeney, who went that extra mile in designing this beautiful book. I offer my humble thanks to you both.

A final word of thanks to Jerry Buirski who, as he always does with my work, cast a hawk-eye on the copy one last time. He always comes up with something … Thanks old man.

Considerable effort was expended in trying to contact those who took photos used in this book. I took quite a few, but there were others - and after almost half a century, it has been difficult to make a connection. If I have erred, it is my fault alone and I invite you to contact the publishers so that future editions are more complete.

There were giants who walked among us, but we never recognised them as such. And now most are passed – and few remarked on …

> American military specialist and author Lester Grau, who wrote the classic *Operation Anaconda: America's First Major Battle in Afghanistan*

It's easier to sell a famine than to effect real, common-sense policy change… and I continue to believe that most aid workers do what they do because they want to make a difference. Nonetheless, a lot of what Oxfam does is to sustain Oxfam.

> Lauren Gelfand – a correspondent for *Jane's Defence Weekly*, based in Nairobi

It was the only time our government has assisted a foreign government killing our own citizens. Why? Because of the massive vanity of senior civil servants who could not and would not be proved wrong.

> Frederick Forsyth at London's Frontline Club, 26 September 2013

Under government pressure both Oxfam [and other British aid agencies] cut off all aid to Biafra in 1968. All BBC radio and TV reporting was stopped. There was an unholy implicit alliance with Moscow when the Russians provided the aircraft and trained the pilots of the Nigerian Air Force. Those pilots refused to fly at night and so left Biafra a nocturnal lifeline down which I flew into Uli, the Biafran airport, over the anti-aircraft guns provided by Harold Wilson and Michael Stewart. There is no more foul a chapter in British history since 1945. A million died.

> Peter Cadogan, who established the 'Save Biafra' campaign in 1968 in a letter to the London *Independent*, 11 January 1998

I have a great affection [for the Nigerians] because they are generally cheerful and friendly, in spite of their maddening habit of always choosing the course of action which will do the maximum damage to their own interests. They are not singular in this: Africans as a whole are not only averse to cutting off their nose to spite their face; they regard such an operation as a triumph of cosmetic surgery…

> Sir David Hunt – Her Majesty's High Commissioner to Nigeria, May 1969

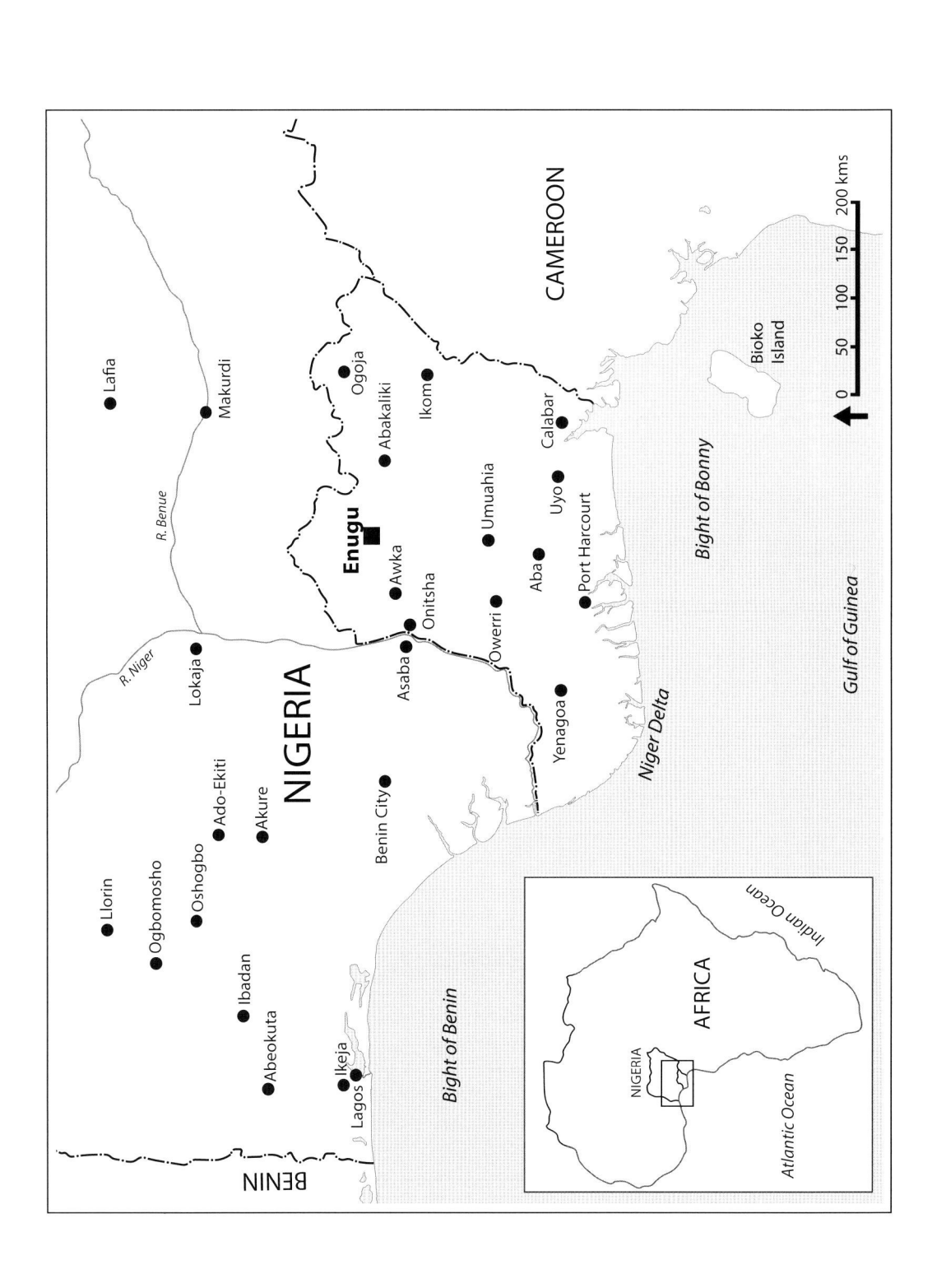

1

Lagos and a Nigerian Army Mutiny

> Anybody wishing to start a Holy War needs only to kill a prominent Islamic personage. As sure as the sun will rise tomorrow, a *Jihad* will follow. Africa's Muslims might not be among the best educated of their contemporaries, but they do have extremely long memories. Thus, when a group of Nigerian Army officers – the majority Christian – murdered some of their country's most respected leaders in the mid-1960s, almost all of whom were of the Islamic faith – their associates waited only months before taking revenge. The bloodletting that followed continues to this day.[1]

The Nigeria of January 1966 was a very different place from the one I had left the year before when I hiked up the west coast of Africa to get to London.

Nigeria had been independent only five years – and what a vibrant, exuberant society it was. I entered the former British colony by dug-out canoe from the Cameroons; spent a few days in a magic little backwater called Calabar; and paid my way in Bush Taxis and Mammy-Wagons through Port Harcourt, Onitsha and Benin all the way to Lagos, where I promptly went down with malaria.

Wherever this white boy from South Africa went in what was then a Federation of Nigerian states, I was feted, fed and displayed to everybody who was curious to know what somebody from the 'Racist South' was like. Even my skin and hair were touched by some to make sure I was real; others plied me with enough Star beer to set up a roadside stall in bids to uncover whatever thoughts about race or black people I might have secreted – and when that did not work, they tried palm wine.[2]

Throughout, I never once encountered any hostility – political or otherwise. Indeed, Lagos in those distant days was among the most secure cities on the continent. We were out just about every night, often on foot moving around the bars on Victoria Island or up Ikorodu Road – often till the wee hours – and a mugging in those days was as alien a concept to the average Nigerian living there as flush toilets in their still-primitive wooden homes.

---

1 One dictionary describes the word '*Jihad*' as a noun, meaning 'struggle'. Another explains that this Arabic word indicates a holy war against infidels undertaken by Muslims in defence of the Islamic faith. A third – Islamic – source suggests a personal struggle of the individual believer against evil and persecution.
2 What I never mentioned (because it might have verged on privilege or possibly self-justification) was that only a few years before, I had published a book on the effects of apartheid on people of mixed blood in South Africa. In this diatribe of 564 pages titled *Coloured: A Profile of Two Million South Africans*, I pulled no punches. Indeed, in the years before it became fashionable to be anti-apartheid, this work was one of the first to slam South Africa's crazily-implemented race laws. Its appearance – under the auspices of Human and Rousseau, an Afrikaans publishing house in Cape Town – earned me an enormous amount of censure within that country's political structure, which included being ridiculed in Parliament in Cape Town. Being of Boer extraction – my father was Afrikaans – I was supposed to be 'one of them' and in some quarters I was labelled a *verraaier* (traitor).

The view of one of the military hangars, as seen from the author's rear office window, with a newly-acquired Czech Delfin jet at its entrance. The initials represent the colonial name of the regional air service: West African Air Carriers. (Author's photo)

Many of these fringed the great lagoon, where a fair proportion of the city's sewage was dumped in a horrendous brown pile that some people viewed every morning from Carter Bridge on their way to work – and that eventually topped 10 or 12 metres.

It was only after the Biafran War – when the real exploitation of the country's oil resources began – that the money started coming in; and with it came graft, malfeasance, greed, corruption and the kind of dislocation of the great colonial administration and many of the fine British traditions that had originally put Nigeria on the international map.

It is worth noting that until independence in 1960 Nigerian tribal enmities that had been kept firmly under control by the exiguous British administration were now becoming serious – but even then, things just muddled along... until the putsch.

What happened was that some junior Ibo army officers – quite a few of them critical of the corruption spiral that emerged after independence; others with strong socialist inclinations, together with a few Yoruba officers – assassinated several prominent northern and western political figures. These included Sir Ahmadu Bello, the Hausa-Fulani Premier of the Northern Region, together with Chief Akintola, the Premier of the Western Region, as well as two Federal Ministers: Sir Abubakar Tafawa Balewa and Chief Festus Okotie-Eboh.

The people killed were the leaders of the nation and the murders shocked the Federation like no other political act before or since independence. Besides their positions in government, some were Islamic spiritual leaders – and as all the news reports declared, this was an extremely serious business. Overnight, the Ibos of the south-east (who had always caused much resentment in the north anyway) were suddenly cast as dangerous enemies of Islam.

During the Imperial period, the Northern Region in particular was largely left to govern itself – a legacy of what was termed Lord Lugard's 'Indirect Rule', which meant that the Islamic faith was

Nigerian troops with a British-supplied armoured car at Ikeja Airport immediately after the coup. The author's office at the airport overlooked this position. (Author's photo)

held in great respect and the British never meddled with it. That the Ibos – of all people – should perpetrate such acts was insufferable to Muslim people everywhere, but in those days it took them a little longer to react. The murders were to cost these Christian southerners dear.

Islam, we all know, is a deeply conservative religion. Even then, Muslims were not at all happy with 'progressive' western social norms – especially with regard to sex. More to the point, the education of the northerners was almost exclusively Koranic; they were, to that extent – by the criteria of their fellow southern countrymen – 'backward', as well as to many in the Western world.

The Ibos, in contrast – a bush and village people – had no such comprehensive Arabic culture as the north had enjoyed for more than a thousand years. Southern communities, in any event, took readily to the sort of education offered by mainly British mission schools; it may have been limited, but at least it turned the Ibo people into employable clerks and government servants. As such, they spread all over the north and people of Muslim faith, with many exceptions of course, offered little in the way of competition.

Northerners had to see good steady jobs filled with these detestable aliens – taking the bread out of their children's mouths, as it were. The not unnatural result was a series of outbursts and quasi-massacres in the Sabon Gari (the Stranger's Quarter) of the old walled cities of Kano, Zaria, Katsina and quite a few smaller towns. So far, this was a sociological matter rather than a political storm, and most believed it would pass; then came independence (that blessed word) – and not long afterwards, oil was discovered on the coast of the Eastern Region. Looking back, it seems always to have been a curse. Most of all, it made the Ibos greedy.

Hitherto, the majority of the Nigerian people had been quite content with their lot within the Federation. It brought them many benefits, but almost overnight, their fellow-countrymen in the

The author with Tony Cusack from Liverpool, who arrived from London on the same plane, also to take up a position with John Holt. Their colleague, Michael Odorro, stands between them. (Author's photo)

Europe's original interest in West Africa was its slaves and Badagry – an hour's drive west of Lagos – was the original slave trading centre (dating back to the 16th century). It was Britain that eventually put a stop to this nefarious business.

The young Queen Elizabeth visited most Commonwealth nations after she ascended the throne – and Nigeria was among the first to be so honoured. During her visit, there were still many British officers and NCOs serving in West Africa.

Colonel Chukwuemeka Odumegwu Ojukwu was a Nigerian military officer and politician who served as the Military Governor of the Eastern Region of Nigeria in 1966 and the leader of the breakaway Republic of Biafra from 1967 to 1970. He was to become a good friend of British author Frederick Forsyth. (Wikipedia)

south east – almost all of them Christians – found themselves standing on top of mind-bending potential riches and their avarice was aroused.

The word quickly spread: the oil is rightfully ours, is it not? Therefore let us keep it to ourselves! Goodbye Federation. It was about then that a lot of educated Nigerians – and quite a few European governments – began to look carefully at some of the military options involved. To many, it seemed clear that the country was headed for civil war; others believed that life would simply go on as before. It was a complicated issue, compounded largely by tribal loyalty.

At the time of independence, only about 15 percent of the officer corps came from the north and the west. Most of those who replaced former white officers were of Ibo extraction. To avoid friction between the three regions, it was then determined that the army should be recruited by quota: 50 percent from the north and a quarter each from the Ibo east and the Yoruba west; but by 1965 the Ibos had filled nearly half of the places offered by the British to Nigeria at Sandhurst.

So once again, the easterners were showing that they were pushier than all the rest – and in so doing, becoming all the more hated. The fact that they seemed to be taking over the whole Federal Army was regarded by some Nigerians as positively dangerous. In the event, the officers responsible for the first military insurrection disclaimed any tribal motive. All they wished to do, they said, was to get rid of corruption in government. Only the armed forces could be trusted.

Many Nigerians were less convinced – especially after an Ibo, Major General Johnson Aguiyi-Ironsi (the General Officer Commanding, or GOC), now became the country's leader. He was vociferous in declaring that he had absolutely nothing to do with what had taken place on 16 January. His protests were heard with great scepticism – and for very good reason.

There was no question that most of those who had taken part in the murders were Ibos. It was there, as plain as day, for everyone to see. The majority of those killed belonged to other tribes. In the event, the coup aroused a general fear of Ibo dominance in the north and west, and Nigeria's newly-ensconced military leader found himself presiding over an increasingly tense and volatile country.

24 BIAFRA'S WAR

Military aircraft that include helicopters, Delfin jets and Fokker F-27s lined up in the military-restricted zone at Lagos' Ikeja Airport. (Author's photo)

Those who have studied subsequent developments in Nigeria tell us that the northerners began to prepare a military counter-coup the morning after the murders of their leaders. That following May, five months later, Hausas and Fulanis set upon Ibos living in the north in a bloody pogrom in which Ibos were targeted: men, women and children; the sick, the lame and the old were slaughtered in their thousands. If you were an Ibo and the mob got you, you were dead. It was as simple as that.

I travelled a great deal in Nigeria in the months after my arrival – among other cities to Kano, Kaduna, Maiduguri and Gusau (all in the north). My work also took me to Port Harcourt, Calabar and Onitsha – that great Ibo city on the east bank of the Niger, which was to become a focal point in the civil war.

Everywhere there was tension. In the Sabon Gari in Kano, I saw places that had been gutted and plundered. Some of the stalls that had been burnt, with their owners dead or gone, were left just as they were, with vultures perched on the roofs.

'If the Ibo comes back again, we shall kill him too,' said one old Hausa veteran of World War II. He was proud of the fact that he had served in the British Army and had been among those who had instigated the riots.

Hardly a town or a village in the north was spared; there were so many Ibo dead. A hundred-thousand more were hacked with cutlasses or set on fire. Most abandoned all their possessions. The survivors fled back to their traditional homes in Eastern Nigeria.

The Premier of the Eastern Region, General Odumegwu Ojukwu (who I had known before the war), watched these events with dismay. He voiced his fears aloud: the north was systematically trying to kill off his people, he said. If the murders did not stop, he declared, the Eastern Region would have to take 'appropriate action'.

The idea of secession was already being discussed in the east of the country – particularly in Enugu and Onitsha. The new-found oil resources in the east, it was generally agreed, would give the Ibos the economic power to secede from the Nigerian Federation. We know now that the easterners had already begun to buy weapons from Europe. Effectively, though none of us was aware of it yet, they were no longer the Eastern Region of the Federation of Nigeria: they were 'Biafra'; then it happened as we knew it would, though most of us got the timing wrong.

Another view of the apron at Ikeja Airport immediately after the coup. (Author's photo)

Suddenly, on the morning of 19 July 1966 as I was on my way to work, I found myself in the middle of what had been – less than an hour before – a bloody battle for Lagos' Ikeja Airport (today Murtala Muhammed). I had just turned off the main road to the airport, where I had my offices, when I saw bodies strewn along the roadside. Armoured cars, Nigerian Army troop-carriers and civilian vehicles – some burning, some capsized – lay all over the place, but I had already made a terrible mistake in turning off the main road. Effectively, I was directly in the line of fire – though by then, the shooting had stopped.

I could, of course, have turned round immediately, but that would have drawn attention – and possibly worse – so I did the only thing left for me to do: I drove slowly and deliberately ahead towards the airport as I had done every morning since I had been in the country.

In spite of the carnage round me, I acted as if it were all a familiar daily occurrence. My radio was on, my elbow was resting on the open window and I tapped on the wheel in time to a high-life tune. I twisted my face into what I hoped would be interpreted as a smile. What else to do?

Then, quite unexpectedly – for I hadn't seen another soul – there they were: half a dozen soldiers prostrate on the ground gathered around a heavy machine gun. I had no idea what kind it was, but it did look pretty formidable from where I was perched at the wheel of my Ford – and it was pointed at me. Worse, I had to go past them before I could finally turn towards the airport. Their position was at the side of the road; I could have ridden over them if I had been crazy enough to do so.

Once abreast of the troops, I lifted a hand and waved. 'Good morning, gentlemen,' I called loudly, still smiling. 'Everything OK?' I kept waving.

They did not react. All of them were grim-faced and silent. I suppose they were nonplussed. I must have been a phenomenon that did not fall within the scope of their very simple instructions: kill anything and everything that approaches the airport.

I was aware, of course, that there had been plenty of killings and murders during the troubles in the months after I had arrived in Nigeria, but this seemed to be a regular pitched battle – and these youngsters (none of them could have been out of their teens) had been responsible – and then, to my astonishment, they let me pass. My office, John Holt Shipping Services in Apapa, knew that I had gone to work that morning, but the phone lines were cut and they couldn't find out whether I

At the time of the coup, Harold Wilson was Prime Minister – and aware that Britain's oil supplies were threatened by Biafra declaring itself independent, he formed an alliance with the Soviets to help crush the breakaway state by supplying the Lagos Government with all the weapons it needed. (Wikipedia)

was one of about 20-odd people killed in the ambush on the Ikeja Road. One of the dead was an expatriate – a Lebanese businessman.

I took no chances on my return that evening. This time I got permission to go back through army lines to the main road that would take me home to Apapa. The officer in charge, a Hausa who had been to Sandhurst and loved it, escorted me and spoke fondly of the rugby he had watched on Saturday afternoons back in the UK as we drove. It was like that in West Africa in the old days.

By the time we travelled that same stretch of road at about five that evening, all the bodies and wrecked vehicles had been removed. Everything seemed peaceful once more. It would have been hard to believe that Nigerian soldiers were, at that moment, slaughtering every Ibo in the country who had not fled. Pax Britannica was only a memory and Africa was itself again – and let's face it, for those who know Africa's west coast, there are occasions in Nigeria when things can be deceptive.

The expatriate community of which I had become a member while working in Lagos was a mixed bunch. Many were there because they couldn't succeed elsewhere else. The Nigerians, by and large, were aware of their shortcomings. These misfits – all of them ensconced in rather easy numbers – were referred to (somewhat deprecatingly) as 'white trash'. Looking back, I suppose some of them were, because their interests rarely extended beyond cheap Nigerian hooch and a never-ending array of dusky floozies.

To get to Lagos' Victoria Island – the heart of the Nigerian capital – you had to cross Carter Bridge from the mainland. Even in 1966 it was often a grind at rush hours. (Author's photo)

Alhaji, Sir Ahmadu Bello was the Sardauna of Sokoto and leader of Nigeria's Northern Region during the last years of British rule. He was also one of Nigeria's esteemed Islamic leaders who died in the 1966 coup.

The majority were British, though there was a fair sprinkling of Australasians, Canadians and other European nationals. There was even a South African technician at Ikeja Airport who was doing specialised work keeping planes aloft, so the Nigerians let him stay, though there was no other contact with the 'Racist South', except that the mail got through.

Our status quo was dictated strictly by the given or implied terms of our contracts. Certainly, the 'tween-ranks pecking order was maintained by a system that smacked of militarism – a tradition that went back a century or more in this part of Africa, both in the erstwhile British and French colonies . Officers simply did not mix with those from lower decks, yet it was a good life. Accommodation – according to your status – came as part of the deal that you were offered before you left 'home'. It was always 'home' – never Britain or England.

Higher echelons got houses. Those lower down the scale, like me, were given apartments. All were rent-free and included a steward. A manager could have three or four servants if he had children or entertained a lot; many did.

There was a complicated array of perks. For those who qualified, there was one or two (or even more) free flights home each year. Also, if you were lucky, the firm paid for your children's education at public schools in Britain. Their travels – two or three times a year between Heathrow and Lagos, Kano or one of the Eastern 'stations' – was also part of the package.

The big expat event of the week in Lagos, Kano, Port Harcourt and elsewhere was the Sunday curry lunch at the club. It was a grand, boozy affair to which few locals were ever invited. In the

This picture was taken very recently of a Lagos lagoon-side suburb. In truth, while this enormous conurbation of what is arguably Africa's most populous city (the Lagos State Government estimates the population of Lagos at 17.5 million), very little has changed in the day-to-day life of the average Nigerian. Huge skyscrapers and glass and marble palaces clutter the skyline, but for those with very little – which means the majority – life is extremely difficult. (Wikipedia)

old days, the clubs had been fairly vigorously segregated along racial lines, even though there was nothing defined; no by-laws stipulating that blacks were not welcome. It was just the accepted thing. Nigerians had their own clubs anyway, it was argued.

That changed quickly once the military took over; it simply had to. When a Nigerian soldier arrived at my 'local' – the Apapa Club – and ordered a Star or a Guinness, he was served with a smile. He wasn't even asked for money. Word quickly got around the barracks.

There were other distractions. The most important of these centred around the fact that in these outlying posts of what had once been Empire, there were few eligible females from back home. Those that were there worked in the embassies, or with various aid or religious missions. Quite a few were Peace Corps or British VSO. There were, of course, many married women – and if you were 'lucky', you hit a homer; but in a small, thoroughly-integrated social environment like Lagos, such liaisons rarely lasted long before people started to talk. Indeed, it was difficult to have any kind of a clandestine life in the former colonies. Every one of us was under some kind of surveillance or other – if not from our bosses, then from the government. As a result, you either cooled it or you were sent home in disgrace.

There were any number of local girls, but in those days, it was just not done to be seen with one of them on your arm in the club. Upcountry, yes, but not in your parlour, as it were – no ways!

These things were happening, naturally, but always well away from expatriate residential areas – and anyway, most of my associates did not advertise their predilection for 'something dark'. That came later in the evening at any one of hundreds of little open-air clubs along Ikeja Road, Yaba, Ebute-Metta or on Victoria Island – and those that did imbibe were discreet about it. Britain had only recently emerged from an age when black people were regarded as inferior – yet some of my colleagues had married black women and weren't any the worse off for it, though the children suffered.

2

A Day Later:
Back in the Firing Line

A lot of things took place in and around Lagos after the second army mutiny that July. A number of people were, as us scribes like to phrase it, 'caught in the crossfire'. I almost became a statistic myself.

It was to the Apapa Club that I went on the morning after my 'escape' at Ikeja. Obviously, nothing quite like that had ever happened before – and the January *coup d'état* was a Wednesday afternoon exercise on Salisbury Plain by comparison.

More ominous with the latest uprising was the fact that the Nigerian army was everywhere. The British High Commission and other diplomatic missions encouraged a low profile for us all. Those not at work gathered at their respective clubs and compared notes, even though the stories did seem to improve with telling as the beer flowed.

By lunch on the second day, I decided to have a look at things for myself. Wilf Nussey, who ran the Argus Africa News Service out of the offices of *The Star* in Johannesburg, had been calling. He wanted to know what was happening, but because I did not have my usual easy access to Ikeja, I wasn't able to file. Certainly, I did not have the facilities of Reuters, the BBC or any of the other news agencies based in Nigeria; I was still very much a backroom boy – and for the moment, that suited me fine.

Discussing it with my friends at the club, I decided that since the largest naval base in the country lay adjacent to Apapa Docks – perhaps a kilometre from the club – there, I thought, I might possibly learn something by visiting the place. Why not? After all, the Nigerian Navy was regarded as the most disciplined and best-ordered of the Nigerian forces.

Also, since I was living there, I had a rough idea of how to get to the base – even though the roads in the area were a mess. They had been laid over what had once been a swamp and followed no set pattern or grid.

After a couple of wrong turns in the car, I eventually came to a road that led directly to the Apapa Nigerian Navy base; it lay dead ahead, about 500 yards away. Its steel gates were shut and the towers on either side, from what I could see, appeared to be manned. Certainly, it looked ominous and I was unsure of what to do next. I had stopped in the middle of the road; that was another mistake.

While contemplating whether to go back or not, a siren sounded. The gates suddenly opened and a squad of about a dozen soldiers – all of them armed – rushed out. An officer appeared and called loudly: 'You there! You come here or we shoot! Now!'

I hesitated a moment; then a shot rang out. It was the officer – pistol in hand. He was firing in my direction; that decided it. I drove ahead slowly – again trying the pasted smile and elbow on the window routine. This time it was a little more difficult.

The British-supplied frigate NNS *Nigeria* at Apapa Naval Base in Lagos Harbour. (Author's photo)

My car moved forward – possibly too slowly. Instead of accepting that I was complying with his order – a lone civilian in a sedan – the officer was getting more excited. I could see by the bars on his whites that he was a lieutenant commander. At that point, he was already ahead of his men waving his pistol wildly in the air. 'Come!' he shrieked. 'Right now!'

What next? I couldn't even make a run for it; the road was too narrow for me to quickly turn around. Anyway, by now he was just ahead of me.

Perhaps 20 yards short of the gate – which I now saw had machine-gun emplacements on them – I pulled up. The man with the pistol was directly in front of me. He was shouting something incomprehensible and, to my surprise, was actually foaming at the mouth. Looking at him closely, I saw a crazed look in his eyes. He was smashed. 'What you want? What you want here?' he screamed – his voice rising an octave or two each time he called. I was terrified, though I dared not show it.

The rest of the troops – in varying levels of undress, rage and stupefaction – surrounded me. There were a dozen rifles pointed at my head and another three or four muzzles pressed against my body. In Nigeria's oppressive heat in those days, you always drove with your windows open.

'Get out! Get out!' the lieutenant commander shouted. Anywhere else in the world, the situation into which I had suddenly been thrust would have been regarded as farcical. Right now, I actually feared that I might be shot. The expatriate community had already taken half a dozen casualties in the past 24 hours.

Many lives were lost in Nigeria in 1966 for no apparent reason. The great majority were Nigerian and not all of them were Ibo; it just happened. There was never anyone who would or could do anything about it. We – the public – only heard rumours, which were often exaggerated. The reason was simple: the moment the military took power, they occupied the editorial offices of all the country's newspapers. Consequently, none of the events that should have been in the news were ever reported. Rumour, of course, feasted on its own excesses. That did not help either.

'Lykes Lines…' I said loudly. I had seen the offices of the American shipping line on an adjacent road as I approached the navy base. It was my only option. The officer stepped back a pace. He clearly hadn't a clue what I was talking about.

Downtown Lagos scene on a Saturday morning. (Author's photo)

'Lykes Lines. The American shipping line,' I called again – louder this time. The man was befuddled, and it showed. My mentioning America must have made an impression. Washington had not looked kindly on the antics of General Aguiyi-Ironsi and his Ibo goons – and the State Department had been quite vocal about it. The Nigerian press had reported the events of the first coup because they were allowed to do so.

'What you mean? Lykes Lines! Lykes Lines! What you mean?' The man was screaming again. I began to get out of the car. He had told me to do so earlier and I was complying with an order, but he moved quickly forward – pistol in my face – and forced me back into the vehicle.

'Stay there… Stay where you are! Do you hear?' There was no argument. It is not only in Africa that you don't argue with a man with a gun at your head!

Then, in a more direct approach, I mentioned the American shipping line once more and pointed towards the company's building across the way. The Nigerian officer turned and looked in that direction. By now, all the soldiers around me were gesticulating wildly. Every one of them was shouting. One of them screamed: 'Kill him! Kill the bastard! He knows he's not supposed to be here!'

Another sailor with a sub-machine gun (he had already stuck the muzzle in my ear) demanded to know why I was spying. 'Who you spy for?' he shouted. It was all so predictable – and also frighteningly intimidating. Looking back, I realise today that none of it had the ingredients of a stage play or a film; it was simply too bizarre. It was also damned repetitive.

Since then, with the kind of work that I do, I have been involved in similar situations half a dozen times. Each time, my skin crawls – as it does now, writing about it. Each experience, I realise, seemed to have been worse than the last; the frenzied rantings of soldiers often high on some substance or other – and most times, completely out of control. There never was any possibility of reasoning with these people. Once they had made up their minds, that was it! Being white in a black man's country did not ease matters either. Also, I was on my own, which hardly helped.

Clearly, I was totally unprepared for what was happening to me on that lonely stretch of road in Apapa. I was aware too that if I did not keep my head, I could be killed – even by accident. By their actions, some of these idiots really seemed to believe that I was up to no good… a

Nigeria's official Navy emblem – prominent at the gate of the naval base at Apapa.

mercenary, perhaps. The papers were full of ghastly stories of mercenaries killing black people; events in the Congo were alive in the minds of these people.

There was a solution of sorts, I suppose. It took a while, but I found that it was often better to counter this kind of hysteria with an off-hand, friendly nonchalance. Any other approach, any belligerence, could lead to disaster.

After I'd mentioned the name 'Lykes Lines' a dozen times – becoming quite vocal in my protestations, even though I smiled throughout – the officer eventually put his hands in the air to silence his men. 'Get back… Get back,' he shouted at them.

'You!' he pointed at me. 'Get out of the car. Now!'

I did, and stood beside it with my hands in the air; then, for the first time, I saw that both machine guns on the turrets besides the main gate had been pointing directly at me. It had been that way probably throughout this horrible pantomime, though if they had to open fire, they would probably have killed all of us in the road in front of the gate. I hoped that those manning it were sober, or at the very least, no less drunk than the officer who was questioning me.

'Now, you say. What is your business?' I could smell he had been drinking. I knew I had little time because his attention span was wavering.

I did so. I explained in as few words as possible that Lykes Lines was an American shipping company. Its ships called regularly at Lagos. I pointed towards John Holt shipping documents which I had on my back seat in a pile. I had taken the more important papers from my office at Ikeja the day before, just in case. The officer looked carefully at me and then peered in through the rear window. What he saw seemed to placate him and then we went through the rigmarole again.

It took at least 15 more minutes of pretty convincing talk to get him to believe me. Even then, he did so grudgingly, but I knew that my smile and my apparent nonchalance did help. I had to convince him that I wasn't really a threat to the security of the nation. In the end, I succeeded.

Eventually, he allowed me to turn my car around. Once more, I did so – very slowly. All the while, I was under the barrels of the machine guns on the turrets above the gates. His men were also still pointing their guns at me – one or two of them with their barrels pressed into my back.

As I drove those last few hundred yards along that lonely road, I could almost sense the aggression. God! I was glad to get away! When I told them at the club, some of the more experienced Old Coasters agreed that I had been extraordinarily lucky. Several Apapa residents had been threatened

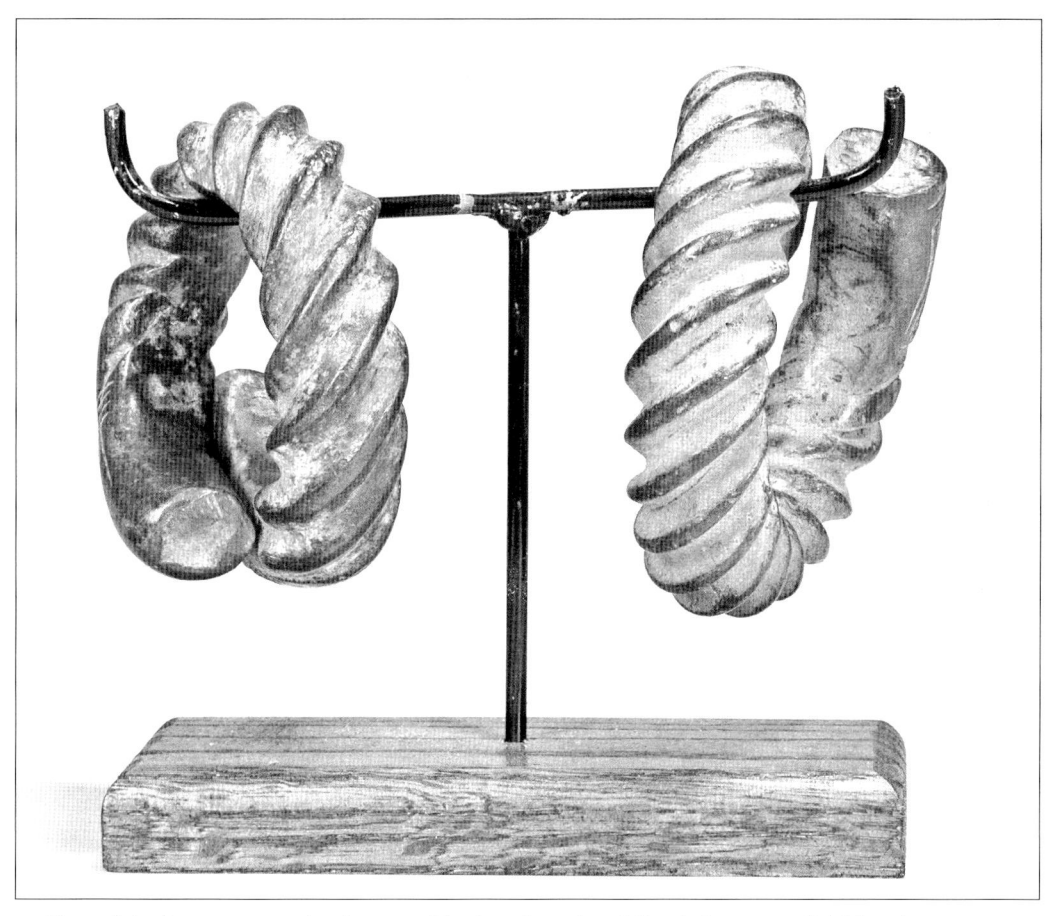

One of the first measures implemented by London when Nigeria became a British colony was to abolish traditional metal currency such as these bronze bangles which, for centuries, were used in trade throughout much of West Africa. Sterling notes with the Nigerian imprint were printed by De La Rue and standard British coins minted.

by troops in the dock area earlier that day, I was told. One of them was wounded by rifle fire for no other reason, apparently, but that he was there; in the wrong place at the wrong time. Nigeria was like that – and by all accounts, not much has apparently changed in almost half a century.

All of us were more cautious afterwards. My steward, David – an Ibo – kept me informed of what was happening using his tribal grapevine as a conduit. Young Ibo males, he told me, were being pressured to return home and undergo military training, even though the Biafran War was still a year away.

With the assassination of General Ironsi in the July coup, his place had been taken by a 30-year-old Army Chief of Staff, Lieutenant-Colonel (later General) Yakubu Gowon – possibly one of the most amiable of all Nigeria's post-independent leaders. 'Jack' – as we got to know him – Gowon was the original 'Mister Nice Guy'. Uncharacteristically (for a Nigerian), he was short on pretention and pomp and believed implicitly in the direct approach. His only flaw – if that be it – was that he was a Christian in a Nigeria that almost overnight had become dominated by the Muslim north. Gowon was the son on an evangelist from the Plateau area of the Middle Belt. He was overthrown five years after the end of the War of National Unity (as it was euphemistically phrased by Nigeria's military leaders) and went back to university in Britain.

I continued to travel throughout the country in my last months in Apapa and a good deal of my time was spent in the east with my John Holt assistant: Silas Anusiem was of Ibo extraction and married to a Yoruba woman.

A quiet, reflective individual who tended to view even innocuous developments with alarm, Silas had excellent connections within government in Lagos; his leaks were always spot-on. I invariably appeared to be ahead of the pack when it came to projections about the future and I was grateful for his help.

Then came an incident that left its mark: I was asked by friends in South Africa to help them in their efforts (as they phrased it) to 'secure a contract'. Someone was in the process of tendering for a contract in Lagos Harbour – a multi-million-dollar project. Because of apartheid, South Africans were banned from commercial contact with just about all of Black Africa – and consequently, the scheme was going to be handled offshore from an office in the Bahamas; at least that was what I was told, but to do so, they said, they needed a complete set of charts of the entire Lagos port area. I was not to know it then, but in any other light, my actions could only have been construed as precarious. Overnight I had become a spy, though I was never paid a penny for it.

It was an odd request. I was to send the charts to the naval attaché at the South African Embassy in London: Commander (later Rear-Admiral) 'Solly' Kramer. I had served briefly under this naval officer in Simonstown. In Cape Town, after I had left the navy, I had met him socially through an old friend of the family, Commander Joe Gower – Head of Naval Intelligence – and Joe and his wife, Elizabeth, were good friends.

Of course, I should have been a little more circumspect and put two and two together, but I did not – and it was some years before I was to discover that the charts were later to be used in an attack on Soviet and East European ships in Lagos Harbour. Most Soviet ships entering Nigerian waters over the next few years were loaded with weapons for the Nigerian war effort against Biafra. It was these ships that were to be bombed with limpet mines as they lay alongside the quays in Lagos Harbour. The operation was inexplicably called off at the last moment.

In all innocence, I had asked Silas Anusiem to buy the charts from the government office responsible for such things in Lagos. Certainly, in retrospect, I could have got us both arrested for espionage. In the heady political climate that preceded the war, we might even have been executed for treason because there was reason enough; the charts were invaluable. Others were shot for a good deal less once the war started, but Silas – with his remarkable network of contacts – was forewarned. Half-way though one of our trips to Onitsha, he turned to me in the car:

'Those charts, Al. Where are they now?'

I sensed that there were more questions coming. 'Why?' I asked in all innocence.

'Because somebody has raised queries asked about them.'

I suddenly realised the implications: I had overstepped the mark security-wise – and that was serious. Moreover, my Ibo associate was well aware of my South African connections. He had apparently been questioned by the Nigerian Special Branch about me. I knew too that my apartment had been searched once or twice while I was away on trips. David had told me.

I explained to Silas exactly what I had done and why I did it. My Ibo associate, normally as black as tan, visibly paled. He never said a word – nor did he ever raise the issue again. He had told me once before that he had a brother in the higher echelons of the Nigerian Navy who served at the naval headquarters in Lagos – and I have no doubt that it was left to him to sort matters out. Once again, I was fortunate.

British armoured cars being offloaded in Apapa Harbour shortly after the coup.
(Author's photo)

It was with Silas Anusiem that I had my last adventure in Nigeria. It was also my last long-road journey through the Eastern Region, which was very different from the rest of the country.

I enjoyed covering the east before the war; the people were friendly. They were certainly more ebullient and there was always something happening. Also, you got things done there. The people were willing to help – and though it cost some, you did not mind paying for good work done.

In Lagos, in contrast, the lifestyle was a perpetual round of haggling, delays, cancelled appointments and very little achieved without dash – the universal system of crossing of the palms with silver, or (increasingly) with large denomination banknotes.

Our route this time took us across the Niger River at Onitsha and then on towards Owerri and Port Harcourt. We were on the second day out, and so far it had been an uneventful journey; then we reached the small town of Nsokpo about 10 or 15 miles from Port Harcourt. Quite unexpectedly, we suddenly came upon a huge crowd – several thousand-strong. They were blocking the road in front of us. It was an angry, ugly mob. Silas suggested that I park next to the road and wait for him; he would go and see what was happening.

Shortly after I had pulled up, I spotted several youngsters throwing stones at cars that arrived along the same road that we had just used. Being white, they ignored me. It was the local fat cats that they were after. Most of these people turned around and roared off; then an army truck with about a dozen soldiers on board came down the road towards us. The mob surged towards them in a fury. In a single roar of disapproval, they converged on the troops – a frightening, shrieking black mass that was altogether terrifying. I thought I knew Africa. I had never seen anything like this before.

The mood had become so menacing that I quickly turned the car around and moved back down the road a short distance. I was afraid that the situation would deteriorate further. I waited half an hour; then an hour. Still no Silas… By now, I was becoming worried. Also, I was hungry. We had been on the road for half the day already.

The author passed through Nigeria on his way to Europe in 1965, which was one of the reasons he went back there the following year. He was already writing at the time and this photo was taken of him by a Peace Corps friend in Conakry, Guinea.

Why not take a photograph? I thought. There was obviously a reason for the disturbances. There might be a good story there, somewhere. Nussey would certainly use it, so I pulled out my camera and, for good effect, climbed onto the roof of my car. I was just starting to focus when a couple of young men near to me noticed the camera.

'No pitcha!' they shouted – the arms raised above their heads.

Ten or 30 young men around them heard the cries and turned towards me – and then they too started shouting. Fists in the air, they screamed: 'No pitcha! You no takka pitcha!'

I smiled, waved – trying to look indifferent and went on with what I was doing. By now, I was attracting an awful lot of attention.

A DAY LATER: BACK IN THE FIRING LINE   37

At that point, there were 200 to 300 people screaming. Moments later, it became a thousand – or it could have been 2,000 because I wasn't counting, except that there was a sea of black faces in front of me and they were all incensed at the presence of this whitey who had intruded on hallowed ground, where some of their people had been killed earlier by the Nigerian Army. That I wanted to take photos only compounded the issue, for such is the volatility of Africa at a time of crisis – and just then, this massive surge of humanity was now heading in my direction. The cry of 'No pitcha' was like a roar. Hell, I thought, this was serious!

I jumped to the ground just before the first wave of protestors reached me. I tried to say something, but it was useless; I was a lone voice against thousands. The shouting had become overwhelming; hysterical.

I think I saved my life by getting into the car at about the same time that they started to beat on my windscreen and roof with their fists. The mob was now shouting at me in the local lingo and I understood none of it. I only knew that I had to get away – and fast!

In a single, fluid motion that comes with practice, I started the engine – at the same time releasing my brakes. A split-second later, I had shifted the car into gear and pulled away. It all happened in a blink and a screech of rubber. Some of the mob was ahead of me. I went right through the crowd without touching one of them. Right then, I was prepared to run them over to get clear. I was 50 yards down the road before the first stone hit my back window, shattering it.

Strangely, the car had been giving me trouble on the trip up. Once or twice, I had had trouble getting it going. Had I stalled then, I would most certainly have been killed. The mob was crazy; out of control. It was a very dangerous position to be caught in. As it happened, the car started in a flash.

Of Silas Anusiem, there was nothing. He was gone – swallowed up by the howling, screaming masses. I stopped about 200 yards further down the road to try to wait for him. Still they kept coming.

It was too dangerous to stick around. I would meet him in Port Harcourt. We had agreed that we would be staying at the Cedar Palace and he would find me there. He did so at about 10:00 p.m. that night. What had happened, he told me later, was that the army had apparently shot a group of striking students at Nsokpo earlier in the day. A riot had developed. More soldiers arrived; more people were shot; then the mob cornered some soldiers. Though the army held its own for a while, they were overpowered, disarmed and killed. It was a ritual; limb by limb, they were pulled apart. It did not help that most of the troops involved in this fracas were northerners. By the time we arrived, the mob had gone totally berserk.

Certainly, said Silas later, if the car had stalled, I would have been slaughtered. The mob was frenzied. They stayed that way until the first Nigerian Army armoured car arrived.

I was never able to discover how many people were killed in that riot on the road to Port Harcourt; it must have been a lot. At that stage, the Hausas were making a dramatic example of southerners who voiced dissent. None of it ever appeared in the Nigerian press.

3
Biafra: The Build-up

It's a truism that for those in the West with expanding communications, the world has shrunk. For Africa, it has grown immeasurably.

As with Iraq – almost 40 years later – Nigeria's oil almost overnight became a priority. As we have seen, it lay at the hub of Nigeria's problems. Huge deposits of fossil fuels had been discovered earlier along the coast of the Eastern Region and Nigeria was forever changed.

Looking back, West Africa's 'black gold' seems always to have been a curse. Even today, there is much squabbling about who owns what – whether title to concessions are legal, or even whether existing oil claims that have been tapped for decades are even valid or obtained 'by other means'. More recently, Nigeria and the Cameroon Republic almost went to war over who owns an obscure stretch of land called the Bakassi Peninsula – a place very few of us had ever heard of before. In fact, nobody knew it even existed until oil was discovered in that area.

There was more sabre-rattling over what exactly constituted the offshore rights of Equatorial Guinea – formerly Spanish Guinea. A botched mercenary attempt to oust the President of that island government (one of the most brutal and corrupt countries on the globe) followed – led by (among others) Mark Thatcher, son of former British Prime Minister Margaret Thatcher and Simon Mann, scion of a prominent English brewing family.

Looking back at some of the events that took place in the mid-1960s, it is clear that the Ibos were way ahead of their Nigerian compatriots at being able to appreciate the bigger picture. Effectively, they did not want the 'Backward North' to enjoy any of it: the commodity was rightfully theirs, was it not?

It was about then that quite a few developed nations – Britain, America, France and Russia in particular – began to look seriously at the military implications involved. It was obvious that Nigeria was headed for trouble, though at that stage, the prospect of a civil war was remote. Nonetheless, it was a complicated issue because internecine strife – as we have since seen in Chechnya, Kashmir, Sri Lanka, Iraq, Afghanistan, Lebanon and elsewhere – usually always is.

Meantime, I'd settled into my new job in Lagos and there were some interesting developments following the army mutiny that had twice caused me a few problems. From my office at Ikeja Airport, despite it being open to large numbers of commercial airlines – including the old Pan American Airways that ran a weekly service between New York and Johannesburg – I could see that the government was starting an arms build-up of its own in anticipation of an Ibo secession. The first evidence was the arrival (complete in Nigerian Air Force livery) of a squadron of Czechoslovakian Aero L-29 Delfin trainer-fighter jets. Some of these trim planes were parked just beyond my office windows.

The eight Delfins bought by the Lagos Government in the mid-1960s were not regarded by NATO strategists as a sophisticated aircraft. Its development came because the Soviet Air Force needed a jet-powered replacement for its fleet of piston-engine trainers and the L-29 provided

BIAFRA: THE BUILD-UP

Civilian refugees head south for their original Eastern Nigerian homeland after coming under severe attack in the Islamic north. (Gamma Press Images, Paris)

something of an answer. Essentially then, it was a Warsaw Pact jet trainer: Czechoslovakia's first locally-designed and built aircraft – originally powered by Bristol Siddeley Viper engines and first flown in 1959.

The first month, following the arrival of the Delfins at Ikeja Airport (which was also the major operations centre for the Nigerian Air Force), these planes were almost mollycoddled. They were carefully washed down and polished every morning and at the end of each day, someone would emerge from the hangars and meticulously close the cockpits and add additional canvas covers so that nothing would be damaged if it rained during the night.

By the second month (probably because there had been a change of command), the covers had disappeared. A month or two later, nobody even bothered about rain, or whether or not the cockpits stood exposed to the elements.

Obviously, the Delfins did not remain operational for very long, though some did see service against the Biafrans after a bunch of Czech technicians arrived and spruced them up again – but by then, Lagos had already been shopping around and eventually bought Soviet MiG-17s which arrived in the country with a large contingent of Egyptian MiG pilots and technicians.

During this period of service with John Holt in West Africa, I travelled a lot. Most of all, I enjoyed heading out towards the east, near the Cameroon frontier. Though unsettled because of the refugee problem – a million Ibos had been forced to return to their roots because they were encountering hardships elsewhere – this was still the most ordered part of the country.

When I first entered Nigeria – impecunious and overland from 'Down South' the year before – I'd managed to visit the delightful little port of Calabar, which nestles like a cherub at the head of a river inlet. It was a tropical hideaway from all the country's travails and I made friends with a lovely bunch of British and American volunteers. As with most of these volunteer communities, a newcomer was always made welcome, though God knows Peace Corps and VSO staff were only paid pittances, but somehow we'd always make do and it wasn't long before I started to savour the delights of palm wine – that West African speciality that is as popular along the coast as Guinness is in Ireland (and in Nigeria, incidentally, where it used to sell almost as well as in the old country).

With not much money, you could easily lose yourself in Calabar for a week or a month because everything you needed was either home-grown or caught – and consequently, cheap – and the natives were friendly. Until then, I'd never experienced anything like it.

Also a charm was Jos – a big place in the interior with its tin mines and strange, primitive tribes who want only to be left alone. It was there that I was initiated into trying to enjoy fu fu and gari – both decidedly acquired tastes and not for the faint-hearted. If you like hot curry, fu fu boils!

The north too was pleasant enough – at least when there weren't people cutting each other's throats. Anyway, we whites were regarded as very much apart from that kind of violence; then things started to get nasty and you couldn't escape the tension. In Kano's Sabon Gari, I saw places that had been gutted and plundered. Stalls had been burnt and their original owners dead or gone.

Throughout, there was much debate in the country – not only about the putsch and the killings, but also about the Eastern Region increasingly looking at turning itself into an armed camp. Politics during this phase was confused, as is usually the case after a revolution, and Nigeria was no exception.

The mainly British expatriate community had settled back into its traditional role of running the various private consortiums active along this stretch of the west coast, but then some uneasy undertones had started to emerge after the coup. The Nigerian armed forces were no longer in the background; they were everywhere – and roadblocks had become commonplace. It was worse outside all major centres, where troops manning them were often drunk or drugged and reports of bribes to be allowed to pass started to come in. This was certainly not the Nigeria of old.

The media obviously took a keen interest in what was going on in West Africa – prompted in large part by the unstable antics of a Ghanaian President who liked to be referred to as '*Osagyefo*', or 'Redeemer'. Kwame Nkrumah was determined to rid Africa of all Western influences – and in this, he found a solid ally in the Soviets. However, his own people quickly saw through that little charade and he was soon deposed – but by then, Africa had become newsworthy and Nigeria was no different. Journalists came and went, though a few stuck it out as things started to deteriorate.

It was in Biafra that I made my first acquaintance with a remarkable young Englishman who was quadrilingual in English, French, German and Spanish and who had flown de Havilland Vampire jets for the Royal Air Force in the days when military conscription was still obligatory in Britain.

'Freddie' to us all, then and now – or (more formally) Frederick Forsyth – had worked for Reuters in Paris and Berlin before accepting a job with the BBC (otherwise known as 'the Beeb') and headed out to West Africa, where he became a friend and confidante of the rebel leader Colonel Ojukwu. This enthusiastic young Brit eventually became so close to the rebel hierarchy that he was actually attached to the main Biafran invasion army that struck out in force in a lightning raid to capture Lagos (then the Federal capital). The fact that he'd fallen out with his BBC

New Biafran Army recruits being put through their paces early on in the war. (Author's photo)

bosses in London because of their partisan approach to the crisis – and which ignored the slaughter of the innocents – had a good deal to do with it.

As he declared:

> The British approach was to try to negate the full implications. This was a domestic issue that would soon be over. 'Play it down. Play it down!' the media was told. London would tell us that it was just an uprising. Unrest, they called it… *30,000 people killed in a pogrom is unrest…?* These people had blinkers over their eyes, which is why I ended up differing so strongly with the BBC… they were whitewashing everything and not only ignoring the real issues, but even worse, also refusing to report them; so I resigned and stayed on in Biafra as a freelancer.

In a 2007 interview with Michael Gould and published in his book *The Biafran War*, Forsyth explained in greater detail exactly why things with the British Broadcasting Corporation turned sour and caused him to support the Biafrans:

> The BBC World Service was funded by the British Government, and I was in Nigeria at the time, reporting on behalf of the BBC. As soon as I tried to balance the picture by giving Biafra's position, problems and issues, I was reprimanded by the Corporation and eventually recalled to London. Once back in London I was effectively demoted and sent to the House of Commons as an assistant reporter. Added to which I discovered that in my absence my London flat had been broken into, and although I found nothing missing, I did discover that some boarding alongside a wall had been disturbed. I am convinced to this day that the security services had entered my home looking for evidence to incriminate me. Because of this break-in and my effective demotion I resigned from the BBC, and with my severance

pay I booked a flight back to Nigeria and presented myself to Ojukwu in Enugu. Ojukwu welcomed me and offered me the use of a caravan, as a home and place to work, parked near to Ojukwu's home, state house, a car and a driver [as well as a] commission in the Biafran Army as a captain. I think the offer of a commission was to allow me the opportunity to freely move round the country in a protected way, so that I could report events as I saw them. I readily accepted this generous offer and for the following thirty months I stayed in Biafra, trying to give the outside world a picture of the country's condition and plight.[1]

As Forsyth subsequently confirmed, beyond the frontiers of the soon-to-be rebel state, Ibos were given an incredibly hard time – especially since the entire defence structure had been 'ethnically cleansed'. Easterners who had survived the initial violent purge were given their marching orders.

The appointment of a new head of state – the rather youthful Colonel Yakubu Gowon – was a welcome development. He was clearly British-trained and, as far as we knew, did not drink or smoke dope, which was an enormous plus because so many of his colleagues did.

I would spot him coming to Ikeja Airport from time to time, but these were quiet, unobtrusive visits that were obviously low-key; they lacked the fanfare of his predecessors. His security detail was, at most times, kept to a minimum – and from what I gathered, his drive to Ikeja (after things had settled down) was usually a two-car affair. Other times, he would be preceded by motorcycle outriders and sirens; then we all had to stop and give way.

At that early stage, there was very little known about the man who had seized power in Nigeria's second military takeover. Colonel Yakubu Gowon was a mild-mannered Christian soldier who originally came from a small northern tribe, the Angas. Though he had a minor role in the July 1966 counter-coup, he emerged as a compromise head of the new government. Frederick Forsyth told me when we discussed the man at my home on the shores of the Columbia River at Chinook that he remembers him emerging out of the escalating chaos as a temperate adjutant of the Nigerian Army.

'He was the typical young Nigerian officer,' said Forsyth. 'More important, he wasn't a Muslim. In fact, he was a devout Christian – and being, as it was termed, 'Middle Belt' (neither from the north nor the south), he couldn't be tarred with a brush of being an Ibo.'

In fact, recalls Forsyth – who covered this civil war from the start – he suited just about everybody:

> As far as the coup leaders were concerned, their attitude was that we can run the country behind this man. So too with Sir David Hunt, the British High Commissioner: he was the perfect choice.
>
> Sir David was very much old Colonial school. He liked the fact that Gowon would snap to attention whenever he walked in… that pleased the man no end. In contrast, there were those among us who regarded the Nigerian military leader as an overgrown boy scout.

Things were very different with regard to the other man in this complex political mix that was making things happen – some of them rather unpleasant. After the tribal pogroms in the north, Lt-Col Odumegwu Ojukwu – Military Governor of Nigeria's Eastern Region – emerged as if from the shadows and almost as if it had been preordained.

In Nigeria today, there is still much debate about the role of the individual whom I'd fleetingly known before the war and who took his people to war against the Federal Government. Everybody kept a close watch on all these events – in large part because having experienced two

---

1 Gould, Michael: The *Biafran War: The Struggle for Modern Nigeria* (London: IB Taurus, 2012).

BIAFRA: THE BUILD-UP 43

One of dozens of camps for children that were established by international air organisations once hostilities had started. (Author's photo)

army mutinies, nobody wanted a third. They got a civil war instead. According to those close to Ojukwu, his dismay was almost palpable as conditions started to deteriorate.

Colonel Ojukwu, an Oxford graduate, was outspoken about the long-term consequences of the killings. The nation was being irrevocably split, he warned. He warned then that war might follow, if only because that the minority were being persecuted – and there was no question that they simply had to do something to survive. Anything!

As he told Frederick Forsyth, the north was systematically trying to kill off his people.

'If the atrocities do not stop, the Eastern Region will have to take appropriate action,' was one of his public pronouncements, he told me. Similar sentiments were voiced shortly afterwards in a radio broadcast from Onitsha – the largest Ibo city in the east.

While Ojukwu always put the welfare of his people first and ostensibly, he did not appear to be interested in the oil imbroglio that had started manifesting itself. The idea of seceding from the Nigerian Federation was already a hot issue in Enugu, Port Harcourt and Onitsha especially, because that city was the fulcrum on which just about everything of consequence in the eastern part of the country hinged.

Among the arguments that this Nigerian Army colonel and his people liked to use was that the boundaries of the country had been arbitrarily drawn by the British Colonial Government a century before – and of course, he was right. Consequently, they maintained, they were of little use now.

Always the pragmatist, Ojukwu did declare that if it really became a matter of survival of his people, the newfound resource would play its role in giving the Ibo *Nation* (it had been the Igbo *People* before and has since reverted to the original – 'Igbo' being a word some people prefer to use) the economic power to go it alone. This was a situation much like that which prevailed in

Rhodesia, which had gone ahead and declared UDI, but Ian Smith (in contrast) had no oil reserves of his own – and he paid the inevitable price.

Just about everybody in Lagos was aware at the time that Ojukwu had already sent his emissaries abroad to buy what weapons they could from Europe – and the reaction was good. The word that came back was that France and several Eastern European countries were willing to sell guns for cash. It was all over-the-counter stuff, but the problem was getting it back to Ojukwu's already-embattled enclave.

Paris, it should be mentioned, was motivated not so much by sympathy for an opposed or threatened African tribal group, but by its own investments in Nigeria – many of which lay under the ground in the east of the country. Also, there were more French cars in Nigeria than those from any other nation (Britain and Japan included). Anybody who spent time in Nigeria after independence will recall that Peugeot taxis were everywhere!

At about this point, things started to move rather quickly. Violence in the northern reaches continued, though not as intensely as before because most easterners had fled, with killings in the Yoruba-dominated west abating markedly over the months that followed. No fools, by now the Yoruba were well aware that this was a largely Christian-Muslim thing, with the preponderant Islamic militants in the north doing what they could to cripple largely Christian Eastern Nigeria. That had a rippling effect on Nigerian society as a whole, and led to some pertinent questions being asked in Lagos and Ibadan: once the Ibos have been dealt with, are we likely to be next? The phrase 'Islamic *Jihad*' was being bandied about by some as if this concept was already a reality. As a result, Nigeria's Eastern Region was soon to be declared the Republic of Biafra: its symbol the rising sun against a black backdrop.

Throughout this period, there was hardly a day when one Ojukwu pronouncement or another did not make the news. Every newspaper in the country – including those in the north – had journalists in the east and they reported the situation exactly as they saw it, though more often than not, with strong emphasis on anything dramatic such as rumours of arms purchases abroad and, once or twice, reports that white mercenaries had been hired to defend eastern borders.

One has to remember that the Congo and its hired guns were still fresh in the minds of most African people, not only in Nigeria, but across the continent – and there was an argument doing the rounds that if Mobutu could use mercenaries to achieve victory in Katanga and elsewhere, then in theory, so might Ojukwu. In truth, it had not yet come to that.

Obviously, the British played an increasingly devious role during this period – using its offices to unabashedly give support to the Federal cause and view Ojukwu with great suspicion (because of the oil, of course). As the former colonial authority, there was regular contact with the east, but these meetings almost never went well or produced something constructive. Also, Ojukwu had an ingrained suspicion about anything that Whitehall might come up with. More to the point, the biggest stumbling block was the High Commissioner himself, who made no secret of the fact that he despised Ojukwu – and this sentiment went a good deal further than politics.

'Sir David's relations with Colonel Ojukwu were frosty,' recalls Forsyth – one of the few observers active in Nigeria at the time that was either willing or able to spell it out:

> The British High Commissioner, to be fair, was very much a product of the old British colonial establishment and he viewed black people in their proper place. Certainly, Ojukwu did not fit into that mould: he came with a British public school education and could actually be regarded as a black Englishman. He'd been to Oxford, played a good game of rugby, his father had been knighted by the King and was a self-made millionaire…this was a man of substance.

BIAFRA: THE BUILD-UP

The Nigerian delegation at a meeting called to discuss the war at the Organisation of African Unity in Addis Ababa was headed by Yakubu Gowon. (Author's photo)

Ojukwu, recalls Forsyth, regarded Sir David Hunt – university don, diplomat, author, archaeologist, TV personality and army officer – with the direst suspicion: 'Well-merited as it eventually turned out,' he recalls:

> From the outset, the British High Commissioner detested the Ibo military leader and the sentiment was thoroughly reciprocated.
> On Hunt's part, there were two reasons. Unlike Ojukwu, Hunt was not public school, despite the brilliant classical brain he demonstrated at Oxford. But he *was* a simply crashing snob and a covert racist. Two, he divorced his wife and married Iro Myrianthousis, the editor of *Lagos Weekly* and the favourite niece of the mega-rich, Lebanese-Greek Nigerian-based tycoon A.G. Leventis… and what complicated matters here was that she had been Emeka's [Ojukwu's] girlfriend, with the younger man vastly better endowed!

In his book The *Biafran War: The Struggle for Modern Nigeria*, Michael Gould – a British academic who had spent part of his youth in Nigeria – has his own views on the rebel leader: he tells us that after several years of education at the Catholic Mission School, followed by a spell at King's College in Lagos – one of the best educational establishments in West Africa and modelled on the British private school system – young Odumegwu was sent by his father to London. That was after Hitler's War had ended and he stayed as a house guest and under the guardianship of John Whiter and his family.

In the United Kingdom, Ojukwu was educated first at Epsom College and then gained a place reading Law at Lincoln College, Oxford. Forsyth mentioned that he was then already aware that the legal profession was not for him, but for the sake of his father, Sir Louis, he stuck to it – filling in time by doing well in sports.

On his return to Nigeria, Gould continues, following interviews with Julia Burrows:

> Ojukwu was almost able to claim by right of birth his position in the elite of Nigerian society, although, with due credit to him, he did not elect to join one of his father's companies where position, status and success would almost certainly have been guaranteed. Indeed, on one occasion in the Whiter household, he proclaimed that there would be uprisings and a war in Nigeria and that he would eventually become king, such was his confidence and arguably his arrogance.[2]

Sir David Hunt never got on with the man he sometimes referred to as 'that young upstart Ojukwu'. In fact, quoting from FCO, Doc 25/232 held in the National Archives, Kew, he was astonishingly outspoken about the rebel colonel:

> Power he has now got in full measure and he is obviously enjoying it; he also enjoys very much contemplating the superiority of his own intelligence and the lack of brains of the Head of the Federal Military Government and the other regional military governors. If I had any confidence in my ability to tell character from appearance, I should say that there was some mental instability in him; apart from his appearance which there seems to be a touch of paranoia in the ease with which he believes unbelievable stories about the secret manoeuvres of his enemies.

Indeed, that was a rather unwarranted statement, since it was an open secret that British Intelligence was doing everything it could to discredit the Ibo leader to the extent of even trying to find incriminating evidence in Frederick Forsyth's London apartment by illegally entering it while he was away and going through his things. Sir David would have been very much in the loop on those SIS machinations.

Later, in the same document, the British High Commissioner goes on to say that he had met Odumegwu Ojukwu six years before as a young lieutenant '… and I thought him polished and intelligent far beyond the average of the Nigerian officer'.

Frederick Forsyth, for his part, during many hours of taped recordings (as well as numerous off-the-cuff comments while we spent time together in Chinook, Washington) never uttered a disparaging word about the former Biafran leader, whom he regarded as a 'close friend'. To the contrary, my immediate impression was that he really liked the man and, after the civil war had ended, the British author contributed liberally towards the education of Ojukwu's children. Though he did not elaborate, I got the impression that, as with other people that Frederick Forsyth helped when he began to make good money from his books, Ojukwu got a share of it.

Possibly the best insight into the man Odumegwu Ojukwu might have come from an article published by the Nigerian magazine *Vanguard* on 2 November 2003. The author was Obi Nwakanma and though many years had passed since the war ended, his recollections present a vivid understanding – even if he is a little ebullient in the telling. I quote some of the more salient excerpts:

---

2   Gould, Michael, Ibid. quoting Julia Burrows – daughter of the managing director of Richard Costain Limited – whom he interviewed on 22 March 2009. Colonel Ojukwu's father, Sir Louis Ojukwu, had powerful business links to the British civil engineering business company active in Nigeria at the time. John Whiter was Costain's managing director.

An exact-to-scale replica Minicon was built by an American enthusiast years after the war ended – complete with Biafra's 'Rising Sun' flag. (Wikipedia)

Primitive efforts at camouflage were made by the rebels – using palm fronds to try to avoid their precious vintage World War II bombers from being picked up by Nigerian Air Force MiG-17s. (Author's collection)

My most vivid memory of Biafra was in its dying days… it was January 1970. My uncle, now a professor of geophysics, but then the Platoon Commander of the Biafran 'suicide squad', a task force under Tim Onwuatuegwu's 'S' Brigade, had found a little time in the raging battles at Owaza to be present at his elder brother's wedding.

I remember because of the ululation that went up that evening, as the sun sank under its balconies, when my uncle drove into my maternal grandfather's compound, battle-drunk, with some of his boys. They bore strange names: 'khaki', 'Man-die-go', 'kill-and-bury'.

They seemed like giants out of the book, the *Grimm's Tales* that my mother found time to read to us, which still echoes deeply in my mind's eye. I remember that evening, mostly because my grandfather's compound shook with volleys of gunshots in the air. Then the song that broke out '*Ojukwu wu Eze Biafra…*' It was heady, a song of innocence. It was a hymnal of faith.

My family was in that war: my father, an operative of the Biafran Civil Defence Forces, my uncles in the Biafran combat zones, my mother, the school mistress, a local organiser of the Land Army. Even my aged maternal grandfather, a knight of the church, a volunteer for the refugee camps, working with Caritas – the Catholic aid group – to feed the displaced from all over the Eastern Region – from as far as Abonema, Opobo, Ikot-Ekpene, who came in search of safety and security in this town secured by ancient forests in Mbaise.

Somehow, the stories of the war came to me, because my house seemed always to be the gathering of many people, my father's friends, mostly displaced from the rest of the Federation, who came to share platitudes, and speak 'great English'. I heard tit-bits that have framed my consciousness in particular ways. I always sat to listen.

One man was usually at the centre of much of that discussion: Chukwuemeka Odumegwu Ojukwu, Commander-in-Chief of the Republic of Biafra.

It seems such a long time now. Ojukwu entered the realm of myth through the front-door, by a single act of will: he chose to stand by the people whom he swore to serve, and to lead. It was an oath he took when he was sworn in, a young man of 32 years, as the Military Governor of the old Eastern Region in January 1966 by the late Supreme Commander, General Johnson Thomas Aguiyi Ironsi.

There is the view that Ojukwu's action was predicated upon the fact that Mr. Udoji was too entangled with significant foreign interests which Ojukwu thought to be too distracting and too deleterious to the administration of the East. Udoji's accounts of that moment, of course, indict Ojukwu as 'too power-hungry'.

Most people in Nigeria have been fed a distorted version of the story of events in Nigeria in which Ojukwu has been painted: as an arrogant, power-hungry monster who deceived an entire people into a tragic war (never mind that the Igbo, especially, are not people you lead easily by the nose).

But let us now put Odumegwu Ojukwu in his proper historical context. Any serious scholar of modern Nigerian history will not fail to conclude that there have been three most definitive figures of modern Nigerian history since 1914: Herbert Macaulay, Nnamdi Azikiwe and Chukwuemeka Odumegwu Ojukwu. These individuals defined the character of their generation in far more significant ways than any of their contemporaries.

Around them and their actions, and the unique aura of their presence, we can tease out the very conditions which frame the basis of modern Nigerian history. In Ojukwu's particular case, he has managed to convoke post-colonial Nigeria as a problematic space.

Born to wealth, shunning wealth for service and choosing the path of stone rather than the paved way which providence prepared for him, Odumegwu Ojukwu is atypical of any leader ever born in Nigeria.

Sir Louis Ojukwu, Odumegwu's father, was a most unusual fellow. A transport mogul and one of the first ethnic multi-millionaires of Nigeria, it was not coincidental that he was an Ibo – and proud of it.

With a powerful tribal orientation, which, in the tradition of Africa of old, has always been more of a *Gemeinschaft* than a *Gesellschaft*, he started life as a working-class man. A good, solid, middle-class sort, he invested all his assets in a single truck at an early age, from where he built up a pan-national chain of transport vehicles that ended up making him a considerable fortune during World War II. For his services and aid to the Empire during wartime, Sir Louis was knighted.

Biafran soldiers on the march. While undergoing training, some of these troops were issued with wooden guns. (Author's photo)

As Obi Nwakanma tells us, Sir Louis Phillipe Odumegwu Ojukwu became the wealthiest Nigerian of his generation – a man who had been chairman of the United Africa Company (Unilever); the Nigerian Stock Exchange; director of Shell-BP; had vast investment in property in Lagos, Kano, Port Harcourt, Enugu, Onitsha and other places; and owned controlling shares in many of the top blue-chip corporations that still operate in Nigeria today. Emeka Ojukwu could have walked naturally into a life of ease and indolence. In fact, by today's set of values, Sir Louis Ojukwu's wealth would be in the range of about 10 billion sterling.

The eternal entrepreneur, it was taken for granted that the majority of people he would gather about him were from the better-educated and not-afraid-of-work Ibo, Ibibio and Ijaw tribal grouping from which he hailed. The trouble was, while this was fine for easterners, other Nigerian tribes tended to consider the Ibos as individuals who, if not pushy, over-ambitious and self-important, liked to regard the rest of their compatriots as inferior. Not for nothing were the Ibo people sometimes called 'The Jews of Africa' – and uppity ones at that. In a word, the Ibos were considered snobs, but unlike the Muslim people in Nigeria's north, they were competent snobs.

Obi Nwakanma, author of the original treatise published in *Vanguard,* continues:

> Returning from Oxford University, Ojukwu turned his back to all that, and chose the service because it was his own path to freedom, and to greatness, on his own terms.
>
> His biographer, the English writer Frederick Forsyth, has given an account in the book, *Emeka,* of how Ojukwu's helpless father had tried to lure his Oxford-educated son to become a director in his company in 1956, and about how he chose instead to enter the civil service.

The international community soon rallied in support of Biafra's starving children. Joan Baez and Jimi Hendrix launched a concert in their support in August 1968. (Mark Press of Geneva)

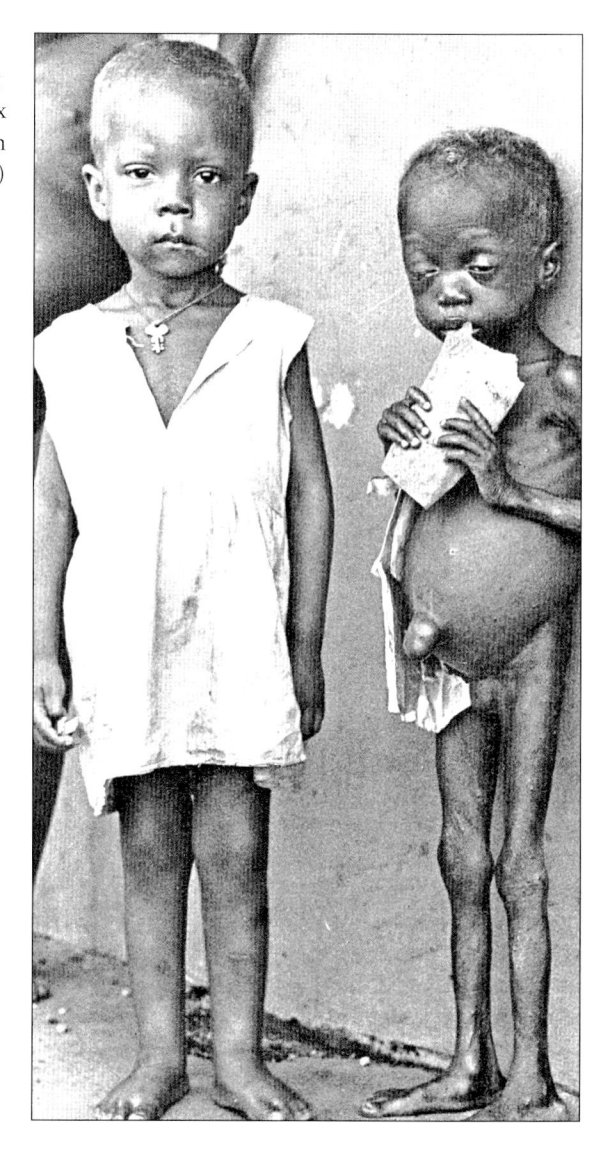

Seeing that his mind was made, Sir Louis goes to his friend, the British Governor-General Sir James Robertson, to try and convince Emeka Ojukwu.

The Governor-General offers Emeka any job he wanted, including as senior assistant secretary in [his personal] office. Ojukwu rejects the offer, and on his own terms secures a rural posting to Udi, in the Eastern Regional Civil Service.

We have also come to know how Ojukwu entered the army as the first Nigerian university graduate to earn a commission. This, at a time when the military was not too sexy, Ojukwu, apparently with an eye on history, sought a commission. His influential father once again intervened to stop his son, using the Governor-General once again to block Ojukwu's commission. Failing to earn an officer's commission, Ojukwu decides to go through the lowly route – he joins as another rank – a Private with a Master's degree in History from Oxford. This is hardly the act of an arrogant, power-hungry person.

It is apparent that Chukwuemeka Odumegwu Ojukwu was driven by a sense of destiny. As a ten-year old boy in Form One at King's College in Lagos, in 1943, he too had already joined the anti-colonial struggle. That year, he joined senior students like Anthony Enahoro and Ovie Whiskey, among others, to stage an anti-war, anti-colonial protest against the colonial administration, for which some of the students were reprimanded, others conscripted to fight, and from which people like Enahoro emerged into national limelight.

Ojukwu was tried as a juvenile in the courts in Lagos for his participation, and two pictures essay that moment: when he lay sleeping at the docks, and when his father, Sir Louis, carries him still sleepy, on his shoulder at the end of proceedings.

Ojukwu's radicalised consciousness was possibly sharpened when his father sent him off to school in England, to Epsom College, soon after the King's incident.

Black, stubborn, and opinionated, Ojukwu might have earned himself some unsavoury record. But he was a sportsman. He was brilliant. He was a rich boy. He was inevitable. In Oxford, Ojukwu joined the socialists, even though he rode about in a Rolls-Royce.

The war that everybody regarded as inevitable became a reality when the secessionist West African state of Biafra unilaterally declared itself independent from Nigeria in May 1967. The split came months after I left Lagos, when tens of thousands of Ibo people in the Northern Region were massacred. Perhaps a million more fled southwards to eastern-dominated areas. In turn, huge numbers of non-Ibos were expelled from the east.

While hostilities started well enough, with the secessionists marching half-way across the country to take Benin and much of the central regions, the Biafran Army was hesitant to push on to Lagos. It was unquestionably Ojukwu's worst mistake of the war. The city was wide open – and government forces, though not in disarray, were on the back foot and would have been unable to respond to the rebel initiative; then came betrayal.

Ojukwu himself today admits that the role played by Colonel Victor Banjo – a non-Ibo, but one of his senior planners – had a significant effect on the outcome of that early, extremely critical phase. His forces were never supposed to have taken the mid-west city of Benin. They wasted weeks and a lot of lives in doing so; then Banjo clandestinely made contact with Federal Army officers in Lagos. It did not work, because Banjo was unmasked, court-martialled and shot at dawn.

As Frederick Forsyth wrote (he spent a lot of time in Biafra and wrote a classic book on the war, *The Biafra Story*): 'It was also clear that the Nigerian Army was a rabble, a shambles from beginning to end'.

Government forces did get their act together after a while – in part – because either they did, or they went down. Lagos' forces then proceeded to blockade all eastern ports in the hands of Ojukwu's troops – and within months the conflict had degenerated into one of the most brutal tit-for-tat wars of attrition that Africa has seen since independence.

Fighting everywhere was vicious and confused. Towns changed hands – sometimes three or four times within months. Eventually, the preponderance of Federal power prevailed and the Biafrans were pushed back – first from the coast and finally into several loosely-linked enclaves in the heavily-forested interior. Government atrocities at the hands of what had become a northern-dominated, mainly Islamic force, soon convinced the rebel nation that secession from the Federation was no longer the principal issue. Rather, it had become an all-out battle for survival.

Once again, in the eyes of their adversaries, the Ibo – as crafty as he was – had shown that he was pushier than the rest. Some Nigerians regarded the fact that easterners seemed to be taking over the Federal Army as dangerous, and so ran editorials in some of the northern newspapers.

4

Hostilities Take Shape

Uncertainty in Federal Nigeria caused all the participants in this developing conflict to carefully examine their options. By then, the major powers – principally Britain, France and the Soviet Union – were formulating contingency measures of their own.

I was to spend a month at Ikeja after that historic battle, which ultimately changed the face of Nigeria forever. The airport was where I'd also started writing seriously – being the only person who was doing any reporting because journalists were prevented by the military junta from entering the country.

There was no shortage of stories – as well as quite a few unexpected 'scoops'. Also, getting my missives and photos out of the country was not a problem – bearing in mind that these were times when the fax machine had not yet been invented, never mind cell phones.

Each time I had something for one of my editors, I'd sidle up to a departing Pan American passenger waiting to check in his or her baggage. Totally incognito, I'd ask them to take my little package out of the country. It would usually contain a roll or two of film – and, of course, my story, but they did not know that and nobody ever refused.

I said something about my mother not having heard from me for ages 'because of the army having taken over' and that I wanted to show her that I was alive and thriving. I would also pass on a slip of paper with Wilf Nussey's phone number at the offices of the *The Star* in downtown Johannesburg – 'my brother', I explained – and told my newfound 'courier' that he'd send someone to their hotel to fetch the packet. It worked like a charm – and it says a lot that not one of my reports went missing, but I don't suggest trying that at any airport today…

Those were interesting times. Apart from Nussey's Argus Africa News Service, I cut my teeth as a budding journalist on stories that went to United Press International in London and Otto Krause's *News Check,* as well as South Africa's Afrikaans-language *Huisgenoot*. Being the only person with any kind of access to what was going on at the time in Nigeria – and obviously the only person willing to chance smuggling news and photos out of the country – I not only made a packet, but learnt a lot about the news-gathering game.

I lasted six months in Nigeria before calling it a day and headed home. I was on probation with John Holt anyway and my British bosses were not stupid when my name kept popping up in various newspapers, so they gave me my notice with a hefty bonus to leave as soon as possible.

Also, one of the company officials caught me taking surreptitious photos of Nigerian Air Force planes at Ikeja, which underscored my naivety. I could easily have been arrested by the army for spying. I would actually be very interested to see what was recorded in my security files in London because there is no question that the British High Commission got wind of my activities, but they said and did nothing. They rarely do, until they have to.

As the war gathered pace during the latter part of 1967 I was determined to get back to West Africa and cover it, if only because my little sojourn in Lagos had provided me with some valuable

HOSTILITIES TAKE SHAPE 53

An early photo of one of the Nigerian Air Force MiG-17s that Moscow insisted Egypt give to this West African state. It was not long before they were being flown by Western pilots. (Ares Klootwyk)

writing connections – and since Vietnam tended to hog the headlines (and most of the more experienced hacks), there weren't too many scribes either eager or willing to go into a conflict that, from abroad, looked like a single step removed from disaster.

Because of censorship on both sides of the front, nobody got the entire picture – and the reason was fundamental. One of the first steps taken by both the Biafrans and the Federal Government was to hire a succession of reputable and extremely expensive public relations companies – initially in the United States and then, for Biafra, in Switzerland. Instructions were clear: they were to push their respective military claims – most of them inflated. There were some battles that took place that – had you to judge by their respective PR and news reports – might have happened on different continents.

One of the persistent consequences of all this was that just about everything about the war – from start to finish – was clouded by duplicity and equivocation. I thought that perhaps because I'd seen developments from the inside, I'd be able to add my thing. I'd been there from the start – right at the core of it. I also knew that the Biafrans would not be an easy pushover. As we now know, they were not.

How to get into Biafra – landlocked by then and only to be reached by air from one of two neighbouring territories – was another matter. Biafra, at that stage, was recognised by only five countries – and then only circumspectly. Tanzania, another revolutionary cauldron perusing its own Soviet-backed revolutionary interests in neighbouring Mozambique, was one of them; the others were Gabon, Haiti, the Ivory Coast and Zambia, though for a long time, it was believed that Mauretania was also in this group.

Having gone to Nairobi, I'd made my way by road to Dar es Salaam and, using my *Daily Express* press card, banged at the door of the Biafran legation. It took time while they checked my bona fides, but eventually a visa came through. From Tanzania, I headed for West Africa.

In theory, I expect I could have covered the war from the Nigerian side, but things there at the time had become ultra-difficult. The media was suspect – some Federal politicians calling them 'Fifth Columnists, spying for Biafra' – and individual Nigerian commanders weren't shy to show their displeasure if somebody reported something contrary to the official line.

One senior Nigerian Army officer, Colonel Benjamin 'Black Scorpion' Adekunle – Commander of Nigeria's 3rd Marine Commando Division – was a psychopathic bully who was quite happy to shoot his own men if he thought he needed to make an example. He did so once in the presence of foreign journalists and dared them to file their stories.

Adekunle often blasted off about the kind of journalism that was then coming out of West Africa – blaming his nation's woes on the CIA, Westminster, the Pope and who knows who or what else. It was worse if the object of his venom happened to be white. Europeans were responsible for all of the ills of Africa, he would proclaim. It was worse when he was drunk.

Mike Williamson, in *A Measure of Danger*, mentions a dinner at which Adekunle drew a pistol and pointed it, in turn, at each of the journalists at the table. Eventually, he pressed it against Williamson's temple and pulled the trigger. It went click. Black joke from the 'Black Scorpion', as somebody commented. With all this in mind, I really did not want to cover the Nigerian side. In any event, the Biafran effort sounded much more romantic; and dramatic –and it was – but how was I to get in there? Aware that I could enter the beleaguered state from one of three places, I had to make a choice. First there was Lisbon, which everybody knew had regular flights to the island of São Tomé, which had been a Portuguese colony for centuries and from where there were nightly, mainly Church-Aid relief flights across the Nigerian coast into Biafra; or I could head straight for São Tomé itself, but that would have meant starting my journey in Portugal anyway.

The only other alternative was Gabon – another of the states that had recognised Ojukwu's cause. Trouble was, most flights into Biafra out of Libreville – the Gabonese capital – were military and that meant getting to the war on a plane carrying explosives. Candidly, I would have preferred something a little more innocuous, though even that became dangerous after one of the Nigerian mercenary pilots flying a Soviet MiG-17 shot down a Red Cross aircraft loaded with baby food.

My opportunity came after I had gone back to West Africa on an assignment to cover a story in the Ivory Coast for a European magazine. I found myself in Ghana shortly afterwards and from there I reviewed my options. For a start, as a freelancer – and a relative beginner –money was tight. I had to budget carefully. I knew that I could afford perhaps one flight to whatever destination I chose – and I'd have to make the best of that.

Gabon, I decided early on, was my best option, but getting there from Ghana was the problem. Any flight between Accra and Libreville would have meant changing planes at Lagos. I hesitated for several reasons – not the least being that I had worked at Ikeja International Airport for quite a while and just about everybody there (including quite a few Nigerian Army and Air Force senior officers) knew me by my first name. Questions would obviously have been asked…

Also, having lived in the country for six months, the Nigerians would have been interested to learn what it was that had brought me back to West Africa in a time of war. They were familiar with what I had done at John Holt before – and anyway, people involved in shipping don't go traipsing about Africa if they had no good reason to do so. Had I needed to, I could have talked my way out of that one, but I did not relish the hassle. Who knew where it could lead?

By then, we were all aware that mercenaries had become an issue. Lagos had its Egyptian, British, Australian and South African mercenary pilots, while Biafra had started recruiting freebooters from all over – many of whom had served in the Congo (including a good few French soldiers of

Biafran troops in bayonet training. (Author's photo)

fortune). Among this number were such illustrious characters as Rolf Steiner and Bob Denard. I feared that I could very easily have been mistaken, even briefly, for one of them – particularly since I was headed for Gabon – so instead of going by air, I did the next best thing and made for Ghana's biggest port at Tema and started shopping around for a berth on a ship heading east. Within hours I found what I wanted: a freighter that would take me to the Cameroons – Nigeria's Francophonic neighbour. My saviour was the Norwegian-registered 12,000-tonne freighter *Titania*.

No, the captain assured me, there would be no layovers in any Nigerian ports – and yes, he said, he was going to Douala in the Cameroons. Problem solved. We discussed a price and with a handshake, we had a deal. I knew I could easily fly from Douala to Libreville. What I had not factored into the bargain was that cargo ships all over the world are subject to the prerequisites of their owners. If there's a cargo waiting to be picked up somewhere along the way and there's money to made by doing so, the master will get his instructions and he would do the necessary – so it was with the *Titania*.

We had barely slipped our moorings in the Ghanaian port when he called me to the bridge to advise of a change of plan. The ship was going into a Nigerian port after all. Some oil-drilling equipment had to be hauled out of the Nigerian delta port of Warri, he explained. We would stop over first in Lagos, he continued, to have our cargo and our papers checked.

As expected, I was closely questioned about the reasons for my visit to Nigeria when the *Titania* berthed at Apapa Docks. My name was on file and so was the fact – very clearly imprinted in my passport – that I'd been in South Africa a short while before. That was a half-hour that was gruelling and uncertain, but eventually the man – clearly linked to one of the Nigerian Intelligence offices – let me continue my journey.

When I disembarked at Douala, my troubles started afresh – largely over what was termed something of a *mercenaire* issue. Many of those who have travelled the West African coast refer to Douala (the city lies in the middle of hundreds of square miles of swamp) as the original 'Armpit of Africa'. It is as hot and clammy as an aardvark's ass, with mushrooms often sprouting on the carpets of your hotel.

The colonising Germans, no doubt, had good reason for settling at the estuary of one of the unhealthiest rivers in Africa, although they've always escaped me. Victoria – the British-controlled enclave along the western fringe of the Cameroons that lies at the foot of the great Mount Cameroon – is a much more appealing setting and is situated further towards the west and the Nigerian frontier. It is also a lot healthier.

One of the tasks given to Cape Town's Ares Klootwyk – then flying as a mercenary for the Nigerian Air Force – was to fly this helicopter out of territory captured by Federal forces. (Ares Klootwyk)

At Douala, in contrast, the river is nearly always shrouded in a tropical mist after dark – and its mosquitoes and other bugs are legion. There was an appalling number of deaths among the colonists in the early years of this century, where most of them died of yellow fever.

Travellers arriving at Douala are greeted by a city that is almost completely surrounded by an almost impenetrable swamp. An aircraft flying to Europe from Johannesburg in the 1960s crashed immediately after take-off, with more than a hundred passengers and crew on board. Although it went down almost within sight of the airport, it took French Army and Navy rescue teams three days to reach the wreckage, though one must obviously ask the obvious: were there no helicopters? Nobody survived and the word went out that crocodiles feasted on the bodies, which was perhaps just as well in that heat, though that was something you could hardly convey to their families.

History repeated itself when a Kenya Airways Boeing jet crashed after take-off from Douala in May 2007. Again, there were more than a hundred people on board – all of them killed – and once more, it took another two days for the authorities (this time working *with* helicopters) to discover the site of the wreck. As with the crash two generations earlier, it came down just a few miles from the airport…

After leaving the *Titania*, my intention was to fly to Libreville from Douala and make contact with the Biafran Embassy in that city. From Gabon, hopefully, I'd be able to cadge a lift on a plane to Uli. That much about my trip, I had been told, had been arranged two months previously by Ibezim Chukwumerije – one of the diplomats at the Office of the Biafran Special Representative in Dar es Salaam.

I had no difficulties in Douala, except that I was kept for an hour by an officious immigration officer who quizzed me repeatedly about my intentions.

'You're not going into Biafra?' he asked in good English. He looked hard at me – and it could not have helped that I was sweating cupfuls in his airless office above the harbour.

The Biafrans soon acquired interests in several aircraft used to bring in flights on nightly shuttles. These included nondescript Super Constellations. (Author's collection)

'Not at all, Sir.' I declared earnestly. 'I'm going south.'

'Strange that you should come through here, through Douala,' was his remark.

Because the man was obviously suspicious, I said something about liking ships. I was only to discover afterwards, that a couple of weeks before, two young Americans had arrived in Douala – very much as I had – though they'd flown in from New York. They'd heard about the plight of Biafra and they said that their intention was 'to help the starving millions' – at least that's what they told an immigration official at Douala Airport. When things started to get tough, one of them pointed to the fact that newspapers all over the world had made it known that Biafra needed medical help. Obviously, these two youngsters were sincere. They were also absurdly untested in some of Africa's quandaries – one of the most immediate being personal security.

In their case, simply mentioning their intention of going to a country at war with a neighbour set off a chain of consequences that they could never have foreseen. First they were arrested; then, for several days, they were interrogated and savagely beaten. The *Agence Camerounaise de la Presse* had declared in a leading story that the two were mercenaries, but that was after they were taken to hospital and the American Embassy in Yaounde had delivered a protest note. There was nothing 'mercenary' about these two youngsters. Both had had solid medical backgrounds and they honestly believed that they could help in a war zone. They were flown out as soon as the American Consul in Douala could get them released – and in order to achieve that, he had to offer some hefty guarantees. One of them spent months in hospital after he got back home.

On my way to Biafra, I eventually got to Gabon, but it was there that my troubles started afresh. Basically, the French were committed to keeping the Biafran War alive. For reasons of its own, the Quai d'Orsay was opposed to a powerful Nigerian presence striding tall across West Africa – if only because the French had enough problems keeping their own former colonies in line without being confronted by an erstwhile British monolith. More to the point, Paris did what it could to curtail this influence, which politically, had become intrusive.

Consequently, it was the French – and not the Gabonese or the Biafrans – that vetted anybody wanting to go into the rebel territory. I was no exception. It took me several days of persuasion to get a flight. Eventually, with the help of one of the South African pilots involved in relief work, I got onto a flight to Uli – at that stage reckoned to be West Africa's busiest airport.

Only a jungle airstrip in the heart of tropical West Africa, Uli Airport – codename Annabelle – became a legend among the airline pilots of the world. Long after it had been destroyed by the

Nigerian Army, it continued to nurture an almost mystical status that fired the imagination of a thousand adventurers.

The building of an improvised airstrip in the bush followed the fall of Port Harcourt to the Federal Nigerian Army in May 1968 for one reason: the Biafrans urgently needed weapons. While an enormous effort was made to save the lives of starving children in the embattled enclave, Uli's prime role was centred on the ability of its army to fight.

Indeed, following the walkout of the Biafran delegation to the peace talks in Uganda in the spring of 1968, a Biafran officer told the British journalist John de St Jorre that: 'If you gave us the choice of 1,000 rifles or milk for 50,000 starving children, we'd take the guns.'

Thus, it was through the Uli airstrip that the first large consignment of French weapons began to arrive. These cargoes – consisting variously of rifles, machine guns and light artillery; as well as anti-aircraft guns, millions of rounds of ammunition, hand grenades, rockets, mortars, explosives and the rest – all delivered serially in 20-tonne loads flown in each night by commercial air freighters, pushed the conflict to its limits.

Uli/Annabelle was originally constructed as a stopgap measure, with every intention of reverting to Port Harcourt Airport once it had been recaptured – which, of course, never happened. It stood on the main road between Owerri and Ihiala – a long, arrow-straight stretch between Mgbidi. The road was widened to 25 metres and modified into a 2,600-metre long runway, along with an adjacent taxi-way that ran parallel to the strip. Capable of handling up to 30 large aircraft every night – and better known among the locals as Uli-Ihiala Airport – it became fully operational in August 1968.

Like most things, everything that went on at Uli was improvised. The runway was lined on both sides by primeval jungle – and anybody not familiar with what was going on there during the dark hours might have believed that the place was an abandoned military base if they passed that way during the day. The airport came alive immediately after the sun had set, with a thousand helpers and soldiers crawling out of their bunkers to do the night's work. They would gather in groups for orders and then be sent out to remove palm fronds that had been laid out over both the runway and camouflaged support vehicles and set to work. With no cranes or forklift trucks, everything was done by muscle-power.

Even then, things did not always happen as intended. When the fuses blew, which happened regularly, they would line the runway with cans of palm oil with lighted wicks floating on top to show approaching aircraft where to come in. It was typically West African Heath Robinson – especially when the wind blew – but it worked.

A similar ploy was adapted years later at the primitive airstrip used by South African Air Force C-130s with Dr Jonas Savimbi's military headquarters at Jamba in Eastern Angola.

Frederick Forsyth describes it well in his introduction to one of the best books to come out of the war, Mike Draper's *Shadows: Airlift and Airwar in Biafra and Nigeria*.[1]

> It was crazy, it was hairy, it was impossibly dangerous; it should never have worked. But somehow it did, night after night. When the planes landed and taxied into the welcome darkness by the side of the motorway-turned-landing-strip, willing hands hauled sacks of milk powder and bundles of stockfish out of the fuselages and away into the feeding centres. That done, the pilots taxied back to the take-off point, the lights flickered on for a few seconds and they were gone…

---

1 Draper, Michael I., *Shadows: Airlift and Airwar in Biafra and Nigeria 1967-1970* (Coombe Corner, Awbridge, Hants SO51 0HN: 1999).

Biafran troops at a holding position on the outskirts of Asaba. At that stage, morale was still quite good among the fighters. (Wikipedia)

Forsyth recalls that this was the story of the strangest air-bridge the world has ever seen. As he says: '… the airplanes used by the aid people were a ramshackle collection of time-expired or phased out workhorses of the skies, culled from bone yards all over the globe'. Had it not happened, he reckoned there would have been another million Biafran children starved into oblivion because the rebel state was blockaded by land, sea and air.[2]

For their part, the Nigerians were just as active. Apart from shooting down the International Red Cross relief plane, mercenary pilots flew hundreds of MiG-17 missions against Biafran ground targets – something dealt with in detail in Chapter 11.

For much of the war, Uli remained the tenuous lifeline between Biafra and the world outside in this grim, internecine war. The 'miracle of Uli', as the hacks referred to it, hosted about 30 flights a night – though sometimes there were as few as five and, occasionally, as many as 40 aircraft – often loaded well beyond internationally accepted safety limits. The transport planes, which were registered in a couple of dozen nations, ferried in tonnes of food and weapons and ammunition.

The planes ran the Federal blockade, but not always without incident, because a few were destroyed either on the ground or in landing or take-off accidents – and quite a few suffered shrapnel damage. Some were hit while taxiing; others were bombed by the Nigerian Air Force

---

2   Forsyth, Frederick, *The Biafra Story: The Making of an African Legend* (London: Penguin Books, 1977).

'Intruder' – an antiquated C-47 Dakota that had been adapted to carry 20-kilo canisters of explosives. Later, the Nigerians bought some surplus American B-25s.

There were several planes also accidentally shot down by Biafran ground fire, though the rebels always denied it. They said it couldn't happen, but it did. We were nearly hit by heavy machine-gun fire from the ground as we came in – and it wasn't Nigerian fire coming up at us because their lines were miles away.

Look at the figures: in church relief flights alone (never mind the arms runs, which were a sizeable tally each night), there were 7,350 freight flights into Biafra in the three years that war ravaged Eastern Nigeria. In this time, almost a million tonnes of supplies – including arms – were taken into the beleaguered territory. During the course of these operations, there were 15 aircraft lost and 25 air crew killed – all buried at a small cemetery adjacent to Uli Airport. Their graves were bulldozed by the Nigerian Army immediately after the war ended. That took place a day or two after Nigerian troops had overrun Uli, so that, as one cocky Nigerian field commander declared to a gathering of foreign correspondents: 'They'll be eternally forgotten…We don't want their families poking about here for their remains afterwards.'

Getting from Libreville to Uli was an event. Suddenly, on day six or seven, the Biafran representative in Libreville told me: 'You're going in tonight. Make sure you're at the airport by three this afternoon and bring along something warm to wear. It gets cold in the air.'

My pilot was a German. 'Herman the German', we called him – a laconic individual with severe halitosis who was much given to brandy, good or bad. Word had it that he drank day and night. When he reported for duty that afternoon, he'd obviously had plenty and I couldn't object because Herman was my passport to an unusual war – and '*Zey*,' he said – implying the Nigerians – 'are *vaiting* for us.'

It was essential to listen very carefully to whatever Herman had to tell you. His English sounded like a send-up of some of those skits that were popular in Britain in the 1960s and that the British were so adept at making. It took a while to work out that '*zem*' was 'them', and who '*zey*' was – especially when he slurred, which was often. It was rumoured that this alcoholic aviator had flown supplies into trapped divisions at Stalingrad, though it was something he would not talk about.

Once on board the unmarked L-749A Super Constellation, with its unmistakable triple tail fins, there were no formalities – and I had no intercom to talk to the pilots up front. My place was at the back – a single solitary seat immediately ahead of the tail, with a toilet that had not been cleaned in months. From where I sat, the cockpit felt a thousand miles away. I should have been comforted by the mountain of baby food between us, but I wasn't.

Herman, of course, was right. The Nigerians *were* waiting for us. As soon as we crossed the coastline somewhere near Port Harcourt, I spotted flashes of artillery fire on the ground that quickly became brilliant orange balls of flak as they exploded a few thousand feet below us. I watched the panoply through the porthole nearest to me – transfixed by the sheer horror of it. I'd never experienced being directly shot at before – and for a time, it was a bit like being at the movies.

Only after the war did it emerge that the nightly shuttle of aircraft from Libreville and São Tomé into Biafra was a giant charade – a chess game of sorts that the Super Powers tended to indulge in from time to time.

Nigerian anti-aircraft guns and their crews were Russian. Somehow, those who made the nightly flights into Biafra were aware that their fuses had been set at 14,000 feet. Meanwhile, we crossed the coast a bit higher at 18,000 feet. Had they wanted to, they could probably have shot us down at any time they chose. Curiously, the Nigerian High Command never protested, although one would have thought that they might have done so, since Lagos was picking up the tab for all this so-called 'gratuitous military aid' from the Soviets.

HOSTILITIES TAKE SHAPE 61

A Nigerian armoured vehicle knocked out by Biafran forces during one of the early rallies by the rebel state. (Photo courtesy of Leif Hellström)

Once we'd crossed the coast, there wasn't a light to be seen anywhere on the ground, apart from some heavy calibres shooting at us from what I'd earlier been warned were 'front lines'. What compounded matters, I soon discovered, was that none of the aircraft approaching Uli used their navigation lights – even though there were sometimes eight or 10 aircraft stacked above and below us. Getting onto the ground, there was a mammoth nightly operation that seemed to work, but (considering the impediments) should not have.

Herman told me before lift-off that our approach to Uli Airport would be made in the dark – not that it made much difference when we eventually got there. Almost all of Africa was clothed in a brilliant, almost incandescent glow from a moon that was almost full.

There was a joke among relief crews: that if they were all to simultaneously switch on their lights while circling Uli, half the pilots would have died of heart attack. Most of these ageing aviators had been in World War II and were flying dangerously close to each other.

The actual landing process was dicey. With time, routines to cope with the unusual demands of the bush strip were developed, with the result that our descent was ultra-steep. Pilots would manoeuvre their aircraft into position before sets of improvised runway lights were switched on for about five or six seconds. That was all the time they had to get their bearings. Meanwhile, Herman was talking to ground control – or rather, I hoped that he was doing so.

Though the world was dark outside, most of the pilots would have some idea of where they were while circling because of the landing lights that flashed irregularly before touchdown. Once into short finals, another few seconds of light was allowed and that was that. It was a pretty precise operation and spoke a lot for the skill of those at the controls of these ageing hulks; many of the pilots were retired airline veterans and were well past their 'use-by' dates.

Meanwhile, it was the job of a Nigerian Air Force bomber labelled 'Genocide' by locals – and also flown by mercenaries – to give these relief planes a battering. The 'bomber' would break into

A Soviet Ilyushin bomber loaned to the Nigerian Government for its Biafran war effort. (Tom Cooper)

the cargo planes' radio chatter and taunt them: 'This is 'Genocide', baby… Come on down and get killed.'

The man's South African accent was unmistakable: obviously another war dog.

As Forsyth still recalls: 'Anyone listening in on the same wavelength could hear mercenary pilots flying the Nigerian bombers jeering at them, daring them to land when the lights flashed those few elusive seconds'.

To begin with, 'Genocide' was an archaic Dakota C-47 'Gooney Bird' that had been adapted to carry canisters of explosives (as mentioned earlier in the chapter). That old plane would hover at about 18,000 feet and wait for things to happen – the idea being to drop his canisters just as an oncoming aircraft came into the approach. Ideally, the explosives would go off just as the plane put its wheels down.

This improvised bomber – and another dubbed 'Intruder' – rarely succeeded in causing serious damage, but when they did, the Nigerian propaganda machine would spin into action and Lagos newspapers would crow that Uli Airport had been crippled. It sometimes took a week to put things right again – and often, Ojukwu's people would find alternate stretches of road; then the process would begin all over again.

A sidelight to these events was that in their final approach to Uli Airport, many pilots would come in so low that their fuselage would sometimes clip the tops of palms. Later, back at base, air crews would compare notes about 'green props'; just about everybody experienced them. There was also the occasional 'red prop'. Since most loading teams were made up of tribesmen who knew little about the dangers of modern aircraft, there were instances of them walking into propellers while the planes were being cleared.

Once on the ground, Biafrans crews (so many of them clearly malnourished) went to work –sometimes with astonishing gusto considering that they were all starving. Obviously, with the 'bomber' overhead, and none of the pilots wishing to spend longer immobile on the ground than

A motley collection of Biafran fighters. This photo was circulated to the media by Mark Press of Geneva.

was absolutely necessary, there was urgency to it all. Air crews would keep their engines ticking over and cargoes would be cleared within minutes.

If it were food, Roman Catholic White Fathers in their long cassocks would direct operations. Munitions were handed by the Biafran Army and canisters and crates destined for the military would be hurried away in trucks.

Meanwhile, other Biafran officials would indicate what or who was to go out that night. Most of the outgoing cargoes consisted of starving – mostly orphaned – children who were sent off to camps in other parts of Africa such as *Kilometre Onze* in Gabon, or to a succession of Roman Catholic Church institutions in São Tomé. The Biafrans were taking out 1,000 tonnes of cacao or copra a month on these planes.

None of us who went in that night will forget the heat and the noise that cloaked us like a sauna once we stepped off the plane. I crouched in a split-pole bunker beside the runway, together with a couple of others, and there was a musty, unwashed immediacy to it all. In time, the senses were sharpened by the stutter of automatic fire along the runway somewhere.

Alongside our position were several tall palms – their foliage blown away. This was all that was left of what was once a substantial palm oil plantation that probably dated from the colonial era. Their trunks looked like thousands of giant naked fingers pointing towards the sky. Alongside, perhaps 30 paces away, was the barely recognisable tail section of a Joint Church Aid Globemaster C-97 that had crashed a month before.

That, the priests in their robes, and occasional bursts of automatic fire – coupled to the roar of engines of aircraft landing and taking off – made for something surreal. Herman did not even bother to wave goodbye; he was airborne again in minutes. For a while, an uneasy calm descended on the jungle – broken now and again by more automatic fire.

An Ibo officer – a captain, I think, with the distinctive Biafran 'Rising Sun' patch on his arm – came towards me at a brisk pace. He cradled a sten gun.

'I take it that you are Mr Venter of the *Daily Express*?' he asked with a salute and an accent more reminiscent of Guildford than Africa; it was all so terribly British.

He introduced himself as Major Charles Ofili. He had been a schoolteacher before the war started, he told me as he led the way to the rest house where I would be offered 'breakfast': an improvised tea and scones that were half-sawdust …

5

Air Attack in Warri Harbour

> The first mercenary pilots hired by the Nigerian government arrived just after the fighting had started… most had left the Congo only weeks before.[1]

I was in my cabin on board the Swedish merchantman *Titania* when the first salvo struck: two powerful blasts in quick succession. It was like a car backfiring, only up close. The impact of exploding rockets reverberated throughout the ship and my immediate impulse was to get myself up top…

Two, three steps at a time, I shot up the companionway and emerged on a deck washed in bright tropical sunlight. I just had time to see two small single-engine aircraft turning low on the water about a quarter-mile away. We were only to find out afterwards that the planes – Swedish-built MFI-9B Minicons – had that morning scored their first major strike against maritime targets in the Nigerian Civil War. Just then, they were heading straight back at us. Two more spurts of smoke from their under-wing pods told me all I had to know: I'd seen enough war movies to be aware that more rockets were heading our way.

There was no thinking about it: my only option was to hurl myself down the same companionway from which I had just emerged. Moments later, more blasts erupted behind the bulkhead – one of them eight or 10 feet above my head. For a second or two, I had the air knocked out of me and it took a little while to get back on my feet. Meanwhile, another projectile hit the ship amidships and then one more above the waterline. Whoever was using these things knew what they were doing.

Though neutral, the Scandinavian merchant ship on which I was a passenger in Tema, Ghana had become a casualty; so had the American steamer moored ahead of us in the roadstead off the Nigerian oil port of Warri. Both freighters had made their way the hundred or so miles up the estuary of the Niger – West Africa's biggest river – and found themselves caught in a conflict that was already into its third year.

Comparatively speaking, the *Titania* had come off lightly. Not so the *African Crescent* – then in the final stages of a West African run out of Houston. Though there were larger-than-usual Stars and Stripes hanging fore and aft (she also sported a Farrell Lines crest on her smoke stack), the American cargo liner had two of its crew members killed and seven wounded. Only afterwards was I able to put together some of it. Having watched the Minicons do their turn over the river and fire a second salvo of what we later discovered were 68 mm rockets, I'd thrown myself down the same narrow set of stairs from which I'd emerged a short while before and landed on top of two female members of the ship's crew making their way up. The three of us collapsed in a heap at the foot of the companionway. The rocket that had detonated nearest to us exploded in the ship's linen

---

1 Draper, *Shadows*.

The author took this photo of the upper deck of the *Titania* while steaming up the Niger Delta to the Nigerian port of Warri.

cupboard – immediately under the stairs behind us. A year's supply of sheets, blankets and towels absorbed most of the blast and we weren't hurt, though my ears zinged for a week afterwards.

As 'fighters' go, the Biafran Minicons involved in that attack against us were modest little aircraft; some called them fragile. They'd originally been designed for training and were never intended to see action in any war. There, the two-seaters – originally built by SAAB – were fitted with under-wing hard-points that allowed them to carry rocket pods, one under each wing. That done, they were secretly shipped to Gabon by sea, where they were reassembled.

It was an eventful morning for everybody. Having gone into action against us at Warri, the Minicons pulled away and banked towards one of four or five tiny airstrips where fortified concrete bunkers had been built deep inside Biafra, but not before they struck again at several oil storage tanks on the outskirts of the port – sending plumes of black smoke thousands of feet into the air. By then, two merchant ships were dousing their fires and I was taking pictures.

Though the damage was real and there had been casualties, as far as the Nigerian Government was concerned, these were events that never happened – nor, insisted the Federal Government spokesman, were a million Biafran children starving; and since I was stringing for the London *Daily Express* and this was an event that needed to get out, I was faced with the dilemma of trying to communicate the news from a country at war.

No, said the captain; his ship was neutral and he could not – or rather would not – allow the radio officer to send 'war' reports from his radio room. I countered with another request: what about *me* transmitting my own copy? I'd done a spell of telegraphy in the navy and suggested that I could push it out to one of my ham friends in Nairobi for forwarding to Fleet Street. That was also unacceptable, answered the Swede – reverting to his customary taciturn mode. He was a mean bastard; the only time I ever saw him smile was when there was skirt about.

Undeterred, I went ashore to try my luck at the local post office – irrespective of the fact that government spooks were to be found at every street corner in town. While the local postmaster was prepared to take my story, as well as the Cable and Wireless card that went with it for payment (sweetened by a $20 bill), my report was never sent. I shouldn't have been surprised because the country's military censors used blue pencils to impose a blanket ban on any news of Biafran air activity. Officially, they maintained, the Minicons did not exist – even though I was told that London's *Lloyds List* covered the incident in some detail afterwards, as it does with all matters that pertain to international shipping.

Not long after the disaster that created the Congo that we know today, the rebel Nigerian 'state' of Biafra became a rallying point for mercenaries from just about everywhere. Their numbers included soldiers of fortune from many European countries, South Africa and Rhodesia, Australia, Canada and Britain – as well as one or two Chinese Nung fighters. There was even a CIA operative eager to get in a bit of action at company expense; experiencing the goings-on in a beleaguered Biafra must have been better than propping up the bar at the Federal Hotel on Lagos' Victoria Island.

There was also 29-year-old Nick Bishop from Philadelphia, who added Biafra to the notches on his belt after he had served awhile under Colonel Mike Hoare in the Congo. With him in this desperate West African enclave was British 'Major' C.C. Watson; he was a claymore mines specialist who went on to develop the appropriately dubbed 'Ojukwu Buckets' that carried enough explosives to fry an armoured car.

Another character to arrive shortly afterwards was a hefty 42-year-old American named Barry 'Hawg' McWhorter. A big man in all departments, he flew an obsolete B-26R bomber for the breakaway Biafrans for a time and then went on to look for something that paid better money. Tipping the scale at a weighty 300 lbs, McWhorter was hardly your typical swashbuckling war dog, though there was lots of swash and more than enough buckle whenever he strapped himself into his pilot's seat. By the time he got to the west coast, he'd already made a name for himself as an opportunist of repute in several theatres of military activity on the African continent.

Barry joined the American based organisation Joint Church Aid to help fly in relief supplies to the rebel enclave from São Tomé at what he claimed was $5,000 a month. Most mercs flying cargo planes ended up there, while others flew from Libreville. Only a handful of this rum bunch worked from Fernando Pó in Spanish Guinea (Equatorial Guinea today).

Not long afterwards, word had it that McWhorter had moved on to Chad to provide support to French units battling rebels in the Sahara. Totally mercenary – all of these aviators – quite a few were also motivated by their faith.

To understand the complexities of the civil war in Nigeria, in which numbers of foreigners eventually became involved – including the erstwhile RAF, as well as Egyptian Air Force pilots; Soviet anti-aircraft specialists; a South African Special Forces group; former French Foreign Legionnaires; and an assortment of other nationalities – one needs to understand both the people who took part, as well as the reason why war happened.

Frederick Forsyth was there at the time and he points out in his excellent history of the Nigerian Civil War how and why mercenaries became involved in this struggle. It was also, he maintains, a development that set the pattern for quite a few other African wars thereafter. He makes the point that far from it being an 'Ibo revolt', there were officers from other Nigerian groupings involved in the putsch – including a good few Muslims. Much of it he details in *The Biafra Story* – regarded by the majority of African scholars as the first (and best) of several books on the Biafran War.

The orientation of these plotters, says Forsyth, was actually much more radical – more left wing than tribal. The bulk of those involved had returned to Africa after having been educated in Europe – and most had inculcated a distinct socialist, egalitarian bias that was reflective of popular institutions like the London School of Economics.

Though not exactly communist, some of the plotters viewed the Marxist-Leninist view of life preferable to the kind of nepotism and corruption then just starting to take a hold on Nigerian society. They wanted change, they declared in statements issued after they had taken over. Rather pointedly, their spokesmen maintained that they were compelled to topple what they viewed as a doddering, out-of-touch bunch of potentates that Britain had chosen to run this West African state after independence.

The politicians in the mainly Islamic north of the country weren't buying any of it. For a start, what the young officers wanted was contrary to the most fundamental precepts of The Prophet (May He Rest in Peace) – and if ever more proof was needed in the eyes of Muslim leaders and their retinues in Kano, Maiduguri, Sokoto and the rest that the January army mutiny was a set-up, then what about the fact that General Aguiyi Ironsi – the army chief who took over from the Civilian Government – was from the Ibo Tribe?

Ironsi headed the country for about six months when the second coup took place in July 1966. The northerners had carefully planned their revenge, and they did so in spades – in the process murdering that newly-appointed leader. Unlike the January revolt, the carnage that resulted from the second coup was both bloody and widespread. It was also worse than anything Africa had yet seen.

The bunch of northern officers responsible for countering the initial army revolt struck their first blows in Lagos at Ikeja Barracks – headquarters of the Nigerian Army. Every Ibo officer in the place was dragged out of his quarters and butchered on the parade square. Concurrently, a massive pogrom erupted in the north, where some 30,000 easterners – men, women and children – were taken out of their homes and massacred, Africa-style. Still more were hacked to death on the roads; in villages and towns; and in the local *Sabon Gari* – the marketplace – of all big population centres.

As Forsyth emphasises, there was not much gunfire involved:

> We are talking about machetes and clubs. The outcome, clearly, was traumatic. It was also deeply shaming for the British Government, because it was totally unforeseen. In fact, there wasn't an American or European intelligence service that had any idea it was going to happen. Therefore London's attitude was to suggest that things weren't as serious as some observers said they were.[2]

'Play down the violence, play it down', British ministers told their media people – stating that it was all just unrest. It was a phase and nothing would come of it, London told the world. We know now, of course – declares Forsyth – that it was nothing of the kind.

The pogrom was so bad that every Ibo that could do so fled. These were people that had been living in every corner of Nigeria: in the mid-west, the western regions and in the north. One and all, they headed back to their eastern tribal homeland which was then under the military governorship of a man who had been appointed after the first revolt: Colonel Odumegwu Ojukwu (Sir Louis' son).

Curiously – it emerged afterwards – Ojukwu Junior had absolutely nothing to do with the January coup. The officers of the first revolt specifically left him out of it because (as one of their

---

2 Forsyth, *The Biafra Story*.

number told Forsyth) they regarded him as an establishment figure. He was more of a 'Pan Nigeria man', they reckoned. In the eyes of his peers, Ojukwu was above tribal conspiracies – and in a sense, they were right.

The youthful Military Governor of Eastern Nigeria now found himself trying to cope with a refugee problem – the likes of which neither he nor anybody else had seen in any African country before (and certainly not in the modern period). Desperate people were resorting to desperate measures and were entering the Eastern Region in hordes. For a while, he was finding it difficult not only to maintain law and order, but to provide support and succour to a society that had lost just about everything.

Totally unprepared for this scale of emergency (because nobody believed that a catastrophe of this magnitude could ever happen), his fledgling Biafra – overnight – needed a huge injection of funds. There were not enough schools; a chronic paucity of clinics and hospitals; and no basic transport infrastructure, which in turn, meant that there was not enough food or the means to distribute what there was. Coupled to this, Ojukwu lacked the administrative infrastructure to counter these inadequacies. In fact, says Forsyth, there was not enough of anything.

The basic population of the region under Ojukwu's command, he explains, was close to 20 million – of which, by now, a fair proportion was fugitive. It was made that much more immediate by the fact that the majority who got back to Biafra arrived penniless.

Forsyth:

> They literally left behind everything. That included their houses; their workshops; their stores; and their little cars. They travelled on 'Mammy-Wagons' and trains, while others walked or cadged lifts home – some badly wounded because they had lost limbs. One woman arrived with her husband's severed head in her lap. Clearly, this was a traumatised community – and they needed medical help far beyond what was available in Ojukwu's fief. He, in turn, needed all sorts of things, but there was nothing forthcoming out of Lagos – and certainly no funds.
>
> This went on until finally the clamour for the secession of the eastern half of the country from the Nigerian Federation became more pronounced. It started with the tribal chiefs, and the call was soon echoed by the majority of refugees. It was then sounded by those who were not refugees, but who roundly sympathised with the roughly two million people who had been displaced.
>
> 'If we are to be treated in this way,' they shouted, 'and if we are not to be given any recourse from Lagos for our misery, then what are we doing in this country? Why don't we just pull out of the Nigerian Federation and go our own way?'
>
> Eventually, Ojukwu did just that. He declared his so-called Unilateral Declaration of Independence (or what the Rhodesians subsequently referred in the politics-speak of the day as UDI) in April 1967 – having delayed 10 months. Because of fading memories and an international media that initially ignored both the violence and the atrocities that had originally caused all this, they came down hard on Ojukwu's decision to go it alone.

Ojukwu and his Ibos – some journalists declared – were just a bunch of maniacs, idiots… It was hardly clever to call Ojukwu an opportunistic power seeker, Forsyth said, because he already had the power.

The response from Lagos finally arrived three months later – on 7 July – when the Nigerian Army invaded:

> The immediate reaction of the north, when the Eastern Region went off on its own, was – in the minds of many of them – good riddance. Most of the Hausa and Fulani tribal people in

A beautiful corner of the globe – now totally polluted by oil effluent. (www.livingearth.org.uk)

Northern Nigeria were happy to see the Ibos go. They did not like them – nor did they want them. They'd expelled them, almost to the last man and woman, and that was that.

This was all very well, until somebody realised that the fledgling state of Biafra was rather strategically perched on almost all of Nigeria's oil reserves. Overnight, this reality became the key: Nigeria's oil was (and still is) its wealth and it was now under Ibo land. Most of the producing areas were along the Imo River; around Port Harcourt; in the creeks; and along many of the tributaries of the Niger River – all again, essentially, under Ibo control.

And when this horrifying revelation finally entered the skulls of the Hausa colonel who commanded the Nigerian Army – and they realised that without Ibo oil, Nigeria was nothing more than a huge impoverished country – a complete about-face took place.

'It all happened in hours,' said Forsyth – and so too in Britain and the United States. There, the collapse of the Nigerian Federal political structure was viewed with alarm. The Cold War was hot – and in West Africa, any kind of upheaval that upset the political and economic status quo tended to worry strategists. More salient, Nigeria was one of Britain's principal sources of crude oil. Who knew what would happen if that flow was disrupted by war, it was asked – and that, basically, was the gist of some of the editorials that started to appear in the British press.

Also, argued Whitehall, if Nigeria were to fragment, hostilities there could ultimately affect other countries not only in that region, but also in other parts of Africa. Here, Ian Smith's Rhodesia had already taken the lead. Remember, this was a time when the fragmenting concept of the Domino Theory was very much in vogue – even though, in those early days, it pertained more to what was going on in South East Asia than to Africa.

Barely mentioned, even in the financial press, was the fact that London and Washington were alarmed that Ojukwu – a young military upstart that nobody had heard of before – was threatening their investments. Consequently, an abrupt turnabout followed. From all the clatter about good riddance and bad rubbish, emerged the shout: 'We must again reunite Nigeria. Ojukwu mustn't be allowed to secede,' which was a farce – as Frederick Forsyth suggests – because the whole thing about the unity of Nigeria was one great big invented fiction.

'There never was any unity in Nigeria,' he will tell you today:

> It was a most divided country. Under Britain's colonial rule, the country was deliberately divvyed up into what was essentially the North and the South (with the Yoruba nation being the other half of the South).
>
> In a makeshift effort, the country was cobbled together – literally five years before independence – and we were all told that it was one country, but in the hearts and minds of the people, it never was the 'One Nigeria' that its politicians said it was, because tribal groupings predominated; and it still isn't a single country to this day.
>
> So the war began, and we were all told (I was a journalist at the time, working for the BBC) this whole thing was going to be over in 10 days. We were also rather candidly informed by London that the Ibos were a bunch of incompetent bottle-washers and that we had this magnificent British-trained Hausa Army of the North that would sweep down and make a meal of Biafra in a week.
>
> What was overlooked was two important things: first, the so-called 'magnificently trained army of the North' was rubbish. It could not fight its way out of a Human Rights convention in Blackpool. Second, as we know today, the Ibos had become a desperate group – and with all the things that were happening around them, they were suddenly given a large dollop of courage, which was something they'd never really before thought they had.
>
> The kind of fear and anxiety that the Biafran people were then experiencing really can offer an individual or a nation a remarkable level of audacity – and let's not forget, it can also result in an astonishing amount of obstinacy.
>
> For its part, Biafran propaganda immediately began to say 'if we surrender, then we'll all be killed; they'll end up finishing the job'. This was fuelled by many voices in the North replying: 'Yes we will! We will wipe you out!' So basically, it was a war of genocide.
>
> Apart from that, the British made two more mistakes – both crucial. If London had realised this was going to be a 30-month war that resulted in a million people dying of starvation, I don't think the British would have taken the position that they did. In fact, I'm certain of that. The other was for the Prime Minister and his advisers not to realise that the rebel Biafrans were just as pro-British, and as much a part of the Commonwealth, as the Nigerians.

Frederick Forsyth was in Biafra when the Biafran Army decided to invade Nigeria westwards, towards Lagos. It was a bold step, this former BBC correspondent recalls, though he broke with that body soon afterwards because of its biased reports about the war:

> Yes, I went in with them. We swept across the Onitsha Bridge and very soon we could see that it was a crazy amateurish kind of war, a conflict, in a sense, of boy scouts.
>
> Here was this huge bridge spanning the great Niger River that effectively connected the Biafran Eastern Region with Western Nigeria. There was a sort of gentleman's agreement in place between the leaders of both sides not to use it. They had another agreement not to destroy it. Certainly, it was accepted by all the participants that it would not be used for any kind of invasion.
>
> Ojukwu was regarded by the Nigerian military leader Colonel Yakubu Gowon as an absolute bastard for breaking that concord by crossing the bridge with an invasion force. In a way, it was a bit like the mouse that roared. How, Gowon asked, thoroughly perplexed, could the tiny little Eastern Region invade Nigeria? But it did – and it was a remarkably successful venture because the newly-appointed Nigerian leader's strategy was a disaster.

OFFICE OF THE SPECIAL REPRESENTATIVE OF THE REPUBLIC OF BIAFRA

Telephone 67829
Telegram: BIAFRAN.
Our Reference BGD/SEC/16/71.
Your Reference ....

10 Hill Road,
Oyster Bay,
P.O. Box 2431,
Dar es Salaam

20th September, 1969.

Mr. Al J. Venter,
c/o Foreign Editor,
Mr. Jag Nicoil,
"Daily Express",
Fleet Street,
London, E.C. 4.

Dear Sir,

<u>Visit to Biafra</u>.

With reference to your application to visit Biafra, we wish to inform you that approval has now been given for you to enter Biafra <u>through Sao Tome</u>. You should make your arrangement direct with the Joint Church Aid for your flight into our country.

2. May I remind you that your stay in Biafra cannot exceed seven days and as you will be catered for by the Biafra Overseas Press Services while you are there, you will be required to pay 35 U.S. Dollars per diem for the duration of your stay. This <u>must</u> be paid in U.S. dollars.

3. Please find attached hereto, a letter of introduction which will facilitate your entry into Biafra. Your photograph should be affixed to the letter.

4. Kindly acknowledge the receipt of this letter.

Yours faithfully,

(Ibezim Chukwumerije),
for Biafra Special Representative,
(EAST & CENTRAL AFRICA).

The author's original document that he used to enter Biafra from Libreville – capital of Gabon. He was working for the London *Daily Express* at the time.

Gowon, by now at the head of the rest of Nigeria, took the entire professional Nigerian Army of only 6,000 men and hurled them across the Benue River (a tributary of the Niger) to the north of the rebel enclave. He then ordered them to turn their guns towards the south and face Biafra, where they promptly bogged down. The result was that there were barely any troops between the bridge across the Niger River at Onitsha and Lagos, Nigeria's capital.[3] The Biafran strike force was faced with an absolutely empty, open road to victory.

Someone got to Ojukwu and said to him: 'Look, we can be in Lagos in 48 hours of hard motoring.' That would end the war at a stroke. I don't know how much persuading he took, but certainly, that was what he finally decided to do.

Since Ojukwu had no armoured columns of his own, the Biafrans got together a bunch of trucks, Mammy-Wagons and oil tankers because they would need fuel supplies. They also grabbed just about every Land Rover in the country and commandeered oil company vehicles and virtually the entire region's agricultural four-by-fours – and what a motley collection that lot soon became, though all these shortcomings did not prevent the force from calling itself 'Ojukwu's Undefeated'.

They hadn't enough soldiers in their territory, because broadly speaking – Ojukwu apart – the Ibos had never really been among the country's soldier class. Nigeria's army, in fact, was overwhelmingly from the north – much as it is today – so what this fighting colonel got in lieu of a combat force was a bunch of ragtag, bobtail volunteers… many of them schoolboys.

So too with his officer corps, which was mainly composed of technical officers. The head of the Biafran Army, for instance, was a former Nigerian Signals Corps man. He was very good with radios, but sadly, he didn't know a damn thing about guns – though they had some artillery officers, because that was a technical discipline, but there was no armour at all. They were literally riding to war in trucks, lorries, tankers and Land Rovers.

So this column, before dawn one morning – as I was to see for myself, because I was with them – drove across that crucial bridge and took the war to the rest of the nation. Without formality, they swept aside the two dozen or so Nigerian soldiers on the western side and plunged on towards Lagos.

They reached Benin City – the capital of the mid-west – within 12 hours, where, amazingly, they lost their nerve. They just could not believe that they had managed to penetrate so deep into Nigeria without encountering any kind of opposition.

Yet even then, they did not stop. This improvised, totally makeshift force – still with me in tow – went beyond Benin, actually to the border between the mid-west state and Western Nigeria, which is a little village called Ore. It was there that some of us realised that the reality of reaching the capital, Lagos, was almost in sight.

Then too, the words 'cut off' began to circulate.

'Cut off from what?' I asked several of them. 'What are you going to be cut off from, in your own country?'

'We're cut off,' they answered – adding that there might be Nigerian troops suddenly appearing behind us.

So I would question where these supposed Nigerian troops were supposed to be coming from.

'There really aren't any there,' I told the commander and his staff.

'Oh,' they answered, 'still, we might be cut off.'

Very soon, the expression 'cut off' became obsessional.

---

3   Only after the end of the Biafran War did Abuja replace Lagos as the Federal capital.

An improvised petrol station in Nigeria immediately before the war. (Author's collection)

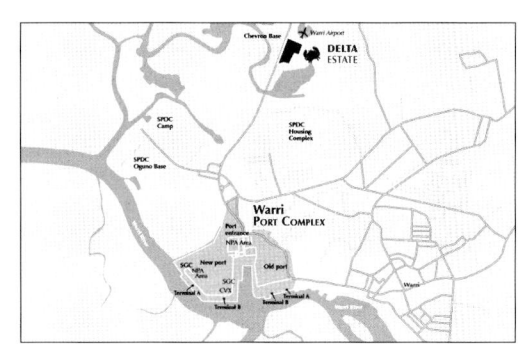

A modern sketch of the Warri port complex. The *Titania* was moored at the Old Port, opposite Terminal B, when she was hit by a pair of Minicons.

At the start of the invasion, Colonel Ojukwu did something rather unusual by appointing one of the very few Yorubas in his army, Brigadier Victor Banjo, as the Commanding Officer of the entire expedition. He thought that because Banjo was a Yoruba, he would be made welcome once he entered his own Yorubaland. What the Biafran leader did not realise was that Banjo had his own agenda… The original intention of this rather enterprising, but devious Yoruba officer – with all this power play then going on – was that he earnestly intended becoming the future ruler of Nigeria.

So Banjo turned traitor. Once the column stopped in Benin City, he used the radio of the British Deputy High Commissioner to call up the British High Commission in Lagos and asked for Gowon to be brought to the microphone. His intention was to negotiate a handover of the country to himself. Banjo wanted to call himself President of Nigeria.

That bit of duplicity stopped the invasion in its tracks, though frankly, I could never understand why. I could never comprehend why this extremely successful invasion force – with a completely empty road ahead – had been halted.

Of course, there were two reasons here: one was a total loss of nerve; and the treachery by Brigadier Banjo, its Commanding Officer.

Throughout it all, the experience – as that experienced British author will tell you – taught Nigeria a very hard lesson. It set in motion the effort, as he states, to recruit, recruit and recruit.

'Within almost no time at all, General Gowon ran his army up from the original 6,000 to something like 150,000.'

Forsyth:

The newcomers came from all over. They scraped dregs out of the prisons, like Lagos' awful Kiri Kiri Prison, which was nearly emptied of every thug, gangster and killer. Murderers were summarily released and put into uniform; then they virtually emptied Lagos University. They put the students in uniform, gave them rifles, and – as was the case in Angola 30 years later – all these men were pushed up to the front. There was never any question of training this new group of improvised soldiers.

Suddenly, further afield, there were other effects. There were people in London and Washington who panicked when they realised that perhaps this Nigerian Civil War thing was not going to be as easy as they'd originally thought.

When I started enquiries about going into Biafra, I came up against a wall on the Nigerian side. They knew me by now and I knew that a lot of questions might be asked about my earlier reports. These things get around – and it could mean problems in the long term. Also, field security within the regular army was lax and led to unnecessary casualties. Priya Ramrakha, a colleague out of Nairobi and working as a cameraman for a British network, was killed in an ambush – and that was big news because we all knew the man. Consequently, I wasn't all that eager to work with the Nigerian Army – especially since I'd been stuck with them for several months while working at Ikeja. Also, my South African connections seemed to foster an unhealthy interest among some Federal Intelligence agencies – particularly after a Biafran officer who had turned traitor made public Pretoria's role in the war.

Finally, I decided on Biafra – and in any event, Ojukwu's efforts against Africa's most populated state were just then starting to look laudable (at least from a distance).

The truth was more basic: Biafra had already became a dangerous option after one of the mercenary pilots working for the Nigerians at the controls of a Soviet-built MiG-17 purposely shot down an International Red Cross DC-7B loaded with baby food. The incident was regarded by many of us as one of the more tragic events of the war. The freighter – piloted by American Captain David Brown – had taken off from Santa Isabel (capital of the island of Fernando Pó).

The Nigerian Government claimed afterwards that its fighters had challenged the cargo plane after it had entered Nigerian air space and ordered it to land either at Port Harcourt or Calabar, near the Cameroon frontier. When he refused, Lagos said, the MiG pilot 'positioned his fighter to the rear of Brown's plane and fired several short cannon bursts'. This caused the DC-7's nose to rise sharply before entering a stall. Shortly afterwards, it crashed.

Frederick Forsyth provides a more likely version:

> At 1738 hours on that Thursday evening, Captain Brown took off from Fernando Pó with his cargo… If he made any mistake, it was in leaving too early for Biafra. The sky was a brilliant blue, without a cloud, and the sun was still well above the horizon. It was habitual for planes leaving São Tomé to depart at this hour, for with the longer journey, they only came over the Biafran coast after 1900 hours – that is, after dark. Dusk is very short in Africa; the light starts to fade around 1830 and by 1900 it is dark – but with the much shorter journey (only 60 miles) from Fernando Pó to the coast, he came over the coast about 1800 in broad daylight. At 1803 his voice was heard on the Fernando Pó control tower and by other Red Cross pilots on the same run. He gave no call sign, and the voice was high-pitched with alarm. He said: 'I'm being attacked… I'm being attacked.'
>
> His switch went dead. There was a moment's silence; then a babble on the ether, with Fernando Pó asking for the identification of the caller. Thirty seconds later, the voice came back on the air.
>
> 'My engine's on fire… I'm going down…'
>
> Then there was silence.

The São Tomé side of the airlift (a tiny place about twice the size of the Isle of Man and which lies about 300 miles off the Nigerian coast) was started by Hank Wharton – a genial cigar-chewing Yank with a penchant for unusual flights and dubious cargoes. Officially, he presented himself as a director of The North American Trading Company – a title that could hardly be more vague. In

One of the few vehicles that was prepared to venture on the roads during daylight hours - this time in Warri - which had just been hit by a pair of Minicons that damaged our ship, as well as an American steamer lying ahead of us in the roadstead. The foliage on the roof was supposed to confuse strafing jets. (Author's photo)

1968 he took a contract with the Catholic relief organisation Caritas to fly six chartered flights into Biafra at $3,800 each. As part of the deal, he would make one flight free. At that time, about 2,000 Ibos were dying of hunger each day – most of them children. Gradually, a number of European governments and the International Red Cross took real interest in their plight and started to do something about it, though it took a while.

Prior to bringing in his Minicons, Count von Rosen had been flying cargoes of food across Nigerian territory in daylight (about 300 feet up). His navigator, Father William Butler, was a missionary who had worked in Rivers Province and knew the waterways like he'd been born there. It did not take long for the Count and Colonel Ojukwu to become fast friends.

As more religious entities took part in humanitarian work, they came to ignore their sectarian differences. Catholic and Protestant churches pooled efforts and resources in São Tomé and worked under the aegis of what became known worldwide as Joint Church Aid.

For their part, the Americans became involved through Catholic Relief Services and the Church World Service – and they ultimately provided four Boeing C-97 Stratocruisers. All were sold to these unconventional operators as surplus for the peppercorn sum of $4,000 each.

6

The Conflict Escalates

To many a man in the line today, fear is not so much of death itself… as of the terror and anguish and utter horror that precedes death in battle.[1]

It was the little everyday things about life in a country at war that astonished those of us who visited Biafra for the first time. We discovered an inordinate will to survive, which was natural enough, except that the odds were powerfully stacked against Ojukwu's people. I saw conditions at fairly close quarters, since my escort – Emeka – and I went just about everywhere on foot. Cars or pick-ups were a luxury reserved for longer trips.

The Biafran social code was enforced with the rigour of an Amish settlement in the American mid-west. Civil and criminal courts were held from Monday to Friday in all big towns in the rebel enclave. The Biafran Supreme Court of Appeal sat in session in Owerri when it was in rebel hands, or in Umuahia when it wasn't. Colonial traditions were strictly observed: wigs and robes for all senior members of the bar, which was absurd in that climate, except that such flummeries still persist in most of the former British territories (except that wigs are no longer worn in British courts) – nor had the prisons been abolished. Inmates could be seen in working parties under guard on the last day of the war.

Ojukwu printed his own money – now of good value among collectors. The notes, gaudy and in every colour of the spectrum, were professionally printed in Europe. A planeload of it disappeared on the way back from Switzerland. Biafra also had its own coins, stamps and postal orders. In spite of restrictions necessitated by conflict and a breakdown in communications, Biafran welfare officers continued to pay pensions to war widows until the end – and postal deliveries always remained efficient (even after hostilities ended).

When an area had to be evacuated – as in the case of Owerri before its recapture (following the fall of Umuahia to the east) – the first to be moved were the wounded and civil prisoners; the latter carrying litters or supplies. Likewise, entire hospitals disappeared into the bush.

Former inmates of mental institutions had long since been released to fend for themselves in the jungle – and from what I heard, they seemed to manage. Federal troops never touched them because African tribal lore disavows anybody doing so; it is very bad *ju ju* to abuse the insane…

The nightly flights into Biafra, which concentrated mainly on the needs of the children and the military, could hardly have been expected to supply the demands of four million people cut off from the outside world. As a result, prices in Biafra were the highest in Africa. A meal of roots at the Progress Hotel in Owerri, for example, cost the equivalent of two dollars; an ounce of meat as much again. Salt for the meal would be priced at one Biafran pound, or two US dollars – all

---

[1] The famous Ernie Pyle reflecting on the horrors of war in his last column – written on Okinawa Island – before he was killed by a Japanese sniper in 1945.

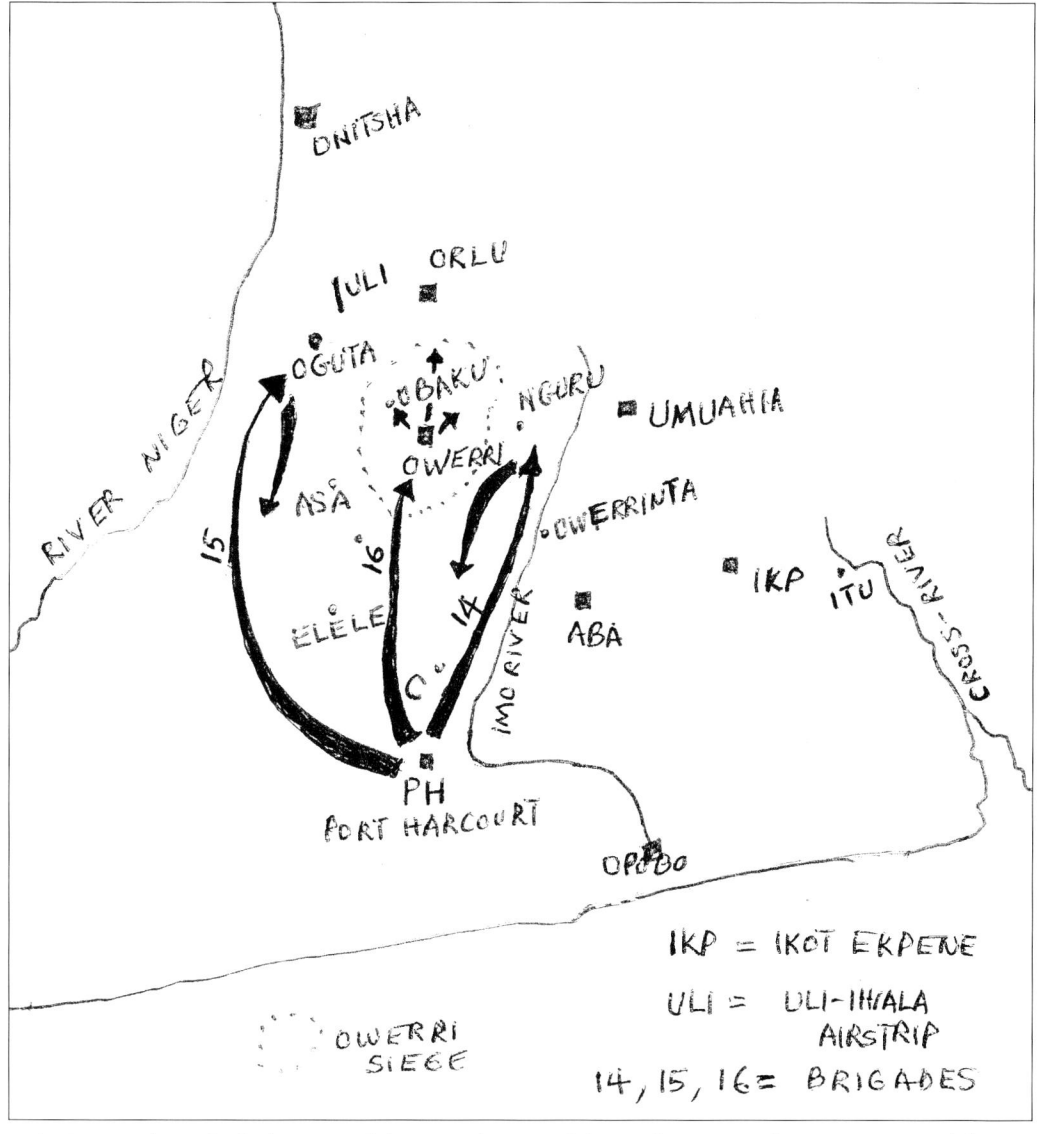

A Nigerian brigadier's diagram of the encirclement of the Biafran town of Owerri. Many of these tactical arrangements were made ad hoc and rarely referred to higher command in Lagos.

of which we had to exchange on our arrival at Uli for foreign currencies (at par with sterling at pre-secession rates). By the end of the war, inflation was rising at several hundred percent a month.

The cost of 'non-essential' goods was greater: a single cigarette in the last two months of the conflict cost 10 Biafran shillings (roughly a dollar); so did a cup of tea with goat's milk (I was surprised that any goats had survived so long). What sugar there was mostly went to mission hospitals, where it was used as a substitute for glucose intended for starving children.

Petrol (as they still called it) was a strategic material and not sold on the open market, although a gallon could be bought easily enough on the black market for $30 or $40 – and then again, only in American dollars. A pair of men's flannels cost $20; a shirt sometimes as much as $50. Second-hand clothes were barely any cheaper, and it puts things in perspective when you realise that almost half a century ago, that was a lot of money!

I was soon confronted by inflation. After breakfast on my first morning at State House, I was told to wait because there was no transport – something I soon got used to. The morning newspaper arrived: a single folded sheet of school exercise paper that – I was assured – had a circulation that ran well into four figures. I was charged a dollar.

'It's the only paper we have left,' said the youthful editor of *Jet,* the Biafran daily, 'but it gives us what we need: objective news of the outside world.'

Anything from Federal Nigeria was tainted: *Propaganda!*

The news was printed in bright red ink, which looked like a compound of shoe polish and ochre – and probably was; they certainly did not have money to spare for the real thing. That particular issue of 4 November 1969 celebrated Ojukwu's 36th birthday. Half-page advertisements on the crammed sheet had been taken by two expatriate companies that had formerly traded in the Eastern Region: the United Africa Company (Unilever) and the African Continental Bank, which then (last heard) still had its head office in Lagos. A two-column advertisement on the last page of *Jet* urged subscribers to book in time for their Christmas cards and New Year's greetings.

All foreign companies that formerly operated in Eastern Nigeria were now managed by their Ibo staff – and though little happened (for instance, at the local office of Caterpillar, or Bata shoes), many were surprised after the war ended to find that nearly every branch office had kept up-to-date books.

In spite of some lighter moments, the grim reality of conflict was omnipresent. Cripples were everywhere – and there were a lot of them. Young boys, some barely into their teens, hobbled legless on crutches. Anywhere else, they'd have been in an institution, or being prepared for prosthetics. Only the very worst cases could be dealt with at Red Cross and government clinics.

I came across several groups of shell-shocked youngsters – and these were experiences that remained fixed in my mind for many years. Huddled in small groups almost like zombies, they communicated with grunts and gestures in an absent-minded sort of way. Most were tended by some older person until they recovered; quite a few got better and some were even posted back to their units. Quite a number, one of the Red Cross people told me, never would. Decades later, some of these poor souls are still afflicted.

It was at the headquarters of Major-General Philip Effiong – the Biafran Chief of Staff – that most of the strategy in this war was planned. In a sandbagged and well-camouflaged camp on the outskirts of Owerri (it would have made a marvellous film set) was the 44-year old Sandhurst-trained veteran of two Nigerian operations in the Congo, while Katanga's Moise Tshombe still strode tall.

The visit promised to be an experience, and we went by car. Because of the MiGs, each of us carefully observed his quarter of the horizon as we drove. I sat behind the driver, so my responsibility was the rear quadrant on my side of the vehicle. The system worked quite well, because with time, the Biafrans had become pretty adroit at recognising distant dots in the sky.

We weren't bothered on that trip. Another time, while travelling to Santana Awo-omama, where I was to overnight, our driver – with a screech of the brakes and a hard right-hand turn – shouted a warning. Even before the car had stopped, all four doors were flung open and we dived into the thick wet undergrowth. A Soviet MiG roared over moments later.

I'd lived in Nigeria before the war and had travelled the length of the coastal belt, and I was always struck by the number of snakes we saw on the roads – especially near the coast, where the country is densely forested. Some of these reptiles were eight or 10 feet long and glistened in the heat as they slithered across the road. My fellow passengers would whoop and scream: 'Kill it! Kill

Biafran NCOs receive instruction in an improvised jungle classroom. The average Biafran recruit was usually far better educated – and motivated – than his Nigerian counterpart. (Author's photo)

it!' as if the driver could have done anything. By then, the creatures were gone – having disappeared into the undergrowth.

How different now that I had to take a dive. I did not even think of snakes, scorpions or any other of West Africa's creepy-crawlies as I shot headlong into the steaming undergrowth. The idea was to reach cover if there was 'incoming'. Had we actually became a target, the bush would have probably counted for little. Three loud explosions a mile or so down the road moments later told us that something else had engaged the pilot's attention. Meantime, we picked ourselves up, joked and laughed at our 'escape', while someone made sure that the jet hadn't turned to make a second run. When everybody was ready, we continued the journey.

The road to General Effiong's camp was littered with the ruins of previous battles – and obviously, the area had seen some pretty intense fighting. Bridges had been destroyed and the burnt-out hulks of a number of armoured cars were scattered along the verge. As at Uli, the foliage of palms and tall trees had been stripped clean by God knows how many shells and mortar-bombs fired by two opposing armies. The bare stumps reminded me of photos that one of my uncles had shown me of Delville Wood.

Near the camp was a petrol tanker that had been strafed from the air; a line of bullet-holes ran its length. Further along, there was a large road safety poster also riddled – a legacy of the pre-war days. 'Better be late than *the* late', it proclaimed. The driver chortled as we passed.

From the road, it was impossible to see the army headquarters until we reached its gates. Suddenly, the car turned into a wide clearing lined with palms and guarded by a machine-gun turret. Everybody saluted as we passed. For all they knew, it might have been Ojukwu himself.

He travelled about unannounced and seldom used the same vehicle two days running. Now and again, he turned up where he was least expected. Discipline was strict: all the men wore freshly-washed khaki and officers' uniforms were starched.

General Effiong – showing none of the egotism that some of us had found on the Federal side – walked at a brisk pace to greet us… his swagger-stick comfortably under one arm; truly a black Englishman – complete with tailor-made uniform. With his trademark smile, he greeted us kindly. We'd risked our lives by coming into Biafra, and he was honoured, he said – his English like something out of the Old Country. His adjutant – a captain – looked us over carefully. We were obviously unarmed, but if there was to be any trouble, this young officer would be ready for it.

Time magazine's James Wilde was spot-on when he wrote about a visit to Major-General Phillip Effiong's headquarters almost at the end of the war:[2]

> … it was the code of Kipling that influenced the conduct of the war on both sides. Until the very end, Effiong looked like a British staff general – polished Sam Browne belt, a sword for ceremonial occasions and a chauffeur-driven, khaki-coloured English Humber car bearing a general's flag. His officers were similarly indoctrinated – moustaches, swagger-sticks, barmen, officers' mess…

It seemed difficult to believe that people like Effiong and Adekunle had actually served and trained together in the Nigerian Army during the pre-secession era. Indeed, the two men were as unlike as their respective armies.

What was his worst difficulty? I asked.

'Air power,' he affirmed.

Federal air-strikes both at the front and behind the lines had created havoc, he admitted. He said he always knew when the next Nigerian offensive was coming.

'They like to soften the place up for a few days with air-strikes. How can our men hold their own against modern jet fighters armed with Russian and British weapons?' he queried.

'Still, we've survived against great odds for two-and-a-half years, so we can't be doing too badly.'

And manpower? How was he coping?

'Not so simple,' he answered.

Speaking from behind a heavy mahogany desk with a little Biafran flag dominating one of the corners, he pointed at a large map studded with coloured pins behind him.

'Biafra is divided into 20 provinces. The central government in Owerri levies men on a quota system – even in those parts overrun by the Feds. It's easy to bring groups of civilians through the lines for training,' he explained. Lagos was asleep when it came to controlling movement, he reckoned, though he did admit to a serious shortage of young men – 'So we've just got to make do with what we've got,' he declared.

'Before the war started, we had the highest literacy rate in Africa. That means we've never been short of men of officer calibre. They lead every attack, just like the Israelis, from the front… most effective way – but we've lost many of our best men as a result.'

As he spoke, we could faintly hear the rumble of artillery: front lines could not have been that far away.

What about prisoners of war?

'Yes, my people take prisoners now and again and hold them,' was all he was prepared to say before he changed the subject. Later, one of his officers told me that the Biafrans would have taken

---

[2] Wilde, James, *Time* magazine (New York: 26 January 1970).

A press cutting from a Biafran newspaper showing Colonel Ojukwu visiting a village. He made a point of maintaining close ties with his community.

many more POWs than they had, but that the Federal Army shot its wounded whenever they were in the retreat. 'A nation of over 60 million can easily afford that sort of thing,' was his parting comment.

It was hard to grasp, as the war continued, that Biafra was completely surrounded by the enemy. At best, 200 tonnes of ammunition was being brought in at night in the airlift. Whenever Uli was knocked out – and it happened fairly routinely – there would be nothing coming in for days; and that, to keep a couple of hundred thousand Federal Nigerians at bay.

Also, throughout hostilities, the casualty rate rose steadily. It puzzled us all, considering that this was a strictly African war, how the Biafrans were able to hold out so long? There were several reasons…

Biafra's ability to survive – it was agreed afterwards by those of us who were able to observe conditions from up front was due largely to the remarkable competence of the ordinary Biafran. This was (and still is) a community that is able to improvise, plan for the unexpected and take the initiative. As we have already seen, their adversaries (often disparagingly) call them the 'Jews of Africa' – and of course, they're right. Ibos like to roll up their sleeves and get things done.

Also, Ibos make money; they work and succeed where others fail. Like the Luo in Kenya and the Mandingo of Guinea, they are sometimes thoroughly disliked by less pushy tribes – much like southerners are wary of New Yorkers. It's a patchy analogy, but you get the picture. In that regard (with notable exceptions), they are – consequently – very different when compared to the average Yoruba, Hausa or Fulani. Success, as they say, breeds distrust.

What I do know is that with time, I became friendly with many Ibos – and any day of the week, I'd put my life in their hands. We, who favoured the Ibos, also shared somewhat in their unpopularity. Frederick Forsyth resigned his job at the BBC not because he was vociferously committed to the Biafran cause, but because the British Broadcasting Corporation ended up being partisan in a conflict where, in keeping with a tradition that went back to its first days on the air, it should have shown impartiality. It was all oil politics, we knew – and in the end, it made a difference.

Richard Hall – one of the most experienced Africa hands – was greatly taken by this rebel community. 'Dick', as we all knew him, was the co-founder and editor of Zambia's *Central Africa Mail* and no newcomer to this volatile continent. His comments about Biafra are instructive: he described Biafrans in the *Sunday Times* of London at the time as:

Nigerian troops enter one of the Biafran towns that has been laid to waste by a Federal artillery bombardment. (Priya Ramrakha)

… a people I respect and like [who] are threatened with persecution and death. I cannot therefore pretend to be impartial, but Biafra is more than a human tragedy: it is the first place I've been to in Africa where the Africans themselves are truly in charge… where there is a sense of nationhood. . . free from the African vices of graft, superstition and ignorance.

It had all suddenly become a furious debate.

Some of the best stories to come out of Biafra were not so much about the ongoing conflict, as the ability of the Biafrans to do their own thing. Certainly, they were ingenious. We could walk through any Biafran town, even towards the end of the war, and discover that life went on almost as if nothing were happening. Shops were open, though their stock was exiguous; post offices were selling stamps and money orders – and, with fair warning, you could even buy foreign exchange in the banks (although you had to have a very good reason).

There were dozens of home industries repairing or recycling old things or making new ones: iron bedsteads, car engines rebored on makeshift lathes, stoves and (of course) the market mammies at their stalls. The army took most of what was left after a proportion had been set aside for the children, so their offerings were skimpy.

That was what you were allowed to see – and obviously, there was much else besides. Behind the towns, in forest and bush clearings, hundreds of factories turned out all sorts of things, such as boots for soldiers and ammunition. Emeka took me on guided tours through some of them. In a factory near Umuahia, engineers were making – or rather recycling – motor parts for an otherwise

A Red Cross delegation visits a Biafran POW facility holding Nigerian captives. The Lagos Government rarely afforded the ICRC such entitlements. (Wikipedia)

Food arrives at Uli Airport from the world outside – and the elation on the faces of these young Biafrans is palpable. (Joint Church Aid)

ageing fleet of army trucks (mostly Mammy-Wagons that had been seized). Brake-linings, I was told, were among the items on the urgent list, which was one of the reasons why some were modified from crashed aircraft parts at Uli.

There were jungle workshops making uniforms. Since there was no cloth, long lines of women were busy making a rough substitute from bark. It was not the best or most supple material – and was probably tough on the skin – but it was better than nothing. The army needed boots – and since there was no leather, they added chemicals to a raw rubber latex mixture and created a strong and pliable material for the uppers. The soles were made from old motor vehicle tyres.

They refined their own oil in cooking-pot refineries – rather like illicit Arkansas gin stills. Up to the end, they produced enough fuel to keep several hundred vehicles running.

The Times in London ran a fairly comprehensive report on 5 March 1969 on Biafra's ongoing local oil supplies, which explained that apart from military needs, church groups, the ICRC and other aid groups all received weekly allocations of diesel fuel which totalled 1,000 gallons. This was significant, it declared, because Biafra had been under a naval and land blockade since the previous July.

'At a Biafran Army divisional headquarters I saw one of their homemade refineries in action' – the man in charge of it (an Economics graduate of Durham University, Mr Nwofili Adibuah,

Biafran troops on patrol near Uli after repelling a Nigerian attack. (Photo courtesy of Leif Hellström)

aged 34) explained: 'The process we use is fractional distillation, using these crude cooking pots'. He went on: 'The petrol comes off first; then the kerosene and finally, the diesel' – adding that his particular mini-refinery consisted of three 'cooking pots' and produced '280 gallons of petroleum, 100 gallons of kerosene and 250 gallons of diesel every day'.

There were even private citizens – who are today refining their own fuel in their back yards so as to keep their cars on the road. Dr Ben Nwosu – a distinguished Biafran nuclear physicist who trained in London and the United States (and worked until recently at the International Atomic Energy Agency in Vienna) – told me:

> Our main refinery, which is considerably more sophisticated than what you have seen, produces 25,000 gallons of fuel per day and we are now investigating the possibility of making our own aviation fuel, but we do more than produce equipment for the army. We have decided to produce what we call 'survival gin', which has palm wine at its base. Until we lost Abakaliki, we were able to produce our own salt. We make our own matches, dyes for military clothing, soap made from palm oil and caustic soda, shoe polish and farm implements.

To me just then, the most interesting aspect of this remarkable ability to continue fighting was the varied array of home-made weapons. These included hand-grenades – almost like the German potato-mashers of the two Great Wars and known locally as the 'Giraffe' – and a primitive rocket with a range of about five miles. There were also anti-personnel mines – and the 'Ogbunigwe' (an improvised device that was probably the most destructive improvised explosive device of all – and developed long before the Iraqi IED) became ubiquitous. The name, in the vernacular, meant 'Kill quickly', but it was referred to by most of those observing the war as the 'Ojukwu bucket'. In simple terms, it employed the same principle as the American claymore – and at peak, the rebel state claimed to be producing about 500 a day (though that might have been an excessive figure,

As in all wars, the aftermath of battle left an enormous amount of disorder after the dead and wounded had been squared away. (Photo courtesy of Leif Hellström)

since their deployment was specialised and there were only so many ambushes in the jungle that could be set on any day of the week).

'Ojukwu buckets' – with a range of about 300-400 yards and detonated electrically – were regularly deployed against Federal road convoys and, considering their lack of sophistication, they were remarkably successful. They were also able to take out the Nigerian Army's armoured cars so effectively that for some time, the Federal forces stopped using their British-built Ferrets in the jungle.

'Ogbunigwes' were also used at Uli. Aircraft of the Federal Air Force regularly bombed and strafed the landing strip during daylight hours – swooping low across it. The devices were placed at various points along the runway and were detonated when a jet passed over. We learnt afterwards that some mercenary pilots in the NAF had some close calls.

Ares Klootwyk – the South African gun-for-hire who had flown as a mercenary in the Congo – told me: 'On two occasions, the blast caught me unawares and my MiG nearly flipped, but the MiG-17 is a strong machine. Had it been a prop-engine, with less speed, they'd have got me.'

Not surprisingly, towards the end, a certain amount of lawlessness became manifest within Biafran ranks; this was particularly evident on the fringes of the fighting. Reports emerged of soldiers waylaying trucks and stealing food intended for children; others took provisions from aircraft off-loading in the dark. Those caught were hauled off into the nearby bushes and shot.

There were many deserters; because of the ever-changing military situation, there was nobody to stop them – not that anybody had the energy to do so, anyway. Entire units were sometimes caught on the wrong side of the front as a Federal attack closed its pincers. The fact is, everybody was starving – not only the children. Soldiers sometimes drove refugees out of their camps and seized their stores.

To be fair, such reports were not as commonplace as they might have been. There was certainly far less lawlessness on the Biafran side than among the Feds. When Nigerian Army rabble went berserk and started killing, looting and raping, there was little their officers could – or would – do.

Unloading ammunition supplies that came in overnight at Uli Airport. (Author's photo)

It says much for President Gowon's command at the end of the war in January 1970 that he managed to hold his Federal forces in tow – and for that, I personally regard him with great respect. Had he not been able to use his station, together with the influence that went with it to achieve that much, a lot of old scores would have been settled. Slaughter might have become the norm, because the Biafrans (by then) were hardly able to defend themselves, never mind retaliate – but then that's another amiable Nigerian trait: they can be enemies one day and friends the next. A few years later, travelling through the Eastern Region, it was as though there'd never been a war.

One of the first journalists who went into the ravaged east after it had all ended was Colin Legum – another old friend from my days as a scribe. He went to the army barracks in Onitsha – that huge Ibo city on the Niger that I so often visited while I lived in West Africa.

'There in the officers' mess', he wrote, 'were the Biafran officers and the Federal officers drinking beer together as though it was the end of a cricket match. They'd fought very sternly and they were now chums again, as they'd been chums before'.

The end, when it came, was mercifully quick. Once Biafran lines had broken, Federal forces overran all that was left of the rebel territory – and it took them all of a day (perhaps two). So much effort; so many dead – and let's face it, how many people these days have even heard the name 'Biafra'?

7

Frederick Forsyth's Biafra

Direct pressure always tends to harden and consolidate the resistance of an opponent.[1]

There is no question that a good deal of what appeared in Forsyth's third novel, *The Dogs of War*, came from time that he spent in Biafra reporting on what he calls 'that dreadful conflict'.

During a series of interviews and discussions on the war that Forsyth had with the author at his home in Chinook, Washington he said that he recalled that there was a steady flow of mercenary hopefuls entering the enclave, though only a handful stayed the distance.

In Forsyth's view:

> … the first group to arrive came at the behest of the French President Charles de Gaulle, who, you will recall, had no real interest in Lagos, Nigeria – it being a former British territory. Having virtually nothing to lose, he made a speech that was not so much helpful, as favorable towards the breakaway Republic. That was followed by an offer of French mercenaries:
>
> Ojukwu told me at the time that he simply had to accept this group because it would have been a considerable rebuff to the French to tell them and their mercenaries to get lost. It was also unfortunate that Paris charged him a hefty quarter of a million pounds, money that he desperately needed for the war effort.
>
> So Roger Faulques, a very distinguished Indochina veteran who'd also been in the Foreign Legion and had every gallantry medal in the book, arrived in Biafra a short while later. The group was comprised of about 35, perhaps 40 men.[2]

As Forsyth remembers, it did not take anybody very long to realise that these veterans actually knew very little – either about Biafra, or the kind of problems they were likely to encounter in the breakaway state:

> In fact, it seemed as if they thought they were going on a picnic. To their horror, on their very first trip south, they ran straight into an ambush east of Port Harcourt.
>
> Ojukwu told me later as we sat talking late into the night with coffee and brandy, that immediately after extricating themselves from that mess, they did an abrupt U-turn and headed straight back to the airport. One of their representatives came into his office, sat down

---

1 Sir Basil H. Liddell Hart.
2 As subsequently established, it was a 100-strong group commanded by Roger Faulques – and at the behest of his Paris-based intelligence-linked superiors, the group of hired guns played a devious political role (something dealt with later in this chapter).

A portrait taken of the British author Frederick Forsyth in 1994. (Wikipedia)

and told him that he wished to withdraw all his men. He had no option but to say yes, he stated. Nor did he get back any of his money either.

Return to Europe the French soldiers did, the following day. Ojukwu said afterwards that it was probably the shortest military assignment in the history of warfare. A couple of the men decided to stay: one, the ex-Foreign Legionnaire Rolf Steiner; the other was Marc Goossens – a burly Belgian national. Both men were to play useful roles in this terrible internecine conflict, though Steiner eventually overstepped the boundaries and was abruptly hustled out of the country. He refused to go, but ended up in restraints – bound hands and feet – when they put him on board an aircraft headed for Libreville.

Meanwhile, a few more unlikely war dogs dribbled in: all of them volunteers. One was Alec Gay – a Scot; there was also Taffy Williams – a South African, though ethnically Welsh. Georgio Norbiato – a former Italian marine commando who had previously fought in the Congo – also showed up, but he was later killed while on a solo op when he went down the Imo River, south of Port Harcourt. Finally, there was Armand Ianarelli, but we will learn a bit more about him in Chapter 18. Another German, Christian Oppenheim, joined the group later. Unlike the others, his job was to fly a twin-engine B-26 light bomber that crashed on its second raid over Lagos.

The Biafrans had no bombs of their own, so they improvised and used hollowed-out fire extinguishers – usually with a couple of fins welded onto them to guide them downwards. Packed with industrial explosives, these devices were fitted with impact fuses – with the hope that they'd land nose-first and explode.

Forsyth:

> That group of guns-for-hire that ended up in Biafra was an unusual bunch. We'd all get together evenings, and after a few drinks Taffy Williams would tell us that we were all crazy to be there and that he was the only certifiably sane person in the group. What he did not tell us was that he'd got the certificate to prove it after being released from a lunatic asylum sometime in his obscure past.

Pivotal to the Federal war effort was its leader, Colonel Yakubu Gowon. A career army officer, Gowon was very different, though he was a contemporary of the rebel leader Ojukwu. The two men actually served in the same units on occasion, and knew and understood each other's foibles, which could have been a reason for the Biafran leader believing that he could pull off his wager.

Whereas the future rebel leader wasn't afraid to go before the microphone to put his views across, Gowon wasn't one for publicity. In fact, it took us an age to get our first interview with a man who I always found extremely reserved and quietly-spoken. Never recalcitrant, he was reticent to talk about his own life – and though he could have claimed one of the presidential palaces as his own, he never did. All his successors did – most times with excessive brass and hoopla. He, in turn, preferred to stay on in the barracks with his family (in part, it has been said, because the presence of his own soldiers offered better security).

Eschewing limelight and controversy, General Gowon was different in other respects as well. The media made a big thing about his having been trained in England at the Royal Military Academy, Sandhurst, as well as in Ghana. The truth, says Forsyth, 'is that while it sounds like the full three-year permanent commission background, it was actually a three-month summer course which Commonwealth officers literally could not fail.'

Gowon did get involved in two tours of duty with the Nigerian Army during the Congo's upheavals and, by all accounts, he did a sterling job in putting down some of the uprisings in the interior; and once the Biafran War had ended, it was General Yakubu Gowon who initiated the remarkable reconciliation that took place between the victors and the vanquished – in itself an astonishing gesture, because it avoided unnecessary bloodshed. That this happened at a time when the Nigerian military clamoured to bring the entire Biafran command and their supporters to trial, made his efforts even more commendable.

There were those who wanted the lot executed. Gowon managed to sidestep this bristlingly emotive issue, which underscores the measure of his resolve. After all, his opponents argued, hundreds of thousands of their own people's lives had been lost in what they regarded a senseless war.

Gowon had a ruthless (and some say, a sensible) side to him that went unheralded. He was the first African leader to hire foreign pilots to fight his war: first Egyptians to fly his Ilyushin bombers and MiG-17s; and then a batch of South African, British, Australian and other mercenaries who were eventually to play a prime role in turning the war around. He was also powerfully opposed to any direct humanitarian aid going into Biafra without the aircraft first landing at Nigerian airports to be checked. As a consequence, he was implacably opposed to organisations like Oxfam and Joint Church Aid, which flew its planes into Biafra from São Tomé.

In the political climate on an unstable Nigeria that was both unpredictable and volatile, General Gowon simply could not last. On a diplomatic mission to Uganda in July 1975 the Nigerian Army deposed him.

Forsyth:

> Both the harsh and the gentle side of Gowon were deceptive because he was, throughout, like a glove puppet; either of the Fulani/Hausa zealots like Murtala Muhammed, or British advice which could spot a brilliant opportunity for good PR. Visiting correspondents and residents like Angus McDermid were constantly briefed by the High Commissioner as if he were in total charge in all matters when he wasn't; he constantly deferred to his British and Northern advisors.

Then came Aburi – and the one crucial effort to prevent conflict. It was staged by the British High Commissioner who held the post immediately before David Hunt, Sir Francis Coming-Bruce (also known to the hack community as 'Cunning Brute'). All the parties involved were represented, with the idea to find a compromise settlement and head off secession and a civil war.

Forsyth:

> Ojukwu turned up at Aburi wholly focused and minutely briefed. While he ran rings around the poor, floundering Gowon, the deal was nevertheless signed to general jubilation and relief, but Lagos had made concessions. The east was allowed to retain its Federal taxes to cope with her almost two million penniless refugees who had fled the north and the west with only the clothes on their backs – leaving behind 30,000 dead and bringing with them the same number of machete-mutilated victims.
>
> Back in Lagos afterwards, the northerners exploded and denounced the concessions. The British briefed the press that Ojukwu had taken gross advantage of the not-too-bright Gowon (who could have brought a team of scholars, but chose to negotiate alone). Lagos then reneged on every point that had been agreed to at Aburi.
>
> Ironically, accused by Sir David Hunt of being a dictator, Ojukwu was the only one of the two who bowed to the will of his people.

The Nigerian attitude, as we have seen, was 'good riddance'… until London pointed out exactly where the oil lay…

Michael Gould adds his own two bits' worth by declaring that after Yakubu Gowon had taken over the Nigerian Government, he revealed very little about his real intentions or thoughts about the gathering storm in the troubled eastern regions of his country. He was always the moderate one within the upper echelons of the army, which was probably one of the reasons why he got the job. His contemporaries believed that if push came to shove, he could easily be ousted – as he eventually was.

A measure of this sentiment emerges from a speech he made in early-August 1966 – and in this I quote from a comment made by Michael Gould, echoing one of Anthony Kirk-Greene's volumes on the war:

> … I have now come to the most difficult part, or most important part of this statement…
>
> As a result of the recent events and other previous similar ones, I have come to strongly believe that we cannot honestly and sincerely continue in this way, as the basis of trust and confidence in our unitary system of government has not been able to stand the test of time… suffice to say… the base for unity is not there or is so badly rocked, not only once, but several

An aerial shot of a section of the Niger Delta north of Port Harcourt. The region is tough and inhospitable. (Peter Wilkins)

A large part of Eastern Nigeria – parts of which became Biafra – was covered in palm oil plantations. (Peter Wilkins)

times. I therefore feel that [we] should review the issue of our national standing and see if we can stop the country from drifting away into utter destruction.[3]

By now, Ojukwu had secretly launched a fairly extensive build-up of arms of his own – involving people like the American Hank Wharton and Rhodesia's enterprising Jack Malloch (of whom we will hear much more later).

Both men – together with arms merchants from France, Holland, Germany and China – worked hand-in-glove with several European governments (including France, Portugal and Spain) to give Ojukwu just about all he needed.

By linking itself to Paris's efforts at subterfuge, South Africa also got involved. The plan orchestrated by Jacques Foccart – the mercurial *eminence grise* in charge of African affairs for President de Gaulle – was to try to help Pretoria out of the isolation that had resulted from its years of race-motivated policies. Soon after hostilities in the Congo ended, France persuaded Pretoria to provide the secessionists with arms and ammunition – largely because French ammunition did not fit 'British standard' weapons fielded by the rebels. The South African Army eventually gave Ojukwu hundreds of tonnes of ordnance, as well as a squad of Special Force troops – all flown illegally into the rebel territory across Nigeria's borders.

Contact had originally been made with the future President Botha, who was South Africa's Defence Minister at the time. He delegated responsibility for the liaison to General Fritz Loots – the original founder of the elite Special Forces unit, the Reconnaissance Regiment (later Commando), or in local parlance, 'Recces'.

Meanwhile, co-ordinating developments in Libreville was Neels van Tonder – a brilliant young staff officer who was eventually to leave his mark on the outcome of the Angolan War.

Other South Africans who got involved included such luminaries as Colonel Jan 'Bruin Man' Breytenbach – one of the finest unconventional counter-insurgency specialists fielded by the SADF (and, surprisingly, the brother of arch anti-apartheid activist Breyten Breytenbach). There was also Chris Moorcroft, Alan Heard and another old hand at this sort of thing, Paul Els – all

---

3 Gould, Michael, *The Biafran War*, p. 167 quoting Anthony Kirk-Greene's *Crisis and Conflict in Nigeria* Volumes 1 and 2 (Oxford University Press, 1975).

The headline says it all: Biafra desperately needed help – invariably unpaid. (Wikipedia)

of whom became involved in the Biafran War – and still more South Africans were linked to training and tactical issues. It suited the Pretoria regime to cause dissension in Africa – largely in an effort to take the heat off domestic problems back home: all part of South Africa's continent-wide programme of destabilisation.

At one stage, there was an operation planned to get one of the South African Daphne class submarines off Lagos Harbour – the idea being to send in an underwater demolition team to blow up Russian freighters then bringing in arms for the Federal offensive. Inexplicably, it was called off at the last moment, which was perhaps just as well.

I deal with the mercenary element involved in this civil war at length in Chapter 18, but little cognisance has been given to the French mercenary role, which, like South African military involvement, is a good deal more substantial than most like to believe.

Forsyth and I discussed this issue at length when he visited me in Washington – and his feelings were that while a French Army veteran, Captain Roger Faulques (who had served with some distinction in the Congo a few years before) arrived at the head of a 100-strong mercenary group, but was then purported to have stayed a day or two before opting out, but this was simply not the case. It was one of Jacques Foccart's duplicitous machinations to make it appear that the French mercenaries were unhappy with the situation and that they had departed; but again, like Breytenbach and his men, this group of fighters was deployed on the far side of the rebel enclave – well out of public view.[4] The truth is that neither Pretoria nor Paris wished it to be made public that their surrogates were involved in an African military struggle in which several major powers were vying for one-upmanship.

The Biafrans were good fighters, but they lacked the kind of practical 'on the ground' tactical advice that these old war dogs could give. The freebooters ultimately had little impact on the outcome of the war, in part, because the Ibos were a proud nation. With some notable exceptions, the mercenary cadres involved would also be faced with an entrenched level of bias from Biafra's officer corps. Most believed that they could do better than a nondescript bunch of hired guns – and they weren't afraid to say so. Also, that the people arriving to take up arms against the Nigerian Army were white did not help either.

---

4   See Chapter 19.

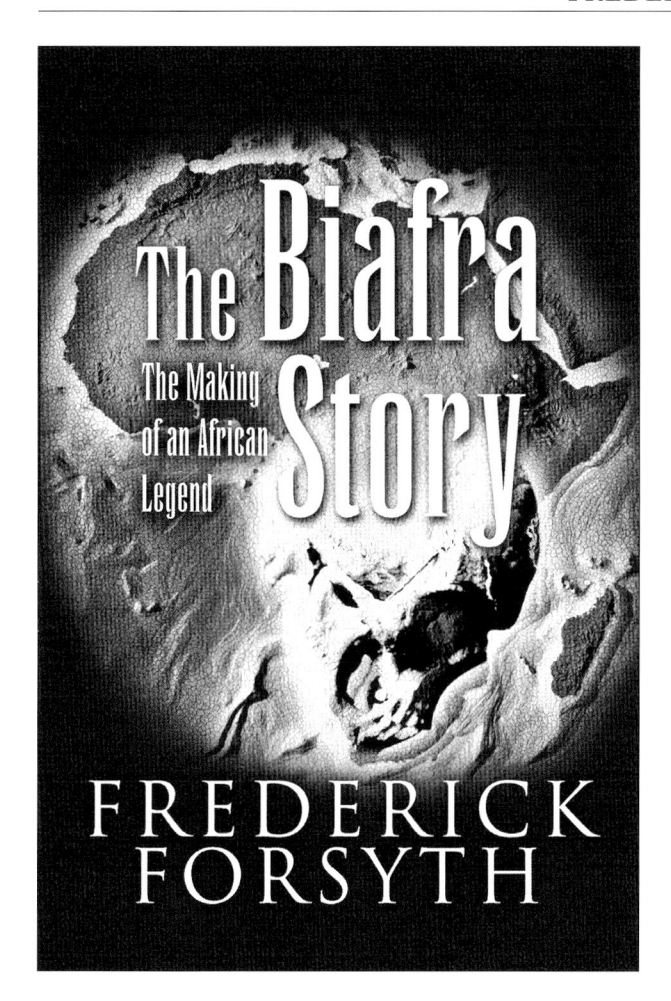

Forsyth's classic book on the Biafran War.

Among the foreigners involved, not everybody turned a coin. Count Gustav von Rosen (a Swedish nobleman of independent means) created an instant air force for the near planeless Biafrans during one of his summer vacations – and he did not charge a penny. When he flew his squadron of second-hand MFI-9B Swedish Minicon trainers into Biafra from Gabon, they were so heavily loaded with extra fuel tanks together with rockets in wing-pods and radio equipment, that some of the aviators present at take-off said they would not get off the ground; well they did – and within the first couple of days had notched up their first successful strikes.

In the first three raids after arriving in the rebel territory, these modest little 'fighters' struck at airports at Benin City and Port Harcourt and bagged several Nigerian Air Force aircraft – including a MiG-17 or two as well as an Egyptian Air Force Ilyushin-28. All of them were blasted while still on the ground. By then, the Nigerians had started using Egyptian mercenaries to fly some of the larger jets, which included Ilyushin bombers. After that, the Biafran pilots had to be more circumspect; there was any number of Nigerian Air Force planes – including MiGs – out looking for them and their bases.

Another figure from Africa's dubious past that arrived in the war was the German mercenary Rolf Steiner – the same man who was later captured by the Sudan Government while fighting for the Christian rebels in the south. Before that – in Biafra – Steiner was appointed Brigade

This was a civilian hospital run by one of the Catholic orders active throughout at Umuahia before it was bombed by one of the Ilyushins flown by Egyptian pilots. Even though the rebels had no effective anti-aircraft weapons, the Arab aviators rarely descended below 10,000 feet when dropping bombs, so this happened more by 'luck' on their part than design. (Author's photo)

Commander and there were mercenaries from many nations who eventually fought under him. An austere, engaging figure, he'd enlisted in the French Foreign Legion after Germany's surrender in 1945. He claimed to have spent seven years in Indochina, where, he said, he'd lost a lung at Dien Bien Phu. Forsyth, in doing a bit of detective work of his own, said that wasn't true.

That did not prevent Steiner scrapping for another five years in Algeria – after which he broke away and joined the anti-Gaullist OAS. While living in Paris, he got wind of opportunities in West Africa. It took him only a few months to make Colonel in Ojukwu's army – a commendable touch, since he'd never been more than a sergeant before.

For all his faults, which included insubordination towards his Biafran seniors, Steiner was extremely tough on his troops. Black or white, they found him a ruthless taskmaster, but somehow, they also seemed to respect him, because while he was unconventional in his approach to most things, he got results.

The proponent of the unexpected till the last, Steiner's favorite ploy was to haul out his Browning Hi-Power pistol and fire it into the air whenever he demanded attention.[5] In Africa, such quirks work. For his personal credo, he adopted the Legion's motto: 'Long live death, long live war'.

---

5   This is slightly elaborated upon in Chapter 18.

Throughout his Biafran escapade, the fighting – though sporadic at times – was as intense as it gets; it was also confused. A town might change hands three or four times in a couple of months – and eventually, the sheer preponderance of Federal might prevailed. It did not take long for the Biafrans to lose their foothold along the coastal areas and be pushed back. Finally, this tiny recalcitrant nation became trapped in a combination of loosely-linked enclaves in the interior – almost all of them heavily forested.

Early in the war, Steiner became involved in an aborted attempt to form a Biafran Navy. With Biafra ringed by conflict on three sides out of four – and the great Niger River and its tributaries running through most of it – it was to be expected that Ojukwu would do what he could to ease the Nigerian naval blockade. Federal forces by then included a Dutch frigate, five Ford class seaward defence boats (SDBs) and three Soviet P6-class patrol boats. At one stage, a Biafran contingent tried to seize one of the SDBs in Port Harcourt Harbour, but those involved were thwarted by the quick actions of a Nigerian support group who sank the boat at its moorings.

In a bid to outdo them, Steiner and Georgio Norbiato commandeered three fast Chris Craft from the Port Harcourt Sailing Club. They mounted machine guns on their prows and set to work. Each could carry four commandos plus a pilot – the idea being that they would ambush small freighters moving upriver.

Their first sortie provided excellent dividends: the booty included five Land Rovers, thousands of uniforms and millions of 7.62 mm cartridges. A later haul brought in 10 tonnes of Soviet and British 81/82 mm mortar shells and tubes, as well as several 20 mm Oerlikon cannons that had been mounted specifically to thwart such actions; then everything ground to a halt after Norbiato was killed in a contact. Until the end of the war, merc elements continued to use the Niger Delta to perform early-warning patrols.

What was also notable about this struggle was that from the beginning, there were very few prisoners taken on either side. Government atrocities at the hands of what had become a northern-dominated – mainly Islamic – force soon convinced the rebel nation that secession from the Federation was no longer the issue; it had become a desperate struggle for survival.

8

A Broader View of Hostilities

War does not determine who is right – only who is left.[1]

Just how competent were the two armies facing each other? We've had Frederick Forsyth, who was right in the thick of it, saying that the Federal Army could not 'fight its way out of a Human Rights convention in Blackpool'. More to the point, they bolted if the enemy showed any defiance whatever.

That these Nigerian troops made pathetic combatants was only part of it. They had their moments, of course, but the fact is that many of their regular officers, who were running the show and making critical decisions (all the way to the top), were not much better. In fact, their job should have been simple because there were few full-blown campaigns while hostilities lasted, but rather, a series of minor or mid-range sorties or skirmishes.

For the Nigerian Army that was just as well, because whoever was handling things like everyday planning, logistics, rations and movements constantly seemed to make a hash of it. There were some operations that were disasters even before they began. In 1967 alone – apart from the Biafran mid-west invasion – these included early reversals at Eha Amufu; various abortive and disastrous Federal attempts to take Onitsha in an assault river crossing; and the loss of previously captured ground like Oguede and the Abalambie Coconut Estate.

In 1968 there were catastrophes such as the loss of numerous logistical vehicles at Abagana; and reversals at Onne, Arochukwu, Esukpai, Aletu, Amaseri, Afam, Enugu-Aku, Ikot-Ekpene, Oguta, Umuahia (Operation '*OAU*'), Adazi and Imu-Ikwu. A year later, there were reversals or disasters which befell Federal troops at Otoro, Uzuakoli, Owerri, Obetete, Obokwe, Omoko, Umuakpu, Ozuzu, Elelele, Omo Nwa Ami, Ovom and Ipo… the list goes on.[2]

We are not talking about a few months here, but for the duration of the war. Much of what happened on the various fronts devolved in a series of debacles – and had the Biafrans not been starved into submission, they might have even won the war. Units would often be left to fend for themselves in total isolation – or more likely, troops would run out of ammunition (in large part because they had never been properly instructed in weapons-handling procedures). Rifles were thrust into the hands of newcomers and they were rushed to the front. As one of the more experienced Federal officers confided to somebody who lived and worked in Lagos after the war, accidental discharges of firearms (ADs) was an everyday occurrence. It eventually got so bad that on returning to barracks, soldiers in many units were forced to unload their weapons and leave all their ammunition at the gates. They were resupplied before they went into battle again.

---

1   Bertrand Russell.
2   Omoigui, Nowa, The Nigerian Civil War File: 'Federal Nigerian Army Blunders of the Nigerian Civil War: Part 1'.

Major-General Philip Effiong – himself a son of a former general in the Nigerian Army – at his headquarters in the bush. He took over the government after Ojukwu had fled and orchestrated the surrender. (Author's photo)

Take something as basic as fire and movement – such tactics hardly ever rated during the normal course of events on any of the front lines. In the overall course of the war, it appeared that nobody had told the average Nigerian soldier that you did not raise your rifle above your head and pull the trigger on full auto. More likely, they were put through the requisite paces, but were simply not listening – or possibly, the men mustered were as high as kites when they went into battle, as was often the case when I spent time with their people in Sierra Leone in 2000.

Worse, those doing the fighting had no experience of the kind of jungle terrain into which they were thrust. Most were city or town boys – with good dollops of jailbirds and academics – who were about as interested in going to war as they might have been in solving equations. To most of them, the jungle was as alien as swimming in the sea; suicides happened a lot.

As for basics such as drills or square bashing, it simply did not rate, which also meant that unit parades – if they happened at all – would almost always be a shambles. One insight came from

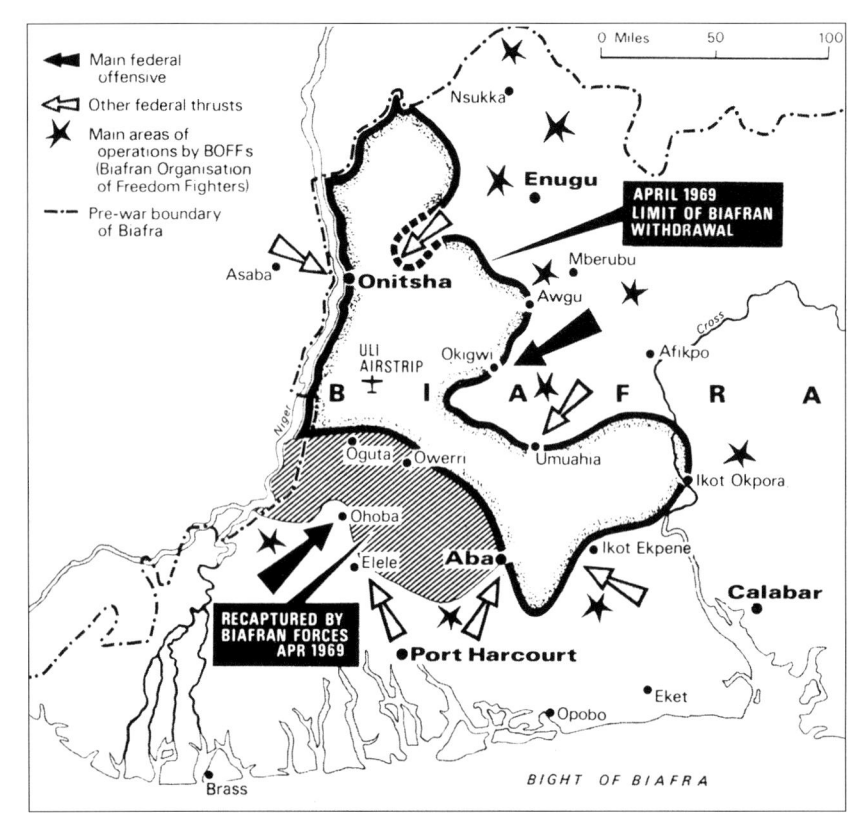

A fairly graphic depiction of how the Nigerian Army progressed towards pressuring Ojukwu's forces in a tiny enclave in the heart of the Eastern Region.

Biafra, where Colonel Jan Breytenbach's small force was training troops. A new intake arrived and during a small-arms training session, one of the recruits was seen firing his weapon into the air. When asked what he thought he was doing, he replied that because his rifle was an automatic, 'the bullets are able find the target on their own.' Those of us who covered other African conflicts are aware that these things happen – sometimes more often than most instructors would like. I have even observed Sudanese fighters closing their eyes when they let rip with the heavy stuff.

For all that, the capabilities of the Nigerian Army could sometimes be as changeable as the West African weather. They would start quite well – taking ground, overrunning towns, defeating rebel strongpoints – and then, a month or three later, would end up losing much of it. It was sheer force of numbers that ultimately made them victorious – by which time they outnumbered their Biafran opposition by something like 10 to one, though there are some who maintained that the margin was significantly greater at the end. Also, the Nigerian Army was issued with rations on a reasonably regular basis, while Ojukwu's troops had almost no food at all – a situation which customarily favours the aggressor.

The case in point here was after having gained much ground in early 1968 the Biafran Army hit back hard and overran the Federal Army at several points. Six months later – in October 1968 – Adekunle's so-called crack commandos lost a third of their number when his force took a serious thumping by the Biafran Army at Umuahia. Taking back Owerri from the Nigerians is regarded in Eastern Nigeria today as one of the touchstone actions of the war – and clearly, the fact that Ojukwu had the support of the locals in this situation certainly played a vital role in his overall strategy.

A BROADER VIEW OF HOSTILITIES

Starving Biafran children. As hostilities progressed, the food problem became more critical, with thousands of children dying every day. (Author's collection)

According to Colonel Robert E. Scott – defence attaché at the British High Commission in Lagos at the time – it was a consistently pathetic performance by the Nigerian Army and something that every military attaché in Lagos could hardly miss. The Colonel went on to write a critical report on the capabilities of the Nigerian Army (or lack thereof) for his superiors in London towards the end of the war. Though classified, it was subsequently leaked to the *Sunday Telegraph*.[3]

Detailed and caustic, Colonel Scott's report caused a huge rift between Britain and Nigeria. Though on solid terms with Yakubu Gowon (they played squash together), this officer was immediately expelled.

Scott's observations are instructive because almost half a century later, they have a considerable bearing on the pathetic performance of the Nigerian Army against the Al-Qaeda-allied Boko Haram terrorist organisation that seems to be able to run rings around Abuja's regular forces – often with impunity if news reports out of West Africa are to be believed. Some critics reckon that what is happening in Nigeria's northern regions today against Boko Haram is almost a repeat of what took place in the late 1960s, with Biafra's much smaller, better-motivated insurgent force maintaining a military precedence against a major African force that had (and still has) the additional advantage of air power for ground support.

Colonel Scott's report – listed as 'Appreciation of the Nigerian Conflict' in the Liddell Hart Centre for Military Archives – reads as follows:

> Tactics employed by the Nigerian Army are basically conventional, but are poorly executed, ponderous, slow, but nevertheless in the long run they prove effective. This is an infantry war fought at platoon or at best company level, with progress dependent upon the going and the visibility in the various sectors. Units regard a vast expenditure of small arms ammunition (the basic weapon being fully automatic) as a substitute for their acute shortage of leaders at the lower level. Effective fire control and conservancy of ammunition are almost unknown throughout the army, apart from in a few units in the 1st Division, which are wealthier in junior NCOs and officers. Normally it is the cacophony of automatic weapons, with most bullets flying harmlessly high into trees, which carries the Nigerian forward. It is said that the Nigerian Army, in the advance, is the best defoliant agent known.

---

3 *Sunday Telegraph* (London: 11 January 1970).

A Nigerian Air Force Delfin jet in action. (A photo from Michael Draper's remarkable book on the war, *Shadows: Airlift and Airwar in Biafra and Nigeria 1967-1970*, which one reviewer said was worth buying for the photos alone.)

Somebody in the Nigerian defence structure must have taken notice of these comments, because Nigerian forces attached to ECOMOG in fighting the rebels in Sierra Leone three decades later were an improvement from before. I was to see some of these units in action when I flew with helicopter gunship plot Neall Ellis in that war. His comments are instructive, because Ellis – who made Colonel in the South African Air Force and has flown helicopters for most of his professional life (including three years in the ongoing war in Afghanistan flying support missions in Mi-8s) – has vast experience in these matters.

In Sierra Leone, he relates, the Nigerians hardly rated when compared to an incredibly small group of South African mercenaries who forced Foday Sankoh's Revolutionary United Front to the negotiating table in Togo. They were able to inflict some damage on the enemy because they were usually less smashed than the rebels. More salient, that regular army held its ground when it mattered (most times, anyway).

Ellis goes on:

> The Nigerians deployed three battalions as part of UNAMSIL (United Nations Mission in Sierra Leone). From this force, they had to concede one battalion to the Guineans, and like any army, with decent training and good leadership, they can do the task given to them.
>
> In Sierra Leone, the legendary Colonel Maxwell Khobe was a no-nonsense leader with good military qualities and was able to provide results. It was under his leadership that ECOMOG was able to drive the RUF from Freetown and secure most of the country with follow-up operations.
>
> Once he was removed from commanding ECOMOG and appointed as Chief of the Sierra Leone armed forces, ECOMOG's force steadily lost ground to the RUF, to the extent that

A Nigerian World War II vintage American-built bomber. (Author's collection)

Freetown was once again overrun in Jan 1999 – in large part because he was no longer a 'hands-on' field commander. If I remember correctly, it took not much more than a week for the RUF to route the entire ECOMOG unit deployed in the east of the country from Kono all the way back to Freetown.

So, in essence, the Nigerians do not make for particularly good soldiers. That can be seen with the ongoing fight against Boko Haram today, where we have a well-equipped army that is unable to carry out successful operations against a rag-tag bunch of radical Islamists.

A few words about General Maxwell Khobe are warranted, because this was one of the few Nigerian Army commanders that succeeded brilliantly where most others failed – even if the timeframe between Biafra and Sierra Leone was separated by decades.

Writing in the *New African* in June 2000 Nigerian journalist Ben Asante, who knew the man well, said that Max Khobe (in Sierra Leone) was a joy to watch at the front:

> He kept encouraging the troops to move forward. Several times we went to the front at first light – only to discover that the men had withdrawn from the positions we left them at the evening before. Many factors caused the pull-back: ammunition was not delivered after they ran out, or no food supplies came through. Other times, rumours circulated that the rebels were coming with anti-aircraft guns, and lacking effective cover, his men just pulled back. Wherever Khobe went, the troops seeing him surged forward and just kept going.

On the fighting ability of the Biafran Army, Colonel Scott was a lot more flattering. In the same confidential report mentioned earlier in the chapter, he declared:

> The [Ibo] soldier has displayed latent military qualities which caused some surprise. This motivation stems from fear for survival, which follows the daily tirade of propaganda which is pumped out by Ojukwu's information service. In sheer guile he has proved himself adept at infiltration and by doing so, has forced the Federals to use caution in their movements and to expend a disproportionate number of men on purely security and defensive tasks. With the Federal formations acting in isolation and lacking in co-ordination, the rebels tend to turn

the traditional disadvantage any force has when operating along inferior lines of communication to their advantage. Apparently, this fundamental fact has never been fully appreciated by Federal planners, who consistently fail to move their three divisions in concert.[4]

My old Nairobi pal Mohammed Amin (he was always full of surprises) once said something about every war having 'a personality' of its own. You cannot argue, because every war is different. Indeed, compared to what is going on in Syria and Iraq today, the Africa of half a century ago bears no comparison.

Of all my colleagues, Amin (as his family called him, though his media pals used 'Mo') was thoroughly familiar with conflict – having seen it from up-close many times. At one stage, he even joined a Palestinian insurgent group based in Jordan on a raid against Israeli forces. That time, he came perilously close to coming short.

Having covered a couple of dozen wars in his life – these events included coups, revolutions and revolts in Africa; the Middle East; the revolution in East Pakistan (what was to become Bangladesh); East Asia and elsewhere – he knew perfectly what it was all about, though he would rarely talk about his adventures (or rather 'misadventures', as he called them). In the process, while working on the outskirts of Addis Ababa in 1991 with the BBC's Michael Buerk, he lost an arm when a munitions dump they were filming exploded nearby. His soundman, John Mathai – standing alongside him – was killed. Before that, he was targeted in Djibouti – France's erstwhile colony on the Red Sea – by what he regarded as an overenthusiastic French Foreign Legionnaire who lobbed a grenade in his direction. Amin was wounded and the shrapnel in his leg left him with a limp for the rest of his life.

Mohammed Amin never covered the Nigerian War, because by then he was paying others to bring him news stories and, in the process, became the wealthiest journalist I had the privilege to know. For developments in Biafra, he relied in part on people like Priya Ramrakha – one of his old Nairobi buddies (then working for an American TV network). That ended when Priya was killed in an ambush.

As Amin once commented, in this business, one needed to thoroughly understand the vagaries of combat, together with the circumstances in which particular wars are fought in order to record or write about them. That, he conceded, applied as much to Iraq; Vietnam; Lebanon; the ongoing insurgency in the Philippines; or Israel's Yom Kippur War as it does to what is going on in Afghanistan today – whether it be along the Tora Bora, or on the dusty plains beyond Kandahar.

With the situation rapidly deteriorating in Biafra, those involved were more or less aware that the Ibo leader had tried to break free from Federal Nigeria after his people had been targeted by the Islamic north. For a while, the situation in this West African state hinged on total dislocation: anarchy, some would call it. Recently independent, hopeful and contradictory and, most important of all, confused by a series of dramatic and violent events that would change its history forever, the country was now faced with a secessionist dilemma.

As Forsyth tells it, once the January 1966 army mutiny became a reality, 'the chaos started'. Every single Nigerian minister, in the wake of the killings, he recalls, 'literally disappeared: 'gone for bush', as they used to say, or vaporised into the jungle.'

The Biafran War, for all its disjointed priorities and mismatched participants, was a near-run thing – especially at its start. In the three years it lasted, there were severe casualties on both sides, with hundreds of thousands of civilians dead by the time the guns stopped firing. More tragic,

---

4 Ibid.

A rural scene on Biafra's roads as the war progressed. With time, many of the young men almost disappeared from view – either serving in the army, or dead. (Author's photo)

only a tiny proportion of those who did the actual fighting lost their lives; most of the casualties were children.

This 30-month West African campaign was also the first of more recent Third World wars to claim an inordinate number of war victims. Even Algeria doesn't rate where numbers are concerned, though in recent years, fundamental Islamic Salafists have been making every possible effort to catch up. While fighting has been going on in the Sudan Republic for much longer, its tally only really soared after the 1980s when modern weapons, jet fighters and chemical weapons were introduced to the frays by Khartoum.

As with more recent African conflicts – Sierra Leone and Liberia included – few prisoners were ever taken in the Nigerian Civil War. Those held, even for brief periods, were displayed solely for propaganda purposes. POW camps, as such, did not exist. In any event, the beleaguered Biafrans had neither the means nor the ability to feed anybody but their own.

We were all aware that Federal forces would murder any of the enemy they captured. In fact, the vast majority of those taken by the Nigerian Army were lucky to survive much longer than a few hours of hard interrogation. There were exceptions, but only when scribes were around. Journalists saw it all in a curious light. As 'guests' – on both sides – they made the best of brief, distorted and slanted handouts; erratic and sometimes dangerous transport (especially in the air); and a front line that could waver by as much as five and, once or twice, 30 miles overnight – never mind vile accommodation (or any accommodation at all) and food that never warranted close inspection. Most of the scribes took their own and nobody entered the country without a wide range of antibiotics.

One of the posters that emerged in Nigeria which condemned Britain's links with the Soviet Union against Biafra. (Author's photo)

There were often scarcely-veiled threats of expulsion if you got the story wrong. You would get a friendly visit from an official and be given the 'message'. Consequently, you rarely gave the whole story as you experienced it, but saved the juicer bits for after you'd left the country.

Intimidation – as with Beirut at its worst – was routine. If you followed the Biafran line while working in Lagos, you found yourself on the next plane out of the country, unless you had first-class contacts within the Federal Government (as was the case with the BBC's Angus McDermid when he first reported on the Ibo secession).

Conflict in Nigeria had as much to do with the people as with the money to fund the fighting. With a population of about 60 million (much more than double that today), the Federal Government had a distinct preponderance where numbers were concerned – and naturally, the ability to acquire as much hardware as Britain and Russia could sell, because Lagos (most times) paid in cash. That was a good deal more than Biafra could muster – even if it had the funds.

While the Federal forces had their 'hero' – the psychopathic Colonel 'Blackjack' Adekunle – the Biafran Colonel J.O. 'Hannibal' Achuzia, who commanded the Biafran Red Commando strike force (one of the best unconventional units of the war), was a totally different kind of military man. In Forsyth's eyes, his role was exemplary.

Achuzia had fought in Korea as a soldier in the British Army – and at one stage, was taken prisoner and tortured by the Chinese. He applied much that he'd learnt abroad to his own tactics in the rebel state and sometimes sent his men on long-range raids. In one attack, his men caught more than a hundred Nigerian Army trucks in an ambush. Munitions and equipment not destroyed were later put to good use by his own forces.

On the circumstances surrounding that strike, Colonel Achuzia told Michael Gould in a 2008 interview that:

> … a lucky shot hit the leading petrol tanker and the ensuing flames spread backwards throughout the column, destroying everything in path. All the enemy's supplies were lost, including all their vehicles and many of their troops. [The event] had a remarkable effect on Biafra's morale and indeed the remains of the attack were left for visiting journalists to inspect and photograph for the remainder of the war.[5]

Towards the end, Colonel Achuzia was ordered to take his force south. It was a last, desperate attempt to stem a Federal advance from the town of Aba across the Imo River. Since his troops were outnumbered 10 (sometimes 20) to one – and his men often down to a couple of rounds of ammunition each, with no artillery support – it was hopeless.

A charming, perspicacious man, Joe Achuzia was married to an English woman and was very much the antithesis of the dreaded Adekunle. Like the urbane former Federal Supreme Court Judge Sir Louis Mbanefo – and the Biafran Chief of Staff, Major-General Philip Effiong (another product of Sandhurst) – he was a gentleman of great dignity. In that regard, the Biafrans were streets ahead of their former comrades-in-arms. Many Federal officers we met were boorish in manner and uncooperative in their dealings with us – and in this regard, Frederick Forsyth was spot-on: they despised and often ridiculed us scribes; how different the Biafrans.

Early on the morning of my arrival at Uli, I was taken to State House at Ihiala, where I was to have my passport examined. The grey-brick building was well-camouflaged from the air, with palm fronds spread over the roof. The Biafrans wanted to confirm that I was who I said I was; the suspicion of infiltrating Federal Nigerian agents had become an obsession. Also, the passport stamp 'Enugu Airport – Biafra' looked a bit incongruous considering that the former capital of the Eastern Region had fallen to Federal troops more than a year before and lay a week's march up the road, were that possible. There I met Brigadier Okorafor of the Overseas Press Service. He was responsible for 'processing' those like me who had entered the rebel territory overnight – 'putting you through your paces', he liked to call it. Some reporters were spared the routine – people like Forsyth, who were there by special request of HE (that is, His Excellency) Odumegwu Ojukwu.

The Brigadier – a distinguished-looking former diplomat – welcomed me warmly.

'You obviously haven't had breakfast; please join me.'

The meal was revolting. He apologised and said it was the best he could offer under the circumstances. Anyway, gari is an acquired taste – especially when it was smothered in eye-watering pepper. I usually gave it a miss, even while I was living in Lagos before the war. The bread offered resembled nothing I'd ever encountered before, and it certainly contained precious little flour, but as the Brigadier tried to joke, it was all part of the daily fare. At least the tea was Earl Grey.

'If you'd come last week,' said the Brigadier, 'I would have offered you an egg. We get three a month. Ours arrived last week. Sorry about that.' He was contrite.

My host himself ate as if we were at the Savoy Grill. I could have done with a steak, but by then, meat was equally scarce in Biafra – and what little there was, invariably enjoyed a dubious provenance. Every cat and dog in the country had long since gone – and rats (especially West Africa's huge cane rats) were a rare delicacy and made for a feast when caught or shot. They were actually not bad as meat dishes go, because I'd savoured some earlier in Togo, where it came with a spinach and hot pepper sauce.

---

5 Gould, *The Biafran War.*

At Ihiala, I met another of the stalwarts who had led the country into war after some of his family had been wiped out in faction killings in Kaduna in the Northern Region. This was Major G.C. Akabogil – a former high school principal; then the security officer at Uli Airport. Genial but tough, 'G.C.' scrutinised all new arrivals. He quoted Virgil like an Oxford professor as he compared the war to the Roman rebellion that ranged against the cruel Etruscan King Mezentius. The analogy was good, he thought, because Yakubu Gowon – in the guise of Mezentius – would ultimately be vanquished, even if it had to be with foreign help. With his excellent English, he sounded rather like a black version of Richard Burton.

Until I had travelled from Ihiala to Owerri, which was to be my base while I was there, I had no idea how badly the war had been going for Ojukwu's people. The Biafran High Command was composed of optimists who constantly spoke of victory. They continued to do so to the very end, even though the Feds were banging on both their back and front doors and, as Forsyth once quipped, 'trying to climb in through their windows as well'.

The country was desperately short of food other than starch – and it showed. At the airport, it took four men to lift a single ammunition case that I could have handled on my own with ease. Likewise, in some of the Biafran towns I managed to get to see, the people were listless and debilitated – their eyes sunk deep into their heads and their pathetic arms and legs displayed little of the kind of muscle that the average Nigerian these days is proud to display whenever the opportunity allows.

It was worse for the kids. Every child that hadn't been placed in one of the scores of camps that were dotted about the territory was swollen-bellied. Most had distinct white patches in their hair – the most visible evidence of *kwashiorkor* (a disease caused by starvation).

'Thank God all the children haven't yet been sent off into the bush. They're our most effective air raid early-warning system,' said one old man. I hadn't been in Owerri for an hour before the first MiG-17 streaked across the sky – its arrival preceded by long, loud whistles. Like domestic dogs (had there been any), the children could hear the whine of jet engines long before we could. The moment their signals sounded, we scuttled like rabbits into improvised underground bunkers. The walls of one that I ducked into early on were crumbling, and I could see sky through the roof.

'Why did they not finish the job?' I asked my escort, Emeka Nwofor – formerly a teacher. His sister was at *Kilometre Onze* in Gabon looking after Biafran orphans.

'Because we haven't got the energy to do it,' he admitted. 'The men take it easy when they aren't working or fighting. We have to conserve what little strength we have. If I want it mended, I must do it myself.'

It was hardly a matter for debate.

At Owerri, I was unceremoniously installed in a caravan: the same standard box-on-wheels in common use all over Nigeria before the war. This one was barely habitable; there was a latrine pit at the back, and for a shower I used a bucket under the palms. Anywhere else in Africa, it might have made for a pleasant safari camp. Several more caravans were clustered together in the shade of some big trees. The exposed sides were also camouflaged with palm fronds, elephant grass and bushes.

My nearest neighbour was the Italian photographer Romano Cagnoni, who – like the Cockney lensman Don McCullin – seemed to have taken up permanent residence in the country. Between them, they were responsible for many of the colour spreads of wounded, dying and emaciated Biafran children that appeared in *Life* and the London *Sunday Times* colour supplement; *Paris Match*; *Bunte*; and others on all five continents. The Biafrans made good use of the stuff – especially since images of dying children stabbed sharply at the conscience of the West. Europe was responsible, not Africa, they proclaimed – and gradually, people started to listen.

A Nigerian Air Force Dornier spotter plane; it was German-built. (Author's photo)

A Biafran soldier with the remains of Nigerian rockets fired on the southern flank. (Author's photo)

Mohammed Amin repeated the process not long afterwards by bringing back the first alarming scenes of millions of starving civilians in Ethiopia. That set in train the largest international aid programme ever – of which Somalia (and the war in Africa's Horn that followed) was an offshoot. He garnered a gong from the Queen in the process.

In Biafra, in contrast, General Ojukwu was effectively helped in his campaign by the public relations firm Mark Press of Geneva. The company thoroughly vetted everybody who wanted to go into Biafra – and again, the paranoia with Federal agents was palpable. Cagnoni and the rest of the bunch of news-gatherers – into which I was thrust at Owerri – lived pretty well. They'd brought with them all the booze they needed and trunk-loads of food. Since I'd been led to believe in Libreville that we would be catered for while we were there – and since we weren't – I all but starved. I should have known better, because pictures of the breakaway state's starving children were in every newspaper in the West. Certainly, the Biafran representative in Gabon failed to warn me that his government not only would not, but (more to the point) *could not* feed me – so while at Owerri, I was almost entirely dependent on Cagnoni's goodwill and, let's face it, he could only help so much. Nobody was sure how long they'd be around, or how long the war would last – and the hacks and those taking the pictures were not taking any chances.

    I ended up famished – and it made for a rather novel, if disagreeable, experience. Everybody (speaking generally) has fasted for a day or two – and you're usually that much the better for it, but when it goes on for a week or 10 days, it starts to get to you; life becomes difficult. I could hardly complain, because the Biafrans had been hungry for two years. By the time I got back to Nairobi, I couldn't stop eating. I also found it difficult to stop hurling myself to the ground each time a car backfired; I was bomb-happy for a while afterwards.

9

Biafra: The Conflict that Created *Médecins Sans Frontières*

It's simple really: go where the patients are. That might seem pretty obvious, but at the time (in Biafra) it was something of a revolutionary concept, because borders got in the way. It is no coincidence that we called it *Médecins Sans Frontíeres*.[1]

Medicines (or rather the lack of them) were a constant problem while hostilities dragged on – and dragged on they certainly did, because for the majority of the population (with no hope, no prospects, and no way out), it seemed that the war would never end.

Whatever drugs were brought into the country went straight into the tummies of hundreds of thousands of sick and starving children. Adults, civilians and combatants had to make do with bush remedies and potions; witchdoctors thrived.

I spent many a night at the French Red Cross Hospital in Owerri watching the forerunners of *Médecins Sans Frontières* (Medicines Without Borders) treating the wounded. There were no formalities and I could walk into the operating theatre at will, with or without a mask over my face. Operations were carried out without anaesthetics, because there were none. Only the officiating surgeon and his theatre sister wore surgical gowns; the rest of us were in our everyday gear. There was no sterilisation – not even scrubbing soap.

The wounded were brought in from the various fronts at night in Mammy-Wagons – the universal means of transport in West Africa. These were (and still are) huge covered vehicles – half bus and half truck – with their distinctive garish billboard-type pronouncements emblazoned over the driver's cab, which has become a feature of transport all over Black Africa. Some were bizarre, like 'God No Get Wrong Ting', 'Man He Get No Rest', or 'Never say Die Today', or the equivalent in the local Ibibio or Yoruba languages. One I vividly recall, because I used it often to get about and the driver was a willing soul, had 'Kiss My Gnash' painted in foot-high letters over the windscreen. It referred specifically to the backside of a human being in the vernacular.

During the day, there was very little movement on Biafra's roads, with MiG fighters constantly overhead (as I was to discover a few times, to my own consternation) an omnipresent threat. The wounded had to wait for nightfall before they could be moved – and for those with gut wounds, the delay could be serious; septicaemia is fatal in about six hours if not treated.

Every one of those covered trucks that arrived at the medical camp had on board something like 15 or 20 casualties. A lot depended on space and who could manage to sit up or not. There were, invariably, three or four of those wounded earlier in the day already dead.

---

1 Bernard Kouchner, Founder of *Médecins Sans Frontíeres*.

Members of the French medical team at a primitive jungle hospital in Biafra. These volunteers – brave people, one and all – were the immediate forerunners of the French-led *Médecins Sans Frontières*. (Author's photo)

BIAFRA: THE CONFLICT THAT CREATED *MÉDECINS SANS FRONTIÈRES*

'We have to work fast when the first ambulance gets here,' said one of the French doctors who'd volunteered to come to Biafra to gain trauma surgery experience.

The wounded – some walking; others supported, as well as a few on makeshift bamboo lifters – were taken to an 'emergency station' (usually an empty room lit by paraffin lamps). The worst cases would be separated from the others, and the young doctors would go to work – often through the night; it was harrowing.

By nightfall, some of the patients would already show the first symptoms of gangrene, which meant that at the makeshift Owerri hospital there were certain set routines in place. Those who offered no hope of survival were put on one side, and there would sometimes be a priest who would offer the last rites. For the rest, arms and legs were hacked off without ceremony. A piece of wood would be thrust between the victim's teeth, several soldiers would hold him down and the doctor would get to work with a saw.

'What else can we do?' said Dr Michel Fontainebleau. 'If we didn't amputate the limb, he'd be dead by morning.'

Bullet-holes to the chest – unless a vital organ had been pierced – were relatively simple by comparison. Many were of large calibre, such as the NATO 7.62 mm, and unless they had hit bone, they would pass straight through the body much more often (by comparison) than was the case with AK slugs. The narrow bullet-holes would be rinsed out with a disinfectant – usually with the help of a narrow garden hose. If there was a large exit wound, that would be something else. Often there would be a vital organ smashed, which even with modern procedures in a Western hospital today, would probably be terminal. For all this, there were some astonishing recoveries – one of which was a young soldier who had been slashed almost all the way through his chest by a large chunk of shrapnel from an artillery shell. Even in Biafra, we came to realise soon enough that miracles did happen.

I'd watch these dedicated young Frenchmen plunging steel rods tipped with a length of lint into a bullet-hole in the chest and push it through to the other side; it was like cleaning a rifle. While most amputees would scream, none of the soldiers given the rod treatment so much as whimpered.

I never found out what proportion of casualties survived, but it must have been a fair number. The Biafrans, I soon discovered – famished or not – were a remarkably tough bunch. They rarely complained – and there was no question that their fortitude was exemplary to us Western softies.

By the time I arrived in the war, there were quite a number of French medical volunteers working in the enclave – almost all of them still in their early-twenties. This was a fragmented community and not that well organised, because these young folk had to make do with what was available and what they had been allowed to bring in by plane – and even that was restricted because of weight. *Médecins Sans Frontières* (MSF), as we recognise that organisation today, had not yet been founded by the time the Biafran War started. In fact, apart from mission and government hospitals, the occasional clinic, and some volunteer medical people from abroad, such facilities were sparse and there was a shortage of everything: drugs, anti-malarial tablets, bandages, dressings and morphine, and pain suppressants especially.

I went into several 'clinics' used by these young doctors and nurses while there, and most played dubious medical roles under extremely rudimentary conditions: what had once been a bedroom would double as an operating theatre, and there was never the possibility of sterilising either the room or the table on which the victim was treated. Instruments like scalpels, forceps, clamps and other surgical paraphernalia would be immersed in a pot of boiling water that had been heated over an open fire once the patient had been attended to, and that would be that. That process would be repeated many times each night – and it could hardly have been ideal from an infection point of view. There was almost no non-essential electricity throughout the country – and consequently, no other option. There always seemed to be enough catgut for sutures to stitch wounds,

A battlefield casualty is hauled back from the front line. Those Biafran troops who might have had a chance of surviving had to wait until nightfall before they were taken to the bush hospital by Mammy-Wagons. (Author's photo)

though perhaps these youthful enthusiasts also used fishing line, because I never saw anybody lifted off or walk away from the tables with an open wound – and they obviously needed a lot.

We scribes knew that if we took a hit, we'd have to leave the country on the first flight out – either that, or we'd land up on the dreaded operating table, which was almost always covered in something dried or drying, and certainly malevolent-looking by morning. Worse, were any of us to take a hit in the torso, the chances of terminal infection setting in within hours made the possibility of survival in that soporific heat pretty slim.

BIAFRA: THE CONFLICT THAT CREATED *MÉDECINS SANS FRONTIÈRES*

There were few opportunities to socialise with these volunteers – mainly because of the odd hours they worked. Also, these were extremely trying times and there is no question that if only for the sake of personal survival, they carefully nurtured their 'down-times'. One couldn't help but be impressed by their dedication because the work was tough, and because of often horrid circumstances – obviously unpleasant. You clearly needed good focus to get through it – often for weeks or months at a stretch, which is saying a lot, because these people were hardly paid very much. They must have had a bit of a social life, because nobody could survive that extremely demanding rigmarole day in and day out without some diversion – if only to lift morale and sagging spirits – though that was invariably completely beyond our ken as outsiders; and anyway, their culture was French – and just about everything else in Biafra followed the strictly traditional British regimen.

Most would start their day when it got dark and the majority would work through the dark hours. Towards midnight, I would sometimes spot one of them taking a quiet break in a corner and they'd fall asleep almost immediately (and stay that way until called for the next procedure by one of their colleagues). Most would have eaten their main meal during late-afternoon, which was when I usually arrived at their base – the principal one being a rambling, bare-roomed old structure that had probably housed the regional British District Commissioner (and possibly his family) during recent colonial times.

Thirst must have been a constant companion for most in that heat – and half a century ago, there was no bottled water as we know it today. I'd arrived in the country with a load of water-purifying tablets, and they must have used them as well, though you had to gag your way through the chlorine taste in order to still thirst. It worked though; none of us were ever plagued by stomach bugs.

On the nights that I went 'medical', I never had to ask permission to hang around – nor to take my pictures. I'd simply pitch up and watch them unloading their charges from the trucks – never a pretty sight, because there was blood everywhere, quite often congealed into oozing crimson or pitch-black puddles of gunge.

At the time, I couldn't help but imagine that this might have been something like those involved in the Napoleonic or Crimean Wars had experienced, because it was all so fundamentally primordial. The eerie part about it all was that there was so very little talking among those involved. Doctors, nurses and their aides would whisper instructions to each other. In fact, I don't think I ever heard one of the volunteers barking an order. Everything seemed to be handled with a quiet, dignified grace –almost as if those involved expected many of their patients to die. The truth is that by the time one of the wounded men had made it to these medical outposts, he would probably survive, because many of those with life-threatening wounds would have passed on by then.

As each patient was lifted off the Mammy-Waggon, he would be given a brief going-over by one of the doctors and one of the local helpers would be told where to take him. There would be a surgical team waiting inside and they would immediately go to work. Though there were women involved in the field with the Biafran Army (many doing their bit of the fighting), it is worth mentioning that I never saw a single female casualty brought in, though obviously there must have been a few – nor was there ever anybody present from the army or the government to check on what was going on.

The group of youngsters who originally founded MSF was a diverse lot. Many had been involved in the Parisian upheavals of May 1968 – after which a group of recently-graduated doctors decided to set up an aid body that would help the victims of conflict and natural disasters. At the time, it was a totally new concept: a new brand of humanitarianism that would reinvent the concept of emergency aid – and though there was a new and undisguised radical political commitment among French youth, a lot of good came out it. As one blogger recently expressed it: 'After the revolt of May '68 burst onto their black-and-white TV screens, the French public soon saw other,

Nigerian so-called 'Mammy-Waggons' were used to bring the wounded back from the front, but rarely during daylight hours because of Nigerian jets that strafed anything on the roads that moved. This vehicle arrived at a bush hospital run by the forerunners of the *Medecins Sans Frontières*. (Author's photo)

more frightening, images. For the first time, television broadcasted scenes of children dying from hunger in remote corners of the world'.

With the war in Southern Nigeria gathering momentum, the French Red Cross issued an appeal for volunteers. Until then, for some years, Max Recamier and Pascal Greletty-Bosviel – volunteer doctors with the International Committee of the Red Cross (ICRC) in Geneva – had been regularly intervening in armed conflicts.

'Contrary to popular belief, the Red Cross is not a medical organisation at all,' Max Recamier said afterwards.

He continued:

> Pascal and myself were the only two doctors they knew because of our previous mission in Yemen, so they asked us to find some doctors for the ICRC.
>
> The first one to volunteer was Bernard Kouchner, who was much younger than I was; he was just finishing his studies and hadn't even finished his thesis yet, but he volunteered to go over there [to Biafra].
>
> A team of six set off on the ICRC mission to Biafra: two doctors – Max Recamier and Bernard Kouchner – as well as two clinicians and two nurses. Being thrown into such a bloody conflict was a real shock for these fledgling doctors, who found themselves having to provide war surgery in hospitals that were regularly targeted by the Nigerian armed forces.

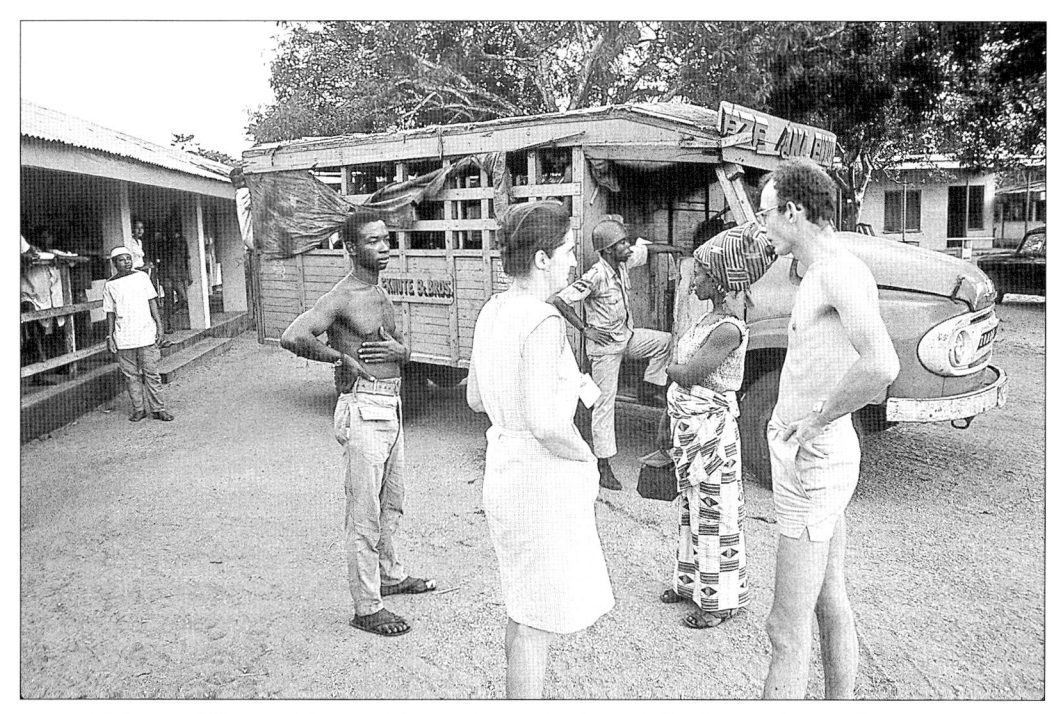

BIAFRA: THE CONFLICT THAT CREATED *MÉDECINS SANS FRONTIÈRES* 115

A Mammy-Wagon with casualties has just arrived – and the doctors discuss their options. (Author's photo)

Recamier and Kouchner believed the world needed to know about the events they were witnessing: civilians being murdered and starved by blockading forces. They openly criticised the Nigerian Government and the Red Cross for their seemingly complicit behaviour.

In the following three years, other doctors began to speak up. These doctors, or 'Biafrans', as they were known, began to lay the foundations for a new and questioning form of humanitarianism that would ignore political or religious boundaries and prioritise the welfare of those suffering.

Bernard Kouchner – one of the prime forces of MSF development – has an interesting background, admitting that the radical Paris riots (which at one stage even threatened the French Government) played a significant role in his life. He was born in Avignon in South-Eastern France – about 80 kilometres from Marseilles – in November 1939. His father, a physician, moved to the suburbs of Paris when he was still very young – and while being educated, he recalls (like many youthful proto-revolutionaries), he was influenced by the works of existentialist philosopher Jean-Paul Sartre and the poet Louis Aragon.

Kouchner qualified for his doctorate in 1964 and subsequently became certified as a gastroenterologist. Four years later, he was still hesitantly finding his way within the arcane corridors of modern medicine – and, according to one source, he travelled to Biafra with about 50 of his colleagues; that was in the summer of 1968.

In retrospect, it is unlikely either that he would find that many professional volunteers to start with, or that the emerging airlift out of São Tomé, would be able to take that many non-essentials into the beleaguered enclave. Most of their cargoes were food for children who were dying in

A still from the modern film *Half of a Yellow Sun*, made on the war. It is based on a brilliant book of the same name by Chimamanda Ngozi Adichie.

the many camps scattered about the jungle – and ancillary services were dealt with according to urgency or need. An enthusiastic bunch of aid workers (no matter that they soon proved themselves invaluable) would have been way down the priority chain. Also, there was limited space on older aircraft like the Super Constellation or DC-6, where weight limitations were further constrained by the tropical climate – so the newfound medical contingent took its chances wherever it could find them.

As a member of an ICRC group, Kouchner admits that his initial attempts to provide adequate medical aid to a suffering population were not at all satisfactory. On his return to Europe – early in 1969 – Kouchner speculated on the problems of the conflict and voiced his disagreement with the ICRC and its policy of not interfering in the politics of the warring countries, which, he felt at the time, was absurd.

How could you not be involved in the face of such blatant suffering and bloodletting? That was only one of his propositions; another was that Geneva should tackle the Nigerian Government about children dying of starvation at source – and that meant Lagos, but the Red Cross was adamant: they would not interfere in Nigeria's internal politics.

It is worth mentioning that something similar took place years later in the civil war in Sierra Leone – and to which I happened to be a party… The South African mercenary group Executive Outcomes was aware of what was going on with regard to children in the interior, and they offered the ICRC space on board their Mi-17 helicopters that were making regular forays into remote places either to take in food, or bring out the mutilated victims. I was in the Freetown offices of the Red Cross when this proposal was made – and the reaction was greeted with undisguised horror.

'Use mercenary transport?' the local ICRC asked. 'Never!' he replied – his face contorted in disgust.

Wounded Biafran troops being wheeled through town to hospital on an improvised litter.
(Author's photo)

The man's reaction was final – and the silly fellow studiously avoided us thereafter, even though we all made use of the same bars, restaurants and hotels in Freetown. What a bloody fool, I thought at the time.

I often thought about that incident over the years and came to realise that through the efforts of one stupid functionary inappropriately handling funds that had been donated by ICRC well-wishers the world over, a lot of lives could have been saved. Today, he has to live with his conscience, because I wrote about that incident in an earlier book.[2] One Swiss individual, who subsequently made contact, said that the person involved was distressed that I had gone public about the matter. 'Fuck him!' I wrote back.

For Bernard Kouchner and his associates, the civil war (and ensuing famine) in Biafra resulted in the founding of GIMCU (*Groupe d'Intervention Medical et Chirurgical d'Urgence*, or Emergency Medical and Surgical Intervention Group). After Biafra, a second disaster – a flood due to a tidal wave in Eastern Pakistan (now Bangladesh) –led to the establishment of SMF (*Secours Medical Français*, or French Medical Relief); then in December 1971 MSF was born from the merger of GIMCU and SMF, with Kouchner as its first director. The MSF today has essentially the same goals as the other two groups: that is, to bring food, medical supplies and, most of all, hope to the needy peoples of the world. Kouchner remained with MSF until 1979, when he left to form a new group, *Médecins du Monde* (Doctors of the World). The goals of this group were essentially those of the previously established groups: putting medicine before politics.

---

2   Venter, *War Dog*.

10

Flying Soviet MiG Fighters in the Biafran War

Constantia's Ares Klootwyk flew military aircraft for most of his career – from learning to fly vintage Harvards in the South African Air Force, to helicopters and jet fighters in the RAF. He was recruited as a mercenary in the Congo, where he flew T-6s, Trojans and Douglas A26s – as well as helicopters. He moved on to choppers and fighter jets in Nigeria, and was the first Western pilot to climb into the cockpit of a Soviet MiG-17.

There is no question that the Soviet Mikoyan-Gurevich MiG-17 (NATO codenamed 'Fresco') was an outstanding fighter jet. During the course of the Vietnam War, the Americans lost something like 70 of their planes in aerial combat to them.

Even though considered obsolete by the mid-1960s – and was denigrated by many Western aviation 'experts' – this stubby, swept wing jet fighter gave an excellent account of itself over Vietnam. Only recently has it been disclosed that in South East Asia, the MiG-17 was secretly flown in combat by Soviet aviators and that it became the favourite combat fighter of most of the top North Vietnamese pilots (including that country's leading ace, the appropriately-named Colonel Tomb).

Because the MiG-17 played a seminal role in air operations against the Biafrans in their 30-month West African conflict, it is important to fully appreciate exactly what this versatile little flying machine could do. The prototype MiG-17 first flew in January 1950 and was reported to have exceeded Mach 1 in level flight, with a normal ceiling close to 60,000 feet. It weighed in at about 13,400 lbs (maximum take-off weight) and was armed with two 23 mm cannons, as well as a single 37 mm cannon.[1]

Pilots flying these jets in Nigeria rarely fired the cannon because it was regarded as slow and had a very poor trajectory. While the MiG-17 packed a mighty punch in its air-to-air combat capabilities, the jet was even more effective when unopposed. It roamed Biafran skies at will – constantly in search of targets of opportunity. These included vehicles on the road; Biafran military emplacements; troops on the move; and, without fail, Count Gustav von Rosen's elusive little Swedish Minicons that could pack an inordinately powerful punch.

Whichever way the pilots turned within the enclave, there was always something to attack. Travelling about the country by road, we were particularly vulnerable and had to keep a constant watch for anything in the air that might be threatening – the MiGs especially.

An interesting sidelight here is the fact that Biafran casualties were never moved to medical dressing stations during daylight hours. The wounded always had to wait until dark before the

---

[1] By comparison, the weapons capacity alone of today's F/A-18 Hornet – the United States' twin-engine supersonic carrier-capable combat jet – is 20,000 lbs.

Cape Town's Ares Klootwyk at the controls of a Soviet MiG-17, which he flew as a mercenary for the Nigerian Air Force. RAF-trained Klootwyk was the first Western fighter pilot to man the controls of this still highly controversial fighter. (Ares Klootwyk)

trucks could trundle out of their jungle hiding places because they would have become easy targets had they tried to traverse the enclave's roads during the day. The result was that anyone who suffered a gut wound in that tropical heat was usually dead within six or eight hours from septicaemia.

By his own admission, Ares Klootwyk was very much against the instructions of the Soviets who had supplied the MiG 17 – and he entered the Biafran War on a whim. He'd received a telegram from Colonel John Peters – a Yorkshireman who had made Corporal in the British Army and ended up as a Colonel in Mobutu's Congo.

As former Congo mercenary biographer Arthur Jones declared, John Peters was a most unusual individual: hated by many, liked by very few and loved by nobody. Those with whom he came into contact tended to defer to him because he was 'so utterly fucking ruthless and unpredictable.' There were several reports of Peters wiping out entire villages in the African bush because he had been told or believed the residents there were harbouring the enemy. Peters was also the man who helped put Mobutu into power in the Congo, and later offered to take him out. He took over command of 5 Commando in Katanga from Mike Hoare and when that was over, he started recruiting mercenaries for the Nigerian Government. Interestingly, his Second-in-Command was Alistair Wicks – a fellow British Army officer who had been appointed Commandant in the Congolese Army and who had begun a rival organisation recruiting mercenaries for Biafra.

Klootwyk standing in the cockpit of his MiG-17 parked in the jungle. (Ares Klootwyk)

Klootwyk never actually met Peters, but in January 1968 he received a telegram from the man which said, roughly: 'If you want to fly in Nigeria at a thousand pounds a month, you will be met at Lagos Airport. Airfare will be refunded, notify arrival or not'. Always the opportunist, Klootwyk admits at being at a loose end just then and thought: 'What the hell, I'm bored; I'm doing nothing and, in any event, I need the money.'

From what he'd been reading in the press, there were some interesting developments in West Africa – and, as he says, that was incentive enough:

> I was also aware that Peters – ex-Congo – had started recruiting some of the guys with whom he'd been involved from about mid-1967 onwards. News went out that he was in London and looking for potential recruits, pilots included, all of it coming by word of mouth because there were never any advertisements in the newspapers.
>
> I was not aware of any company involved, but we knew that he wouldn't be getting into that war himself, physically that is… he'd done all the fighting he'd needed in the Congo and, by all accounts, was pretty bloody ruthless at it…
>
> Also, with Whitehall working hand-in-glove with Lagos, British Intelligence simply had to be aware of what Peters was up to. In fact, they probably helped him get started.
>
> What emerged after I'd got to Nigeria was that that country was in serious need of professional pilots, both for helicopters (which I'd flown in the Congo and elsewhere), as well as

FLYING SOVIET MIG FIGHTERS IN THE BIAFRAN WAR

BEFORE T/O
TRIMS — N
AIRBRAKES IN
FLAPS 20°
INSTS. NORMAL
OX. IF REQ.
CONE OFF
BOOST LEVER ON

AFTER T/O.
RAISE U/C.
REDUCE POWER
RAISE FLAP

CLIMB 10,500 — 800   TAS. 620
OR 11,200 (690   720
COMBAT 11,560 JPT   750
                MAX

CRUISE 10,800
ENDURANCE 320 IAS
GLIDE 600 TAS — 450 IAS.

FORCED LANDING: DROP TANKS AND STORES — UNPRESS COCKPIT — OPEN CANOPY — SWITCHES OFF — IN ROUGH, LOWER NOSE WHEEL.

EMERG U/C: CHECK CIRCUIT BREAKER — PUT U/C LEVER UP, THEN NEUTRAL, PULL LEFT & RIGHT EMERG HANDLES, PUT LEVER DOWN, OPEN AIR SYSTEM.

EMERG BRAKE: CENTRALISE RUDDER & PULL LEVER.

EMERG FLAPS: PUT SELECTOR DOWN + OPEN BOTTLE.

CANOPY MIST. PRESS. ON HOT.

SMOKE IN COCKPIT: OPEN FRONT VENT, OPEN LEFT SIDE EXTRACTOR (CLOCKWISE OPEN) CLOSE AFTER.
SURGING: THROTTLE BACK, OPEN SLOWLY.
ENGINE FIRE: RED WARNING LAMP ON, SMOKE ASTERN, JPT RISES, SMOKE IN COCKPIT. THROTTLE BACK, HP COCK OFF, SPEED 300-350, PRESS EXTING. UNPRESS COCKPIT, OPEN FRONT VENT + EXTRACTOR VENT.
ASI FAILURE. CHANGE PITCH ATTITUDE TO CHECK. PUT ON PITOT HEAT. CHANGE TO STANDBY PITOT.
GEN FAILURE: LIGHT COMES ON. PUT OFF ALL UNNESS. CIRCUITS, LAND. BATTERY OK FOR 18-20 MINS. NO INSTS.ON
ICING ON CANOPY: USE DEICER, DECREASE HEIGHT.
RELIGHT IN AIR: 2000-6000 METRES, RPM 1200, PUT ON RELIGHT SWITCH, HP COCK ON AFTER 10 SECS, OPEN THROTTLE SLOW, IF NO START, WAIT 30 SECS.
TAKES 45 SECS TO START. MIN HEIGHT, NOT BELOW 2000 METS. MIN. EJECT HT. 500 METS.

FUEL PRESS 45 ± 6   CONTROL BOOSTER
OIL PRESS   4   PRESS 60
OIL TEMP   75   THRUST 2270 KG
GEN   28·5   + A.B. 3380 KG

GREEN FUEL PUMP WARNING ON:
AVOID USE OF AFTERBURNER, NEG G, HARSH USE OF THROTTLE. + DESCEND BELOW 9000 METS.

HYD PRESS GAUGE 120
EM. U/C - 50 EM. FLAP 120.

A 118·1
112·5
122·7
140·0

(MIG 17)

Ares Klootwyk's personal notations about flying the Soviet fighter.

Klootwyk at Lagos Airport with one of the Nigerian Air Force helicopters he also flew.
(Ares Klootwyk)

fixed-wing pilots who could fly combat in some of the Nigerian fighter jets. Also, it was pleasing to be told that my salary would be paid in any currency and into any bank in the world. Essentially, for us guys, it was very much a win-win situation – and the added bonus was that Biafra had no fighter aircraft which might be used to oppose us.

The deal was basic: we worked five months on, with a month off on full pay, together with a return ticket back to where we had originally come from, or the equivalent amount towards any other destination of choice. The small-print that each one of us signed indicated conditions while on operations and included a life insurance policy if we were killed or wounded.

From the start, we were housed at good hotels and fed three meals a day. The downside was that we had to pay for our drinks, which was perhaps just as well, because some of the fellows would have drunk the bar dry had they been given the choice.

He disclosed too that individual pilots were able to take their wives, mistresses or girlfriends to Nigeria – and (also paid for by the Nigerians) return tickets, accommodation, food and all (with everything supplied by the government). The women were even allowed to accompany their men as far as Port Harcourt.

Nigerian Air Force, Makurdi 1968. From left: An Egyptian Air Force technician, Major Falope, a medical doctor, two Nigerian pilots and Ares Klootwyk. (Ares Klootwyk)

Klootwyk:

On my first posting to Makurdi – immediately to the west of Biafra and which had a fairly large air force base – I lived in a guest house there which offered adequate housing. The food was a bit dodgy; typical African fare – mainly rice and goat meat. In Lagos, we stayed at the same Airport Hotel where I'd been taken when I arrived. Port Harcourt also hosted us at the Airport Hotel, which was equally good, and a real treat because we had free access to the wine cellar at no cost.

There were approximately 16 mercenary pilots hired by the Nigerian Air Force over the duration of the war – comprised mainly of British, South African, French, Australian, Polish and possibly one or two more nationalities as the war progressed. At any period, there were perhaps five to eight active pilots on contract.

I arrived at Lagos' Ikeja Airport on the 11th of January 1968… Can't remember the airline, but I came in direct from Jan Smuts, so it was probably Pan American, which stopped in Lagos twice a week on the New York run. I was met by Yorkie Grimes – a former British serviceman who had Royal Navy helicopter technical experience and whose day job was to look after Nigerian Air Force helicopters. He escorted me to the hotel, booked me in and then hauled me across town to Nigerian Air Force Headquarters near the harbour in downtown Lagos. There I was well received, gave my banking details, but was offered no real briefing as to what was expected of me. All I was told was that I would find out everything I needed to know from the other pilots. Moreover, when required, I would fly air force helicopters.

We weren't issued with uniforms and, for a long time, wore civvies and donned overalls for flying. Eventually some of us got some camouflage gear.

An example of the kind of orders that Klootwyk and his mercenary colleagues might expect prior to going out on strikes. (Author's photo)

> *Memorandum*
>
> *From* GOC
>
> 04 MAY 19 69
>
> To Capt. Alfa
>
> Go on the farm settlement furing your second sortie. You will go on the Ohekelem - Olakwo run. Fire the Houses. They are all in there.
>
> Our own tps are in Okpuala. The en are now in Objs 1 to 4. They are your tgets.
>
> Serious attacking going on now. Hurry.
>
> COL,
> GENERAL OFFICER COMMANDING,
> 3 MARINE COMMANDO DIVISION.

Just about everything that happened in that West African nation was fairly haphazard and unplanned – like the 30 minutes of dual instruction I was given on a Westland Whirlwind Mk-2 helicopter after the Nigerians acquired eight from the Austrian Air Force. Immediately afterwards, I was posted to the air base at Makurdi to fly general duties, but then this was Africa – and you went along with it because you were expected to make things happen… something we were all pretty good at.

Because the Soviets were involved in Nigeria (supporting the Lagos war effort against the Biafrans), it is axiomatic that Klootwyk would have had some contact with these people, but certainly not enough to become familiar with, because he had flown in the RAF and was still regarded as a potential enemy in the context of the Cold War.

Before Klootwyk arrived in Nigeria, a large group of Egyptians had arrived in the country to provide support for the war – flying MiGs and their two Ilyushin-28 bombers and doing maintenance on these aircraft: 'I'd already converted from choppers to flying the Czech Delfin L-29 trainer/fighters in August 1968, which was handled by Charlie Vivier – a South African mercenary aviator with whom I'd previously served in the Congo.'

But, says Klootwyk, it was obvious from the start that the Nigerians weren't impressed by the Egyptian commitment. They were rarely prepared to take any chances – invariably flying at high altitudes when they dropped their bombs:

A Nigerian MiG-17 force-landed near Opobo in June 1969 by British mercenary pilot John Pallister. (Ares Klootwyk)

> It seemed their bombing and strafing was not at all effective – and consequently, they had poor results. At frontline airfields, the mercenaries had Egyptian technicians for servicing the MiGs and Ilyushins, while Nigerian ground personnel on the airfields only refuelled and moved aircraft around; then somebody at Air Force Headquarters in Lagos got the idea that it might be a good idea to get some of us involved with the MiGs. The Egyptians were pretty useless, so this could only be an improvement – and anyway, most of us already had good combat experience with fighters and it was a natural progression.

In October 1969 eight Soviet Antonov-12s each delivered one MiG-17 to Kano International Airport. These were the so-called 'MiG-17 Glatts' and came from East Germany, because that country was retiring its MiG-17As from service. The 'Glatt' bit came from 'gloss pipe' (in German), which indicated these jets were not equipped with afterburners.

According to Klootwyk, the first problem to be faced was that Moscow was never keen on supplying MiG-17s to the Nigerian Air Force:

The Soviets were actually dead-set against us Westerners getting anywhere near their planes – in large part because the operating parameters of the MiG-17 were still secret.

By then, Jimmy Webb – another British pilot – and I were already active against the Biafrans. We were flying armed Czech L-29 Delfins and the day came when we were quietly told by our Nigerian Air Force commander that we were to fly the MiGs – very much against the wishes of the Soviets, who were then supplying the Lagos regime with much of its military hardware.

The two of us had been flying ground attack roles in the Delfins and were ordered up to Kano to meet our instructors. Mine was Major Jibrin, a Nigerian Air Force instructor, and Jimmy had an Egyptian pilot put him through his paces.

Our conversion consisted of three flights each in tandem dual-seat MiG-15s: total dual instruction time of about an hour and 50 minutes. A 15-minute solo flight on a MiG-17 followed; easy enough, we thought, when Jimmy and I compared notes afterwards.

That was followed later by a 30-minute instruction in Soviet gunnery procedures on one of the MiG-15s. It consisted of going in fast on a ground attack and firing our machine guns and the jet's sole cannon.

We then did a further 45 minutes' general flying and an hour of gunnery practice on the MiG-17 before returning to Lagos and on to Benin, where we became fully operational in the war. It was one of the quickest conversion sessions I have seen any pilot undergo, but being young, we were quick to learn.

Klootwyk explained that the MiG-17 had a conventional cockpit layout, except that the instruments and cockpit instructions were in Cyrillic script and that the instruments were marked in kilometres per hour and in metres:

After a simple pre-flight routine, we discovered that the MiG had very good visibility, was an easy starter and simple to taxi – as against the RAF Vampire, which had similar brake and peddle actuation, but was a bit more difficult to control.

My first take-off in a dual MiG-15 was a cinch, but with such a superior performance to the L-29 – which I'd been flying until then – I found myself at 300 metres before I remembered to retract the undercarriage, such was its superior thrust. Airborne handling was no problem – and neither of us encountered any difficulty in touch-and-go landings or full-stop landings.

After three short flights with Major Jibrin, I soloed on the MiG-17 – and not using the afterburner on take-off, I found no real superior performance compared to the MiG-15. What the MiG-17 did have was a good rate of climb – and coupled with easy handling and ease of landing, it was an excellent fighting machine.

On our operations over Biafra, there was never any need – unless ferrying an aircraft – to go above 3,000 feet, as our operations were mainly ground attack. Flight time on internal tanks was no more than 40 minutes, and with two drop tanks of 100 gallons each, we could remain aloft up to 80 minutes.

We also found that the aircraft's 23 mm machine guns were very effective, since every third round or so was a tracer, which meant that you could easily remain visually on-target. The 37 mm cannon was, in contrast, disappointing. We hardly ever used it because of the unsatisfactory trajectory of its cannon shell, which one could see dropping practically the moment it left the barrel.

On subsequent take-offs – sometimes using the afterburner – there was a greatly increased acceleration and shortened take-off run. It was quite a step up from the Czech Delfins which

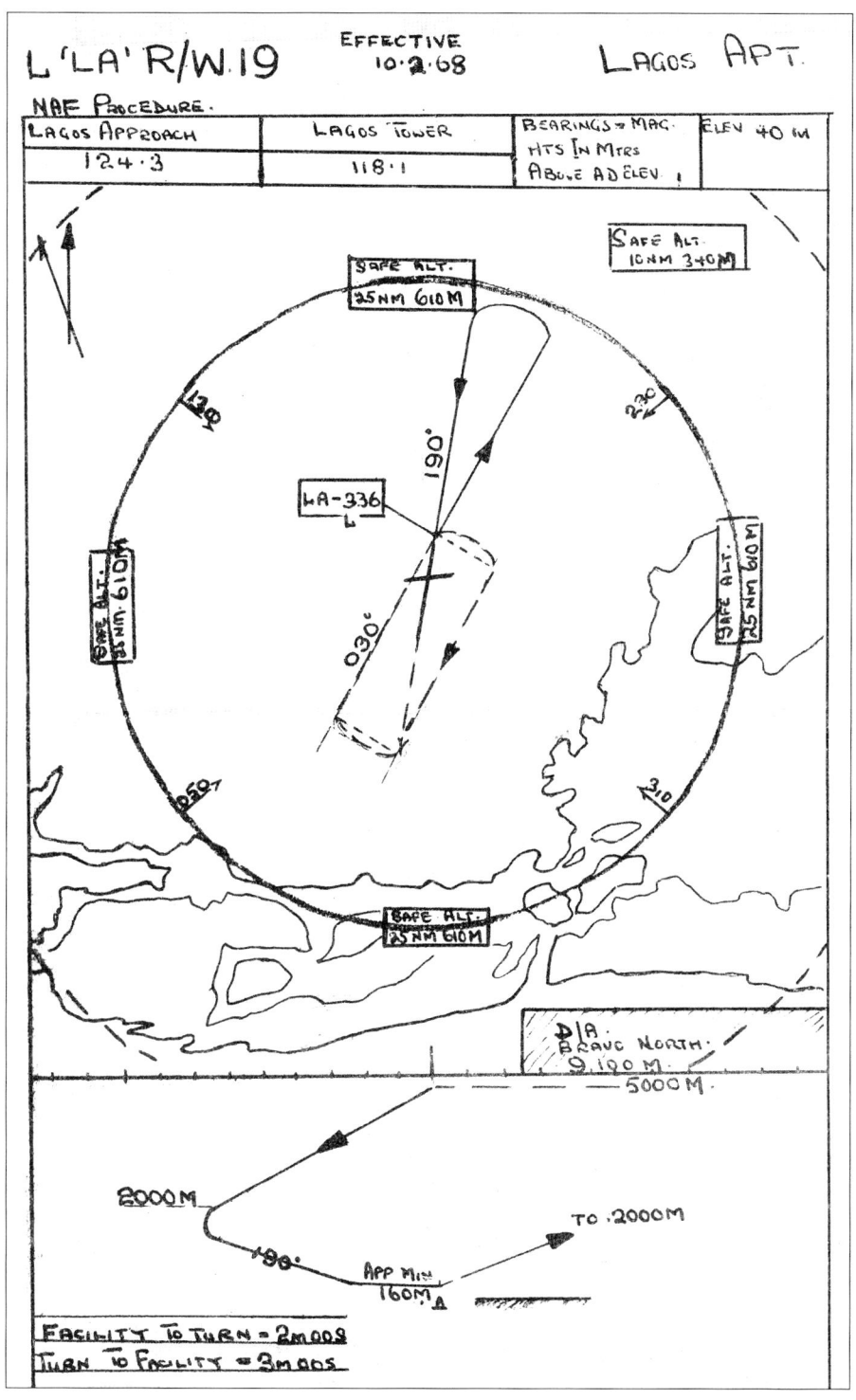

The South African mercenary's Nigerian logbook produced this interesting document about Lagos Airport. (Ares Klootwyk)

we'd been using in ground attack roles. The Delfins were efficient, but not all that effective because they were, essentially, light training aircraft and armed only with four rockets.

There were rarely any glitches when handling the MiGs operationally, says Klootwyk.

Though the Kano posting for Klootwyk and Webb was brief, things did not go exactly according to plan, because the Nigerian Air Force base there was also manned by Soviet technicians arming and servicing the MiGs. As Jimmy Webb says, 'they must have been surprised to find that the fighter jets suddenly had new drivers… but perhaps because it was already *fait accompli*, things were allowed to slip.'

According to Klootwyk, it wasn't quite that easy. The Nigerians 'were not eager to rock any boats. In fact, they were keen to avoid any kind of Soviet or Egyptian confrontation about the conversions, which was why they rushed putting us through our paces.'

Jimmie Webb recalls a rather hasty Central Hotel check out in Kano and the dash to get them to Kaduna Airport to board a DC-3, which flew back to Lagos 'in part because we'd all suddenly become aware that the Russians were on the lookout for us in Kano… I'd imagine they became suspicious when the MiG cannons were being armed for our range sorties.'

What also emerged was that the Nigerians had never asked Moscow for permission to let Klootwyk and Webb fly these still top-secret MiG fighters. As Klootwyk stated, that was also confirmed by Terry Peet – another of the mercenary aviators: 'Permission was never asked of the Soviets – nor was it ever given.'

The Nigerians used a variety of ploys to harass the Biafrans – one of the more effective being night-time raids over the rebel airstrips in which a DC-3 was converted to dropping improvised bombs and incendiary devices. Some transport pilots landing at Uli, Uga and other strips referred euphemistically to the aircraft as 'Intruder', while others used harsher language. Klootwyk and his fellow pilots had little contact with these unconventionally-minded mercenaries, who soon acquired a reputation (if not for accuracy) then for a measure of ruthlessness:

> The 'Intruder' DC-3 was flown by Henri Laurent – a Belgian pilot – and usually with co-pilot Francois Reip (also a Belgian). Their Bombardier was a South African, Jimmy Calderhead – all three of whom had seen service in the Congo. We saw them infrequently at various airports, Port Harcourt, Lagos, Benin and elsewhere. Calderhead now lives in Cape Town at the Salvation Army home in Greenpoint.

As to coming under Biafran fire while flying operationally, it happened of course – as it does in any conflict – but in Klootwyk's case, more often while at the controls of helicopters, which he flew in Nigeria prior to going onto jets:

> In February 1968, while based at Makurdi with a Whirlwind 2 helicopter, I was airlifted to Enugu to have a look at what I was told was a French-built and supplied Alouette III, which the rebels had been using to drop home-made bombs, and which was subsequently captured intact by our forces.
>
> I was flown across to the riverside city by a Dornier twin to find a Westland Widgeon helicopter emblazoned with a Bristow helicopter's markings camouflaged under palm fronds… did the a pre-flight inspection and because it looked 'flyable', a Jeep battery was connected to start it. Though I'd never flown this type, it came from the same Westland stable as my Whirlwind 2; I was able to run it up and hover for a while.
>
> Since everything seemed fine, I said I'd fly it to Makurdi, which I did. En route and at a fairly low level, my Nigerian mechanic and I came under small arms fire, which we later

A tail-end view of one of the MiG-17s about to take off from a jungle airstrip near Benin. (Ares Klootwyk)

learned had come from our own troops. They were under the impression that the helicopter was still being operated by the Biafrans. I don't remember that we were actually hit in any way by ground fire, but it was close.

On another mission, also in the Whirlwind out of Makurdi, I was flying to our troops at a frontline position. When the soldiers on the ground heard us approach, they really let rip and only stopped when their officers told them to do so – realising that we were 'friendly'.

On shutting down on the ground afterwards, I found that they had put two rounds through a rotor blade, which could have had fatal results. Westland rotor blades are not of a solid construction, but made in what are termed 'joined pockets' that run the length of the blade behind the main spar. One was shot off, which meant there was a part that measured roughly 20 mm by 20 mm altogether shot away from the blade. Another bullet was embedded in a main spar, but I managed to land safely without too much vibration; then I judged that it would probably be OK to fly home, which I did. A replacement rotor blade was later sent up from Lagos – and the all-purpose specialist Yorkie Grimes arrived to install it.

Things were very different at Biafra's Uli Airstrip, where Nigeria's mercenary pilots always experienced ground fire – usually when they arrived in the morning to see what aircraft had been left behind overnight. That would happen if a plane couldn't take off because of unserviceability or mishaps, like being hit by 'friendly' ground fire when landing (which happened all too often), or possibly bomb damage from the Nigerian Air Force DC-3 which arrived over the airstrips just about every night:

A report in a Nigerian newspaper about a successful air operation in which the mercenaries were involved. (Author's photo)

Two rebel planes shot down

TWO rebel "Minicon" aircraft spotted by the Nigerian Air Force over Obirikom last Saturday morning were chased back to their secret landing strip at Ozubulu where they were destroyed as they landed at about 10.45 a.m., it was announced yesterday.

A reconnaissance flight carried out by planes of the Nigerian Air Force over the air strip immediately afterwards showed the aircraft still burning.

It will be recalled that the "Minicon" planes which the rebels have been using to rocket some parts of the Federal territory were flown into Nigeria by Count Von Rosen, a Swedish ace-pilot, and his group, many of whom are still known to be within the rebel enclave. What is not known however, is whether Count Von Rosen or any other of his co-mercenary pilots were in the destroyed rebel planes.

The tactics we used with the MiGs was for the leader to come in at about 400 mph in a left-hand circuit at an altitude of roughly 1,000 feet. Number Two would follow about 10 seconds behind.

We'd have quite a bit of ground fire – usually ack-ack and machine-gun fire coming up at the lead aircraft, but with no lead offset being allowed for by the gunners. The rounds would burst and traverse between the two jets and the second plane would then dive down and fire on the enemy position, which would immediately be silenced. We would pretty well have *carte blanche* to take out any other targets on the airstrip.

We must have been quite lucky, because we were almost never hit in those sorties. The only casualties we experienced were when the Biafran Minicons and Harvards attacked our planes on the airfields – and as compact as those tiny planes were, they sometimes caused quite serious damage.

There was no question that the Nigerian Air Force MiG-17s soon became a significant factor in the internecine war being waged in West Africa. Reports that subsequently emerged suggest that the Soviet planes made a significant change to rebel tactics – in large part because almost all movement on the enclave's roads during daylight hours were halted.

MiG-17s 'parked' out in the open along jungle airstrips made enticing targets for Biafra's Minicons. Quite a few were destroyed in surprise raids by these tiny Swedish 'fighters'. (Ares Klootwyk)

While flown by Egyptian pilots, neither the MiGs nor the Ilyushin IL-28 bombers made much difference. They bombed and strafed as required of them of course, but always at altitude, while the mercenary aviators in Lagos' pay preferred the low, fast and accurate option.

A good deal has come to light about the MiG-17 in recent decades – including the fact that its listed range was 870 miles, which in Vietnam gave it an enormous advantage over American escort fighters in their sorties. Most times, they were allowed only minutes over the target areas.

According to documents released by the Aerospace Museum of California (Volume VIII), the MiG-17 fighters frequently tangled with American jets during the early days of conflict in Vietnam – and one report is emphatic: 'Due to its high manoeuvrability and light weight, the tight-turning MiG-17 was often a difficult target to hit. American F-4C Phantom IIs and Republic F-105 Thunderchiefs, although substantially faster (and heavier), could not [safely] successfully engage the small and dangerous MiG-17 in close dogfights'.

The report goes on:

> ... thus the only sure way to kill a MiG was through use of air-to-air missiles at a safe distance... in part because early production MiG-17s were fitted with the VK-1 engine – a Soviet copy of the Rolls-Royce Nene.

Fortunately, most American fighters had sophisticated search and targeting radars and a range of AIM type missiles to employ in this role.

Later versions of the MiG-17 could also carry two Atoll AIMs on wing-pylon stations; IR/heat-seekers almost identical in design and function to the US-made 'Sidewinder' missile of the period, which meant that the MiG-17 SP-2 version had roughly similar capabilities to the US F-86D 'Sabre-Dog' interceptor.

As with most contemporary fighters from all nations, the MiG-17 had a pressurised cockpit and was typically 'over-built' in the conventional sturdy Russian manner. With heavy-duty landing gear designed to be used on rough or poorly-prepared [Third World] landing strips and solid, rugged aluminium construction throughout, the MiG-17 could be easily maintained in the field by ground crews.

More salient, most maintenance problems could be fixed with simple equipment and ordinary tools. Consequently, by the time that Ares Klootwyk and Jimmie Webb climbed into the cockpit of this 'still unknown' aircraft in Lagos for the first time, Western intelligence agencies were very much on the tails of both aviators – eager to get their views not only on how this Soviet fighter performed, but also in hopes that they might be able to pinpoint some of its shortcomings.

'Though it took a bit of time, we didn't disappoint either the Americans or the British,' Klootwyk is happy to confirm today.

Obviously, the MiGs were no match for the Minicons (and vice versa) because the jets were simply too fast and sophisticated for the little prop-driven jobs that usually flew only metres above the jungle. Klootwyk recalls a run-in with the Minicons, though he was on the ground at the time:

We were all at Port Harcourt when the Minicons staged their first attack – and they caught just about everybody by complete surprise. I was taking a nap after lunch in the Airport Hotel when a series of strange popping sounds woke me. I went to my balcony, from which I could see the airport, and in a befuddled state I thought I saw an aircraft about the size of a Cessna-150 buzzing around the airfield. It didn't really register just then that the airfield was under attack, and I went back to sit on my bed to consider what the hell was going on. Only then did I become aware of what was actually happening. I took another look outside to confirm my fears, got dressed, phoned another of our pilots and told him to meet me outside as soon as possible. Something very strange was happening at the airfield, I said.

We jumped into one of our Mini-Mokes, drove to the airfield and found an Africair DC-4 on fire at the terminal. We then hurriedly drove over to our hangar, where there were more fires – including one of our MiGs burning furiously. The enemy Minicons had gone by then, but the damage these little planes inflicted was remarkable considering that they weighed only a few hundred kilos.

At another time, we were having lunch in the hotel when I heard a sound that was very familiar because I had originally trained on them: it was a T-6 Harvard approaching the airport at a fairly low level – and when it passed over the hotel, it fired a long machine-gun burst which we later learned was at a truck in the road, and which killed the driver.

It disappeared after that and we couldn't find it following the 20 minutes or so that it took for us to scramble.

Many pilots had stories to tell after the war ended: a former RAF pilot ran out of fuel after having overflown Port Harcourt Airfield (see photo). He attempted an engine-off landing on a narrow surfaced road to the immediate south of the airfield. Unfortunately, after safely touching

One of the pictures of a starving Biafran child that was circulated worldwide during the course of the war.

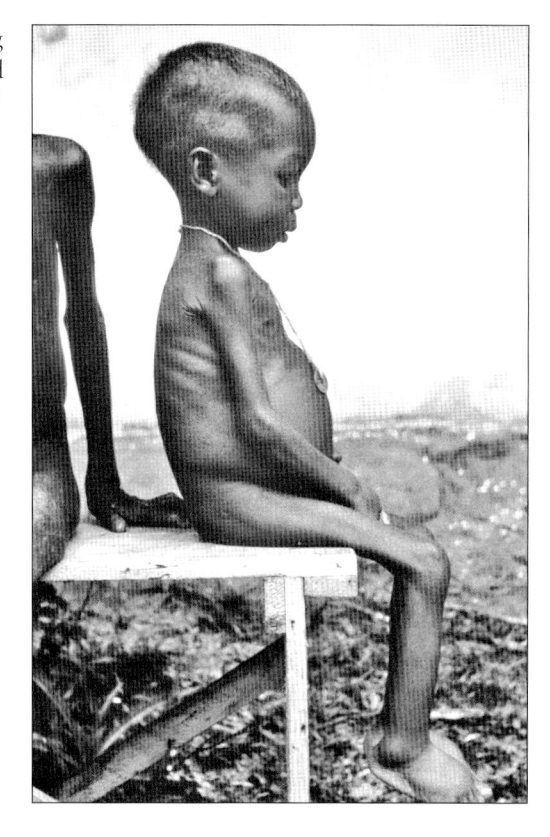

down and before coming to a halt, his starboard wing struck a palm tree next to the road. That cart wheeled him directly into the bush – damaging the aircraft enough to make it a write-off.

Another pilot, upon returning to the airfield at Port Harcourt, ran out of fuel on the final approach. He hit the ground a few hundred metres before touchdown and was killed; that fighter was also a write-off – otherwise, recalls Klootwyk, there were no ditchings, landings or bailouts behind enemy lines.

It is also telling that Nigerian Air Force routines were exceptionally low-key. Klootwyk maintains that with briefings before flights, the pilots normally received no more than a hand-written note from the army commander (see photo) that would provide little more than cursory instructions as to what he required (like strafings); what targets were to be bombed; reconnaissance work; and anything else that might be required. These details would be passed on to the pilots by hand; then the war ended – and to Ares Klootwyk, recollecting today from his home in Constantia Valley, it was something of an event:

> I was at the pool at the Airport Hotel at Ikeja when we got word that the Biafrans had surrendered and that the war was over. Francois Reip flew a lone Harvard back from the front somewhere and landed it at Ikeja – and a few days later, us pilots were all asked where we would like to go and to which destination they should make out our airline tickets. Our services were no longer required, we were all peremptorily told. I opted for London and left Nigeria shortly afterwards.

11

Biafra's Aerial War of Attrition

> Considering that Nigeria is again – almost determinedly – sliding into another self-perpetuating civil war, it is perhaps appropriate to look back at how the war was fought in the air from the Biafran side. It was a minimalist effort, because Colonel Ojukwu had very little foreign exchange with which to buy modern fighter aircraft – but in the course of events, some things did happen…

The introduction I did for my final article on the Biafran War – shortly after I'd emerged from the fighting there late in 1969 – just about says it all: 'It was only a jungle airstrip in the heart of tropical West Africa, but Uli Airport – codename 'Annabelle' – became a legend among the airline pilots of the world'.

Like most things in that dreadful conflict, everything that went on at Uli – the hub of the Nigerian Civil War for three years in the late 1960s – was improvised. As we have seen, Uli's 'airport' runway – lined on both sides by primeval jungle – had once been a stretch of main road between the towns of Aba and Onitsha in Eastern Nigeria.

Forsyth, who was down with malaria when I got there, recalls that this was the story of the strangest air bridge the world has ever seen – in large part because the airplanes used by the aid people who every night flew in Biafra's supplies and munitions were a ramshackle collection of time-expired or phased-out workhorses of the skies.[1]

The freebooters that flew them were recruited through a single company in Switzerland. The Egyptians, in contrast – who manned their Ilyushin IL-28 bombers, which were notable for their inability to achieve anything spectacular – came direct from Cairo at the behest of President Gamel Abdel Nasser. As a close ally of the Soviets, this 'dictator in all but name' had already launched a series of insurrections that included the invasion of the Yemeni Republic.[2] Coming to the aid of Nigeria, which effectively made him a British 'ally' in that struggle, was viewed with great suspicion by other Western powers – including France and the United States. That said, the performance of his Egyptian Air Force pilots was dismal. His bomber pilots would rarely drop below 10,000 feet for fear of ground fire, which – at best – was pretty marginal because there was so little heavy ammunition being airlifted into the country.

The overall picture of what was then going on in this West African military struggle was that the single common denominator in this bloodletting was similar to what we see in Israel today: both sides despised each other with a religious-driven fury that even today defies description. At the end of it, a singular difference emerged: once the Biafran War ended, both sides were able to get

---

1 Draper, *Shadows*.
2 Hart-Davis, Duff, *The War That Never Was: The True Story of the Men who Fought Britain's Most Secret Battle* (London: Century – a division of Random House – 2011).

Biafran pilots August Okpe and Willy Bruce in front of one of the MFI-9B 'Minicons'. (Gunnar Haglund)

together, if not reasonably amicably, then without having to resort to violence to settle outstanding differences.

With the war in Vietnam becoming more intense by the month – and claiming the bulk of international media attention – few people spared a thought for what was going on in Africa at the time, even though it was the biggest military conflict the continent had experienced since the end of World War II. From the start of hostilities, the Biafrans weren't altogether inactive in countering the Nigerian air offensive, though the rebels were able to offer only limited resistance with a tiny air force called the 'Biafran Babies', which had been put together at the behest of the swashbuckling Swedish philanthropist, Count Carl Gustaf Ericsson von Rosen.

Von Rosen had a rather persistent delusion that Africa was going through a phase: 'growing pains', he called it. He also believed that he could change things for the better and, as heaven only knows, he tried. It was Africa that killed him in the end when he died in a guerrilla attack in Somalia's Ogaden War in 1977.

Von Rosen clandestinely brought five Swedish-built Malmö MFI-9Bs to the breakaway Nigerian state and created the Biafran Air Force. Initially, the planes were ferried into Biafra from Libreville. Because of losses, American Intelligence sources disclosed later that these were supplemented by several more – totalling eight Minicons by the time the war ended. As 'fighters' go, the Minicons were among the smallest modern combat aircraft built. 'Von Rosen's Vengeance' – as the modest prop-driven planes were called by the media – proved astonishingly effective.

One blogger, who calls himself 'Srbin' (all we know about him is that he was born in 1986), commented that:

Biafran bombers made several strikes on Nigeria's eastern port city of Calabar. (Wikipedia)

… even the Skyraider was like an SR-71 compared to the little putt-putt plane around which von Rosen built his force: the tiny Swedish trainer looked like those ultra-lights that people build in their garages. This plane could park in sub-compact spaces at one of Stockholm's shopping malls … it had a maximum payload of 500 lbs; or, as he said: 'me plus a couple of medium-sized dogs.' Lucky those Swedes are so skinny…

… in Gabon, von Rosen slapped on a coat of green VW paint to make them look military and on each aircraft, he installed twin wing pods for French-built Matra 68 mm unguided rockets; then he and his pilots – three Swedish volunteers who took time off from their civilian jobs, together with three Nigerian Ibos – flew them back to Biafra and this unlikely septet immediately went into combat, the next day apparently. More Minicons were bought later, again paid for by this Swedish aristocrat.

They blew the hell out of the Nigerian Air Force, as well as the Nigerian Army. These little fleas were impossible to bring down. Not a single one was knocked out of the sky, although they'd buzz home, sometimes riddled with holes… they flew three missions a day and their list of targets destroyed included Nigerian airfields, power plants and troop concentrations.

Caught napping on the ground, they also knocked out two, possibly three Soviet MiG-17 jet fighters (and damaged another two); one Ilyushin-28; a British-built Canberra bomber (as well as one more damaged); the 'Intruder' (the twin-engine DC-3 transport plane manned by the South African mercenary who called himself 'Genocide' and who would bomb civilian aid aircraft as they landed in the dark); as well as two helicopters, with one more damaged.

That, declared 'Srbin', was hardly a bad tally for a rebel air force that the Lagos Government – throughout two-and-a-half years of hostilities – routinely declared 'did not exist'.

At one stage – in a bid to supplement his Minicons – the Biafran leader bought a dozen World War II surplus T-6 Harvards, but they were in a poor condition, because only four were airworthy. During their initial transit flight from Gabon to Biafra, two were lost. The remaining pair was used in strikes – usually in conjunction with the MFI-9s (nine of which were then still in service). During the latter part of the war, two MFI-9s were destroyed – presumably to ground action, which could sometimes be intense.

Interestingly, Artur Alves Pereira – a Portuguese mercenary pilot (and at one stage, a Portuguese Air Force squadron leader in that country's colonial wars) – flew T-6s as well as Minicons for Biafra. He was the last freelance pilot to fly out of the beleaguered enclave on 9 January 1970 and was dropped off in Gabon. From there, he headed home to Lisbon – and although the war was over and all rebel offices in Portugal were closed, the now non-existent Biafran Government sent him a final paycheque which covered all the war missions he had flown, as he told friends, 'down to the last penny'. He commented afterwards that this small example showed how special a people the Igbo [Ibos] are: 'Which country in the world, let alone in Africa, would bother to fulfil its commitments to this extent? Which messenger wouldn't feel tempted to keep part, or even all, of the money?' The amount that he received, he admits, was quite a lot at that time – especially when the future seemed so uncertain to everybody involved. Obviously, he concluded, there would have been no court to which to complain.

Another significant comment was that with experience gathered over time at the 'Sharp End', the tiny Minicons – in true guerrilla style – turned their weaknesses (small size and low speed) to their own very effective advantage. They were so slow that they simply *had* to fly really low, which made them almost impossible to hit in the jungle, since you never saw them until they were almost on top of you. Their modest speeds made for much better aiming capability than the sleeker and faster MiGs: almost half of the approximate 400 rockets they fired hit their targets, which is an amazing tally for unguided aircraft munitions. (There used to be a joke in the United States Air Force during World War II and Korea that if it wasn't for the law of gravity, unguided rockets fired from aircraft wouldn't even hit the ground.)

Clearly, these minuscule MFI-9Bs packed a decisive punch. Apart from the Harvards, there was also a surplus World War II American-built B-26 bomber which had mixed fortunes before it crashed on a bombing raid over Nigerian lines. After the war had ended, a Biafran Air Force de Havilland DH-104 Riley Dove (serial unknown) emerged. It was discovered in wrecked condition on the playing fields of a school in Uli. Tom Cooper told me that this was a bit of a revelation, as the authorities were only aware of a single Dove – a US-registered Riley Dove N477PM delivered to Port Harcourt from Switzerland by Andre Juillard/Girard/Gerard after having been impounded for a while in Algeria in the summer of 1967. The 'new' Dove carried a unique camouflage pattern that comprised patches in khaki outlined in black over a turquoise-green backdrop. The lower surfaces were mid-blue, which in anybody's book, was unusual.

With time, the Biafran conflict devolved into a series of holding actions, with the majority of the population doing their best simply to survive. In reality, after the first year of the war, the food situation in Biafra had become so critical that the entire nation was starving. The only way to get food in was by an air bridge operated either from São Tomé or from Libreville. The International Red Cross flew some flights from Fernando Pó and from Cotonou (in what was then still Dahomey), but that was not a regular event, and was eventually halted in June 1969 when one of its planes was shot down by a Nigerian MiG-17.

By mid-1968, international relief organisations were carrying out flights on a limited scale – using the same planes that ferried weapons from Europe to Port Harcourt and later onwards to Uli. When one of the American pilots refused to go in because of risk, Count von Rosen made a flight for the German Caritas welfare group in August that year. The air connection from São Tomé was organised by a Scandinavian group called Nordchurchaid – and by January 1970 more than 5,000 flights had done runs across the Nigerian coast and back again.

The ICRC – sometimes also operating from Fernando Pó and Cotonou – hauled in 20,290 tonnes by June 1969 when flights were finally suspended from that island. Once in Biafran air space (always after dark), following the first few months of hostilities, things often got hectic – extremely so at times.

The following is an extract from a flight report from one of the aid pilots, dated May 1969:

> … spent one hour and four minutes waiting in the air over the Uli field… made five aborted approaches. Nigerian bombers were harassing as usual; the landing lights came on too late or were turned off on final approach. The Intruder, i.e. the bomber, released his first bomb when we were at the end of our final approach.

Biafran ground troops had no effective counter-measures against Nigerian MiGs that took out their targets almost at will. The best they could manage was using rifles against the jets. (Author's photo)

When we first got clearance from the ground to approach at an altitude of 2,500 feet – from the east and towards the airport – we got instructions to return to the beacon we came from, EZ. An aircraft was being observed between us and the ground. The plane flew south.

From Uli Airfield we were told that this plane probably was GJE (New Zealand DC-6 from Cotonou). What he was doing there and who gave him clearance to go there I do not know.

Uli Airfield was bombed incessantly during some periods, but the damage was quickly repaired. A total of 11 aircraft were destroyed and 21 members of aircrew killed. That figure included nine aircraft and 13 pilots belonging to church groups.

In November 1968 a Joint Church Aid DC-6 was damaged by a 20-kilo shrapnel bomb that exploded alongside the aircraft. Five people were killed and many injured – including the co-pilot, Jan Erik Ohlsen and the pilot, Captain Kjell Bäckström. Ohlsen was flown out by a Red Cross plane, but Bäckström decided to try and do the impossible and take his damaged aircraft out. It had 50 shrapnel holes along one side and two of its engines were leaking oil. Despite his injuries, Bäckström succeeded in getting himself, his crew and his aircraft to São Tomé, where he was operated on at the local hospital by Portuguese surgeons. Three pieces of shrapnel were removed from his body.

Eight crew members of the Red Cross were killed in a crash in May 1969 and in an aircraft shot down by Nigerian forces in June 1969. Joint Church Aid lost a total of 13 crew members. Four men died when a German aircraft crashed in July 1968 but that was before Joint Church Aid was formed. On 7 December 1968 a German DC-7 crash-landed at Uli – killing four; then on 4 August 1969 a Canadian Canairelief Super Constellation went down – killing its crew of four. Five

Americans died in an air crash on 26 September 1969. Thereafter, four additional aircraft were totally destroyed without loss of life and two more damaged beyond repair – all at Uli. In spite of these losses in crews and machines, the air relief programme was an enormous success.

Early in the war, Egypt sent 15 MiG fighters to the Nigerian Air Force. To the Egyptians, this was almost routine, since Cairo was then supporting a host of revolutionary groups (including many from Southern Africa's revolutionary wars). The most determined effort in usurping power was in the Yemen where, for several years, Nasser's subterfuge was countered by Britain's Special Air Service, with the help of mercenaries (including the French mercenary Bob Denard). Later – helped by Algeria – Cairo again assisted Nigeria by providing more Ilyushin-28s. In addition, 12 L-29 Delfins came from Czechoslovakia; two Jet Provosts from the Sudan; a couple of Westland Whirlwinds from Austria; and a pair of Gnome Whirlwinds and an FH-1100 from Britain.

While I worked for John Holt in Nigeria, the Delfins were parked on the runway outside my office – and since the second Nigerian Army mutiny took place while I was living in Lagos, I deal with these episodes in considerable detail in one of my books, *Barrel of a Gun*, which was published by Casemate in the United States and Britain in 2010.[3]

Shortly after hostilities started, the Nigerian Government decided to recruit mercenary air crews – largely because Nigerian pilots were unable to manage the intricacies of modern fighters and bombers. These 'guns for hire' came from a dozen countries. What followed, starting in 1967, were a huge number of attacks by the Nigerian Air Force on schools, hospitals and marketplaces – and although there were sporadic halts, the aerial strikes continued until the end of hostilities.

Virtually every hospital in Biafra was blasted at some stage or another (sometimes many times over) – underscoring observations made by independent observers, which included members of the church who worked in the enclave. All concluded that these were 'terror' bombings and had absolutely no military value. Indeed, it was confirmed long afterwards by others who put pen to paper that the attacks served only to strengthen the Biafran resolve to resist. Had such things happened today, those responsible would almost certainly have been arraigned before the International Court of Justice in The Hague on human rights transgressions.

During the first few months of the war, Biafra had certain advantages in the air war especially since they had pilots who were better trained and fought with greater motivation (if only because their survival was at stake). Most Biafran Air Force (BiAF) pilots and mechanics had previously served with Nigerian Airways or the fledgling Nigerian Air Force and, obviously, though Scandinavians and European mercenaries were hired by the rebels, they all played significant roles.

An important contribution was also made by Friedrich 'Freddy' Herz – an old friend of most of the Biafran pilots trained in Germany. On the outbreak of this West African struggle, Herz was living in West Germany. He received letters from his Biafran friends asking him to come over and 'lend a hand'. After some deliberation, he went to the Cameroons, got permission to enter Biafra and from there he was taken to Enugu – the newly-created Biafran capital – by his friends. Since this was his first visit to Biafra, he was carefully vetted. Only after several weeks did he actually get to meet the BiAF Commander, Colonel Zoki, who believed his explanation that he wanted to help the Biafrans with no other compensation than free food and board.

At this time, the situation at Enugu was critical. The Nigerians were pushing in hard from the north and were close to the town. At Enugu Airport, the Biafrans had two B-25 Mitchells and one B-26 which had also been christened 'The Marauder'. All three aircraft had to be flown out of Enugu to prevent them being captured by the approaching Federal forces.

---

3   Venter, Al J., *Barrel of a Gun: A War Correspondent's Misspent Moments in Combat* (USA and UK: Casemate, 2010).

Cape Town's Ares Klootwyk took this photo over Biafra of his wingman, who was also flying a Soviet-built MiG-17.

Freddy had never flown these types before, but together with Colonel Ezilo, he managed to fly the first B-25 to Port Harcourt and then return to Enugu by road to save the remaining B-25. The B-26, however, caused more problems: its wheel brakes were faulty and the Biafrans did not want to permit it to take off. Because both the airfield and Enugu were taken by Nigerian troops soon afterwards, that bomber was lost in the fighting that followed. A few weeks later, Colonel Zoki was killed. During this phase of the war, Freddy also participated in a ground operation at Onitsha on the Niger River, where he helped Biafran soldiers erect rocket launchers.

Freddy later arrived at Port Harcourt, where the two B-25s were now stationed. Together with the Biafrans and a Cuban pilot, Freddy checked the aircraft carefully and then did test runs on both. Shortly afterwards, he carried out a number of raids using both B-25s – as well as a DC-3 Dakota converted to a bomber. The targets were enemy positions and formations – primarily in the south-eastern quadrant of the rebel enclave and in the mid-west region, towards Benin. This was done in co-operation with the army, and it was noted afterwards that these actions significantly delayed the Nigerian advance on the Southern Front.

Late in 1967 a night raid was carried out against the Nigerian port city of Calabar (then in the hands of Nigerian troops). As detailed in Gunnar Haglund's book – published in Swedish by Stockholm's Bokus AB in 1988 and titled *Gerillapilot i Biafra* (*Guerrilla Pilot in Biafra*) – the raid was to be carried out with the DC-3, one of the 'liberated' B-25s and a newly-delivered B-26 said to have been flown to Biafra directly from South America. After dark, the three crews prepared for take-off. The DC-3 and B-26 had already been refuelled and loaded up with incendiary bombs – many of them home-made. Orders were that the DC-3 and the bomber would depart first, find their targets (which were designated as Calabar's industrial area and airfield) and drop their incendiaries. In the light of this envisaged carnage, Freddy would arrive over the target in his B-25 and drop conventional high-explosive bombs on factory buildings and hangars. The three aircraft took off and formed up over the airfield before setting out towards the east at a relatively low level. The crews, survivors said afterwards, were tense, since Calabar was known to be ringed by heavy anti-aircraft emplacements.

Just before arriving over an astonishingly well-lit Calabar – conventional military 'blackouts' during the Nigerian War were never effectively imposed by either side – the DC-3 and B-26 climbed to a little over 3,000 feet, dived and dropped their loads. This action caused a number of blazes and, said one of those involved afterwards: 'Parts of the area was lit up almost like it was day.'

Freddy later recalled that he could easily make out the factory buildings they were after. He came in low at about 500 feet and dropped his HE bombs, but was greeted from the ground by fairly intense ground fire. His aircraft took a number of hits, but as he admitted afterwards, the plane emerged reasonably intact and none of the other three men on board were injured. He made a steep turn with his B-25 and headed back towards Port Harcourt at low altitude – in part to avoid Nigerian Air Force MiGs that might be circling the region. It wasn't long before his instruments told him that his fuel tanks were leaking; their aircraft had taken a good deal more of a hammering than he first realised.

They finally managed to make contact with air traffic control at Port Harcourt and were given immediate clearance to land after one of the aircraft directly ahead of them. By now, he recalled, the fuel gauge was registering almost zero: from good experience, he was aware that he had very few gallons of fuel left in the tank. At this point, they were close enough to the airport to see the runway lights stretching out ahead of them, which was when air traffic control gave them clearance to go in directly rather than complete the usual circuit. Freddy reduced power and that, in itself, was a huge relief.

Haglund records the event as follows:

> Their old B-25 made a short turn in towards the runway and descended a bit more… flaps were extended to reduce speed, then the landing gear. The other aircraft, which had been just in front of them all the way, had reached the point where it was in the process of landing and Freddy's aircraft had only a few hundred metres left to touchdown.
>
> Suddenly, the traffic controller called over the radio: 'Abort landing! Abort landing immediately!'
>
> Apparently, the plane just ahead had crashed on the runway – blocking it.
>
> As Freddy recalled, everything suddenly began to happen very quickly. 'We had to interrupt our landing and climb again, raise our landing gear, pull up flaps and moderate the throttle to avoid wasting what little fuel remained.'
>
> The cockpit crew feared the worst. Freddy prayed that it might just be possible to go around the field, just a small circuit, so that ground crews could get the crashed aircraft off the runway – but then, not entirely unexpected after half a circuit, one of the engines coughed… then the other did as well…
>
> Both engines stuttered again in unison for a few seconds and fell silent. Freddy and Ezilo prepared for a make-or-break emergency landing in the dark – turning on their landing lights in the process – while sinking fast towards the ground.
>
> Freddy spotted a clearing in the bush diagonally in front of their flight path, but it was too late because the bomber was just above the ground when one of its wings hit a tree. A moment later, the aircraft ploughed into the ground, bounced a few times and slid along into a clearing. Freddy remembered multiple thuds, the screech of metal-on-metal, together with scrapes and creaking noises everywhere.
>
> 'Finally, there was a terrible bang and almost as if somebody had thrown a switch, everything went quiet.'

He and his co-pilot woke to find themselves in the Port Harcourt hospital. Sammy, their navigator, had been killed instantly. The rear gunner was a lot more fortunate, because on impact, he had been hurled out of the aircraft and came away from it all with an injured leg.

Despite all this (the records tell us today), the raid on Calabar had been an unmitigated success. Numerous targets were destroyed, and the airport and the city's factory area, as well as a fuel depot (all in the same vicinity) were devastated – largely because they had been set alight by incendiaries.

According to Haglund, Freddy's nerves had taken a pounding and he wanted to get away from the war. After almost three weeks in hospital – and with his leg mending fast – he returned to Europe, but like most veterans bored with domesticity back home, it seems that this aviator couldn't keep away from where everything was happening… By January 1968 he was back in Biafra; by then, Nigerian forces had taken Port Harcourt – as well as the two surplus American bombers which were left standing at the airport – and there was nothing for him to fly.

The year 1968 passed without Biafra acquiring any new aircraft. Several times there were attempts to buy old surplus planes from different sources – both jet and propeller aircraft. Most deals came close to being closed – with the aircraft prepared for delivery – but each time, the transactions failed. Those deals ended up costing the Biafrans bucket-loads of precious foreign currency, but they still did not get the planes they so desperately needed.

After the Biafrans had lost Port Harcourt to the Nigerian Army and Navy, they launched several attacks on the city – usually centered on its airport. As with the Calabar raid, these details come from Gunnar Haglund's diary, which was originally published in *Gerillapilot i Biafra*.

I quote:

> In the morning, Thursday 22 May, we checked the aircraft extra-carefully. Each one had selected an aircraft earlier on and knew its peculiarities, such as the calibration of the rocket sight. We checked the loading of the rocket pods, which we had only fired once previously. Our mechanics looked over the planes a last time, which gave us a certain feeling of security. The co-operation between pilots and mechanics had been excellent.
>
> The aircraft were fully tanked and loaded. We put water bottles in the cabins for the long flight. We realized that the aircraft would be very heavy in the air. It was 35 degrees warm and the jungle steamed in the heat. Light clouds slowly passed across the sky.
>
> At 11.00 we took off. CG would fly as number one and took off first. While Martin, who was number two, rolled out on our primitive runway, I got settled in and started the engine. The aircraft felt heavy already, but with CG's first test flight in fresh memory, I still realised that I would have better odds during this take-off. Besides, I was 50 lbs lighter than Martin, and if he managed to get up in the air…
>
> After me came August and Willy. When everybody was airborne, we gathered in an open formation over the jungle and then set out on our first leg. CG and Martin were ahead of me and when I turned around, I saw August and Willy just behind.

Once he got up in the air, Haglund became quite calm. The others later confirmed that they had the same relaxed feeling. They were all in good shape and confident in the team. The tactics for this first attack was to fly very low in order to avoid being seen on radar. Radio silence was also observed. They were soon out over the sea – out of sight of land – and the flying was pretty boring:

> To pass the time, I lined up some biscuits beside me and decided to eat one every quarter-hour. By the eighth biscuit, we should be passing the coast just south of Port Harcourt.

Nigerian Air Force mercenaries at Benin in 1968. From left (in white overalls) is former RAF pilot Mike Thompsett, who flew his MiG into the ground and was killed at Port Harcourt; South African Charlie Vivier; and Klootwyk. (Ares Klootwyk)

> I took bearings on the sun and the island of São Tomé, which was visible far away in the distant haze. I estimated the drift and tried to calculate our position over the water. As far as I could tell, we were following the planned route. CG made course correction twice during the flight – the first time to compensate the drift; he estimated the wind velocity by looking at the waves. CG later also ordered a change of course to avoid an area with heavy rain.

They were flying very low (at about 15 metres) and their radio traffic was not yet likely to be overheard. Haglund passed on von Rosen's instructions in English to August and Willy, who were now lagging some five minutes behind, out of sight. Willy was apparently unhappy over the low altitude and kept talking on the radio all the time. August tried keeping silent, but felt that he had to answer Willy.

At this point, Haglund was getting concerned that perhaps the transmissions were being picked up by the Nigerians, and MiGs scrambled to intercept. When they approached the deserted coastline, the altitude was decreased to only a metre or two:

> Would we really cross the coast on the spot we had decided the evening before, when we stood looking at the map? Would we, after several hours' flight at minimum altitude over the sea cross the coast exactly where we had planned? How would the coast greet us? With a hail of bullets from anti-aircraft guns, or just as peacefully as it looked from here?

NIGERIA'S MERCENARY PILOTS

(By Al Venter)   Lagos

Eleven mercenary pilots – including a few Royal Air Force World War II veterans – played a crucial role in finally smashing Biafran resistance last month. Flying Russian-supplied MiG-17 jet fighters, General Yakubu Gowon's mercenaries cooperated closely with Russian and Egyptian ground crews to keep up around-the-clock bombardment of the beleaguered territory during the last week of the 2½ year civil war.

The British pilots, who included RAF trainee Paul Martin and Nobby Armstrong, were helped by three white South Africans, Calderhead, Charles Vivier and Ares Klootwyk, two Belgians and a Frenchman, each earning £1,000 a month. No Nigerians were allowed on operational duties in MiGs, the white fliers said.

According to one of the mercenaries, who asked to remain anonymous, many were hired by former Congolese freebooter Major John Peters. All were required to sign three month contracts, though some – particularly South Africans – were on their second and third tours of duty. The fliers were allowed one week's paid leave after three months.

"We were paid to hit the Biafrans and hit them hard – both military and civilian targets," one of them told me in Lagos. "And if anyone tells me he would not do the same for the kind of money we were earning he is lieing", the pilot said.

If the war had continued much longer, they would have resorted to shooting down civilian relief planes the mercenaries maintained. British pilot Mike Thompsett shot down a DC-7 carrying food for starving Biafrans – near Calabar on June 6 last year. Thompsett was later killed in a night landing at Port Harcourt.

In the two and a half years Federal Nigeria has been in state of civil war, General Gowon has built up a formidable jet air force – one of the most powerful in Africa. Except for British helicopters, it was almost entirely Communist supplied. At the end of hostilities the Nigerian Air Force consisted of about 30 MiG-17s (eight new ones delivered a month ago via Cairo), 6 new Czech Delphin fighter trainers, and four Ilyushin 18s with 4,000 lb. bomb loads. Bombers were flown exclusively by Egyptians. ("But they're rotten shots" said another of British mercenaries, "we had to finish off many of their raids for them," he maintained.

Egyptians were also responsible for training Federal fliers. However, 30 Nigerians were sent to Cairo last year on an eight month Ilyushin conversion course. When they arrived back in Lagos, the Nigerians had not been on a single flight. This resulted in considerable disillusionment with the UAR war effort in top Federal circles.

Relations between Nigerians and South Africans had been fine, said a Pretoria-born pilot. "They know where we come from but leave us alone. As long as we do their killing for them they're happy. They pay us to do the job well," said another of the South Africans, a South African Air Force veteran who had fought in Congo for Tschombe before joining the NAF.

What would happen to them now that war was over? The mercenaries would not comment. Said one of them as we parted "We may have to find another war. That should not be difficult in Africa."

A cutting from *Wings* magazine in February 1970, with an article by the author on Nigeria's use of mercenaries.

I took the last biscuit and noticed that the water bottle was almost emptied. CG climbed with his aircraft over the coastline and then descended again, before we flew in over the beach and the trees. The first tributary we passed inland seemed to agree with the map and I was sure that we had arrived in the right spot. Strange…

CG must have had some luck as well, I said to myself. It is not possible to navigate like this otherwise. The difference to the planned route could not be more than a hundred meters.

Further inland, some huts and canoes were spotted, and some fire from heavy automatic guns heard. Haglund temporarily lost the other two aircraft from sight, but found them again after five minutes:

A few minutes later, CG told us over the radio that we had the airport straight ahead. We now flew on an easterly course. At the same moment, I saw the windsock of the Port Harcourt Airfield. CG and Martin had increased speed somewhat and I lagged behind by some 30 meters. CG disappeared from view, but Martin lay straight ahead of me and started diving towards the runway, but without shooting. Instead, I saw small puffs of white smoke blossom up from the field near the end of the runway, from a bunker, and I realized that an anti-aircraft gun was firing on Martin. I waited and felt irritated that he did not turn away so I would be able to shoot.

'Turn damn you, Martin, you are blocking my target,' I said over the radio. Martin instantly turned away and I fired my first two rockets. They flew away at an incredible speed, but went too low and hit the ground in front of the bunker, from which there was continuous fire. The next salvo hit just beside the ack-ack and the third penetrated straight inside it. I was now very close and saw how the whole emplacement lifted a little at the explosion.

At the next moment, I was in a steep turn to the left, away from the runway and out among the bushes at the side of the field.

Some soldiers with weapons in their hands stood among the palm trees next to some huts. They looked up at the aircraft. I was afraid that they would start firing at me, but when I lowered the nose of the aircraft, straight towards them, they threw themselves on the ground. CG was talking over the radio. I caught sight of one of our aircraft just above the trees, and then another one.

'Now we take the control tower', CG said.

Martin and I acknowledged over the radio. This time we came in almost side by side and shot from a very advantageous angle. Any rockets missing the tower would continue into the hangar behind it. I had time to think that it might be considered revolting to shoot at a control tower, but by this time, those possibly in the tower ought to have figured out what was going on and removed themselves to a safe place. Under any circumstances, the control tower was a military target – not a marketplace.

I hit the tower with a few rockets, while the rest went past and hit one wall of the hangar; then turned a little to shoot at two MiG aircraft which I had spotted on the apron, but I was out of rockets and turned away.

From the corner of my eye, I saw Martin's aircraft. By a quick climb in the turn I managed to avoid colliding with him by less than a meter. It was a reflex maneuver, both Martin and I reacted correctly. Martin paused in his shooting, but when I was above him, he continued to fire his rockets. If he had not restrained himself and paused at the right moment, he could have hit me.

Thanks, Martin, I thought.

After we had turned away, I did not see any more of the target – only smoke from explosions. The object now was to get home as best as we could.

The three Swedes formed up again, but there was no sign of August or Willy. They passed over the front south of Owerri. They then got contact with August and heard that he had carried out his attack (at 1415 to 1420). The attack by von Rosen and the others took place at 1405 to 1415. Four hours after take-off, they landed at the jungle base called Camp II and parked in shelters beside the runway. Two minutes later, both the aircraft and runway had been camouflaged. The Biafran ground crews were very happy and curious about the mission. August landed soon afterwards, but there was no sign of Willy, who had become separated from August before the attack. He had become lost and eventually landed at one of the alternative fields in Biafra:

> During the attack, I had hit the anti-aircraft position at the end of the runway, the tower and the hangar. The two MiG aircraft I had spotted, but which I had not had enough ammunition to attack, had instead been fired upon by CG, Martin and August. We could therefore note two Nigerian aircraft as probably destroyed or damaged.
>
> CG thought he had seen camouflaged Ilyushin aircraft at the edge of the field, but had by then run out of rockets. Martin had never spotted the anti-aircraft position I had hit, which was why he had not fired when in position in front of me.
>
> News reports from the BBC and Radio Lagos confirmed their assessment, but added that an Egyptian Air Force (with Soviet origins) Ilyushin bomber in the hangar had been destroyed.[4]

---

4 Haglund, Gunnar, *Gerillapilot i Biafra* (Stockholm: Bokus AB, 1988), pp. 50-56.

A military bunker – at the edge of an airport – from the Biafran War.

The role of Count von Rosen and his Swedish Minicons, which played such a significant role in this conflict, cannot be over-stressed. A few more words about this remarkable aviator are warranted:

During the Italian invasion of Abyssinia in 1935-36, the Count flew a Heinkel HD-21 and later a Fokker FVII that had been equipped as ambulance aircraft; then, following the Russian invasion of Finland in 1939, he donated a DC-2 and two Koolhoven FK-52s to the Finnish AF. The DC-2 was rebuilt as an ad hoc bomber by SAAB in Trollhättan, Sweden with a dorsal-gunner's position and external bomb racks. Apparently, the DC-2 was actually considered for a bombing sortie on the Kremlin. During that war, von Rosen flew several sorties in Blenheims, as well as the DC-2.

12

The Rebel State and its Bombers

The Feds acquired Eastern Bloc fighters and bombers, and the rebel state had its own bit of muscle with a couple of A-26 World War II bombers that caused a few problems. As with much else in this war, Biafra had to improvise where it could; simply put, it had no option to do otherwise. British historian and aviation specialist Michael Robson sets the record straight…

While much of the war that enveloped Nigeria's eastern regions was land-oriented, both sides mounted air offensives. Initially, that did little to change the course of the war. The Federal Nigerian Air Force was comparatively well-equipped with combat aircraft including MiG-17 fighters and some L-29 jet trainers – as well as six Ilyushin Il-28 jet bombers – all flown by mercenary crews.

For Biafra, the situation was very different. Isolated both geographically and politically, Odumegwu Ojukwu was unable to obtain aircraft by conventional means. The upshot was that he had to rely on the often shady world of the arms dealer and, as a result, ended up with a motley collection of aircraft. His two Invaders were certainly the most interesting of the larger planes – and the subterfuge involved in their acquisition would make for an excellent thriller…

The first of the two was a Douglas B-26P twin-engined light bomber and attack aircraft. It was originally designated a bomber – thus a B-26 – but then reclassified as an attack aircraft, which is why it became a Douglas A-26. What gave this remarkable aircraft an edge was that it was both fast and capable of carrying twice its specified bomb load. Also, it was generally accepted that a range of guns could be fitted, and that made it a formidable ground attack weapon – so much so that a limited number of A-26s were still serving in combat almost a quarter of a century after the end of World War II.

This particular Invader had been operated for a number of years by the French *Centre d'Essai en Vol* (CEV) at Brétigny-sur-Orge, where it was used for radar calibration. It was disposed of to *La Service des Domaines* (Government Property Agency) and on 9 September 1965 it was sold to a David Lau of Pan Eurasian Trading Co. in Luxembourg, who purchased it 'as an investment'.

Indications at the time were that the aircraft was probably acquired for its engines, because Pan Eurasian sold it for almost 10,000 French francs to the American aircraft engineer Ernest A. Koenig, who was also an aircraft broker. His name was to appear frequently in conjunction with the illegal aircraft procurement programme not only for Biafra, but also for some of the elements active in the Congo.

Koenig applied for US registration in September 1966 – and if, as it has been averred, the Biafrans paid him $320,000 for this plane, then his profit margin was remarkable. The Invader was flown to Lisbon by a Belgian pilot by the name of van Reiseghem and took off for Nigeria in late June 1967 – arriving in Enugu after first putting down at Port Harcourt. Both cities were then still in Biafran hands, but that was soon to change.

Biafran pilot Jonny Cliukure at the controls of his Minicon. (Author's collection)

Another pilot involved in the delivery of some of Biafra's illegal aircraft was Jan Zumbach – a Polish ex-RAF Spitfire pilot who wrote about his experiences in his book *On Wings of War*. Zumbach tells us that he learned to fly the A-26 after a quick study of the factory manual and a chat with the Belgian delivery pilot. He also stated that he had been paid $4,000 for the flight – a lot of money in those days when all your other expenses are taken care of. In fact, in the driver's seat was a Frenchman – Jacques Lestrade – and Zumbach would have been his co-pilot. Lestrade was certified on the Invader and had flown the civilian aircraft in France, so it made sense that he was in the driver's seat.

As soon as Washington got word that Biafra had acquired a light bomber or two, they started investigations of their own and demanded details from Koenig. He returned the certificate of registration to the American Federal Aviation Authority with a declaration that the aircraft had been sold to a 'Moises Broder' of Port Gentil – Gabon's oil port. The Americans could find no trace of anybody by that name and concluded that it was unlikely that this so-called 'Moises Broder' ever existed. Koenig eventually got away with this deception because the Invader was, essentially, a civilian machine. To facilitate its export from Europe, it was described as a survey aircraft destined for an organisation in Gabon. Its registration documents also stated that it carried no offensive armament, which was correct, because these were only fitted after the arrival of the plane in Biafra.

The B-26 used in the Nigerian Civil War on arrival at Enugu in June 1967. On the left stands the famous Jan Zumbach and to his right his co-pilot (known only as 'Jacques'). (Author's collection)

It is notable that this plane had an unusually-shaped 'solid' nose – originally installed by the French for their research work. It was ferried in its original bare metal colour scheme, but was quickly camouflaged in Biafra with a two-tone green/brown scheme on the upper surfaces and pale blue undersides. Painted onto the fuselage was a distinctive shark mouth (vicious rows of teeth and all), as well as a glaring eye – something that found much favour with the enthusiastic Biafrans. The rudder was painted in the three national colours – black, green and red – with a Biafran 'Rising Sun' insignia superimposed on the middle section.

The Invader's electrical bomb release mechanisms were still in place when it left Europe, but were designed to function with conventional bombs of a certain configuration and weight. Biafran bombs, in contrast, were makeshift affairs often fashioned from oil drums and gas cylinders and were not compatible with the relatively sophisticated wartime systems that came with the Invader.

Biafra's second Invader was an RB-26P and had French registration papers. Its sale to the Biafrans – linked to many of their arms purchases – had been engineered by the French arms dealer, Pierre Laureys. A French photo reconnaissance version, with the extra window in the nose, is almost certain to have been one of five Invaders based at Creil (near Paris) in the mid-1960s for photographic survey work – and registered to a survey company known as *Etablissements Carta*. Painted black and still carrying its French civilian registration, the bomber was picked up from Le Bourget by Red Mettrick – an American pilot who had never flown the type before. Mettrick was an experienced pilot, having flown for the US Weather Bureau (as well as the Rhodesian carrier Air Trans Africa), so ferrying the Invader to Biafra presented few problems, apart from getting the plane out of Europe.

After a couple of handling flights, Mettrick was satisfied that the plane was sufficiently airworthy for the first leg to Lisbon, where it could receive a more detailed assessment. His co-pilot has never been conclusively identified, apart from Biafran contacts remembering him as 'Captain Mick', or 'Captain Mike'. His job throughout the flight was to manually pump fuel into the aircraft tanks from two 44-gallon drums secured in the fuselage. Mettrick later recalled that the additional

DOUGLAS B-26R INVADER "THE SHARK," BIAFRAN AIR FORCE

The first real combat aircraft acquired by the Biafrans was this reconnaissance Invader, previously the property of the French Air Force and used at their CEV testing center. Although it was sold to a trading company for only 9,720 Francs, the Biafrans may have paid as much as $320,000 U.S. for it.

Once painted in the colors above, the aircraft began operations in the summer of 1967, flown by Jan Zumbach (left), a famed World War II Polish fighter ace who almost single-handedly ran the Biafran Air Force that summer. Zumbach returned to his home in France that September, by which time "The Shark" had become inoperable. It became a parts hack until captured by the Nigerian Army at Enugu on October 4.

ILLUSTRATION BY AKHIL KADIDAL

'plumbing' had been installed in Lisbon, courtesy of the Portuguese Air Force. After stopping at Dakar in Senegal and at Bissau, the A-26 eventually arrived intact in Enugu.

Using the two bombers in this highly unconventional war presented numerous problems: because Biafra had no regular bombs, Zumbach – who, by this time, was calling himself 'Johnny', or sometimes, 'Kamikaze Brown' – had no choice but to instruct his 'bombardiers' to physically hurl whatever explosive devices the aircraft had on board out of the open bomb bay. The improvised Biafran explosives dropped by the A-26 were almost all made by a Biafran artificer, Willy Achukwe, whose former trade (it was rumoured) lay in the manufacture of fireworks. Those who were able to examine this ordnance from up-close reckoned that they were indeed marvels of ingenuity (and even included delayed action devices).

Zumbach describes one of his 'creations' as having a base containing phosphorus suspended in an insulating liquid. A Bickford fuse ran from this compartment through a partition (plugged with wax) into a second stage. This compartment contained gunpowder and a third compartment was crammed with scrap metal. Two big nails protruded from the base of the device – the idea being that impact with the ground would result in detonation.

As Achukwe explained to one of the journalists who had an interest in such matters, the insulating liquid, on impact, was forced out of the resulting nail punctures and thus allowed air to access the combustibles. In turn, that ignited the phosphorus and melted the wax and the fuse, which detonated the explosive compound – simple, if you know how…

While there were no machine guns that might have been suitable for aircraft-mounting in Ojukwu's breakaway enclave, the Biafrans – from the start of the war – displayed some remarkable abilities for improvisation. Following a visit to the government armoury, from where he was invited to take his pick, Zumbach returned to the airfield with two antiquated army issue Czech-made machine guns. Biafran mechanics soon had the first one hitched up-front on the bomber, with the barrel protruding from its nose. The hapless forward gunner was obliged to crouch in the dim recesses of the nose cone, without any view of the outside world and without any voice communication with his pilot – and here too, Biafran ingenuity came to the rescue. .. A length of cord was attached to the gunner's arm, with the other end threaded through to the pilot's station. Zumbach – equipped with a simple home-made gun sight – simply tugged once on the cord to

Nigerian Civil War
BIAFRAN Air-to-Ground Victories

Date	Unit	Aircraft	Pilot	Place	Victim	Result	Country
10.7.1967	BAF	RB-26P	Zumbach, J.	Makurdi airfield	"several" DC-3	dam./dest.	NAF
19.8.1967	BAF		unknown	Kano airfield	"several" MiG-17	destroyed	NAF
20.8.1967	BAF		unknown	Kano airfield	"several" MiG-17	destroyed	NAF
22.5.1969	MFI Sq.	MFI-9	unknown[*]	Port Harcourt airf.	MiG-17F NAF620	dam./dest.	NAF
22.5.1969	MFI Sq.	MFI-9	unknown[*]	Port Harcourt airf.	MiG-17F	dam./dest.	NAF
22.5.1969	MFI Sq.	MFI-9	unknown[*]	Port Harcourt airf.	Il-28	dam./dest.	NAF
25.5.1969	MFI Sq.	MFI-9	unknown[**]	Benin City airf.	MiG-17F	dam./dest.	NAF
25.5.1969	MFI Sq.	MFI-9	unknown[**]	Benin City airf.	Il-28[+]	dam./dest.	NAF
26.5.1969	MFI Sq.	MFI-9	Haglund, G.	Enugu airfield	MiG-17F	destroyed	NAF
26.5.1969	MFI Sq.	MFI-9	Lang, M.	Enugu airfield	MiG-17F	destroyed	NAF
26.5.1969	MFI Sq.	MFI-9	unknown[*]	Enugu airfield	MiG-17F	dam./dest.	NAF
26.5.1969	MFI Sq.	MFI-9	unknown[*]	Enugu airfield	Il-28[++]	dam./dest.	NAF
8.1969	MFI Sq.	MFI-9	unknown[*]	helicopter airf.	helicopter	destroyed	NAF
8.1969	MFI Sq.	MFI-9	unknown[*]	helicopter airf.	helicopter	destroyed	NAF
8.1969	MFI Sq.	MFI-9	unknown[*]	helicopter airf.	helicopter	destroyed	NAF

Statistics from the first 29 attacks (5 abandonded for different reasons) May-Aug:

432 rockets fired, more than 50% hitting targets. No own aircraft or pilots lost.

	Destroyed	damaged
MiG-17	3	2
Il-28	1	
Canberra	1	1
Intruder	1	
2 eng.transport		1
Helicopters	2	1
Trucks	7	
Radar	1	
ATC tower	1	1
Terminal bldgs		2
Power plant	1	
Amm. storage	1	
Headquarters		3
AAA	2	
Oil pump station	1	

Enemy losses: 300 men at airports, 200 men at the front

Source: Haglund, Gunnar: *Gerillapilot i Biafra*, Allt om hobby AB, Stockholm, 1988.

10.10.1969	MFI Sq.	MFI-9	unknown(***)	Bebibg City airf.	MiG-17F	destroyed	NAF
10.10.1969	MFI Sq.	MFI-9	unknown(***)	Bebibg City airf.	DC-4	destroyed	NAF
11.11.1969	BAF	AT-6 Harvard	unknown(#)		DC-4	destroyed	NAF
11.11.1969	BAF	AT-6 Harvard	unknown(#)		MiG-17F	damaged	NAF
11.11.1969	BAF	AT-6 Harvard	unknown(#)		L-29 Delfín	damaged	NAF
12.11.1969	MFI Sq.	MFI-9	unknown(***)	Port Hacourt airf.	MiG-17F	dam./dest.	NAF
12.11.1969	MFI Sq.	MFI-9	unknown(***)	Port Hacourt airf.	MiG-17F	dam./dest.	NAF
12.11.1969	MFI Sq.	MFI-9	unknown(***)	Port Hacourt airf.	MiG-17F	dam./dest.	NAF
12.11.1969	MFI Sq.	MFI-9	unknown(***)	Port Hacourt airf.	DC-1	dam./dest.	NAF
12.11.1969	MFI Sq.	MFI-9	unknown(***)	Port Hacourt airf.	DC-4	dam./dest.	NAF
12.11.1969	MFI Sq.	MFI-9	unknown(***)	Port Hacourt airf.	Do-27	dam./dest.	NAF
12.11.1969	MFI Sq.	MFI-9	unknown(***)	Port Hacourt airf.	e/a	dam./dest.	NAF
12.11.1969	MFI Sq.	MFI-9	unknown(***)	Port Hacourt airf.	e/a	dam./dest.	NAF

Comments:
- (*): Carl-Gustaf Ericsson von Rosen (Sw), Gunnar Haglund (Sw), Martin Lang (Sw), Willy Murray-Bruce (Biaf), Augustus Opke (Biaf).
- (**): Carl-Gustaf Ericsson von Rosen (Sw), Gunnar Haglund (Sw), Martin Lang (Sw), Augustus Opke (Biaf).
- (***): Friedrich Merz (Ger), Ibi Brown (Biaf), Alex Agbufane (Biaf), "Benny" (Biaf).
- (#): Portugal mercenary.
- (+): In fact Douglas DC-4.
- (++): In fact Douglas RB-26P Invader destroyed in 1967.
- BAF: Biafran Air Force.
- NAF: Nigerian Air Force.

Sources & Literature

1. Researcher Håkan Gustavsson.
2. Berns, Lennart: *Děti z Biafry... Air Force o pěti letadlech*, in Revi, No. 2, 1994.
3. *"Biafran Babies", A Noble Swede: From Relief to Raid*, http://www.kwenu.com/biafra/biafran_babies.htm.
4. *Biafran Invaders*, The Douglas A/B-26 Invader http://vectaris.net/id307.html.
5. Cooper, Tom: *Civil War in Nigeria (Biafra), 1967-1970, Air Combat Information Group*, http://s188567700.online.de/CMS/index.php?option=com_content&task=view&id=218&Itemid=47.
6. Gustavsson, Håkan: *Biplane Fighter Aces from the Second World War*, http://www.dalnet.se/~surfcity/index.html.
7. Haglund, Gunnar: *Gerillapilot i Biafra*, Allt om hobby AB, Stockholm, 1988.
8. Housworth, Gordon: *Asymmetrical air force symmetries: Biafra Babies and Air Tigers, part II*, http://spaces.icgpartners.com/index2.asp?NGuid=DA8D6DADD9DD4F59AED1AD1F66DA147B.
9. *Operation Biafra Babies*, The Swedish military aviation page, http://www.canit.se/~griffon/aviation/text/biafra.htm.
10. Petz, Daniel: *MFI-9, trpaslík mezi bitevníky*, in Historie a plastikové modelářství, No. 10, 1993.
11. Polák, Tomáš: *Okřídlený tulák Jan Zumbach*, in Aero Plastic Kits Revue, No. 49, 1996.
12. Runarsson, Kristjan: *Fleas versus Falcons over Biafra, Short history and assessment of the MFI-9B "MiniCOIN" in Biafran air force service*, Part I, The Pogrom, War & Starvation, http://thepogrom-war-starvation.blogspot.com/2007/06/fleas-versus-falcons-over4-biafra.html.
13. Slizewski, Grzegorz - Comas, Matthieu - Cony, Christophe: *Jan Zumbach un sacre canard dans la RAF*, in Avions, No. 124, 2003.
14. Жирохов, Михаил - Моногону, Обунигве: *Прощай, Биафра! Воздушная война в Нигерии в 1967-70 гг.*, Авиамастер, № 4, 2002.

instruct the gunner to start firing, and twice when he was to stop. A simple solution, the second machine gun was rigged to fire through the open bomb bay.

July – only weeks after the Invader had arrived in the war – saw Zumbach and his Biafran crew heading north for Makurdi (a Nigerian Army supply centre some 125 miles north of Enugu). Biafran air crews had been alerted by tuning into radio transmissions from Nigerian aircraft, and were made aware that a number of transport aircraft were inbound for this northern town from Lagos. The crew consisted of co-pilot/radio operator, Godwin Ezeilo; a navigator/forward gunner called 'Freddy'; a rear gunner above the bomb doors; and two 'bombardiers'. Approaching the target, Zumbach had Ezeilo call Makurdi Airport on the radio link to ask for landing instructions – effectively giving the ground station the impression that the Invader was a routine Nigerian flight. The ploy worked and ensured that the Nigerian anti-aircraft batteries did not fire.

A number of bombs were dropped manually by the 'bombardiers' on the first sweep down the runway and appeared to have had some effect, with both machine-gunners blazing away as long as the target remained in sight. Elated, the crew returned to Enugu, where they were feted as heroes. Zumbach the pilot was dubbed 'Saviour of Biafra'. Not long after this mission, Zumbach mounted an attack on a motorised column travelling with supplies from Kano, which resulted in his being hit by ground fire. Landing at Enugu, he discovered that the aircraft had suffered damage to a flap and that a tyre had been punctured. Because of the siege, aircraft tyres were unobtainable in Biafra, and so he was forced to make an unscheduled trip back to Europe to find spares. On his return – and encouraged by the air force's modest successes – Ojukwu called for Zumbach to plan an attack which should be made on the only capital ship in the Nigerian Navy, the NNS *Nigeria*, which was moored in a secluded estuary off Port Harcourt. There was, by then, a tangible fear that the Nigerians might be planning a landing to cut Biafra's lifeline to the ocean, which happened soon after – but for this task, Zumbach conceded, heavier bombs would be required (and which were duly produced by the Biafran master-artificer).

The raid – flown by the A-26 and with a Biafran DC-3 in support – began at first light, with Zumbach leading the attack in the Invader. On going in, he put the bomber's nose down and dived on the former Royal Navy destroyer – dropping his supply of small bombs and strafing the length of the warship with machine-gun fire. On his tail followed Ezeilo in his DC-3 – loaded with two of the artificer's 'special bombs'.

The first landed astern of the destroyer, and the second about 30 feet to her port side. The explosion of the two bombs covered the *Nigeria* with clouds of spray – and there was no retaliation from the Nigerian Navy; all the sailors had run for cover. Ordnance exhausted, both aircraft returned to Enugu and prepared for a second attack. Again, the bombs failed to hit the target, but they had the effect of making the destroyer up anchor and make hastily for the open sea.

Predictably, the attacks were well-hyped by the Biafran publicity machine in Switzerland, but, it transpired – several weeks afterwards – that the *Nigeria* had simply withdrawn to the mouth of the river. There it stayed until the end of the war – effectively blocking access to Port Harcourt.

As the months progressed, Zumbach found that his meagre air force (it now consisted of a Fokker F-27; a De Havilland Dove; and the trusty old DC-3 – as well as the Invader, which had now been christened 'The Shark' because of the artwork on its nose) was unable to cope with the demands being made by Ojukwu and his commanders. At that point, Zumbach hit on the idea of dropping some ordnance on enemy positions in a bid to demoralise the Nigerians. Thousands of leaflets were dropped – all of which announced that selected villages were to be bombed, which in turn, resulted in a widespread exodus and a great deal of confusion not only for the civilian population, but also for Nigerian ground forces.

A month later, Zumbach was again summoned to Ojukwu's headquarters and treated to a discourse on the importance of Biafra's oil industry. Biafra produced about half of Nigeria's

Minicon crews with their flying machines. These tiny Swedish aircraft played a significant role in the jungle war. (Author's collection)

crude oil – and it was no secret that the commodity was the single biggest contributor to Biafra's exchequer. As Ojukwu had declared in a closed session earlier, as long as it lasted, his little country could probably hold out. At the Zumbach meeting, he stated that the only way the Nigerians would be able to reverse the situation was to convince the oil companies not to deal with him. There was no question, it was acknowledged on both sides of the front lines, that in order to succeed in his war, the Biafran leader simply had to maintain this inward flow of revenue. He would do that first by defending Biafra, and then by preventing any suggestion of a deal with Lagos.

The first targets in this switch of tactics was to hit oil storage tanks at Bonny. While these were on Biafran territory, Ojukwu's argument was that such an action would bring the oil companies to their senses and stop diluting their financial contributions to Biafra. It was both a logical and a dangerous reasoning; in fact, as it later emerged, the move was a colossal gamble.

By this time, a consignment of Portuguese 50 kg bombs had arrived in Enugu, which were far more compatible with the Invader's release mechanisms. It also allowed for an attack to be planned with Jean Bonnel – a newly-arrived French pilot – and a Biafran crew. They would make diversionary attacks in the Dove and the DC-3 on Nigerian supply columns near Onitsha, while Zumbach was to fly the Invader bomber to Bonny and make an attack on the oil installation. Unfortunately, the rains had started – and in West Africa, can sometimes limit visibility to metres. Still, several strikes were made on Bonny, with the A-26 returning to Port Harcourt to reload. Some sporadic Nigerian anti-aircraft fire was encountered, but the weather deteriorated further and Zumbach could not be sure if he had actually hit his target. Finally, Ojukwu agreed that further attacks would be futile, but he trusted that his initiative had had the desired result.

August 1967 proved to be a busy month for Biafra's A-26 bombers. Before the arrival of Biafra's infamous Invaders, a few desultory strikes were made on Federal targets using a De Havilland Dove twin-engine executive aircraft which the Biafrans had appropriated from one of the petroleum companies then operating in Nigeria. A general-purpose machine gun mounted in the open

THE REBEL STATE AND ITS BOMBERS

doorway – plus a few home-made bombs – comprised the offensive armament. In the early stages, the aircraft was crewed by expatriate and Biafran pilots, which included Jimmy Yates, Elendu Ukeje and Uwen Oyoho. Jan Zumbach also undertook a few missions in this aircraft.

Surely the most crazy operation took place in October 1967 when the rebel air force mounted a bombing raid on Lagos using a civilian airliner. In April of that year, two enterprising Biafran pilots hijacked a Nigerian Airways Fokker F-27 Friendship on a regular service between Benin and Lagos. The plane was forced to land at Enugu and the passengers were transported to their destination by bus. Because the Biafrans had almost no hydraulic fluid, the F-27 was little used until it took off for Lagos carrying a load of makeshift bombs. The crew consisted of mercenary pilots Andre Cessou and Rene Leclerc, accompanied by their girlfriends and some Biafran officers, whose role it was to dispatch the bombs through a primitive hole that had been cut in the floor.

An oft-repeated story maintains that this operation was the outcome of a drunken party at the Biafran's Enugu base, but Michael Robseo's interview with August Okpe – then nominally in command of Biafra's air force – suggests it was a carefully planned operation.

The aircraft appeared over Lagos Lagoon and appeared to be heading for Nigerian Army Headquarters. It dropped some bombs, which fell on the Bordpak factory and onto the premises of the United Africa Company. On turning for a second run, the aircraft exploded dramatically, with parts of the airframe falling into the lagoon. Much was also made of the story that the body of one of the crew crashed through the plate-glass windows of the Czech Ambassador's residence…

The bodies of the crew – especially those of the European pilots, who were in Biafran Air Force overalls – were displayed in Lagos, which provided something of a spectacular public relations coup for the Nigerians.

While most stories about Biafra's bombing operations focused on the Douglas Invader aircraft, it should be mentioned that in the closing months of 1967 these aircraft were supplemented by the efforts of one, or possibly two, North American B-25 bombers. The origins of these aircraft are somewhat obscure. It appears that the first one – a TB-25K model – was bought from American war surplus stocks by John Osterholt of Homestead, Florida, for use by his company, Aerographic Inc. How it eventually arrived in Biafra is uncertain, though it might have been sold to Tripoints Associates – another American aviation accessories firm – whose president, Robert Cobaugh, was instrumental in sourcing various items of equipment for the Biafrans. Even less is known about a second B-25 – if indeed it ever existed.

The first B-25 arrived in Biafra in August 1967, where it was to be flown by a Portuguese pilot, Gil Pinto de Sousa. In the event, this pairing never transpired and the command of the aircraft passed to the German pilot Friedrich 'Freddy' Herz. Under Herz's command, the B-25 flew sporadic missions against Federal troops and ships of the Nigerian Navy. There was also a bombing raid on Kaduna Airfield in Nigeria's north, which killed a German – ostensibly a civilian working for the Dornier aircraft company, but actually part of a German (possibly East German) military component helping the Nigerians.

There were additional strikes on the airfield at Kano – and that damaged some of the recently-arrived Nigerian Air Force MiG-17s. Thereafter, both Invaders bombed and strafed the Lokoja ferry on the River Niger and, four days later, they attacked columns of Federal troops attempting to cross the Ofusu River.

A Biafran air gunner, Tony Alaribe, stated at the time that the aircraft became unserviceable in late August as a result of wheel brake trouble. Consequently, the emphasis switched to the second Invader, which had been undergoing modification to carry rockets. The original A-26 never flew again and was captured by the Nigerians at Enugu when the town fell in early October 1967. The second Invader was little used and, following a bombing raid with one of Biafra's two B-25 aircraft,

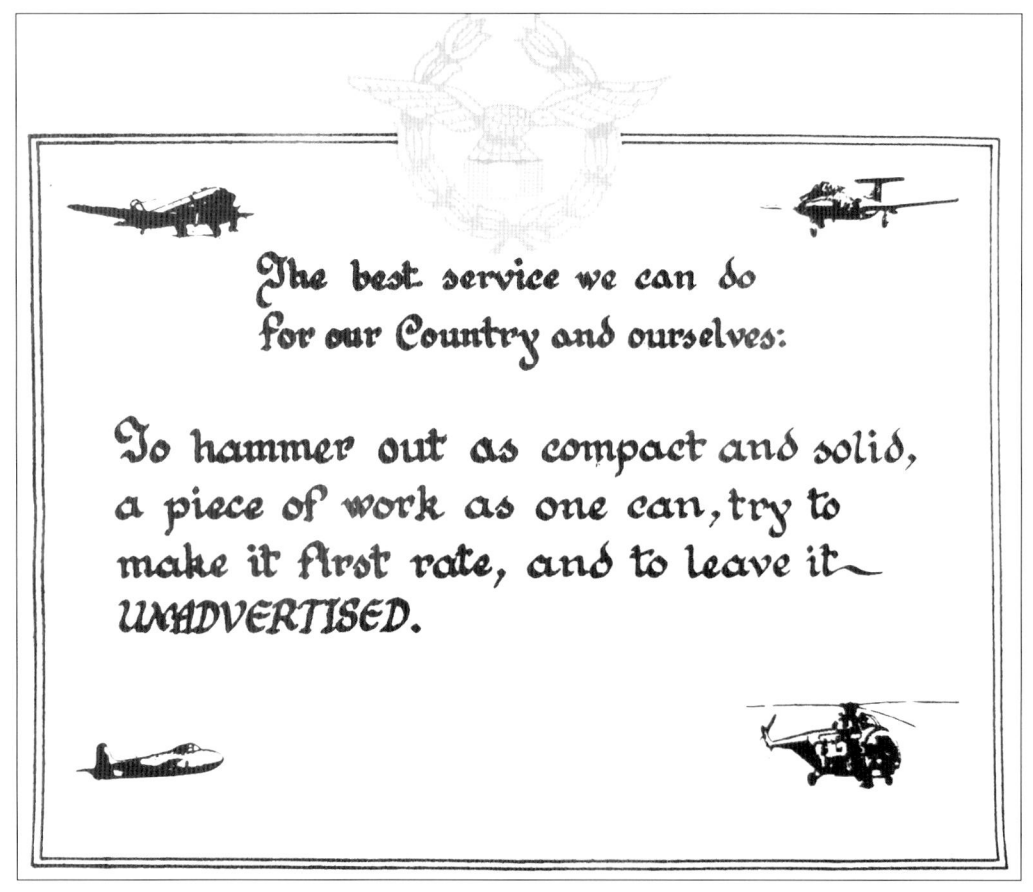

> The best service we can do
> for our Country and ourselves:
>
> To hammer out as compact and solid,
> a piece of work as one can, try to
> make it first rate, and to leave it
> UNADVERTISED.

Aware that there were 'spies everywhere', the Nigerian Air Force circulated this poster to all its bases for display. Apart from trying to boost morale, it also warned against idle chatter. (Author's photo)

was damaged in a wheels-up landing at Port Harcourt the following December. Despite the efforts to repair it, the aircraft fell into Federal hands when they overran the city.

It is interesting that Nigerian technicians actually tried to repair the damaged plane with the intention of using it against its former owners. As a result of monitoring enemy radio messages where spares were requested, the Biafran High Command was alerted and a commando detachment from the BiAF Regiment was sent to sabotage the aircraft. There is no record as to whether this attack was successful.

By now, Zumbach had begun to realise the futility of the Biafrans' struggle and reached the conclusion that despite his best efforts and those of the enthusiastic collection of Biafran air crews, their missions were fruitless. As 1967 drew to a close, he left Biafra and returned to Europe. Soon afterwards, Biafra's efforts in the air had come to a standstill. Both Invaders had been captured, and the remainder of Ojukwu's rag-tag air force lacked any serious offensive capability. The two B-25s soldiered on for a short while longer before becoming grounded through a shortage of spares. The following year saw very little Biafran aviation activity – and it was not until mid-1969 that the enclave returned to the offensive. Count von Rosen's Minicons had arrived!

Jan Zumbach

Jan Zumbach had an interesting career that spanned many decades and several wars. The son of Polish-born Swiss parents, Zumbach was registered as a Swiss citizen and hid his nationality in order to join the Polish Army in 1934. He served as an infantryman until 1936 when he transferred to the Polish Air Force. After graduating from flying training in 1938 he was posted to *111 Eskadra Mysliwska*.

Zumbach did not fly during the German invasion of Poland due to a broken leg, which he received in a flying accident during the summer of 1939. He returned to his unit – only to be evacuated to France through Romania. While in France, he flew the Morane 406 and Curtiss Hawk 75s with GCII/55. In June 1940 he travelled to England by boat, and in August that year he was posted as one of the founding members of the No.303 (Polish) Squadron Royal Air Force.

During the Battle of Britain, Zumbach scored eight confirmed kills and one probable – mostly against Messerschmitt Bf 109 fighters. A *Luftwaffe* pilot flying a Bf 109 shot Zumbach down over Dover in May 1941 while returning from a mission. Fortunately, he bailed out unharmed.

Zumbach became one of the first Allied pilots to experience combat with the German Focke-Wulf Fw 190 when he damaged (and was damaged by) a 'single radial-engined fighter'. By then, he had returned to his squadron as a flight commander. In May, he was promoted to Squadron Leader and took command – a post he held for 18 months. During this period, he flew three Spitfire VBs. Zumbach's victory tally was marked with German crosses under the cockpit on the port side; confirmed kills were outlined in white, probable kills in red and damaged aircraft with no outline.

After handing over command, Zumbach spent a year in staff appointments – including a post at the Polish Air Force Staff College. He then returned to flying duties as the commander of the 2nd Polish Air Wing, No.133 Wing. On 25 September 1944 he scored his final victory of the war – a probable kill against an Fw 190 over Arnhem in Holland.

While flying an Auster that was customarily used to visit units under the group's command, Zumbach made a navigational error and ran out of fuel. He force-landed in enemy territory and spent the final month of the war as a prisoner of war. His final victory tally was 13 confirmed kills, five probables and one damaged.

Zumbach was demobilised in October 1946, but continued to fly for a living. Under a Swiss passport, he flew contraband around Southern Europe and the Middle East. In January 1962 he was contracted to organise and command the key segment of secessionist Katanga – commanding it until December 1962 (KAT French-built Fouga Magisters became operational during July 1961). By October 1961 the Avikat was reinforced by the acquisition of five West German Dornier-28s.

He went on to deal in second-hand aircraft before again becoming a mercenary – organising and commanding the minuscule Biafran Air Force. While flying the B-26 Invader, he used the *nom de guerre* John Brown. In 1975 he published his autobiography – originally available in French under the title *Mister Brown: Aventures dans le ciel*. It was subsequently published in German and English under the title *On Wings of War: My Life as a Pilot Adventurer*. He died on 3 January 1986 in France and was buried at Powązki Cemetery in Warsaw, Poland.

For his endeavours, Jan Zumbach was decorated with the Silver Cross of the *Virtuti Militari*[1]; the Polish Cross of Valour (with three bars); and the DFC (with bar).

---

1 *Virtuti Militari* crosses are the most prestigious Polish military awards.

13

Gibson and Son: Into Biafra on Supply Runs

Two of the air crew involved in the Biafran airlift were a father-and-son team – both of whom started flying in their early-twenties. Only 21 at the time, Mike Gibson already had an interesting early life as the only son of Squadron Leader John Gibson DSO DFC – a Battle of Britain RAF and RNZAF fighter ace (and later personal pilot to the RAF chief Lord Tedder and head of the British Army, Viscount Montgomery). John Gibson passed away in the UK in 2000, aged 83.

John 'Johnny' Gibson, although born in Hove (near Brighton), England was brought up in New Zealand by his mother. He joined the Royal Air Force in 1938 shortly before war was declared with Hitler's Germany.

While training as a fighter pilot on Spitfires and Hurricanes in England, he met and married Ethel – the youngest sister of George Formby (the famous ukulele player/film star and highest-paid British performer of the time). The union ended in 1954 – with Johnny awarded custody of his seven-year-old son, Michael.

As John was about to leave Britain to take up a civil flying position in Southern Africa, it was mutually agreed that young Mike would be better off in New Zealand, where his grandmother could take care of him and pay for his education at Auckland's Kings School and College. At the time, BOAC (forerunner to British Airways) was operating Lockheed Constellations on the London-to-Sydney route – and the seven-year-old was sent unaccompanied to the Antipodes. The crew and captain, an ex-RAF friend of Johnny, took him very much under their wings in the cockpit and allowed the boy to handle the Connie controls.

Not many years later (in his early-twenties) Mike would be flying African and international skies in command of an L1049G 'Super Connie', as well as other four-engine piston, turboprop and jet aircraft – culminating as a DC-8 Captain with more than 10,000 hours by the early 1980s, which is when he chose to retire from flying.

Shortly after Mike left England in 1954 for New Zealand, his father took up a position in South Africa as Chief Pilot for Africair (Wenela) based in Francistown, Bechuanaland – ferrying in native labour from the surrounding region for the Rand gold mines by air.

In 1965 – prior to independence from Britain –Johnny had been commissioned by the newly-named Botswana's first President, Sir Seretse Khama, to form a national airline using Douglas DC-3 and DC-4 aircraft capable of operating into the mainly dirt airstrips in the country at the time. Mike would eventually fly with his father – first at BNA as a co-pilot after attaining his commercial pilot's licence in Salisbury, Rhodesia (today Harare, Zimbabwe); they would later share a DC-4 cockpit flying into Biafra, with potentially disastrous consequences.

In early 1964 (having completing his schooling in New Zealand) Mike joined his father and new stepmother, Isabelle, in Francistown, Botswana – a two-hour drive from Bulawayo, Rhodesia – where he spent a couple of years working as a bank clerk and mostly hating it. During this time, the Rhodesian Prime Minister Ian Smith – also a wartime RAF Spitfire pilot – famously declared independence from Britain, which resulted in the swift imposition of economic sanctions. Mike remembers hearing Smith announcing UDI on 11 November 1965 while sitting in his car listening to the news during a lunch break at the Standard Bank. A few months later, his father made him an offer he could not refuse: would he like to become a commercial pilot? Gibson Junior didn't have to think about it; those exciting times were likely to get even better!

First he needed a commercial pilot's licence – including 200 hours' flying experience. This would cost money, which he would be expected to pay back once qualified and working. His dad pointed him in the direction of one of his Salisbury friends: Captain Bill Church – a South African who was flying Viscounts for Central African Airways (later Air Rhodesia). He had achieved fame as a distinguished SAAF fighter pilot in Korea, where he flew American Sabre jets. While still with Air Rhodesia, Church formed a small instruction unit called the Rhodesian Commercial Flying School, which employed former Royal Rhodesian Air Force pilot David Hume as an instructor – and young Gibson was on the first full-time student course in 1966. The next course included Bill Wragg, who also flew for BNA and later crewed with John Gibson on Biafra flights.

Before the end of the year (still in his teens), he was fully licensed. As planned, Mike joined BNA, where his father, who was also a flight instructor, converted him to the DC-3 to fly as co-pilot (and later, DC-4s). The airline also had partial use of the twin-engined Beechcraft Baron – given by the United States personally to the Botswana President and his family.

Also, alternating as 'Presidential Pilots', apart from Sir Seretse and Lady Ruth Khama, Mike and Bill flew the Khama children to and from their schools in South Africa – including a very young Ian, who was later to become the fourth Botswana President in 2008.

During 1968 – after protracted management disagreements over future aircraft for the fledgling airline – the Gibsons left Botswana for new experiences elsewhere; fate decreed still more developments that were to shape the future. Captain Jack Malloch – another former RAF Spitfire pilot and legendary African aviator, as well as a long-time friend of his father – was about to become an integral part of the youthful Mike Gibson's flying career. Prior to the Biafran debacle, Malloch had been heavily involved in the Congo conflict, as well as sanctions-busting operations for Ian Smith's 'rebel' government. After Zimbabwe's independence – and under Robert Mugabe's Zimbabwe – his cargo airline eventually became 'legitimate'. Sadly, for Jack Malloch, that was to be short-lived. His untimely death occurred in 1982 when the Spitfire he and his engineers had taken years to rebuild in his hangar was taken out on a flying demonstration, which then disappeared into a thunderstorm, crashed and disintegrated near Harare.

In the opinion of many of the veteran airmen active at the time, Jack Malloch was one of the most illustrious aviators to have emerged in Africa after World War II. Like his close friend Ian Smith, he too had been honed on Spitfires.

Having always struggled to keep his various commercial airline ventures afloat, the always-enterprising Malloch needed a bunch of new challenges. He found them among some of the contacts involved in conflicts within Africa and beyond, and soon emerged as a major player in that kind of work. Malloch flew many clandestine missions linked to Cold War operations in Africa and elsewhere (in fact, wherever Washington and London were attempting to counter Soviet efforts at insurrection).

Alan Brough (who, for a long while, was writing a book on Malloch's multifarious career) also disclosed that sanctions apart, he was deeply involved with the British Intelligence and handled several military support flights into the Sudan for Whitehall; then followed clandestine military

Captain Mike Gibson did his flight training in Rhodesia and then joined his father as a co-pilot on many trans-Africa flights. He went into Biafra with his dad when still only 21 years old.
(Mike Gibson)

flights into the Saudi Arabian desert in the early 1960s when he delivered weapons and supplies for Colonel Jim Johnson's British SAS operation against Egyptian ground and air forces in the Yemen.

At one stage, the Central Intelligence Agency (CIA) orchestrated United States Senate approval to sell him DC-8 freighters with jet conversion training for his crews in America. Mike Gibson was one of many among this remarkable group of aviators –spending 10 weeks in Denver at United Airlines' training facilities and simulators in the early 1970s. Sadly, this episode was also regarded by some as an unsavoury remnant of American undercover politics (made worse because it was sponsored by the wife of Claire Chennault – the founder of the CIA's Air America).

Originally involved in the turbulent days of post-independent Congo (Katanga included), Jack Malloch also had close links with Rhodesia's Special Air Service – sometimes dropping its operatives many days' trudge behind enemy lines in Mozambique, Zambia and even Tanzania. Most of the 'secret' work in which Jack was implicated, says Brough, was with the French Secret Service. The *Palais de l'Élysée* was linked to a series of events in the newly-independent Congo and in Katanga (once the mercurial Moïse Tshombe had taken over) – and since Paris was also supporting the breakaway Nigerian enclave of Biafra, his planes went there as well (quite a few times, with at least one of the Gibsons at the controls and sometimes both). It was not surprising therefore that another of Malloch's good friends over the years was the French mercenary Bob Denard. In fact, it was left to Malloch (again with French collusion) to airlift Denard and his group of fighters into both Dahomey and the Comoros Archipelago (which was the second time Denard took that Indian Ocean island country by force).

UNITY AND FAITH, PEACE AND PROGRESS

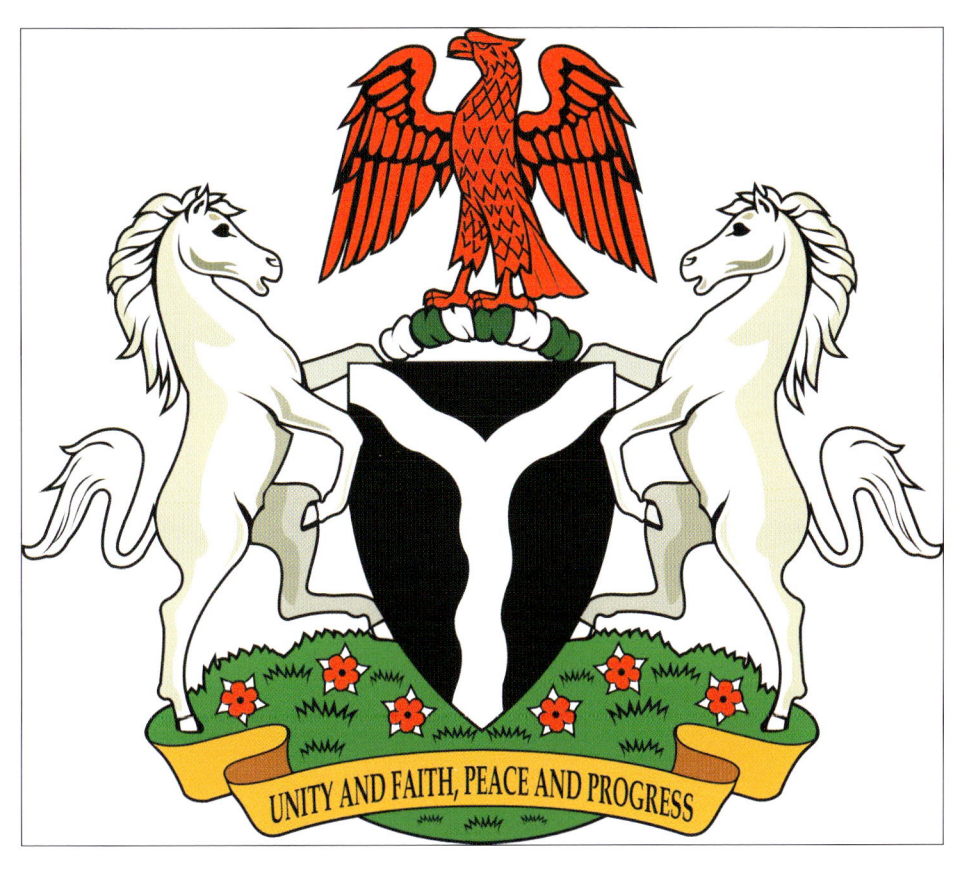

Freedom Justice Peace

LANDING AT
"ANNABELLE," ULI AIRFIELD

When the beacon is passed, aircraft lowers flaps 20° and reduces speed to 165 mph.

The circuit is joined at 1,500 ft, on a course that will take the aircraft parallel to the radio beacon.

If lan
aircra
circu

The Landing Phase: The aircraft flies at 150 mph, flaps down 30°, loosing 500 ft of altitude every minute.

The aircraft comes down to 1,000 ft and makes a hard right turn to align itself with the runway

200ft

30 sec.

At this critical point, the plane calls for night runway lights to be flashed and either continues on to land or aborts.

90 sec.

105 s

60 sec.

Author Akhil Kadidal's magnificently detailed sketch of Uli Airport in the heart of beleaguered Biafra. Most aircraft bringing in relief supplies for the war landed there – and because of Federal bombing raids, quite a few crews were lost.

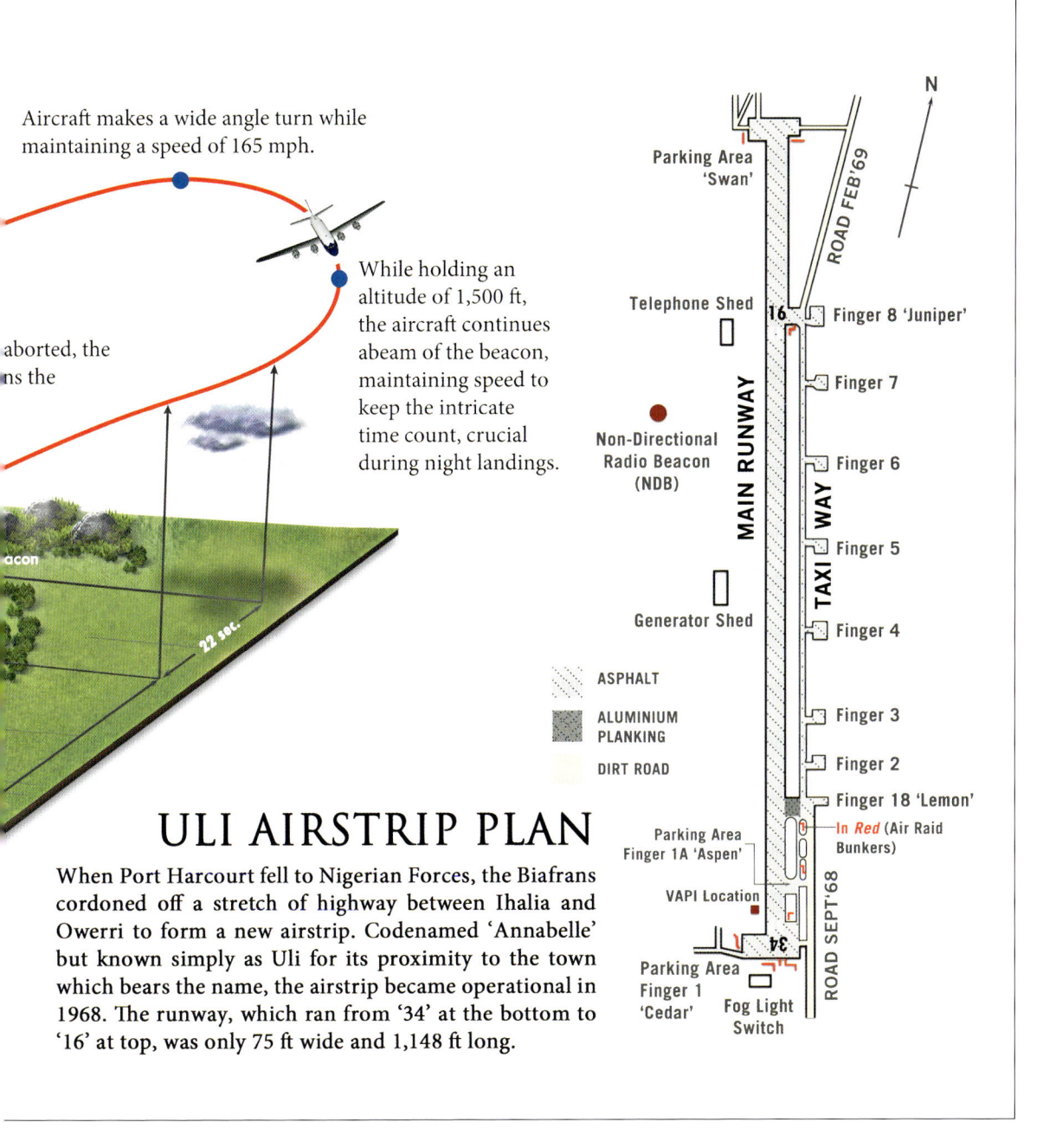

Aircraft makes a wide angle turn while maintaining a speed of 165 mph.

While holding an altitude of 1,500 ft, the aircraft continues abeam of the beacon, maintaining speed to keep the intricate time count, crucial during night landings.

aborted, the
ns the

22 sec.

Parking Area 'Swan'

ROAD FEB'69

Telephone Shed

16

Finger 8 'Juniper'

Finger 7

Non-Directional Radio Beacon (NDB)

Finger 6

MAIN RUNWAY

TAXI WAY

Finger 5

Generator Shed

Finger 4

ASPHALT
ALUMINIUM PLANKING
DIRT ROAD

Finger 3

Finger 2

Finger 18 'Lemon'

Parking Area Finger 1A 'Aspen'

In *Red* (Air Raid Bunkers)

VAPI Location

Parking Area Finger 1 'Cedar'

Fog Light Switch

34

ROAD SEPT'68

N

ULI AIRSTRIP PLAN

When Port Harcourt fell to Nigerian Forces, the Biafrans cordoned off a stretch of highway between Ihalia and Owerri to form a new airstrip. Codenamed 'Annabelle' but known simply as Uli for its proximity to the town which bears the name, the airstrip became operational in 1968. The runway, which ran from '34' at the bottom to '16' at top, was only 75 ft wide and 1,148 ft long.

ABOVE: A Joint Church Aid (also colloquially referred to as 'Jesus Christ Airlines') Stratocruiser lifts off on its evening flight from the Portuguese-held São Tomé Island and heads north towards Uli Airport in rebel-held Biafra. (Author's collection)
BELOW: A domestic scene in Aba, Central Biafra. Most of the Biafran vehicles had palm fronds or foliage over their cabs as an improvised kind of camouflage against air attack – not that it helped much. (Author's photo)

ABOVE: Ojukwu managed to buy half a dozen World War II surplus American T-6 Harvard ground support/trainer aircraft in Europe, but only two finally made it to this African conflict. (Michael Robson)

BELOW: His Royal Majesty *Eze* (King) A.E. Chukwuemeka-Eri (*oji offor* custodian of staff and rods in Biafra).

ABOVE: For many, life went on as usual – despite the war. (Björn Larsson-Ask)
BELOW: The Nigerian Fokker F-27 passenger plane seized at Enugu at the start of the war. It crashed when it was used in a bombing raid on Lagos – the then capital of the country. (Michael Robson)

ABOVE: Red Cross supplies being loaded in preparation for the nightly flight into Biafra. (Björn Larsson-Ask)
BELOW: A domestic scene in a Biafran village during the war, with residents making their way to a building that had just been bombed by Nigerian Air Force jets. (Thurfjell)

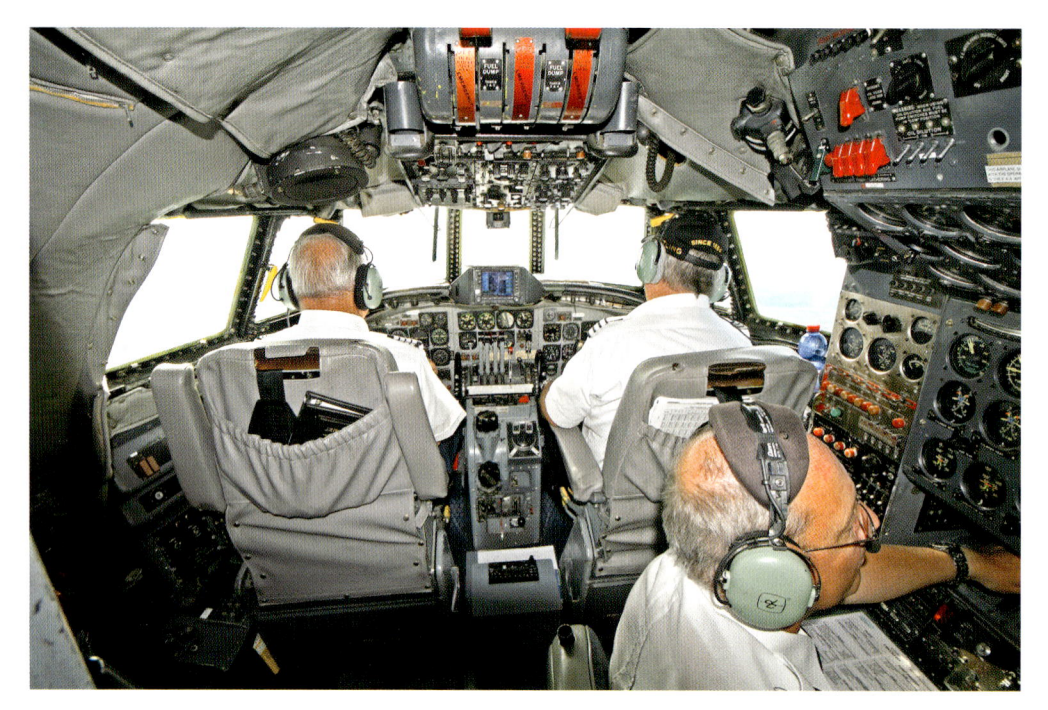

ABOVE: The cockpit of a Super Constellation of the type routinely flown into Biafra by Rhodesians Mike Gibson and his father, John. (Mike Gibson)
BELOW: One of several Super Constellations used in the Biafran airlift that was left behind on São Tomé Island after hostilities ended. The aluminium air frames were almost completely eroded by the island's tropical climate. (Author's collection)

ABOVE: Count Gustav von Rosen seated in the cockpit of one of his Minicons. (Author's collection)
BELOW: A Biafran-modified heavy weapon at the Nigerian War Museum. (Photo source unknown)

ABOVE: A typical country road in Eastern Nigeria – ideal ambush country during the war. (Author's collection)
RIGHT: In attempting to get into Biafra, the author sailed on board the m.v. *Titania* – a Norwegian freighter that called at Warri in the Niger Delta. On the second morning – lying in the roadstead – the ship and an American Farrell Line steamer out of Houston (like us, tied up to buoys) were hit by rockets fired by Biafran Minicons. The *Titania* was hit amidships several times. (Author's photo)

Nigeria has a great cultural heritage that goes back centuries and can be seen in most of the great museums of the world. This 'Queen Mother' pendant mask in ivory – presently in the Louvre – dates from 16th century Edo culture in the country's Central Benin Region.

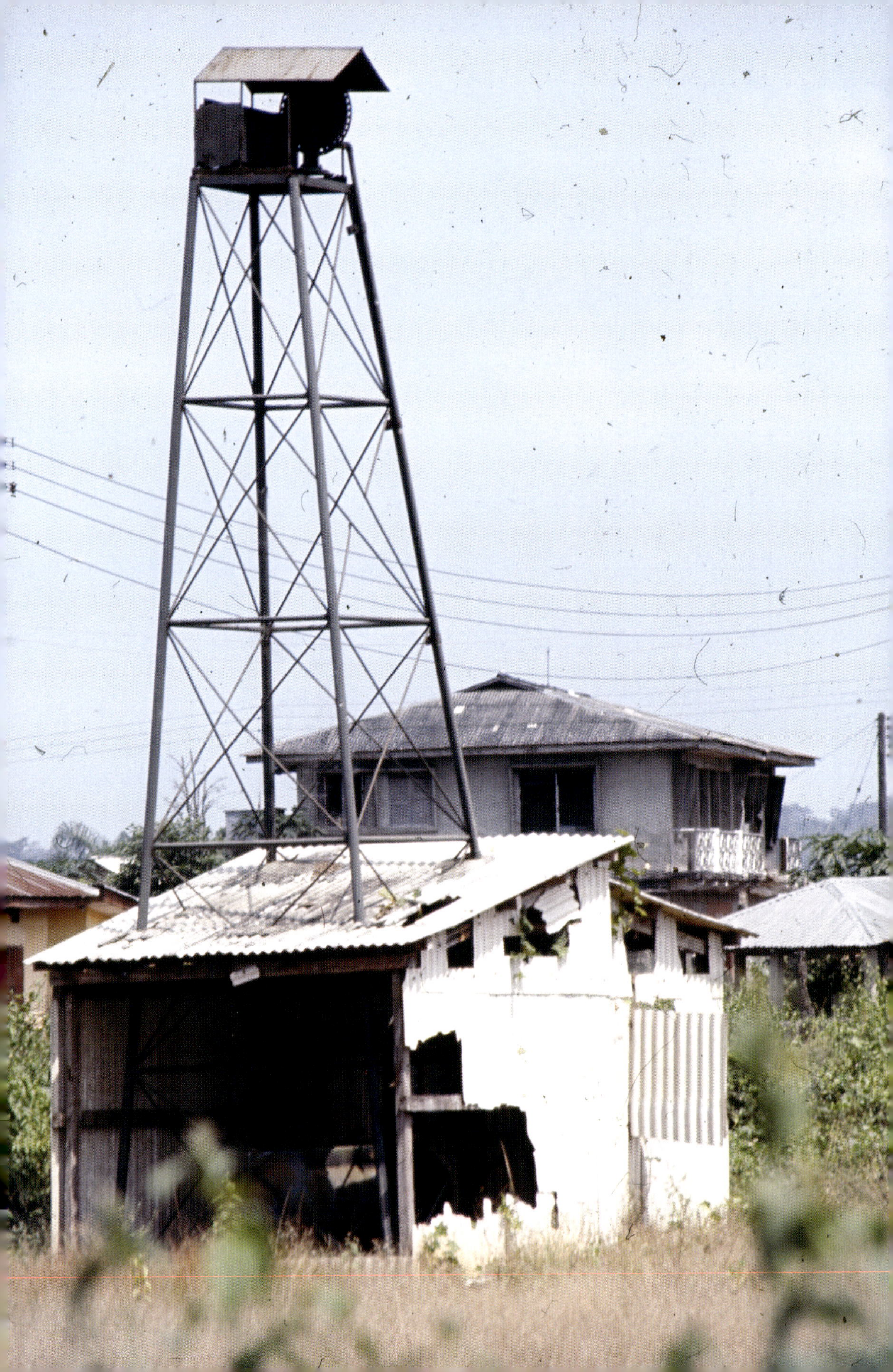

LEFT: A Biafran air raid siren atop an improvised tower. By the end of the war, there were few buildings in the towns still held by the rebels that were not damaged by enemy action. (Author's photo)
ABOVE: Improvised armour – today standing at one of Nigeria's museums. These devices were primitive, but under the circumstances – in a conflict that was often quite primitive – reasonably effective. (Wikipedia)
BELOW: A group of young Rhodesians doing their flying training in Salisbury before the war. Some, like Mike Gibson (who took the photo), ended up flying commercial airliners in the Biafran airlift.

ABOVE: Biafran recruits being put through their paces prior to being sent into war. Towards the end, they would be lucky to get a full week's training before seeing action. In the top right-hand corner of this photo, a mortar group is shown how to handle and aim the tube. (Author's photo)

BELOW: Light machine-gun training was always completed without live ammunition. (Author's photo)

RIGHT: Just about everything in the war on the rebel side was makeshift. You had a helmet if you killed somebody wearing one (surmising it was still usable). Uniforms were threadbare and made from primitive jungle fibres and again, if you could lay your hands on a camouflage jacket, you donned it. (Author's photo)

BELOW: Anti-aircraft fire – again without live ammunition – was hardly adequate against Soviet MiG-17s that pummelled the Biafrans every single day. (Author's photo)

ABOVE: As hostilities drew to a close, the physical condition of troops serving in the Biafran Army had deteriorated markedly. Starvation was the norm – in and out of the army – and I sometimes saw four men trying to handle an ammunition case that two men would easily have lifted. (Author's photo)
BELOW: An everyday scene in a Biafran town – this one Owerri, which changed hands several times. (Author's photo)

YEAR 1969		AIRCRAFT		PILOT, OR 1st PILOT	2nd PILOT, PUPIL OR PASSENGER	DUTY (INCLUDING RESULTS AND REMARKS)
Month	Date	Type	No.			
—	—	—	—	—	—	— TOTALS BROUGHT FORWARD ...
MAY	19	DC4	F.BBDD	GIBSON J	SELF	BUGA - FOOO
	20	"	"	"	"	FOOO - FOOB
	20	"	"	"	"	FOOB - FOOO
	20	"	"	"	"	FOOO - BUGA (R/W 8)
	20	"	"	"	"	BUGA - FOOO
	21	"	"	"	"	FOOO - BULI
	21	"	"	"	"	BULI - FOOO
	22	"	"	"	"	FOOO - BULI
	22	"	"	"	"	BULI - FOOO

Mike Gibson's logbook entries for his flights into Biafra in May 1969.

Mike Gibson recalls that at the time, very few people in South Africa or Rhodesia had any idea of what was going on in the rest of the continent – especially in West Africa and Nigeria. The media spoke of starving Biafran children and genocide but, as he remonstrates, unless you were directly involved, who really cared? There was a lot of talk that it was more about oilfields owned by the French and that they were paying (through the French Government) to keep their assets in this West African state intact. This made sense, because Biafra was indeed 'sitting' on one of the largest crude oil 'lakes' in the world – trouble was, the rebel state was surrounded by a belligerent Federal Nigerian Army that had the resources to fight for as long as it took; Biafra did not.

Gibson's role – as with other air crews involved in the Biafran airlift – was to keep the rebel enclave supplied with arms and ammunition. Food to keep the nation alive was another part of it. Still more aviators – many associated with the ICRC – were concerned with humanitarian aspects, together with a variety of religious charities that were attempting to help Biafra's starving millions.

Very little information other than fundamentals was forthcoming when Mike Gibson was offered a job as co-pilot on supply flights into Biafra from Libreville. Believing he would be on the 'correct' – or appropriate – side of this conflict (most observers regarded Biafra as the underdog – much like the Rhodesians' perception of the treatment many of its citizens in Rhodesia were receiving at the hands of Harold Wilson and David Owen's British Labour Government) and relying on his father's belief in Jack Malloch's personal integrity, Mike accepted the job after a briefing at Jack's home near Salisbury Airport. There was no contract forthcoming – indeed, no commitment at all on either side – but, he was assured, he would be paid well for each flight completed; and indeed he was. Young Mike was given open return tickets for a flight to Johannesburg and from there on to Libreville, where UTA stopped on its Johannesburg-to-Paris legs. Issues like potential personal risk and danger were not discussed.

Compared to typical pilot salaries, the rates in those days were phenomenal. Crews were paid cash in US dollars and, of course, it was all tax-free! Aircraft captains received $750 for each round trip – roughly $5,000 today – and return flights were either empty or the plane took out hundreds of refugee children who would be cared for by Gabonese-based international aid groups. Co-pilots like Mike (who himself logged more than 80 sorties) were paid $600 and flight engineers $500 – plus all expenses including accommodation, food, drinks and even cigarettes at their hotels. Since there were sometimes two or three aircraft making trips on most nights of the week, the amount of cash earned by these air crew was enormous. As Mike recalls, there was a small problem in that there were no safe storage facilities at the hotel or at the airport – and some of the air crew would carry thousands of dollars on them when they flew; others were content to hide it in their rooms, but, he stresses, he never heard of any theft.

Mike's first 'stint' began at the end of November 1968 when he flew to Jan Smuts Airport, Johannesburg – and at the departure gate he was joined by South African flight engineer Bob McIntyre. At least he had someone to talk to on the flight about the upcoming African venture, but unfortunately, Bob knew even less about what was going on in Biafra at the time, or even the risks they were likely to face.

At Libreville, they were met by a group of French Secret Service types who took care of their entry formalities. Very few of them spoke any English and Mike's eight years of schoolboy French came in handy at times, as not many of his crew members could understand French either. Their hosts arranged everything from pre- and post-flight briefings and radio codes for Biafran air traffic controllers, to (most importantly) the money they were to receive at the end of each week. The two were driven to the hotel on the beach where the other crews were staying, and the welcome was kindly. The operation had been going for several months, with crews coming and going – and if you, as an aviator, could contribute, so much the better:

> It was all very hush-hush and no one was to discuss anything with anyone –especially Americans, who were all assumed to be CIA, and who we were led to believe were 'enemy informers'.
>
> We were booked two to a room: firstly at the Hôtel de la Rèsidence – a rundown, ramshackle line of wooden cabins built under tall coconut trees on the beach, with noisy, rusty old air conditioners that could barely cope with the heat and humidity of Libreville, just 26 miles from the Equator, but the food was not bad. The hotel was run by a pleasant French woman named Jacqueline, who was mentioned in an article that appeared as a cover story in *Time* magazine and which described our nocturnal flight activities. Frankly, the piece was more amusing than factual, but it did provide some background.
>
> The magazine was dated Friday, December 26 1968 and the article headed 'Keeping Biafra Alive'. I quote:
>
> 'Perhaps the most important single reason for battered Biafra's continuing survival against the attacks of the Nigerian Federal Army is a steady infusion of French military aid.
>
> 'Although the French will not acknowledge their role, one of the worst-kept secrets of the war is the fact that armaments are flown into the secessionist state almost nightly from two former French colonies: Gabon and the Ivory Coast. Hard proof of responsibility for the arms lift, however, is hard to come by, as *Time* correspondent James Wilde reported from the Gabonese capital of Libreville:
>
> 'Everybody in this shabby capital knows about it, but few will talk. The unmarked planes, however, are there for all to see: four DC-4s, three DC-3s and a single Constellation, parked on the palm-lined seaside tarmac. Patient research shows that the aircraft have varied registration: French, German, Belgian, Zambian, Biafran and Gabonese.
>
> 'Each afternoon, three or four planes taxi to the nearby military airfield for loading and then take off for Biafra at 6pm sharp. They return around midnight, after the 900-mile-round trip. Just as predictable as the flights is the black Citroen, owned by the French security police, that follows me to the strip.

'There are two sets of pilots flying the Biafra run – one English-speaking and the other French – and they are carefully segregated. The English-speaking flyers are housed in the dilapidated, mosquito-ridden Hôtel de la Rèsidence run by a waspish French brunette named Jackie, whose sole virtue seems to be that she is able to count in English.

'Eighteen of the pilots are Rhodesian and South African – all clad in the uniform of the British colonial in Africa: highly polished shoes, long socks, neatly pressed shorts and starched bush jackets. Carefully holding themselves apart are several ex-RAF types, moustached and bearded, who punctuate their clipped, casual conversation with dated bits of Battle of Britain slang like 'wack-o', 'bang-on', 'piece of cake'.

'At the Rèsidence bar one night, a cheerful group strolled in after, as one put it, 'delivering the goodies'. Though the flyers had obviously been ordered not to talk about their employers, some relaxed sufficiently after several pink gins to joke about their cargoes of 'birth-control pills', or ammunition.

'You only need one of them, mate,' a pilot chuckled.

All the pilots have one thing in common: they fly to get a stake.

'I'm only in it for the money,' one sad, balding man told me. 'I've got a wife and five kids and I want to put a down payment on a house in Salisbury.' Another Rhodesian had a second motive: 'That Harold Wilson is a bastard. He's against Biafra and he's buggering us too. This is a chance to bugger him.' Everyone roared with laughter.

'The few French crews have a much pleasanter home. They are housed in the ultra-modern Hotel Gamba, where they spend their off-duty time devouring expensive meals ($25 and up) and socking away wine at $15 a bottle. Clad in soiled shorts and sweat-stained shirts, their bare feet stuck into rubber Japanese *zoris*, they look to be a much scruffier lot than the colonial swells at the Rèsidence. They are much more close-mouthed as well. All attempts to start any kind of conversation fails: their thin, long-nosed Gallic faces remain blank.

'Despite serious problems in obtaining sufficient high-octane aviation fuel, the French seem determined to carry on. An abnormal number of tankers recently unloaded at Libreville. The cargo included long, rope-handled wooden boxes of the sort France uses to transport ammunition. The cases were taken in a French Army truck to the military airport, where several other boxes marked 'Army Rations' were in evidence.

'There are rumors that France may have decided to take over the entire mercenary show in Biafra. The Biafrans have expelled Colonel Rolf Steiner, the German ex-Legionnaire, who had commanded their crack mercenary-led unit (*Time*, Oct. 25). On arrival here in Gabon, Steiner refused to answer questions, but an aide admitted that the Steiner party had been escorted to the Biafran airport in handcuffs.

'The speculation is that Steiner was fired because the Biafran military had grown increasingly jealous of his privileged position with Colonel Odumegwu Ojukwu and had done their best to see that Steiner's troops did not get their share of ammunition and rations. The German, in retaliation, supposedly commandeered a food convoy – a deed that led to his ousting.

'The French do not want publicity on their role in Biafra, but why are they so intent on keeping the war alive? A businessman here says the reason is Biafran oil: 'A million barrels of oil a day, or about one-third the production capacity of Kuwait. That kind of oil production is worth gambling for, even if the odds are against you.'

In addition, Charles de Gaulle relishes any chance he finds to annoy the British, who are backing the Nigerian Government. A third reason may well be that a united and progressing Nigeria would be a threat to the French economic dominance of West Africa. Seemingly, the French cannot lose.

'If Biafra wins, they may get a good deal on the oil. Should events take a turn for the worse, France probably will help Biafra set up a government-in-exile here in Gabon. If, as seems possible, French arms shipments succeed in prolonging the war one or two years, and even if Biafra is defeated, an exhausted Nigeria will not be a threat for some time to come – and the joy of it all is that France is not directly involved, or at least no one so far can prove that Paris is.'

Shortly after publication of the *Time* article, we were moved to the less obtrusive and slightly better appointed Hotel Louis run by an affable Dutchman called John, who spoke good English and who had obviously been well-briefed by our French SS 'minders'.

He was also well paid and happy to ply us with whatever we wanted to eat and drink at the bar on evenings when there were no flights. Chivas Regal scotch with Perrier became my tipple of choice; the South Africans, who liked brandy and coke, had to settle for the best French cognac, while others drank champagne by the glass; some of the smokers developed a taste for foul-smelling *Gitanes*.

For familiarisation, a new air crew member was expected to make one unpaid flight as an observer. Mike's was in Jack Malloch's Super Constellation and, as he recalls:

… it was very different and exhilarating compared to bumping along in a hot DC-3 around the Okavango Swamps – flying low over herds of elephant, giraffe, zebra and buffalo – but apart from flashes of AAA fire from the ground when crossing the coast near the Niger Delta, most of the flight was uneventful until the plane approached Uli – a remote jungle airstrip inside Biafra. The captain misjudged the final approach, missed the runway and was forced to make a visual circuit at low level.

Downwind, we heard strange noises – and after landing and parking, it turned out that palm fronds had stuck in the main gear and left a series of vivid green pigment on our inner prop tips.

Chief flight engineer John Hodges was not amused. After discovering how close they had come to careering into the bush, he dubbed the portly aviator 'Twiggy' (after the skinny, well-known English model). The name stuck – as had the palm fronds.[1]

---

1 Mike Gibson:
Some years after Biafra, but still operating under sanctions in Rhodesia, John Hodges saved our skins by expertly managing to keep two of the DC-7's Wright Cyclone engines (with the problematical power recovery turbines) running after the other two failed a couple of hours into cruise and had to be shut down and the props feathered. This was on a late-night flight from Libreville back to our home base, with a refuelling stop at the Angolan capital, Luanda.

Even after F/O Alan Partington and F/Eng Dave Goldsmith – also on board – managed to jettison several tonnes of chemical fertiliser bags over Zambia through the rear emergency exit hatches (flying on a hot African night on only two engines), we had gradually descended from 11,000 feet down to about 3,000, which we could barely maintain. Salisbury (Harare) was at nearly 5,000 feet, so an alternate was necessary.

Our route took us close to Kariba Dam on the Zambezi River and its airport, which were only 1,600 feet ASL. Air Rhodesia also had scheduled flights through Kariba, but only during the daytime. In 1978 a Viscount was brought down by a terrorist ground-to-air missile between Kariba and Salisbury.

I knew Kariba fairly well – having flown Dad's Cessna 310 which was based there – operating game viewing flights and trips to Bumi Hills on the southern shore of the lake. One of the hazards at both Kariba and Bumi was wild game – from baboons to sable – and smaller buck, warthogs and even elephant sporadically wandering across the landing strips.

Gibson continued:
Although closed to civilian aircraft after dark, Kariba was also FAF2 (Forward Air Field) of the Rhodesian Air Force which, at the time, was under the command of Squadron Leader Cyril White. He was also a good friend

```
AFRICA'S AIR CARGO LINE
AIR GABON CARGO No.  046
NOM DU TITULAIRE/NAME OF HOLDER
Michael John GIBSON
Date de Naissance/Date of Birth        Position
31.12.1946                  PILOT – CAPTAIN
Date de l'edition/Date of Issue
28.04.1977
Autorise par/Authorised by:
                                       DIRECTEUR/DIRECTOR

Compagnie Gabonaise d'Affrètement Aérien
B.P. 484 Libreville, République du Gabon
```

Mike Gibson's 'licence' to fly airlifts into Biafra out of Libreville Airport. It was actually a French security precaution. (Mike Gibson)

In a historic report titled 'Biafra Was The Beginning' – published by AfricaFiles – Hugh McCullum wryly commented that it was officially called 'Jointchurchaid' (JCA):

> … but the daredevil pilots called it the 'Jesus Christ Airline' with a swagger of pride and hint of awe.
>
> For almost two amazing years, JCA kept a small, breakaway West African state alive – refusing to allow starvation to be used as a weapon of war. It flew 5,314 extremely dangerous missions – carrying 60,000 tonnes of humanitarian aid and saved millions of lives.

---

of Dad's and we had drunk a few beers together in the past. If all went as planned, hopefully we could open a few more a bit later!

Radio contact was made via our own base communications, and ATC and I was informed that we could land using gooseneck flare runway lights and Land Rovers with headlights shining across both ends of the landing strip. Luckily – as by now, the remaining two engines were overheating – the first approach went well and I landed as near to the threshold as possible (it being quite a short runway for the DC-7 – over twice the size and weight of a Viscount). We were parked out of the way and met by the relieved RhodAf commander and my father, but I doubt we would have made it without the skills of a superb flight engineer and great friend. RIP John Hodges – and we did drink those beers!

The profile of the American-built Super Constellation – still one of the most beautiful aircraft of that that era.

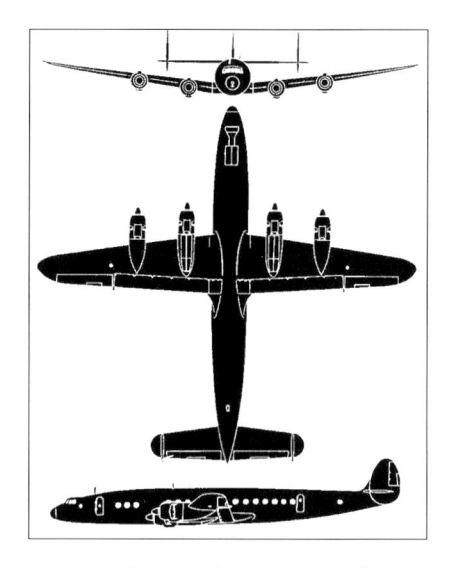

The lumbering DC-7s and temperamental Super Constellations flew at night from a Portuguese island off the coast of West Africa into a tiny airstrip… skimming blind over trees at 2,000 feet to avoid the guns and fighters of the enemy.

Each of the old planes had its own JCA logo: two fishes – one of the earliest symbols of Christianity – but each had its own name; the best known in Canada was Canairelief, whose four 'Super Connies' were an integral part of JCA, but there was also Nordchurchaid (from Europe) and the Holy Ghost Airline (run by the Irish Catholic Holy Ghost Fathers).

JCA soon became the darling of the media – attracting journalists from all over. For the first time in history, famine and starvation – as well as the humanitarian response – were seen nightly on world television.

Supply flights were made into Biafra from many African and European points of departure. Planes took off from Libreville, and many more from São Tomé. Still more arrived from Abidjan (the Ivorian capital city) and Fernando Pó, as well as several European airports (including Lisbon).

There was often confusion about aircraft, crews, cargos and even destinations. McCullum recalls that Ottawa eventually sent three Hercules freighters as part of an ICRC relief effort 'in an act of incredible incompetence or political venality, because two went to Lagos and one to São Tomé'.

Nigeria – at war with Biafra – impounded the two planes that arrived at the country's biggest international airport and never let them off the ground while hostilities lasted. The C-130 that landed at São Tomé was sent back to Canada after another ICRC plane was shot down by the Nigerians.

When based in Abidjan, Jack Malloch's crews were housed in villas in the Presidential Palace compound – lavishly furnished for VIP guests with period furniture, gold-plated cutlery and crystal glassware engraved with the national coat of arms… indeed, strange surroundings for most of the Rhodesian and South African mercenary crews.

Weapons, ammunition and a huge variety of supplies to help the Biafran rebels to survive emanated from numerous sources. Mike once flew with Jack Malloch in a convoy of three DC-7s from Abidjan first to Faro, Portugal and then on to Tel Aviv to pick up cargo – in this case, military stuff – and freight them back. He makes some interesting observations about the two main airstrips inside Biafra – Uli and Uga – where they would bring down their loads: 'Though operating as fully-fledged 'airports', the landing strips were actually long stretches of surfaced roads

– but even that had limitations, because the 'runways' were routinely bombed by the Nigerians and the Biafran rebels didn't have the ability to fix them properly, though it was clear that they did a marvellous job with what little was available.'

He goes on:

> Although we saw very little other than the part of the highway roughly marked out as a landing strip, Uli and Uga were just long enough for heavy incoming freighters like DC-4s, DC-6s, DC-7s and Super Constellation flights.
>
> We understood that the 'control tower' was actually a bunker several metres underground – and perhaps a kilometre from the 'runway' – in order to avoid or withstand regular bombings by the Nigerian Air Force, which also employed foreign mercenary pilots.
>
> As the Biafrans were well aware that the Nigerians were closely monitoring the airlift, all 'airport' equipment and locator NDB was moved from time to time – either after being damaged by daytime air strikes, or to avoid being permanently destroyed. The incoming freight would have been loaded straight onto trucks and moved away from the strip as soon as possible. Also, the Biafrans would sometimes erect tents to provide a measure of protection from the many tropical storms that would thunder through the region.
>
> The immediate area surrounding both airstrips was mainly palm trees and jungle, which meant that there were few – if any – ancillary lights in the vicinity. That made sense because the rebels didn't need to give their Nigerian bombing adversaries any fixed markers which might be used to get their bearings.
>
> At the beginning of the each week, we were given new codes and other information to use on the radio during approach and descent – and considering there were usually dozens of arrivals and departures each evening, with all sorts of flights from a score or more operators working out of airports to the south and west of Nigeria, it was remarkable that there weren't more incidents or near-misses. As it was, about two dozen aircraft and crews were lost during the course of the war. It also says much that this entire airborne set-up was run by local controllers, who managed without any use of radar or other navigational aids besides low-powered non-directional beacons. However, it stands to reason that there must have been some co-ordination with the agencies providing the flights and supplies.

Mike Gibson describes a typical approach to one of the strips – in this case, Uli Airport, which was actually little more than a lengthened and widened stretch of road. Following the fall of Port Harcourt to Federal troops of the 3MCDO on 19 May there was an urgent need for the Biafran separatist government to establish another airport through which weapons could be flown in – thus on the main road from Owerri to Ihiala, the long straight stretch between Mgbidi and Uli was widened to 25 metres and modified into a 2,600-metre-long runway, along with a parallel taxi-way. This airstrip – capable of handling up to 30 large aircraft every night (codenamed 'Annabelle', but better known as the Uli-Ihiala Airport) – became operational in August 1968 and would later assume a mythic stature in the story of the Nigerian Civil War:[2]

> After descending from an approach altitude of 18,000 feet – high enough to be able to cross the Nigerian coast and technically out of range of the Nigerian anti-aircraft gun positions between Calabar and Port Harcourt – we would see bursts of flashes some distance below us

---

2 For details, see future essay on Uli-Ihiala Airport.

The Gibson family at their Rhodesian home, with Mike's mother in the middle. The American flag came from other operators who worked with them.

as we overflew, but there was really nothing to do but ignore them. Fortunately, these were before the days of SAMs and heat-seeking rockets.

Pilots would be ordered to join the 'holding pattern', while previous incoming flights (at lower flight levels) were doing the same – each one of them waiting for clearance to land on the single 'runway'. It was one plane at a time – and only when it was safely down and moved into improvised holding pens in the adjacent jungle would the next freighter follow.

Outgoing flights would have to be phased into this routine – and it wouldn't be too long before there was very little space left on the ground for parked aircraft. There was also the additional danger of air attack or, in the latter stages of the war, ground assault by Nigerian forces.

Eventually (sometimes it would be 30 or 40 minutes in the hold), we would be cleared to final approach and landing, which would happen once the aircraft ahead of us had reported clear of the runway.

Using only the ADF needle pointing at the NDB signal (affected by electrical interference from any nearby thunder cells), we had to confirm that we were lined up on final approach when we were less than a mile from touchdown – and we did this by flashing our landing lights; only then would the controller turn on his runway lights. The strip would rarely be straight ahead – and very swift corrections were then needed to line up before the approach and landing were made. If that didn't work, the process would have to be aborted and the entire rigmarole would start from scratch again.

Almost as soon as we'd touched down, the dim and sparse runway lights would be switched off and we would be signalled by ground crews to taxi to a paved area. Invariably, we were guided by our own lights – as well as torches waved by Biafran personnel on the ground.

Once the engines had been wound down, the flight engineer would open the doors and a host of bodies would appear silently and almost like a horde of ghosts out of the gloom. They would arrive with rickety steps or ladders and the offloading process would be accomplished as quickly as possible.

GIBSON AND SON: INTO BIAFRA ON SUPPLY RUNS

A three-man crew was needed on regular 'Super-Connie' ops. It included an engineer (seated in the foreground). (Mike Gibson)

There was always a Biafran Army officer assigned to meet our flights – most times a Captain Christopher, who was 21, about the same age as me. A very well-spoken and polite young man, he was much concerned about our safety and welfare.

After running the gauntlet across the Nigerian coastline numerous times, the flights settled into something of a routine. Although the risks were obvious, Mike and his colleagues had come to no harm; he was earning serious money – especially for a youthful (but by now, a reasonably experienced) co-pilot: 'I finally managed to persuade my father to join me in Gabon. I'd already had quite a few sorties under my belt, so it was an 'age versus experience' thing in reverse. He arrived in due course, but wasn't overly impressed with the operation, or the French organisers.'

After several routine flights together, an event followed which neither of the Gibsons ever forgot. Mike's air crew log book shows entries for the night of 20 May 1969 with father Johnny as pilot-in-command and Mike as first officer. There were two engineers (Dave Goldsmith and Bill Rheeder):

> We left Libreville, Gabon late in the evening for Uga. This was normally a three-hour flight in the DC-4 and a bit further into the Nigerian interior than Uli – codenamed 'Annabelle' – and also less used, as it was not really suitable for the larger DC-7 or Constellation aircraft. It was our sixth (and what was to be our final) flight into Uga – having flown both Jack Malloch's Gabonese-registered DC-4 TR-LNV, as well as the ex-Air France F-BBDD into Biafra extensively in April and May that year.

Planes used to run the blockade came from all over. This
Constellation had Colombian markings. (Wikipedia)

We approached Uga normally and began descending in the holding pattern – having been radioed earlier that there might be what was termed 'an enemy bomber' in the area. In fact, this is exactly what happened and, as we later learned, it was a Dakota – apparently flown by an Englishman named Mike Smith, who was in the employ of the Nigerian Air Force.

We had heard that the DC-3 was armed with under-wing incendiary bombs, but had no idea how big or how many there were. It was also possible that bombs were manually dropped out of the aircraft doors.

Nervous by this time, but still committed to putting our bird on the ground, we continued on down. With the runway and aircraft lights on immediately before touchdown – and too late to overshoot – we saw an enormous flash on the ground ahead of us, a little to the left of the runway; and then, a few seconds later, there was another blast to the right, but immediately behind us. We were committed to land, but our instinct just told us to stop at the end of the strip, turn round and take off again. I was all for getting the hell out of there.

After landing, the engineer would normally shut down the outer engines – the two inners being needed for hydraulics and braking. However, Dad quickly ordered these engines to be restarted so we would be able to quickly swing our nose around and get airborne before the bomber made his second run. We turned around and lined up at the end of the runway – still waiting for the fourth engine to fire up; then there was another flash, followed by a huge explosion just a few hundred metres ahead of us… the Nigerian 'bomber' had scored a direct hit on the runway. The bastard had now cut off our escape route, which was especially worrying, because we still had a full load of cargo on board.

It was a shock just then to realise that we were, as the saying goes, 'sitting ducks' and unable to get airborne. We assumed the bomber was right overhead and lined up; all we could do was put our heads down, pray and wait for another bomb do what it did best – but it didn't happen. The Nigerian Air Force DC-3 – distinctly recognisable by the sound of its Pratt & Whitney R-1830 engines – passed right over us, but then it began to recede into the distance. We asked ourselves: was he was coming back or not?

Cutting the mags and fuel and switching off all four engines, we made a frantic scramble to abandon ship – jumping from the cockpit by sliding down the emergency escape rope. Dad was a bit long in the tooth for that, but I think at least one of the engineers made it before an old ladder was quickly placed on the door sill by the loaders.

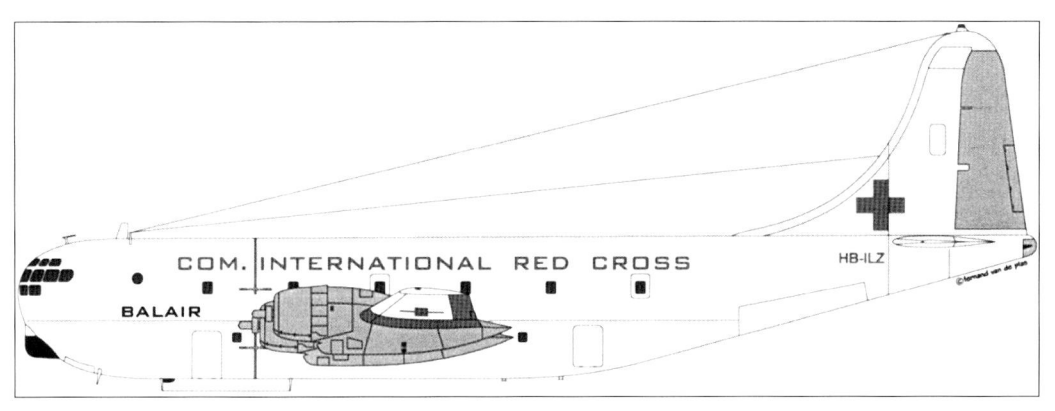

A diagram of a C-97 Globemaster used by Swiss company Bel Air (not Balair, as shown) and flown by American volunteer pilots. The company also used French-built C-160 Transall aircraft.

Once on the ground, we were met by our trusty friend, Captain Christopher – almost in tears with relief when he saw who the crew was. He quickly escorted us away from the aircraft and we waited to see if anything else would happen – but all remained quiet. However, our problems were not yet over…

When it seemed apparent that the bomber was probably returning to base and our DC-4 was being offloaded, Dad and I walked down the runway to inspect the damage. We also paced the distance to see if we would be able to take off again at all before a repair.

About 800 metres from where we were parked near the runway threshold, we came to a sizeable crater where the bomb had detonated, just off the runway's centre line. It was about two metres wide by a metre deep, and there were fragments of the still-warm steel casing clearly visible in the light of the moon. We dug chunks of metal out of the ground to take home as souvenirs; there was nothing large enough to identify the origin or size of the bomb. Fortunately, being empty and using a short take-off technique under Dad's supervision, the runway was long enough for me to lift the plane off the ground and fly the two-and-a-half-hour leg home.

The following night, we were back in the air again in F-BBDD for another (luckily, uneventful) flight to Uli. We never did return to Uga – and I'm not sure whether it ever went back into service. Soon after, Dad decided – for family reasons – that we should not fly together and he continued with Bill Wragg as his co-pilot.

After a flight with severe thunderstorms in the area and temporary loss of radio contact, Dad felt he had had enough. He used some of the money he'd made to buy an old (but serviceable) twin Cessna 310, together with spares and extra engines, which could be serviced by Fields in Salisbury. He flew the 2,000-mile trip home via Luanda with a single VHF radio and NDB for navigation.

After full refurbishment and zero-hour engines, he applied for an air charter licence to operate from Kariba – calling it 'JagAir' (after his initials). In later years, I acted as relief pilot.

Along with many of Jack Malloch's pilots, both Gibsons were also appointed as Reserve pilots for the Rhodesian Air Force and given the rank of Flight Lieutenant. John Gibson also flew Dakotas on counter-insurgency support operations.

LOCKHEED L-1049H SUPER CONSTELLATION

New airlift records were broken by international aid relief flights into Biafra. Two major aid organizations took part in the campaign: The International Red Cross and Joint Church Aid (JCA), otherwise nicknamed Jesus Christ Airlines by wiseacre pilots and aircrews. The JCA was funded by Catholic, Presbyterian and Protestant churches.

Flying for the JCA was this Superconstellation (CF-NAJ), operated by the Canadian firm, Canaireleif, on the behalf of the Canadian Presbyterian Church and Oxfam Canada. Initially, it was Canaireleif's sole aircraft, having been purchased for $C108,000, but was later joined by four more "Connies." Flights began in January 1969 and continued for several months with the aircraft experiencing several close calls at the legendary Biafran airstrip at Uli, little more than an appropriated stretch of widened highway.

On the night of August 3, CF-NAJ hit some trees while trying to land on the darkened runway and crashed, killing all onboard, including three crew members and their popular pilot, Capt. Donald Merriam (on right).

ILLUSTRATION BY AKHIL KADIDAL

Akhil Kadidal's classic depiction of the Lockheed Super Constellation used by Joint Church Aid in their Biafran relief flights.

During the rest of 1969 flights lessened as Biafra became too expensive for the French to continue picking up the tabs. Even a small country at war was an expensive business – and somebody in Paris probably didn't see an end to it. Bill Wragg flew the remainder of his flights with Jack Wight in command until the night the aircraft was lost after attempting to take off the wrong way without sufficient runway available (in spite of the warnings given by Bill). Jack Malloch's DC-4 ran into the jungle and caught fire, but the crew were able to escape unharmed.

After Biafran operations came to an end in 1969 Mike Gibson continued flying for Jack Malloch's various companies until his retirement from aviation. He received his first captaincy on the DC-7s at the age of 23 – followed by the Super Constellation, Canadair CL44 (swing-tail cargo turboprop) and the two DC-8 jet freighters which operated all over Africa, South America, Europe and the Middle East. Most of this work involved countering sanctions against Rhodesia sanctions (until 1980 – when the country was handed over to Mugabe as Zimbabwe).

Jack's aircraft flew under various flags and liveries – requiring air crew licences for several countries: Rhodesian Air Services; Air Trans Africa; Afro Continental Airways; Air Gabon Cargo; CargOman; and Affretair, which eventually became the official cargo airline of Zimbabwe after independence in 1980.

After Jack's death in his Spitfire crash in March 1982 his airline would eventually be integrated with Air Rhodesia (then disbanded). Partly from the effect of Jack's death on the company, Mike Gibson decided to retire from flying while still in his thirties. Later that year, he moved to South Africa to pursue his growing interest in personal computer technology.

14

Nigeria's Enigmatic Leader: General Yakubu Gowon

The trouble with military rule [in Africa] is that every colonel or general is soon full of ambition. The navy takes over today and the army tomorrow.[1]

It is almost ironic that the 'Good General' Yakubu – or 'Jack', as he was known to those of us covering Nigeria's civil war – is almost better remembered for his quote about the ambitions of military leaders in Africa than he is for his role in the Biafran War.

Though many people originally trusted this seemingly devout Christian northerner – in large part because he put his mind to trying to resolve some of the ethnic tensions that threatened to fatally divide Nigeria – the consensus today is that he did not do enough. History tends towards the view that he believed that if he didn't go along with what a manifestly Islamic regime wanted, his head would be the next to roll. It did in the end – figuratively, that is.

The Ibos had started it all, of course, by leading the January 1965 putsch that overthrew Nigeria's first legally-elected government. That revolt was led by an easterner, Major Kaduna Nzeogwu, together with other junior army officers. Called 'The Coup of the Five Majors', they launched a kind of violence that modern Nigeria had never experienced before. To those of us on the 'outside' as it were, the revolt was both stupid and brutal because the plotters murdered two of Nigeria's most revered northern political and spiritual leaders. The first to die was Sir Abubakar Tafawa Balewa, followed by his premier, Sir Ahmadu Bello. Several other prominent figures in various parts of this vast West African state were also targeted.

There was no question that these actions had tribal connotations: the Ibos wanted to rule the country – and in this they succeeded for a little more than six months. When their largely Muslim-orientated adversaries did eventually retaliate, because Muslim people the world over do not easily forget slights (even minor ones), they did so with a vengeance that surprised everybody; we know that many easterners died as a consequence.

Within months, the country was enmeshed in a seemingly irrevocable conflict. It was clear from the beginning that ultimately, the only outcome would be victory for one side or the other, which, essentially, is how it turned out after two-and-a-half years of fighting. When that reality finally struck home, both in Lagos and in an overwhelmingly Islamic Northern Nigeria (and also in London and Washington), the next problem faced by this nation – which had been independent for less than a decade – was who would be tasked to achieve this aim? It could hardly be one of the hard-line Muslim commanders, though there were precious few of them in the ranks – nor could

---

1   General Yakubu 'Jack' Gowon.

it be a Yoruba: the third (and extremely vocal and politically astute) segment of Greater Nigeria, whose people occupied most of the south-west of the country; a compromise had to be sought.

Akhil Kadidal, foreign affairs editor on a major Indian newspaper and a military historian of note (his most recent book, with which he is still busy, deals with the Nazi siege of Malta during World War II – prior to which he was working on another on the Nigerian Civil War), phrased it best when he declared that Gowon's role in the early days of the second *coup d'état* was largely unknown. Although he was the country's Army Chief of Staff, said Kadidal, Gowon was essentially an obscure, unknown officer outside headquarters. Although from the north, his origins (strictly speaking) were from the Plateau state in the middle belt, and he was a Christian from the Angas – a minor tribe in Nigeria's middle belt, where tribes had as many qualms about northern dominance as it did with southern arrogance.

Gowon, born on 19 October 1934 near the town of Bauchi, was the fifth of 11 children birthed into a deeply religious family. His father had been a Methodist minister and a mission-trained evangelist – and accordingly, Gowon had been sent to the St Bartholomew Christian Mission School in Zaria for his early education. Zaria was to become his most venerated place of education, for he remained to attend the Government College.

At the age of 19 young Gowon joined the army – training initially at Teshie in Ghana from 1954 in the Regular Officers Special Training School. This was done at the multi-battalion field force the Royal West African Frontier Force, which had been formed by the British Colonial Office in 1900 to garrison the West African colonies of Nigeria, the Gold Coast, Sierra Leone and Gambia. He was then fortunate enough to be selected for additional training in 1955 and 1956 – first at Eaton Hall and then at the Royal Military Academy Sandhurst, Surrey. In the interim, he was assigned twice to the Congo as part of the United Nations Forces (first in 1960 and again in 1963) – spending the time in-between at the British Staff College at Camberley.

After 1963 he became the first African Adjutant-General in his army's history, but then returned to England for another staff course at the Joint Services Staff College. He had just got home again when 'The Majors' Coup' was launched, but was not a participant (which was one of the reasons why he was regarded with trust by most of his contemporaries when the time came to choose a leader). In the meantime, he played a significant role in helping General Aguiyi Ironsi quell the ongoing anti-eastern Nigerian uprisings.

Unlike the majority of his colleagues, Jack Gowon was a bachelor. He was neither a smoker nor a drinker and, in contrast to some of them (as Kadidal declares), handsome, dapper and easy to smile. He was also easily charming because of his youthful good looks and, invariably, impeccably groomed.

Certainly, says Kadidal, it must be acknowledged that for all the vilification Gowon conjured up in the east when the war began, he was inherently a decent man with an abhorrence for bloodshed. If he hadn't upheld his rank or commanded the authority that he did during these difficult times, northern violence against people of eastern (Ibo) extraction would have continued.

Kadidal:

> To British vexation, the north – with whom they had a long association – seemed uncaring of oil wealth, but to be fair, there was also another fear permeating US and British foreign policy when it came to Africa: that of 'Balkanization'.
>
> While neighbouring French colonies – the Cameroons, Dahomey, the Niger Republic and others – had been carved up into narrow slivers of companionable and largely peaceful states, the British High Commissioner Cumming-Bruce and United States Ambassador Elbert Mathews tended towards the argument that a similar development in Nigeria would be problematic. First, they averred, a break-up of the Federation would be a major political

and economic disaster for the Nigerian people; and second, it would be a severe setback to independent Africa. The consensus in Britain was that in Africa, Nigeria – in terms of potential – was the proverbial 'Jewel in the Crown'. They were eventually proved right – even though it took this burgeoning West Africa half a century to overtake South Africa in terms of economic growth.

US Ambassador Mathews also made it clear the United States would cease its aid to the north and, with hostilities looming, such threats could hardly be ignored.

The argument was also made that that once the north seceded, it would be cut off from the sea and become landlocked. Furthermore, the south now began to realize that because some of the mutineers from the middle belt had behaved so brutally during the initial army mutiny, their ethnic minorities would be subject to strong northern dominance.

As one of the junior mutineers from the Tarok Tribe later conceded: 'A bigger Nigeria will check such excesses. So the bigger Nigeria is, the freer my tribe and myself will be.'

For his part, Colonel Ojukwu was all for letting the north go. 'If that's what they want,' Ojukwu snapped at Brigadier Odungipe – who was still trying to patch things together in Lagos – 'I agree. Let them go!'

In retrospect, the coming civil war could have been averted if the north had indeed been allowed to go its own way at that moment, but things were held together by Gowon's insistence that Nigeria must remain whole. Coupled with the threatened loss of Western aid, the mutineers dropped secession from their list of demands; next to follow was the task of selecting a new military leader of an extremely troubled Nigeria.

Ojukwu argued that as Ironsi's fate had not yet been uncovered, the next logical leader should be Brigadier Odungipe. In reality, Gowon and many of the mutineers knew that Ironsi had already been murdered, but this was not disclosed to the public for six more months. Sir Ibrahim Kashim, the former Governor of the north, was of the view that it would be tantamount to stupidity for the north to hand back executive power to the south 'on a platter'. If that happened, he said, retribution against northern troops who had committed the killings in the second military uprising would certainly follow.

Many of the mutineers made no secret of their contempt for Ogundipe's rank. Indeed, many had been infuriated after discovering that he had been the one to send in troops and armour attached to the Lagos Garrison Organisation (LGO) in a bid recapture Ikeja Airport (see the author's involvement on the fringes of that skirmish in Chapter 1). They also rejected the next in seniority: Commodore Joseph Wey of the Nigerian Navy (like Ogundipe, also a southerner). Wey felt the tide of northern disdain pressing on him and ultimately declared that: 'If they [northern soldiers] cannot take orders from an army officer, they will not take it from a naval officer.'

Infuriated by northern impertinence, Ogundipe finally absolved himself from consideration. 'It is not in the nature of officers with my upbringing to want to interfere in politics,' he later declared with a characteristic air of resignation. 'We are taught to be good soldiers – not politicians.'

The next most obvious choice was Gowon. Ojukwu, at 32, was a good year older than his army colleague and also his senior in rank – and it was to be expected that he might have been upset by the decision. He called Gowon shortly afterwards to ask him what he intended to do. Gowon replied tersely that he and a cabinet of northerners would 'stay in Lagos and take over the running of the country.'

Ojukwu started to protest, but was cut short by Gowon, who told him directly: 'Well, that's what my boys want – and they're going to get it.'

With all the killings of his people, Ojukwu's patience was limited. Using Enugu's radio station, he framed a public challenge of Gowon's authority. If Ironsi was dead, he argued, then Brigadier

International media reports – including a major report in the American magazine *Life*, which was distinctly biased towards the secessionists – did not make Gowon's job any easier.

Ogundipe would be legally next in line to succeed him. The future rebel Biafran leader also pointed out that only the mutineers and 'their northern supporters had been consulted in the formation of the 'New Government', and that was hardly the act of an impartial state… in spite of the fact that the only representations made at these ceasefire negotiations were those of the rebels.'

Ojukwu continued: '… it was agreed to accept those terms to stop further killing. I now consider that the next step will be to open negotiations at the appropriate level to allow further sections of the Nigerian people to express their views.'

Clearly, Ojukwu was determined to reject Gowon's leadership, but for his part – and without answering Ojukwu's charges – Gowon began setting up a residence for himself at the Dodan Barracks (the former residence of the Nigerian Minister of Defence).

A day later, the bodies of Ironsi and his colleague, Fajuyi, were declared found adjacent to the Iwo Road near Ibadan – and the first public images of the dead Ironsi stunned southerners (especially the Ibo people). The two men were initially buried at the Ibadan Cemetery, but in early 1967 were reinterred at their hometowns with full honours. Many in the government hoped that the memories of summer would be buried along with the dead, but – as we now know – that was not the case.

To many international observers, Gowon was a bold new face in African politics. On the same day that Ironsi's death had been announced, Gowon pulled together 60 correspondents for a press meeting at National Hall – home to the original Nigerian 'Westminster-style' parliamentary sessions before the coups. In this briefing, he acknowledged the release of several political prisoners from the Action Group, including that of Chief Awolowo – appearing progressive, but making no mention that Ironsi had actually sanctioned these releases before his death. This display of deference to civilian rule was, however, blunted by Gowon's vague responses over when he intended to return the government back to civilians. Still, Gowon represented the picture of optimism. Only 31 years old, he was Africa's youngest Head of State.

'I believe there is nothing impossible for a young man to do if he possessed sense and a willingness to accept advice,' he told the reporters. 'Look at the inspiration we have of President John F. Kennedy. People said he was too young, but in his three brief years as America's President, he gave us something the world will always remember' – but Gowon was also quick to repeat his opinion that 'unitary government has failed here when put to the test.'

While this was welcomed in the north, in the south, leaders were more concerned with the continuing violence and harassment of easterners (despite Gowon's insistence that a good measure of control had been established). By now, Ojukwu had reached the conclusion that although he disputed Gowon's rise to power, he would try to co-operate with the new regime in order to keep the peace. Publicly, at least, he made an effort to commend Gowon. Speaking to reporters on 9 August he told them that 'there must be no more bloodbaths,' and that Gowon had personally intervened just days before in saving eight Ibo soldiers who were to be executed by Hausa troops.

'This is an important gesture of good faith,' Ojukwu declared. 'We are on the phone all the time. When he first called, [on] the day of the mutiny, Gowon wept…'

Many easterners who had escaped southwards on foot had spoken glowingly of Gowon's moderate attitudes – and Ojukwu was publicly thankful to Gowon for not categorising the escaped men as 'deserters'. Gowon had even put the men on 'leave status with full pay'. Ojukwu was also hopeful that all his tribespeople in the army would be repatriated, who could then be used to form a new eastern army battalion. This betrayed his own belief in separation – if not outright independence.

As Ojukwu said: 'I grieve for the failure of national unity, which we in the army tried so hard to forge – but we did fail and we have to face it.'

At a subsequent conference, attended by 26 prominent Nigerians, the east proposed a loose association of states with autonomous governance.

As Ojukwu had himself said three months earlier: 'It is better that we move slightly apart and survive. It is much worse that we move closer and perish in the collision.'

For his part, Yakubu Gowon put forward four options: a Federal system with a strong central government; a Federal system with a weak central government; a Confederation of independent states; or 'an entirely new arrangement of association most particular to Nigeria, which has not yet found its way into a political dictionary.'

By now it was clear that Colonel Gowon was being both supported and briefed by the British High Commission in Lagos. Many of his views concur with those of Whitehall in this period – the Americans clearly following suit. The north appeared to lean towards a Confederation, and even proposed the model of the East African Common Services Organization which, until then, was working quite well, though it was soon to fragment.

Nigeria's General Yakubu Gowon addressing the media in Lagos during the war.

'Recent events have shown that for Nigerian leaders to try and build a future for the country on rigid political ideology will be unrealistic and disastrous,' a Northern delegation put forward.

'We have pretended for too long that there are no differences between the peoples of this country. The hard fact which we must honestly accept as of paramount importance in the Nigerian experiment – especially for the future – is that we are different peoples brought together by recent accidents of history. To pretend otherwise would be folly.'

The north even requested that a clause be written into the new constitution that would allow 'any member state of the Union… to secede completely and unilaterally from the Union and to make arrangements for co-operation with the other members of the Union in such a manner as they be severally or individually deem fit.'

For once, both the west and east agreed with the north on the necessity for a four-state Confederation – perhaps even a Commonwealth of four independent nations (as proposed by the west). The only dissenter was the mid-west, which wished to continue in a Federation, but as the mid-west had the least amount of political clout it seemed that Nigeria was destined for its new incarnation as a Confederation.

Gowon was openly critical of such a development and called on the northern delegation to reconsider. Under this pressure from the newly-ensconced Head of State, the delegates ultimately called for an adjournment of the proceedings. When the conference resumed a few days later, a complete about-face to northern policy emerged. This abrupt change was what Walter Schwarz – one of the most prescient Western observers of Nigerian politics – later termed 'A Third Coup'. As Schwarz stated, the north was now calling for a strong, central government and even forwarded an endorsement of the creation of new states to minimise the threat of secession. Under stern pressure from Gowon, the north's delegates also categorically rejected a regionalisation of the armed forces. Pressure from the British Government could also have been exerted to prevent the disintegration of the Federation, but when Gowon declared publicly on 12 September that: '… after six years of independence, we seem further away from national unity', he'd made his most accurate assessment to date.

In anticipation of eastern secession, Gowon moved quickly to weaken the support base of the region by decreeing the creation of a dozen new states to replace the four regions. Six of these contained minority groups that had demanded state creation since the 1950s. Gowon rightly calculated that the eastern minorities would not actively support the Ibos, given the prospect of having their own states if the secession effort were defeated; many of the Federal troops who fought the civil war were members of minority groups.

The war lasted 30 months and ended in January 1970. In accepting Biafra's unconditional ceasefire, Gowon declared that there would be no victor and no vanquished. In this spirit, the years afterwards were declared to be a period of rehabilitation, reconstruction and reconciliation. The oil-price boom, which began as a result of the high price of crude oil (the country's major revenue earner) in the world market in 1973, increased the Federal Government's ability to undertake these tasks.

One of General Gowon's off-the-cuff comments that would come back to haunt him after the war was that: '… my heart bleeds to see that [film] clip with those *kwashiorkor*-stricken children. God knows how much effort I made to send food to those children, but it was sabotaged by propaganda that the Federal troops had poisoned the food.'

In view of the million innocents who died in that horrific conflict, the majority starved to death; it was uncalled for and, if not out of character, symptomatic of the kind of duplicity that emanated from both sides before, during and after the war.

On 19 July 1975 – a little more than five years after the Biafran War ended – while General Yakubu Gowon was in Uganda attending an Organisation of African Unity summit meeting with fellow heads of state, the army removed him from power in a bloodless coup (one of several to follow). He was exiled to Britain and stripped of his rank for allegedly participating in the assassination of his successor – northern military officer General Murtala Muhammed – in 1976 (after whom Nigeria's main Lagos airport – at Ikeja – is now named).

His period in limbo did not last long: following his studies at Warwick University, he was eventually declared innocent by a Nigerian court; returned to his original rank; and is today regarded as one of the country's respected senior citizens.

15

How Washington Assessed Nigeria's Civil War

By 1969 it had become clear to everybody involved in this bloody struggle that – simply put – Biafra would never be able to hold out indefinitely. It was only a question of time (and who knew how many more lives lost) before the rebel enclave collapsed. It was not only Nigeria's preponderant manpower that had taken effect, but Ojukwu's inability to get enough guns, ammunition and, most important of all, food, to maintain the status quo. In a word, Biafra was starving.

Because of Nigeria's significant oil potential, America's CIA had a vested interest in the outcome of this war. Langley's best brains and the most astute analysts and investigators were delegated to examine every detail that pertained to the conflict in this divisive West African country.

It was not surprising that Ray Cline was involved: a regular agency man, he had, eight years before – as the Head of the Directorate of Intelligence (the CIA's analytical branch) – been among those who had concluded that the Russians had installed offensive-missile bases in Cuba. Cline carried the news to President John F. Kennedy and, as a consequence of this and other perspicacious assessments that were proved right, was among the most highly regarded intelligence people in the United States.

It was an appropriate choice: as the *New York Times* said in his obituary notice some years later, Ray Cline 'made his strongest mark at the CIA as a thinker, a ruminator, a worrier. As chief of the agency's staff on the Sino-Soviet Bloc from 1953 to 1957, he accurately predicted that Beijing and Moscow would go their separate ways'.

Cline had a somewhat colourful history of examining the world's trouble-spots. As the *Times* pointed out, he was an archetype of the young men who joined the agency in its infancy: high school football captain, Harvard man and wartime operative in the OSS (the nation's chief intelligence agency in World War II) – so it was perhaps not at all surprising that he should have turned his attention to Nigeria.

I never met Ray Cline, but our paths did cross. His daughter, Sibyl, was married to my good friend, Bob MacKenzie who, as a mercenary with the rank of Colonel, ended up in command of one of the more active battalions in the war against Foday Sankoh's rebels in Sierra Leone; that came almost 30 years after the Biafran debacle had ended.

Bob was killed in his very first action against a Revolutionary United Front (RUF) ambush group at Mile 91 on the road out of Freetown. Wounded, he was taken prisoner; tortured; killed; and then parts of his body – including his heart, because he was regarded by these barbarians as an extremely brave fighter – eaten. It was an ignominious end to this fine soldier, who had been badly wounded in Vietnam, where he was left with a withered arm. Undeterred, he joined the

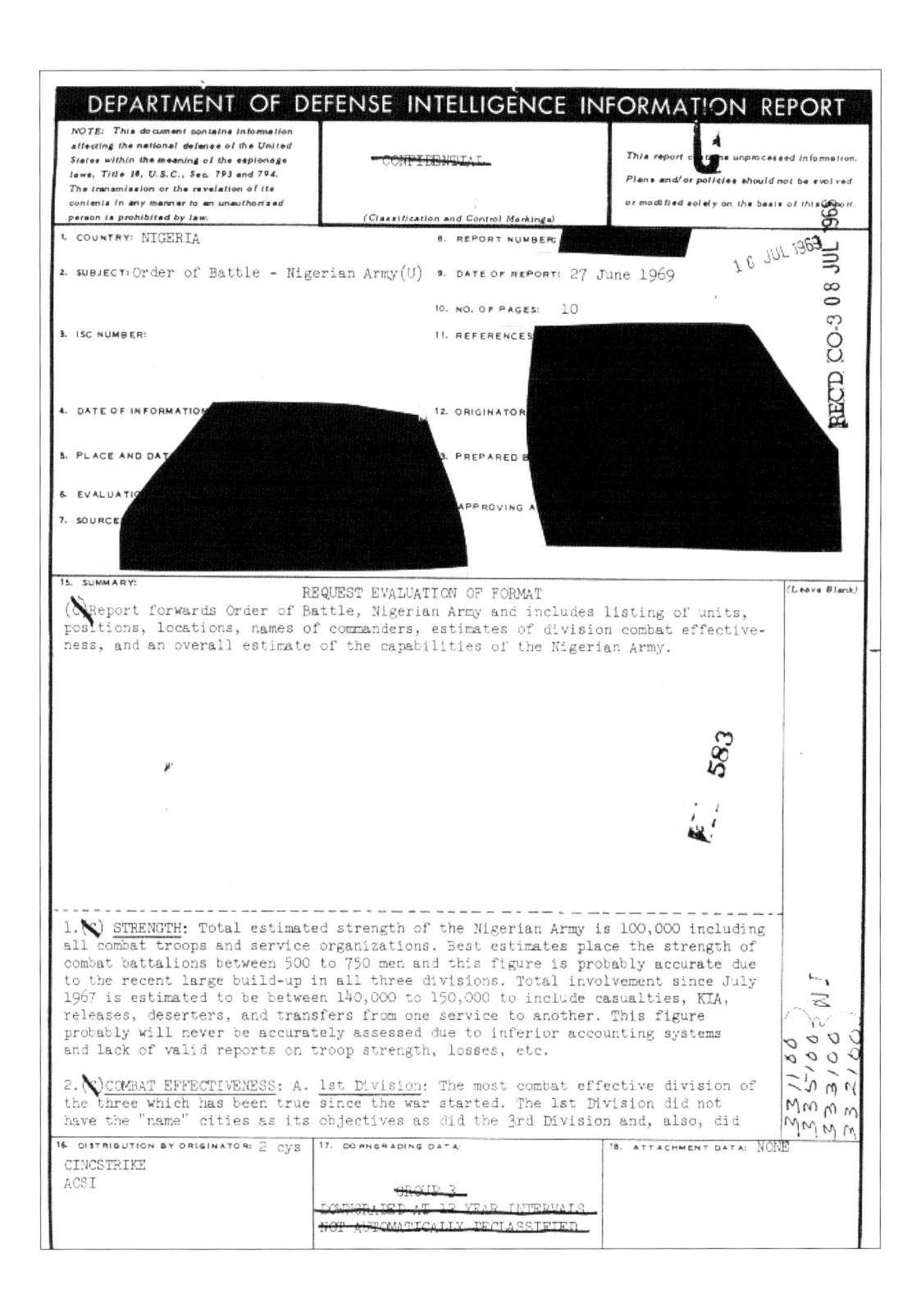

DEPARTMENT OF DEFENSE INTELLIGENCE INFORMATION REPORT

NOTE: This document contains information affecting the national defense of the United States within the meaning of the espionage laws, Title 18, U.S.C., Sec. 793 and 794. The transmission or the revelation of its contents in any manner to an unauthorized person is prohibited by law.

~~CONFIDENTIAL~~

(Classification and Control Markings)

This report contains unprocessed information. Plans and/or policies should not be evolved or modified solely on the basis of this report.

1. COUNTRY: NIGERIA
2. SUBJECT: Order of Battle - Nigerian Army (U)
3. ISC NUMBER:
4. DATE OF INFORMATION
5. PLACE AND DATE
6. EVALUATION
7. SOURCE
8. REPORT NUMBER:
9. DATE OF REPORT: 27 June 1969
10. NO. OF PAGES: 10
11. REFERENCES
12. ORIGINATOR
13. PREPARED BY
14. APPROVING A

15. SUMMARY:

REQUEST EVALUATION OF FORMAT

Report forwards Order of Battle, Nigerian Army and includes listing of units, positions, locations, names of commanders, estimates of division combat effectiveness, and an overall estimate of the capabilities of the Nigerian Army.

1. (C) STRENGTH: Total estimated strength of the Nigerian Army is 100,000 including all combat troops and service organizations. Best estimates place the strength of combat battalions between 500 to 750 men and this figure is probably accurate due to the recent large build-up in all three divisions. Total involvement since July 1967 is estimated to be between 140,000 to 150,000 to include casualties, KIA, releases, deserters, and transfers from one service to another. This figure probably will never be accurately assessed due to inferior accounting systems and lack of valid reports on troop strength, losses, etc.

2. (C) COMBAT EFFECTIVENESS: A. 1st Division: The most combat effective division of the three which has been true since the war started. The 1st Division did not have the "name" cities as its objectives as did the 3rd Division and, also, did

16. DISTRIBUTION BY ORIGINATOR: 2 cys
CINCSTRIKE
ACSI

17. DOWNGRADING DATA:
~~GROUP 3~~
~~DOWNGRADED AT 12 YEAR INTERVALS~~
~~NOT AUTOMATICALLY DECLASSIFIED~~

18. ATTACHMENT DATA: NONE

not have a "newspaper reporters dream" for a division commander, ▮▮▮ who have visited 1 Division have always stated that this division appeared to possess some semblance of a military unit in that there was some visible evidence of discipline and control. Colonel SHUWA now is the most seasoned division commander and apparently Lagos shares the high opinion of him illustrated by the recent re-adjustment of boundaries with 2d Division. The troop strength is at an all time high and is probably close to a total of 30,000 troops. Recent reports from ▮▮▮ who have visited 1 Division state that troops are seen in large numbers everywhere and are well equipped with both arms and ammunition. A large number of SHUWA's troops are from the inept, ill-led 2d Division and it will take time and patience to mold these units into capable, combat organizations. Of interest was SHUWA's reply to a question recently asked by ▮▮▮ ▮▮▮ as to the combat capability of soldiers from different tribes. He stated that the Hausa-Fulani soldier was very good in the offense; however, the Yoruba soldier was much better in the defense and that he was in the process of mixing up the tribal composition of his battalions. This is the initial insight into capabilities by tribe and also indicates that battalions have had a definite preponderance of personnel from one geographic section of the country. SHUWA has recently stated again his displeasure at the lack of guidance and control from Lagos regarding concerted actions with the other divisions. His wrath for the 3d Division is obvious and he has stated that his forward battalions would have attacked 3d Division troops if they had been successful in their ill-fated attempt to earn a share of the publicity during the fall of Umuahia. Although it was announced formerly by the government and in the press, SHUWA has apparently been successful in retaining command of his division with Colonel I. D. BISALLA remaining at Supreme Headquarters as the Military Secretary. He openly admits his serious shortage of leadership and is upset at the disparity in the number of Lieutenant Colonels in his division as compared with the 3d Division. One can readily agree with this comment when lieutenants are commanding battalions.

B. 2d Division: This "group" of people who are attired in soldiers' uniforms is perhaps the most inefficient, inept, poorly-led organization to have ever been called a military unit. This feeling is obviously shared by the Lagos high command illustrated by the recent change in commanders and reduction in mission, capability and responsibility of the 2d Division. It should be pointed out that the rebel threat in the Mid-Western State west of the River Niger also has had a part in the readjustment of division boundaries and responsibilities. Tales of this divisions' shortcomings are many and are typified and include officers bribing troops with money to go to the front, units abandoning their posts, and the vast consumption rate of "Star Beer" by the personnel of this division. The mission of 2 Division is security of the Mid-Western State based on recent rebel actions in that area. Whether the recently appointed division commander, Colonel JALO, is able to improve the effectiveness of this unit remains to be seen.

C. 3rd Division: Reports ▮▮▮ say that the changes for the good are readily apparent in this division since the arrival of Colonel OBASANJO and departure of Colonel ADEKUNLE. The previous commander left the division in such a poor state that it probably will be some time before any degree of combat effectiveness is attained. LTC Godwin ALLY has been given command of 1 Sector, removed from his position as second in command of the division; however, he still goes by the title of Chief of Staff and will probably be a cross for OBASANJO to bear for the time to come. Reports indicate that the last few months of ADEKUNLE's tenure as division commander created havoc with what was once a fairly effective fighting organization. ▮▮▮ in the last two weeks have presented some insight into the disastrous happenings at Owerri and Aba. Evidently ADEKUNLE took the 6-7,000 troops provided by Lagos for the relief of the surrounded 16th Brigade at Owerri, formed a new brigade, and used this new brigade in an attempt to gain some of the publicity from the capture of Umuahia. This new brigade was all but decimated (reports vary but go as high as 5,000 troops killed) by the rebels at Aba. As a result of this attempt to get his name in the press, the 16th Brigade at Owerri was left to fight its way out with a resultant high casualty rate. ▮▮▮ state that ADEKUNLE made a deal with the rebels (arms and ammunition) to get the 16th Brigade out of Owerri. Prior to ADEKUNLE's reassignment, two of the 3d Divisions brigade commanders were in

Two extracts from a restricted American Intelligence report on Nigeria's 'Order of Battle', which today allows a fascinating insight into how the United States viewed the war.

Rhodesian Army as a mercenary and went on to serve with distinction in Rhodesia's Special Air Service – after which he went to the Transkei with Ron Reid-Daly, who had originally founded and commanded the Selous Scouts.

Being CIA, Bob had covered a lot of other insurrections – including a lengthy training spell for irregular fighters involved in the war in the Balkans, as well as involvement in Mozambique's civil war against Renamo, but it was 'Uncle Ron' that blew MacKenzie's cover while he served under him in the Transkei. That, as they say, is a story for another day – though Reid-Daly did tell me afterwards (when I spent time at his house in Dorries Road, south of Simonstown) that once he had accosted him about his 'double role' as an intelligence operative for the Americans, Bob came to him the following day with a request: he said he had to rush back home because one of his children had been hurt in a car accident. It was nonsense, of course, and MacKenzie took the gap.

The last time I saw the lovely Sibyl was at Bob's memorial service, which was held in the chapel at the Coronado Amphibious Base across the bay from San Diego. It was a surprisingly well-attended affair, with people coming in from around the world to pay tribute to a brave man. Many of those present were familiar faces like Colonel Robert K. Brown – the owner and publisher of *Soldier of Fortune* magazine – and author Jim Morris. Also in the party was Mike Borlace, who had worked with Bob for a time in Rhodesia before he was arrested in Lusaka, Zambia, and jailed on charges of espionage. There were also several who spoke to nobody; Langley's unobtrusive few paying special tribute to a fine colleague.

Like her Dad, Sibyl was characteristically quiet-spoken, so she surprised me when she voiced the opinion that in the Sierra Leone ambush at Mile 91, Bob had been killed by his own men. She felt that her husband was simply too streetwise to be taken by surprise by a bunch of rookies, but he was and, in the process, he was killed – something I deal with in great detail in Chapter 19 in *War Dog*.[1]

Consequently, when I chanced upon Ray Cline's final Biafra report for the CIA – dated 14 November 1969 – it was of more than a passing interest because it signified the level of involvement that Washington had in what was largely a tribal conflict in West Africa. His assessment was interesting for three more reasons: the nature of its content; the fact that he had reached the conclusions that he did less than two months before Biafra was vanquished; and the fact that it was probably the last project he ever handled before finally leaving the CIA, which he did months later.

The document, compact and precise, makes for interesting reading – though by then, he must have known that he was stating the obvious (even though it is doubtful that even Ray Cline could have sensed that the war in Biafra would end so soon).

The contents of this document are reproduced in full:

> To: The Secretary
> Through: S/S
> From: INR – Ray S. Cline
>
> Subject: NIGERIA-BIAFRA: New Weapons May Delay Peace Talks
>
> Biafra has received new aircraft that will extend significantly the striking range of its air force. Nigeria in turn has new long-range guns that increase its chances of destroying the principal Biafran airfield. Both sides probably will intensify their military activity to exploit these new

---

[1] Venter, *War Dog* (4th edition, 2008); Chapter 19 – 'An American Warrior Dies in Africa', pp. 445-460.

weapons. While they are doing so, there will be less desire by either to undertake serious peace talks.

Planes for Biafra. Since May 1969 the Biafran air force has been carrying out attacks on Nigerian targets, particularly oil installations, with its Swedish-designed, single engine 'Minicon' aircraft, of which it presently has 11.

Although these attacks have not altered the military balance, they have led to a decrease in Nigerian petroleum production, and shown Nigeria's vulnerability to offensive air action. In early November 1969 Biafra took delivery of two T-6 [Harvard] aircraft. North American Aviation Inc. built over 15,000 of these planes during World War II for use as trainers. The Biafran models, which may have been acquired from the French, are fitted with weapon mounts for combat. Their normal operating range is about 870 miles.

Five more Biafran T-6s are in various stages of readiness outside the enclave. In addition, one British-built Gloster Meteor jet fighter is believed to be in Bissau, Portuguese Guinea, awaiting delivery to a point from which it can be used against Nigeria.

Guns for Nigeria. Nigeria has received 24 Soviet-made 122 mm field pieces having a range of 13 miles. Some of them are assembled and Nigerian crews are being trained. If the Nigerians can bring these guns close enough to targets in Biafra, they might be able to do more damage with them than they have with the 20-25 Soviet jet aircraft they now have in operating condition.

New Offensives for Both. Biafra apparently has already used its T-6s in action against Port Harcourt. If they are able to keep them flying, the Biafran authorities will almost certainly use these aircraft to attack Nigerian airfields. Oil installations, many of which are beyond the range of the 'Minicons', will also be targets. Every target of military significance in Nigeria is within range of the T-s, including Lagos. Biafran authorities have threatened to bomb civilian targets in retaliation against Nigerian Air Force raids.

The Federal Military Government is supposedly preparing an offensive intended to put its new field guns within range of the principal Biafran airport of Uli. The Federal First Division has as its objectives Nnewi, to the north of Uli, and Orlu, to the east. The Third Division's objective is Oguta to the south. These three points are all within 13 miles of Uli. Biafran attacks on the southern front might delay the Third Division's offensive. (See map.)

The Nigerian Air Force will probably give priority to the destruction of the T-6s. If they fail in this effort, as they have in their attempts to shoot down the 'Minicons', they might in frustration endeavor to destroy another unauthorized relief plane.

Negotiation Prospects Unchanged. Continuing and determined efforts by several nations are under way to bring the belligerents to the negotiating table, but it is not likely that either side will negotiate seriously until it is hurt sufficiently to force concessions or loses confidence in its longer range military position.

Other government bodies in the American capital had their views on the war. The report below encapsulates the views of the National Security Council and was delivered in February 1969 – almost a year before hostilities ceased:

NATIONAL SECURITY COUNCIL BRIEFING ON NIGERIA

THE WAR:

The Nigerian Federation united three major ethnic groups and about 250 smaller ones. From British colonial tutelage, it developed reasonably workable political cohesion and decidedly promising economic prospects through five years of independence. But the corruption and indecisiveness of first generation politicians triggered a coup in 1966 by young army officers, mostly Ibos from Eastern Nigeria. The tribal implications of that coup triggered in turn a sequence of assassinations, tribal atrocities and polarization culminating in Eastern Nigeria's secession as 'Biafra' and the outbreak of war 19 months ago. The war is now stalemated with Federal Military Government (FMG) troops surrounding a 7,000 square mile Biafran enclave, or about a quarter the 30,000 square miles the rebels began with. The enclave contains 5 to 7 million people. Despite Federal military superiority in men and materiel, there is very little prospect that either side, by itself, can win militarily in the next six months unless Biafra's arms supply is cut off. The two sides are fighting a total war and subordinate humanitarian to political objectives. Moreover, mutual tribal enmities complicate and embitter the political issues.

FEDERAL MILITARY GOVERNMENT:

General Gowon leads a fragile, relatively moderate and regionally balanced coalition, determined to preserve national unity and convinced that rebel success would tear apart the country. The military stalemate accentuates inner stresses and strains (tax riots, tribal dissidence, increasing war-weariness), but the common interest nevertheless continues to hold the coalition together. In the eyes of the Nigerian public, the international (predominantly white) relief operation helps to keep the rebellion alive through food deliveries and the cover its relief flights provide for arms flights. There is some popular sentiment for expelling it on the Federal side, but the FMG, conscious of international implications and its own need, has thus far co-operated reasonably well with the relief efforts in its own area. It has also reluctantly acquiesced in the night relief flights into Biafra. Yet mounting frustration and incipient xenophobia threaten to make the relief effort a scapegoat for FMG military failure. There are some on the Federal side who would not be averse to winning by starvation.

BIAFRA:

Ojukwu has the strong support of a people (1) whose' morale appears high, (2) who are determined to win self-determination or independence, and (3) who are convinced--with some past justification--that unconditional military defeat by the Federal forces could mean genocide. The Biafran leaders have successfully exploited the issue of starvation to win political sympathy abroad. They believe time is on their side and that either (a) the FMG coalition will collapse or (b) outside sympathy for their plight will bring about a solution favorable to them.

NEGOTIATING POSITIONS:

The FMG insists on one Nigeria and has announced guarantees for the survival of the Ibos and their integration into national life. The present government is unlikely to survive a truce or an unconditional cease-fire which only prolongs rebellion. For its part, Biafra insists her sovereignty is not negotiable and dismisses the FMG offer of guarantees as not credible. It proposes an unconditional cease-fire that would facilitate relief measures. In short, the positions of the two sides appear irreconcilable.

THE ISSUE OF GENOCIDE:
If the FMG overruns Biafra, at least some excesses against the Ibos are inevitable. However, the reports of the international observers have stated that there is no evidence that the FMG is pursuing a policy of genocide. But there are historical reasons (perhaps as many as 30,000 Ibos slaughtered in Northern Nigeria in 1966 before the civil war began) for Ibo fears. Moreover, uncertainties regarding rank and file discipline in the Federal army qualifies FMG official assurances and creates a potential for undisciplined excesses if the war is concluded by military means.

THE POLITICS OF RELIEF:
About two million people in Biafra depend on night-time airlifts operated by the religious voluntary agencies from the Portuguese island of São Tomé and by the ICRC (Red Cross) from, until very recently, the island of Fernando Pó, and now from Cotonou, Dahomey. Deliveries could be increased substantially by either daylight flights or a surface corridor into Biafra. The FMG opposition to night flights, in which it has acquiesced in the past, is hardening because of arms flights tailgating relief planes into Biafra for protection. It has endorsed the principle of both daylight flights and a land corridor into Biafra with outside supervision to avoid military violation by either party. But it insists that: (a) the relief airlift should be inspected for arms and (b) the land corridor should not interfere with military operations. FMG suspicions of all foreign relief agencies are growing. It prefers that all international relief to Biafra be channeled through Nigerian territory.

Biafra refuses daytime flights into its one working airstrip for fear FMG aircraft will tailgate to the airfield. Biafra also values the protection given night-time arms flights by the intermix with relief flights which the FMG is either reluctant or unable to interdict. It has thus far opposed (or countered with proposals unacceptable to the FMG) every land corridor proposed by the FMG on the grounds that it would be militarily exploited by the FMG and that the food might be poisoned.

Religious voluntary agencies (some U.S.-some European) have little or no leverage on the FMG because of the latter's belief that their sympathies are with the Biafrans, among whom the percentage of Christians is higher than in the rest of Nigeria. They have been reluctant to press the Biafrans to accept daylight flights or corridors because (a) their airlift from São Tomé is operating well and they do not want to jeopardize it; and (b) some of the participants, at least, share the view of the Biafran leadership that such arrangements would work to the political or military disadvantage of Biafra.

INVOLVEMENT OF OTHER POWERS:
The British back the FMG with non-sophisticated arms sales. But Wilson is under heavy parliamentary and public pressure to stop. They have tried often and in vain to get serious negotiations started. The British will probably continue cautious support of the FMG, but will want to appear active diplomatically to mitigate parliamentary criticism. They have only marginal leverage with the FMG despite their arms supply--virtually none with the Biafrans.

The Soviets became major arms suppliers to the FMG at the outset of the war when the US embargoed arms to both sides and the British hesitated.* The FMG gives frequent assurances that the Soviet involvement is only a matter of wartime necessity and portends no political realignment of Nigeria's traditional pro-Western stance. We have no evidence that the FMG has thus far granted any significant political concessions in return for Soviet arms. However, Soviet prestige and acceptance has increased. Soviet intentions are unclear. They probably consider Nigeria a target of opportunity to extend their influence at Western expense and relatively little cost to themselves. Whether requested or not, they have not gone beyond the provision of military equipment, including aircraft and the training of pilots. Although disappointed and perhaps somewhat embarrassed--at slow FMG military progress, they appear willing to continue their support in the belief that prolonged fighting and FMG frustrations will increase the political value of their help.

The French decision to supply arms clandestinely to Biafra probably saved the rebellion when it appeared near defeat last summer and continues to sustain it. De Gaulle's motives are mixed, but he is probably influenced by the possibility of the breaking up of an Anglophone federation which could have exerted a powerful influence in a West Africa in which French interests are so strong. There are also indications that French oil interests are supporting Biafra in the hope of acquiring British and American concessions in the Federally-held but Biafran-claimed minority coastal areas. So far, the French have stopped short of outright recognition. They deny giving arms. We simply do not know how far the French are prepared to go in support of Biafran independence.

The Africans see Nigeria's situation as a manifestation of the problem facing most governments on a continent where colonial boundaries enclosed, usually arbitrarily, almost 2,000 ethnic groups in 41 states. In the Organisation of African Unity (OAU), all but four members (Ivory Coast, Gabon, Tanzania, Zambia, which recognized Biafra in 1968) support the FMG and regard the civil war as an internal question which should be solved within an African (Organisation of African Unity) frame-work.

DEPARTMENT OF DEFENSE INTELLIGENCE REPORT

ORDER OF BATTLE – NIGERIAN ARMY – 27 June 1969
Summary: Report forwards Order of Battle, Nigerian Army, and includes listing of units, positions, locations, names of commanders, estimates of division combat effectiveness, and an overall estimate of the capabilities of the Nigerian Army.

STRENGTH: Total estimated strength of the Nigerian Army is 100,000 including all combat troops and service organizations. Best estimates place the strength of combat battalions between 500 to 750 men and this figure is probably accurate due to the recent large build-up in all three divisions. Total involvement since July 1967 is estimated to be between 140,000 to 150,000 to include casualties (and killed in action), releases, deserters, and transfers from one service to another. This figure probably will never be accurately assessed due to inferior accounting systems and lack of valid reports on troop strength, losses, etc.

COMBAT EFFECTIVENESS:
1st Division: 'the most combat effective division of the three', which has been true since the war started. The 1st Division did not have the 'name' cities as its objectives as did the 3rd Division and, also, did not have a 'newspaper reporter's dream' for a division commander.

Colonel Shuwa now is the most seasoned division commander and apparently Lagos shares the high opinion of him illustrated by the recent re-adjustment of boundaries with 2nd Division. The troop strength is at an all time high and is probably close to a total of 30,000 troops. Recent reports from (*redacted*) who have visited 1 Division state that troops are seen in large numbers everywhere and are well equipped with both arms and ammunition.

A large number of Shuwa's troops are from the inept, ill-led 2nd Division and it will take time and patience to mold these units into capable, combat organizations. Of interest was Shuwa's reply to a question recently asked by (*redacted*) as to the combat capability of soldiers from different tribes. He stated the Hausa-Fulani soldier was very good in the offense; however the Yoruba soldier was much better in the defense and that he was in the process of mixing up the tribal composition of his battalions.

This is the initial insight in capabilities by tribe and also indicates that battalions have had a definite preponderance of personnel from one geographic section of the country. Shuwa has recently stated again his displeasure at the lack of guidance and control from Lagos regarding concerted actions with the other divisions. His wrath for the 3rd Division is obvious and he has stated that his forward battalions would have attacked 3rd Division troops if they had been successful in their ill-fated attempt to earn a share of the publicity during the fall of Umushia.

Although it was announced formerly by the government and in the press, Shuwa has apparently been successful in retaining command of his division with Colonel ID Bisalla remaining at Supreme Headquarters as the Military Secretary. He openly admits his serious shortage of leadership and is upset at the disparity in the number of Lieutenant Colonels in his division as compared with the 3rd Division. One can readily agree with this comment when lieutenants are commanding battalions.

2nd Division: This 'group' of people who are attired in soldiers' uniforms is perhaps the most inefficient, inept, poorly-led organization to have ever been called a military unit. This feeling is obviously shared by the Lagos High Command illustrated by the recent change in commanders and reduction in mission, capability and responsibility of the 2nd Division.

It should be pointed out that the rebel threat in the Mid-Western State west of the River Niger also has had a part in the readjustment of division boundaries and responsibilities. Tales of this division's shortcomings are many and are typified and include officers bribing troops with money to go to the front, units abandoning their posts, and the vast consumption rate of 'Star Beer' by the personnel of this division.

The mission of 2 Division is security of the Mid-Western state based on recent rebel actions in that area. Whether the recently appointed division commander, Colonel Jalo, is able to improve the effectiveness of this unit remains to be seen.

3rd Division: Reports say the changes for the good are readily apparent in this division since the arrival of Colonel Obasanjo and departure of Colonel Benjamin Adekunle.

The previous commander left the division in such a poor state that it probably will be some time before any degree of combat effectiveness is attained. Lieutenant-Colonel Godwin Ally has been given command of 1 Sector, removed from his position as second in command of the division; however, he still goes by the title of Chief of Staff and will probably be a cross for Obasanjo to bear for the time to come.

Reports indicate that the last few months of Adekunle's tenure as division commander created havoc with what was once a fairly effective fighting organization, (*redacted*) in the last two weeks have presented some insight into the disastrous happenings at Owerri and Aba.

Evidently, Adekunle took the 6-7,000 troops provided by Lagos for the relief of the surrounded 16th Brigade at Owerri, formed a new brigade, and used this new brigade in an attempt to gain some of the publicity from the capture of Umuahia. This new brigade was all but decimated (reports vary but go as high as 5,000 troops killed) by the rebels at Aba.

As a result of this attempt to get his name in the press, the 16th Brigade at Owerri was left to fight its way out with a resultant high casualty rate. Our sources (*redacted*) state that

Adekunle made a deal with the rebels (arms and ammunition) to get the 16th Brigade out of Owerri.

Prior to Adekunle's reassignment, two of the 3 Division's brigade commanders were in Lagos; refused to return to the division and only did so when Colonel Obasanjo assumed command. It is safe to say that if two brigade commanders more or less deserted their units then the enlisted men must have also departed in large numbers.

Overall Effectiveness: Any newly established army that increases ten-fold in a two year period is bound to have serious problems due to the raw material with which it must use for expansion.

Many of the senior, schooled, and experienced officers were lost during the two coups in 1966 and many of the remaining officers of any stature heeded the call of Ojukwu to serve the rebels. The remaining small nucleus of qualified officers in Nigeria directing military operations are continuing to press on with the war but have been unable so far to apply whatever military expertise they do possess to defeat the rebels on the battlefield.

Yesterday's second lieutenant is today's' lieutenant colonel, and today's junior sergeant is tomorrow's second lieutenant in front line divisions. This point is well illustrated by the age and experience of the most effective division commander, Colonel Muhammed Shuwa of 1 Division who is 29 years old and currently has some lieutenants assigned as battalion commanders within his division. (*redacted*) encountered a battalion commander at the front who had attended a military school in the country (*redacted*) and asked the Nigerian officer why he had his battalion strung out in one long line with no defense in depth, reserve, supplementary and alternate positions as he was instructed to do while attending school.

The Nigerian replied that he had attempted to place his troops in tactical positions as he had been instructed; however, when the rebels attacked, the troops in the rear of his forward companies inflicted more casualties on his own men than the enemy did so he now places them all in a line with no one in front of the other. This is but one example of the difficulties encountered by unit commanders.

As the war progresses, the Nigerian Army should become more proficient simply based on the experience they are obtaining. Many officers on pass to Lagos have voiced complaints at having continuous duty at the front; however, there are recent indications of attempts to rotate officers back and replace them with others who have been working in Lagos and other headquarters away from the front.

The war is still being fought during bankers hours where little activity occurs after 1400 hours and no night operations are ever carried out to include the simplest form of night patrolling.

Eight months ago there were reports of line crossing and fraternization between federal and rebel soldiers; however, these reports are now declining although the practice probably still occurs. 'Star Beer', is issued to the troops gratis by the government in true British tradition, apparently is the subsistence mainstay of the Nigerian soldier and, it has been rumored, would increase the combat effectiveness of front line troops 25 percent if discontinued. (*redacted*) reports that there are 'girls in every hooch at the front' and this, too, is indicative of the mild way in which the war is being conducted.

There are indications that communications among the divisions and the Army Headquarters in Lagos are improving. As the two new Division Commanders become more aware of their division's capabilities, coupled with the build-up and reorganization of all three divisions, it is expected that the combat effectiveness of the field units will gradually improve.

16

The Media and Biafra

Journalists who entered Biafra during the 30-month war came from just about everywhere. Called 'scribblers' by some of the Biafran intelligentsia, it was a term of affection rather than of approbation. Because we took the risk of running the Nigerian 'gauntlet' – the air blockade – it was assumed that we were on their side, if only because these were desperate people; they were totally dependent on us to put their case before the world. Either that, or oblivion…

Not everybody who entered the rebel state was regarded as a friend – even though we were all treated even-handedly. Frankly, that was the way that Okjukwu did his thing.

Quite a few of the British reporters who went in did so at the instigation of Whitehall – the prospect often sweetened by financial gain. One of the immediate consequences was that these supposedly objective news-gatherers vociferously opposed both Ojukwu and his rebel country – never mind the starving millions. Their reports made it clear that they rejected the concept of an independent Biafra – and it didn't matter how many lives were lost along the way.

Several of these characters – each one of them under dubious cover – nurtured cleverly-concealed Soviet connections. For most of us faced with the reality – harsh and as totally uncompromising as it was – it was that these were people who were being systematically starved into extinction. While in the enclave, it was happening all around us and could hardly be ignored.

Just about everybody (except the pliable British Government goons) who went into the rebel territory with open minds ended up altering their approach to these issues after a single visit to a camp. There, for the first time, they saw what this war was all about. You could hardly ignore hundreds – sometimes thousands – of starving children who though being helped by aid groups, were struggling to survive from one day to the next. The lucky ones made it onto the nightly flights to Gabon or São Tomé, where Caritas had set up reception and feeding camps (the biggest being in Libreville at *Kilometre Onze*).

What happened next was that journalistic ethics simply went out the window. After a week or two in this appalling environment, with our minds skewered by the horrific reality of what was plainly an extraordinary human disaster, most of the hacks had had enough and asked to go home. The majority of journalists who spent time in Biafra were very different people afterwards, as I suppose are those who survive a visit to Aleppo today. For many otherwise unbiased, rational and thinking scribes, it was a 180° about-turn on principles – never mind morals – and quite a few came to identify with the terrible tragedy that had emerged in West Africa.

It disturbs greatly that exactly the same happened to me while covering the civil war in Sierra Leone three decades later. I spent an afternoon at the Murray Town amputee camp on Freetown's outskirts, but revolted by what had been done to some of the victims, I opted out after the fourth or fifth child was brought to me. Some were without legs and others with no arms. One little girl of about 18 months had had her arm chopped off by one of Foday Sankoh's drug-crazed juvenile combatants, who, it was said, was about 13 at the time[1] – yet some of these psychos are today being feted in the West because they 'survived the horrors of war'. One even went on to write a best-seller of his experiences and made a lot of money from the proceeds, but nobody mentions their victims.

In Biafra, for the majority of us transients – including several British Parliamentarians and people like *Time* magazine's James Wilde; Antony Terry and Susanne Cronje of *The Times*; veteran Africanist Richard Hall (who, like me, occasionally wrote for Tom Stacy's Gemini News Service, but was then doing his thing for the *Guardian*); as well as Walter Partington of the *Daily Express* – it took effort, risk and time to become aware of this escalating disaster. The British author John de St Jorre, then an *Observer* journalist (who went on to write a book about the conflict)[2], should also be mentioned in this context because his efforts in creating an awareness of what was going on was well beyond the norm.

Some of these individuals were present when an Ilyushin-28, flown by an Egyptian pilot for the Nigerian Air Force, dropped his bombs on the market town of Aba and killed 80 people – leaving more than 100 wounded (many of whom subsequently succumbed). It was an atrocious event because there was hardly anybody in uniform around – and the journalists (the group included Hall, Partington and Norman Kirkham of the *Daily Telegraph*) left little to the imagination of their readers, which resulted in the first real wave of public consciousness of what was then going on in West Africa.

Others who arrived subsequently were the *Sun*'s Michael Leapman; Stanley Meisner, who was the Africa correspondent for the *Los Angeles Times*; and scores more – very few of them not experiencing events that can best be described as 'cathartic'. Michael Leapman's reports were powerful enough to have resulted in a not-so-subtle government-orchestrated campaign against him and whatever he reported about what was going on in the rebel state at the time. In a letter to *The Times*, Leapman related how a Commonwealth official had taken the liberty of phoning the assistant editor of a major provincial newspaper to warn him against believing what Leapman – after three visits to Biafra and one to Nigeria – had reported. He also disclosed that there had been a very subtle campaign (in British press circles) that he was in the pay of the Biafrans, which was twaddle.

Other scribes were also attacked, with some labelled 'duplicitous' – and several more, including Forsyth, accused of being 'corrupt' and in the pay of the rebels, which was rubbish. Decades after that war ended, you only have to spend a short while with Freddie Forsyth before he lets loose – sometimes vituperatively on the subject, as he did among my friends when he stayed over with us in Washington State while conducting research for *The Afghan*. He is also outspoken about these episodes in his excellent book *The Biafra Story*, which has gone into several editions both in the UK and the United States.[3]

Forsyth takes strong issue against the role of the supposedly neutral BBC – especially its external service – which was to become a powerful pro-Nigerian and anti-Biafran lobbying medium for the duration of the war. He had been working for the BBC in West Africa – and when the supposedly august news service started going overboard on behalf of Lagos, he resigned. As he relates, editorial-type comments were liberally infused with what were supposed to be factual news reports from Lagos – and within a short time, most (white and black) living in Biafra and tuning in

---

1 I report at length on this issue in my book on the mercenary war in Sierra Leone – especially the brutalities meted out by the rebels (see Chapter 3 in *War Dog*).
2 de St Jorre, John, *The Brothers War: Biafra and Nigeria* (Boston: Houghton Mifflin Company, 1972).
3 Forsyth, *The Biafra Story* (reprinted 2011).

nightly to the BBC became convinced that there existed a strong pro-Nigerian bias in the coverage of these events.

Forsyth goes on:

> Graphic accounts were related of things alleged to have happened in the heart of Biafra which had not happened, towns were described as having fallen to Nigerian troops long before the Nigerian soldiers actually entered them and some far-fetched speculation was attempted, apparently on the basis of little more than gossip or over-optimistic hopes of the Nigerian authorities.
>
> For example, there was speculation after Colonel Ojukwu (a devout Roman Catholic) had gone into a week's Lenten retreat in 1968 that he had fled the country or been the victim of a coup…

So much of it was plain stupid – and certainly, that kind of professional lassitude was no credit to the (until then) outstandingly even-handed reputation of the British Broadcasting Corporation.

There were exceptions: *The Times* in London kept its reputation relatively unsullied by almost always reporting facts and not hearsay or propaganda that emanated from either of the belligerents. Among the most objective commentators working for that paper was Michael Wolfers – a British Marxist of the *soixante-huitard* left – who I got to know quite well in the early days. We even attended an Organisation of African Unity summit together in Addis Ababa – supping off gold-plated plates and drinking more Tej than was good for us on the last night of that lavishly ostentatious event. I attended as the correspondent of Cape Town's *Die Burger* – an Afrikaans newspaper – and, as a consequence, was kept under heavy surveillance by the Ethiopian security police for the duration; I was even hauled in for questioning at one stage.

Forsyth concurred with regard to *The Times* keeping its reports both accurate and objective. It was the only newspaper that managed to keep up consistently high reporting standards, he said. In this regard, he referred to the recently departed Michael Wolfers:

> … who showed up by contrast the inability of some of his colleagues to file dispatches out of Lagos without becoming the mouthpiece of any Nigerian or British High Commission spokesman with something crass to say. Confining his reports to factual information about what was happening under his eyes in the Nigerian capital and eschewing speculative guesses as to what might be happening 400 miles away, Mr Wolfers turned in a file of copy during his sojourns in Lagos in 1969 that was *in toto* an object lesson on how foreign reporting should be done.

Touché!

There were many things about the Nigerian Civil War that were totally new to the majority of us scribes: for a start, getting into the beleaguered enclave was remarkably different, which was why so many journalists took their chances and entered Biafra several times. As far as I know, nobody from the media was killed on the Biafran Front, though there were a few wounded – and one journalist committed suicide in Johannesburg shortly after he returned home. In contrast, there were several media people who died while attached to Federal forces – including an erstwhile colleague from Nairobi, photojournalist Priya Ramrakha, who was killed in an ambush while in the company of CBS correspondent Morley Safer.

Once in, the majority of writers and photographers seemed to muddle through the daily air strikes, very little food, suspect drinking water and some top-heavy press briefings that might easily have had their origins in United States Army-skewered media reports out of Saigon. There was no question that it was a tough assignment, because front lines were constantly on the move and you sometimes hurriedly grabbed your things and made a dash for it in the face of the advancing Federal Army – and add to that malaria and other tropical diseases; unreliable guard and listening posts (because those manning them sometimes hadn't been fed for days); and the occasional artillery shell that went awry.

Quite a few of us ended up with amoebic and other problems – usually from dodgy food (or from the lack of it) – and several more with typhoid or fever. Indeed, shortly before the end of the war, when I again tried to make contact with Frederick Forsyth for the last time (he had been in Biafra off and on almost since the beginning of the war), I was told that he was in hospital with malaria – and since that was a dodgy day's drive there and back, and Nigerian MiGs were everywhere, I decided to give it a miss.

Biafra was a very different kind of war from most of those on the go at the time. In some of the sporadic Israeli forays against the PLO, if you were one of the chosen few who could approach the front lines, your IDF minder was always right there alongside you – yet while we operated in West Africa, few of us were subjected to security checks. Most of the media crowd would have an escort of sorts (more to keep them from harming themselves, or wandering into some dodgy no man's land close to the front), but generally, we were able to go just about everywhere we pleased.

If I wanted to head up past Uli towards the north, my 'guide' would check the situation with the local military office and, if it was 'safe', he'd try and find us a car to share to get there –no easy task in a country on the bare bones of its backside when it came to fuel; then, once we had a vehicle, we'd each be given a 'section' of the sky to watch for enemy aircraft that would usually strafe or bomb anything that moved on Biafra's roads during daylight hours. It was hairy, but as exciting as hell, and once we'd picked ourselves up after decamping into the slimy, steaming jungle – alive and rattled, but elated – it would be all jokes and congrats all round.

If a MiG did appear from nowhere (all were flown by mercenaries), the driver would slam on the brakes and stop within seconds; then helter-skelter, we'd all pile out and throw ourselves headlong into the jungle. Once he'd sounded the all-clear, we'd get in again and go on with the journey. A simple 10 or 15-mile journey on a bad morning often resulted in at least one bailout (sometimes more).

It was a different matter if we wished to see one of Biafra's senior army commanders. Of course, everybody wanted a bit of time with Ojukwu, but you had to have a good reason or very good connections to end up at his headquarters – and few of us did. Frederick Forsyth was one of the chosen few and, by his own admission, he shared many a bottle of good cognac with his old friend as the war progressed. The best I ever did was briefly to visit his deputy, the Biafran Chief of General Staff Philip Effiong – a charming gentleman who had originally joined Nigeria's Colonial Army under the British in 1945. A competent officer, he quickly rose through the ranks until he received the Queen's Commission in 1956; that followed his officer cadet training at Eaton Hall in Chester, England. Effiong later served with the British Army on the Rhine, West Germany.

In several other respects, Biafra was a different proposition from most other wars of that period, because like Vietnam, Biafra brought modern warfare into our living rooms. With what was going on in South East Asia, it was the first time that the world at large – on both sides of the Atlantic – was able to observe the progress of a war while eating dinner. This could sometimes be disturbing, because observing conflict at close quarters could be gruesome. Ultimately though, Biafra's legacy was not so much about conflict, as about a nation that was being starved to death. Moreover, this was being done jointly through the vigorous efforts of both Britain and the Soviet Union. Although in totally different ideological camps, it was in the interests of both powers to gain access to Nigeria's oil – and to do so as quickly as possible. In order to achieve that, they needed to work in tandem, which they did, very effectively indeed.

It took a while for the international media to become accustomed to these ploys, but once horrific images of distended and horribly emaciated people started to emerge from West Africa, there were a few consciences pricked. It wasn't long before the Biafran conundrum started to vie with South East Asia for the evening's headline news – much more so in the United Kingdom than in the US. It was a forceful effort – and some of the sad images of these pathetic souls can be viewed within these covers. More recently (in 2003), Time Warner published a selection of some of these historic pictures in a landmark book titled *100 Photographs That Changed the World*. Among these were black and white photos taken in Biafra by British photographer Don McCullin, who covered many conflicts during his half-century of activity (including a more recent visit to Syria's Aleppo that worried his Muslim hosts a lot more than it did him, because he was so frail).

In Biafra, Don was joined (among others) by Romano Cagnoni, with whom I shared a hideout in my own little caravan perched precariously in a jungle patch – discretely camouflaged with palm leaves to prevent our being attacked by Ares Klootwyk and his pals. While there, I would often give Romano a shout after a day's outing – usually for a chat and, more hopefully from my point of view, whatever he could (or would) offer me in the way of food and drink. That problem was of my own making, because I was stupid enough to have entered the beleaguered territory inadequately prepared. At the end of it, both McCullin and Cagnoni led the international pack with their pictures that were circulated around the globe – and played a much more powerful role in changing opinions than a hundred radio or TV reports a day could ever do.

In a blog hosted by the Honors Humanities Program at the University of Maryland – and authored by Rachel Pak in April 2013 under the heading 'Thinking in Public' – she maintained that 'after witnessing the civil war that was taking place between the newly-seceded Ibo state and the rest of Nigeria in 1969, McCullin began to document the famine that ravaged Biafra at the time,' as she declared: '… it was these images that preyed especially on young children.'

She goes on:

> One of McCullin's most notable photographs from this public tragedy is '*Biafra 1969*', which was one of the many images that sparked public interest. With these pictures, the international community became outraged and responded by protesting – contacting government officials and sending aid to Biafra. McCullin created an effective image to provoke social change regarding [this] conflict; however, the ethics of the journalist's role and [the] media's portrayal of the conflict are questionable.

Pak stresses that the composition of '*Biafra 1969*' was extremely successful in stirring emotions and provoking outrage in the international community – causing people to take action:

> Firstly, McCullin focused in on a few individuals rather than a mass of people… [which] encourages a more personal connection with the viewer, rather than facing an anonymous mass of people. Further, McCullin chose to focus especially on a starved albino boy,[4] who is not only a victim of famine, but also an outcast because of his genetic condition. The extreme marginalization of the boy causes the viewer to feel even more discomfort and sympathy than usual.
>
> … People felt guilty when confronted with these images – and McCullin himself admitted that the photos made, 'one feel guilty every time one eats.' Public guilt transformed into outrage, and inspired a series of actions toward social change. Frederick Forsyth, who

---

[4] Used in the colour section of this book.

reported on the Biafran famine, recalls the 'meetings, committees, protests, demonstrations, riots, lobbies, sit-ins, fasts, vigils, collections, banners, public meetings, marches, letters' sent to anyone in a position of influence to activate change. The public's reception to '*Biafra 1969*' and the resulting worldwide reaction are known to have given rise to the modern humanitarian-aid industry. Forsyth also commented that the State Department received, 'as many as 25,000 letters in one day by citizens demanding that action be taken in Biafra.' Soon many NGOs and other non-profit organizations were providing aid in Biafra, and their efforts most notably resulted in the Biafran air bridge, which flew in food every night to Biafra…

We see the same sort of thing with Ebola today.

While the war lasted, no country beyond the Iron Curtain States was inviolate to this propaganda effort. A West German group, *Gesellschaft für bedrohte Völker* (Society for Threatened Peoples International), was among the first to highlight what was going on in the enclave; its approach was totally uncompromising.

The first of its works, labelled 'Documentation of the Genocide', appeared in 1968 under the title *Biafra: Todesurteil für ein Volk* (*Biafra: Death Sentence for a People*), to which the international historian Golo Mann wrote an introduction.

An excerpt reads:

> … A war in which British 'Imperialists' and Russian 'Communists' pull together on the same rope of crime, in which a former colony is fighting for the supposed unity of its state against a tribe which is not even 'Socialist' is quite uninteresting – Lenin had nothing to say about this. But there are situations in which theory is useless, in which all theory is indeed harmful! All twisted artificial thinking must then be thrown out of the window…

That was followed by a treatise written by several German correspondents (Werner Holzer, Klaus Natorp and Klaus Stephan), who together with a military commission made up of British, Canadian, Polish and Swedish military personnel, questioned Nigeria's genocide. Their *Komitee Aktion Biafra-Hilfe* published a list of 171 personalities, journalists, politicians, Red Cross helpers, clerics and scientists from across three continents who were witnesses of these grotesque excesses.

As this society stated, no international institution ever actually counted the number of victims who died in this genocide, but the final figure is reckoned to be considerably more than a million civilians – above all children (the majority of whom died from starvation and illnesses caused by hunger):

> There were also several thousand civilians killed in massacres and in mass and individual shootings, mainly carried out by the Nigerian Army. Thousands fell victim to the bombing raids of the Nigerian Air Force with British and Soviet planes.
>
> The British Sunday newspaper *Observer* reported in the spring of 1968, for example, 48 bombing raids against civilian targets. [As a consequence] hospitals were destroyed in nine towns, ten colleges and schools as well as 16 urban estates. British eye-witnesses reported the shooting of many prisoners and massacres of non-combatants.

These findings were again published in 2014 with the declaration that:

> … in Nigeria there has been, to this day, no admission of the crime of genocide and no attempt to come to terms with the past. Very many of the Biafran elite have settled abroad, mostly in the United States. The places where the fighting in the Biafran War took place in

Thoughtless and insensitive commercial exploitation of the disaster.

Central and Eastern Nigeria, which are mainly inhabited by the ethnic group of the Ibo, belong today to the regions which are as regards economy and infrastructure the least developed regions of Nigeria.

It also states that in 1967 there were more than a million pupils in Eastern Nigerian primary schools and 65,000 in secondary schools. Effectively, when the war started, Biafra had as many pupils as the rest of Nigeria put together – whose population, they pointed out, was three times as large as the rebel state. In addition, there were 33 commercial training colleges, with 5,000 students; the University of Nsukka, with 3,000 students; 500 Biafran doctors; 700 lawyers; and 600 engineers – and those figures were never again matched in the almost half-century since the conflict ended.

In one sense, the group maintains, the Biafran War goes on. It is in the interests of the Federal Government to subjugate the more enterprising people of Eastern Nigeria, they aver, which is why not a single week goes by without more Eastern Nigerian Christians being murdered and their places of worship desecrated by Hausa and Fulani Islamic northerners.

Frederick Forsyth had a very personal take on what went on in this extremely troubled Nigerian enclave: once the war ended and he started to make money from his books – including some of his personal experiences in Biafra, which formed the basis of his novel *The Dogs of War* – he wasn't shy to assist old friends when he was asked to do so; as he said: 'If I was in a position to help, I did – simple as that.'

Though he wasn't specific about amounts, I gathered that he gave his old chum Odumegwu Ojukwu – then in exile in the Ivory Coast – regular amounts of cash which I reckoned to have been well into six figures sterling. Interestingly, he also came to the aid of some the mercenaries who had been involved in Eastern Nigeria while he was there and when they were in need – but then, that was always Freddie: not shy to answer the call when it came. This work has not ended. Frederick Forsyth is constantly asked to write forewords or chapters for books on this West African struggle – and he does so willingly and without reward because he believes that some terrible wrongs were committed by the British Government. Indeed, he gave me several hours on tape for my own efforts – recording in great detail exactly what went on in the Biafran War.[5]

An interesting aside to all these developments was the extensive use that both Biafra and Nigeria made of international public relations companies. Their role, simply put, was to spread propaganda. Clearly, the starvation issue was the seminal message – something that the Federal Government had to contend with from the start. It was a losing battle because it is difficult to refute real-life images of children dying – at first in dozens, and then in their hundreds, and eventually, thousands.

By June 1968 the *New York Times* had already run a report that the main issue facing Biafran children was *kwashiorkor* – a debilitating disease that stems from severe protein-energy malnutrition. Most kids with *kwashiorkor* display enormously distended bellies that sometimes conceal enlarged livers with fatty infiltrates – a truly noxious condition that without prompt treatment is invariably terminal…

Biafra wasted little time in appointing Mark Press of Geneva (run by expatriate American William H. Bernhardt) who, by all accounts, effectively 'sold a war'. Hardly the archetype American his enemies like to portray him, Bernhardt was soft-spoken – and with a quiet dignity and a predilection for English country clothes, he had everything about the 'Lord of the Manor' about him. Before Biafra, he had been involved in a project that sold the ill-fated American F-104 Starfighter 'Flying Coffin' to the West Germans and, following a curious set of circumstances, he had once handled a Western Nigerian account.

As the war progressed, Bernhardt immersed both himself and his company into propagating both Biafra's plight and Nigerian Army brutalities to the point (one report had it) that Lagos considered taking out a contract on his life. They desisted when the Federals were warned off by British Intelligence, who had got wind of it.

Bernhardt was an extremely thorough individual – and there were few photographs that passed through his hands that didn't reach the five or six major news agencies, as well as thousands of people that mattered on every continent. His list included the entire United States Congress (and both candidates in the 1968 presidential campaign), as well as every member of the British House of Commons. To this end, he even managed to go into Biafra at least once to sort out niggles that had crept into his contract – and this he did with Ojukwu personally (after which he had a telex installed in the Biafran leader's home that connected him directly with the action on a daily basis).

---

5   It encompasses several chapters in one of my books – published in 2011 by Casemate under the title *Barrel of a Gun: A War Correspondent's Misspent Moments in Combat*.

Bernhardt was an outstanding operator – and his story would still be an excellent guideline for modern PR aspirants.

The Lagos Government, in turn, did what they could, but it was an uphill fight against the basic tenets of humanity that they could never win. They initially hired a British company – Galitzine, Chant and Russell – in early 1968 after trying for some of the bigger names in London, who refused to even consider the contract because of potential adverse publicity. An American PR firm – Burson-Marstellar Associates – followed, but they gave up less than a year later because neither they nor their British associates could effectively penetrate the obscurantist bureaucracy of the Federal Ministry of Information. It says a lot that exactly the same condition holds today with regard to the Boko Haram *Jiyadi* threat in Northern Nigeria; some things in Africa never change…

Auberon Waugh was one of the most outspoken commentators about what was taking place in the Biafran War – and though he went on his own 'Long Walk' a while back, he needs no introduction within these covers.

For those not in the know however, 'Bron' (as his friends called him) was the eldest son of the even more illustrious Evelyn Waugh and became most famous for his *Private Eye* diary, which ran from the early 1970s until 1985 – and which he described as 'specifically dedicated to telling lies'. His work as political columnist on *The Spectator* coincided with Biafra and he spent a good deal of time strongly criticising the Harold Wilson Government – especially Foreign Secretary Michael Stewart for colluding in the use of mass starvation as a political weapon. Waugh was sacked from *The Spectator* in 1970, but with the support of Bernard Levin and others, he won damages for unfair dismissal in a subsequent action.

'Hail Biafra' – an insightful piece written for that magazine and published on 1 August 1968 – is well worth a mention. I've let it run because it provides an excellent backdrop of what went on in the enclave from a British perspective.

> … Of the many journalists who have visited Biafra and attempted to give some picture of what British foreign policy is achieving there, I think I was the first political correspondent.
>
> When our party landed at the airstrip in one of Mr Hank Wharton's Constellations – our plane brought in seven tonnes of ammunition and we had taken it in turns to sleep on a mattress thrown over the ammunition boxes – I was straight from the Government's moral crusade in Westminster.
>
> I had heard Mr Michael Stewart assure the House of Commons that if he could be persuaded that it was the Lagos Government's intention to commit genocide against the Ibos, then he would 'more than reconsider' his decision to provide arms for the purpose. Both Mr George Thomson and Mr Wilson had expressed a willingness to fatten the Biafrans up before allowing them to be killed by the weapons they supplied to the other side, and seemed upset when Colonel Ojukwu refused to let them demonstrate their compassion in this way.
>
> Our plane was met at the airstrip by a party of missionaries who were hoping for food and medical supplies. Unfortunately, on this occasion, we had brought them only the Catholic Bishop of Port Harcourt – a most amiable man who created a scene in the dining room at São Tomé Airport when they tried to give him Coca-Cola instead of beer.
>
> There was also another African priest and Father Butler – an Irish missionary working for Caritas who had come over from São Tomé just for the ride. His sang-froid rather annoyed one journalist, who swore that we were being shot at every time the plane shuddered.
>
> The pilot was a highly capable American mercenary called Robbie who, like all Mr Wharton's pilots, had a huge cigar permanently stuck between his teeth. Goodness knows

why he chose this method of earning his living, but I would like to take this opportunity of putting a little free advertisement for Mr Wharton's Air Biafra.

If my dispatch from Lisbon last week seemed a little curmudgeonly in this respect, it may have been coloured by the fact that we had failed to get a plane three nights running – on the last occasion, Mr Wharton explained with commendable frankness, that his navigator was drunk. But once aboard, the cheerfulness and competence of Air Biafra's pilots make it an unbeatable advertisement for the American merchant adventuring spirit.

The first sight which meets the eye at Umuahia Airstrip is a formidable anti-aircraft gun flanked by two Biafran soldiers standing to attention. This covers the runway's direct approach, and as Nigeria's Egyptian MiG pilots do not like being shot at, they have always tried to hit it from a diagonal approach, with no success.

With extraordinary speed, working under the arc lights in the muggy haze at two in the morning, men unload the ammunition boxes into army lorries, the plane is turned around and passengers are shepherded inside for the return trip. Meanwhile, we are taken to a concrete shed about half a mile away for the mild farce of passport and immigration control. Our luggage is searched, passports stamped and an anxious health official asks for certificates of inoculation against smallpox and yellow fever. On being told that we have none, and that we should consider it indelicate to show him them in any case, he goes away looking misunderstood.

Much of Biafran officialdom's time is spent making lists, and we had all been listed about half a dozen times when we set off in a convoy of four cars on the sixty-mile journey to Aba. The roads in Biafra are extremely good, and one only had time between roadblocks to receive a fleeting impression of coconut palms rising above the dripping vegetation.

These roadblocks are a major feature of travel in Biafra. They are approached by nine-inch earthworks across the road, over which one has to drive very slowly or break an axle, although, of course, they would not make the slightest difference to a Saladin, or even a Ferret.

They have been manned day and night for fourteen months and one is never quite sure of one's reception. Sometimes a terrifying figure in camouflaged denim uniform would thrust a sub-machine gun through the window, cocking it as he does so and demand to see my papers. At others I was waved on by a sleepy figure, bare to the waist in the pouring rain, or dressed in an ankle-length raincoat and floppy hat, leaning on an upside-down Lee Enfield from the First World War.

The words 'World Press' are usually greeted with great grins of welcome, patriotic salutes and, occasionally, little dances to the refrain of 'Hail Biafra'.

All the government rest houses have been re-named Progress Hotels, which seems as good a name as any.

Since the fall of Enugu, Aba has become the administrative capital of Biafra, although everything has been decentralised as much as possible. The place possessed neither electric light nor water when we arrived, although water started flowing at about six in the morning.

Everybody unpacked by candlelight: torches, pills to make poisonous water drinkable, mosquito repellent, things to remove stones from a horse's foot. The Germans brought knives to carry in their boots and electrical gadgets for every occasion. They had an insolent way of shaving themselves with battery-powered machines during any lull in the conversation.

At any other lull, an incredibly boring young Swede would explain the Swedish way to health and happiness. He said he spoke in an American accent because he found it easier. He was far too intelligent to be taken in by Biafran propaganda, so we all resolved to poison him as soon as the first Red Cross supplies came through.

We were summoned at seven o'clock for breakfast – fried plantains and mushrooms –by a servant called Michael, who called one 'master'. At the home of Mr Oti, the local representative of the Ministry of Information, we were told that as the Biafran pound had not 'devalued' last November, we should receive only 16s 8d in Biafran money for our English pounds, and American journalists would have to pay $2.80 for a Biafran pound. Also, we were to be charged about £12 a day for board, lodging and share of a car.

We were asked what in particular we wanted to see. Everybody said they wanted to have a personal interview with Colonel Ojukwu and see at least one of the fronts.

To see the Colonel, it is necessary to fill in a long form listing one's educational qualifications, the readership of one's newspaper, other countries visited, religion and number of children in one's family. Perhaps my family did not come up to scratch, because I never heard any more about it – nor indeed did any of the other journalists. In any case, the Colonel was away when we arrived, at the abortive talks in Niamey, and just conceivably the fellow was rather busy on his return. Only the Swede seemed to mind, claiming that he represented the second most important newspaper in the South of Sweden.

The Eastern Nigerians – largely through their own carelessness in the matter – have always chosen to live on the borderline of protein sufficiency. Their normal food, of cassavas and yams (flavoured with various highly peppered gravies), has very little protein content indeed, but it has always been supplemented by some 3,000 tonnes of stock fish (dried cod) imported from the West every month, and some 2,000 head of cattle imported from the North.

In 1965 the Queen Elizabeth Hospital, Umuahia, treated 100 patients suffering from malnutrition throughout the whole year. In 1967 the figure was 800 patients. Last week, on a bad day, the staff treated 1,700 patients, nearly all suffering from oedema, or swollen feet, a characteristic of the last stages of protein deficiency.

While everybody – or nearly everybody – is now living on a virtually protein-less diet, it is inevitably the children who are struck down first. The outpatient department was jammed solid with mothers nursing their babies – not skeleton-thin, with stick-like legs and distended stomachs, as in Oxfam advertisements, but curiously puffy, with a reddening of the skin, a paling and straightening of the hair and a total listlessness.

'I should say it's most dubious whether this one's going to live,' said Dr Shepherd, a quiet-spoken Scottish Presbyterian in charge of the department. 'If I had to choose, I'd feed up this one.' Of course, he has no choice. Only the extreme cases can be treated at all, and they are rationed to one scoopful of powdered milk per fortnight.

The most impressive thing about it was the way in which mothers accepted that this was just, that no more could be done. It was only when one saw the pain and hopelessness in the mothers' eyes that one began to understand what every unit in the casualty figures represented in terms of personal agony.

I also visited the casualty wards, which had received some forty patients from the Degema-Igrite-Port Harcourt front on the day before (thereby giving the lie to Lagos' claims that there was both a lull in the fighting and that all resistance in these areas had been crushed). As the hospital specialised in thoracic surgery, most of the cases involved bullet wounds in the chest – occasionally sniper fire, but mostly from the machine guns of the Saladin, Saracen and Ferret armoured cars supplied by the British Government.

Without these armoured cars, the Nigerians would have very little chance of pushing through to Umuahia. The Biafrans have no defence against them, except land mines and the more desperate method of climbing under them with napalm grenades to put on the outside of their petrol tanks. One did not feel particularly proud of being English on this occasion.

While there is a certain amount of anger against England among the Biafrans, there is far more incomprehension. They keep returning to the fact that England is a Christian country, that they learned their Christianity from England (and Ireland) as well as their cricket and also, perhaps, their sense of fair play.

It is this sense of fair play, as well as Christian fatalism, which is the strongest impression one receives in Biafra. How is it possible, they ask, that Mr Wilson does not understand what will happen to Biafrans in the event of a Nigerian victory?

I reply that he believes that nothing will happen to the Biafrans, he thinks that talk of genocide is so much false propaganda put about by Colonel Ojukwu and those who covet Port Harcourt's oil in order to stiffen Biafran resistance. But the roads are jammed with non-Ibo refugees fleeing from the Federal Nigerians.

However, the Hausas from the North do not distinguish between Ibo and non-Ibo Easterners, with the result that, when large numbers of them had been murdered and others rounded up into concentration camps, those remaining started the long trek into what remains of Biafra where they now add to the appalling refugee problems.

Mr Wilson's thesis that we are all the victims of skilful propaganda could not survive a visit of half an hour to Biafra. In the course of my travels I must have talked to about fifty people directly concerned with ministering to the hungry and the dying. They were missionaries, doctors, camp organisers and local Red Cross workers.

I asked all of them, first, whether they did not think the risks of surrender would be preferable to the certainty of starvation, and, secondly, whether they did not think that too much priority was given to arms in the aeroplane flights, and not enough to food and medical supplies.

Without a single exception – and my informants included pacifists and humanists, as well as Catholic and Anglican missionaries, nurses and schoolteachers – they all said that the probability of a massacre was too great to make surrender thinkable.

More surprising still, there was no suggestion among the army officers that greater priority should be given to arms and less to powdered milk. They, too, have seen whole companies cut down by Nigerian artillery and machine-gun fire without being able to return a single shot. They have no choice but to fight, and everything which can be done is being done.

Even the journalists – and British journalists at that – who were eating valuable meat and burning valuable petrol, were welcomed wherever they went. So great is the Biafrans' faith in the justice of their cause, and so great their faith in the basic fair-mindedness of human nature, that they welcome journalists as saviours. This is not only among government officials, army officers or white welfare workers, but in every single Biafran home.

One may doubt whether many English homes would show such sophistication in similar circumstances.

Any Commonwealth Office official who is prepared to spend half an hour talking to Biafrans will learn that, after what has happened, there is not the slightest chance of Biafra voluntarily rejoining any except the very loosest Nigerian Federation.

The only prospect in sight, if Britain continues to pursue its lone policy of one Nigeria – shared somewhat half-heartedly by America, whose Assistant-Secretary of State for African Affairs, Joseph Palmer, made his name as ambassador to Lagos with high, glowing reports of Nigerian stability, unity and permanence – is that the war will drag on indefinitely from the bush.[6]

---

6   Waugh, Auberon, 'Hail Biafra' – *The Spectator* (London: 1 April 1968).

Auberon Waugh in his later years.

Biafran soldiers.

Some interesting comments, both about Waugh and about Biafra, came from Alex Mitchell (who flew with him into the enclave) – the renowned Australian journalist possibly best known for his long-running political column in Sydney's *The Sun-Herald*. Mitchell moved to Britain in the late 1960s and worked on Fleet Street papers and then on television. All of this appeared in one of his recent books, *Come the Revolution*, under the chapter heading 'Chance to be a War Correspondent'.[7]

Mitchell left Lisbon in one of Hank Wharton's lumbering freighters and his travelling companions included Auberon Waugh, John de St Jorre and Guy Rais from the *Telegraph*. As he states: 'We were their guests on a mercy flight to bring news of the starving and beleaguered Biafran people to the British public. Our American pilot, Hank Wharton, was dressed in work shorts, a T-shirt and elastic-sided riding boots. He had a .38 pistol stuck in his belt.' On closer inspection, he revealed, their cargo wasn't dried milk, rice, flour, baby food, medicine or bandages: it was tonnes of Czech-made small arms and ammunition.

Mitchell continues:

> Before leaving, I decided to consult the *Sunday Times*' war photographer Don McCullin, whose excruciating pictures from the war zone had been published in that paper's colour magazine a month earlier – accompanied by an essay: 'Biafra: The Darkness in Africa', written by Chinua Achebe.
>
> When I told McCullin my aim was to interview Ojukwu and join up with a Biafran Army unit to bring back news of the fighting, he shook his head dismissively and replied firmly: 'Don't get involved with the Biafran Army. The officers are fucking useless and the soldiers are just kids who don't know what they're doing.'
>
> As a travelling companion, Waugh was immense fun. It was as if we'd been placed in a time capsule and were reliving *Scoop* – that wonderful newspaper novel written by his illustrious

---

7 Mitchell, Alex, *Come the Revolution* (Sydney, Australia: University of New South Wales, 2012).

father, Evelyn Waugh. When Bron imperiously and ostentatiously ordered his meals at the hotel restaurant, it was if William Boot of the *Daily Beast* was reborn in Ishmaelia – the fictional location of his father's 1938 book.

We made an incongruous band of war correspondents; what we shared was an enthusiastic, if emotionally-driven support for Biafra – which was undoubtedly why Mark Press [Biafra's public relations agency] selected us.

Bron was the most zealously pro-Biafran, and his wife, Lady Teresa Onslow, had named their recently born fourth child Nathaniel Thomas Biafra Waugh. Looking back 40 years later, de St Jorre, my immediate rival from the Astor-owned *Sunday Observer*, wrote to me: 'We were a mixed bag: upper-class, eccentric, Catholic Bron with a famous name; Guy, lower-class, Jewish home reporter more used to kicking in the door in places like Streatham and getting the story on a grisly murder than jumping on a plane to darkest Africa; me, the eager-beaver, bleeding-heart liberal Africanist; and you, the Trotskyist in Lord Thomson's wolf's clothing'.

One of Mitchell's interesting asides came as a result of an impromptu outing while the group was still awaiting their departure orders in Lisbon:

> The three of us decided to go swimming, but not Bron. He held back, but we eventually persuaded him to climb into his swimming costume and join us. His pale, frail body looked as if it had never had an audience with the sun. His waiflike physique was made more alarming by a savage scar which swept across his abdomen and chest and halfway up his back.
>
> 'What happened to you?' we chorused. Bron explained that during his National Service with the Royal Horse Guards, he had been sent to Cyprus to wage war on Archbishop Makarios' EOKA independence fighters. On patrol in the Troodos Mountains in an armoured car, Lieutenant Waugh attempted to fire off a few rounds from the machine gun mounted on the front of the vehicle. When it jammed, he leapt from the vehicle, grabbed the barrel with both hands and shook it vigorously.
>
> His spontaneous act of bravery ended badly: the shaking action unjammed the trigger mechanism – letting loose a salvo of shots at point-blank range. After the medics patched him up, Bron had lost his spleen, one of his lungs, several ribs and one of his fingers.

Alex Mitchell said long afterwards that he remembered little about his exploits in Biafra. His partner, Joy, recalled 30 years later that he had told her about the mercenary plane ride and the landing at Uli Airstrip, but nothing else. 'You didn't want to talk about it, so I didn't ask,' she said.

Mitchell: 'At an informal debriefing session at the *Sunday Times*, I was unable to discuss the horrors I had witnessed. Some things, I discovered, are too horrible to recall: unable to cope with them, we have the ability simply to bury them in the hope they will go away.'

17

A Retrospective Nigerian Military View of the War

In 1992 – almost a quarter-century after the Biafran War ended – Major Abubakar A. Atofarati (a Northern Nigerian officer attending the United States Marines Corps Command and Staff College) wrote a thesis titled: 'The Nigerian Civil War, Causes, Strategies and Lessons Learnt'. With the benefit of hindsight, he makes a number of interesting, if weighted, observations…
(Courtesy of United States Marine Command, Quantico, Virginia)

The most salient point comes on his opening pages, where he states that the Federation of Nigeria 'has never really been one homogeneous country, for its widely differing peoples and tribes'. This obvious fact notwithstanding, he declares:

> … its former colonial master decided to keep the country one in order to effectively control her vital resources for their economic interests. Thus, for administrative convenience, the Northern and Southern Nigeria were amalgamated in 1914. Thereafter the only thing this people had in common was the name of their country, since each side had a different administrative set-up. This alone was an insufficient basis for true unity.

As he states, under normal circumstances, this amalgamation ought to have brought the various peoples together and provided a firm basis for the arduous task of establishing closer cultural, social, religious and linguistic ties vital for true unity among the people – but it was not to be. Instead, there was division, hatred, unhealthy rivalry and pronounced disparity in development.

The growth of nationalism in the society and the subsequent emergence of political parties were based on ethnic/tribal (rather than national) interests, and therefore had no unifying effect on the peoples against the colonial master. Rather, it was the people themselves who were the victims of the political struggles which were supposed to be aimed at removing foreign domination.

At independence, Nigeria became a Federation and remained one country. Soon afterwards, the battle to consolidate the legacy of political and military dominance of a section of Nigeria over the rest of the Federation began with increased intensity. It is this struggle that eventually degenerated into coup, counter-coup and a bloody civil war.

History of the Nigerian Army Before 1966

What is known today as the Nigerian Army was – before 1966 – a part of the British West African Army called the Royal West Africa Frontier Force (RWAFF). This force included the armies of the Gold Coast (Ghana), Nigeria, Sierra Leone and Gambia.

At this time, there were eight indigenous Nigerian officers in the entire force – the rest being British officers. The role of an army in a developing country was not fully realised by the nationalist leaders struggling for independence – hence, there was no effective pressure on the British Government to train Nigerian officers in preparation for independence. Even at this stage, it was clear that the future stability of a nation such as Nigeria depended on (to a large scale) the existence of a reliable army. One result of this short-sightedness was that the first Nigerian to command the Nigerian Army – Major-General J.T.U. Aguiyi-Ironsi – was not appointed until 1965 (nearly five years after the country achieved its independence). When that happened in 1960 it soon became obvious that the group that controlled the army could aspire to run a stable Nigerian Government. Either by coincidence or by design, almost all the military installations were concentrated in one area of the country: the north. To illustrate this fact, below is a list of major military installations in Nigeria and their locations before the January 1966 coup:

Northern Nigeria:
1. 3rd Battalion, Kaduna
2. 5th Battalion, Kano
3. 1 Field Battery (Artillery), Kaduna
4. 1 Field Squadron (Engineers), Kaduna
5. 88 Transport Regiment, Kaduna
6. Nigerian Defence Academy, Kaduna
7. Ordinance Depot, Kaduna
8. 44 Military Hospital, Kaduna
9. Nigeria Military Training College, Kaduna
10. Recon Squadron and Regiment, Kaduna
11. Nigerian Air Force, Kaduna
12. Ammunition Factory, Kaduna
13. Recruit Training Depot, Zaria
14. Nigerian Military School, Zaria

Western Nigeria:
1. 4th Battalion, Ibadan
2. 2 Field Battery (Artillery), Abeokuta
3. 2 Reconnaissance Squadron, Abeokuta

Eastern Nigeria:
1. 1st Battalion, Enugu

Even at this stage, there were no military units in Mid-Western Nigeria, and those in Lagos were either administrative or ceremonial – although the LGO did field a combat unit backed by armoured cars that was used in a bid to counter the second army mutiny at source at its Ikeja Airport core (unsuccessfully as it transpired).

Recruitment of soldiers into the Nigerian Army was based on an ethnic quota system. Under this system, Northern Nigeria provided 60 percent, Eastern and Western Nigeria 15 percent each and Mid-Western Nigeria the balance. This was done to encourage the northerners, who had not been interested in joining the army initially. The standard of entry into the army was consequently lowered to favour northerners. As a result, the north in 1966 had the absolute majority within the rank and file of the army, but there was a cost, because standards fell and soldiers became more politically conscious. As one observer pointed out, 'in order to ensure the loyalty of the military established in this manner, the criterion for promotion and advancement was based more on political considerations than either efficiency or competence.'

The involvement of the military in politics took a turn for the worse during the Western Nigerian elections in October 1965; politicians blatantly courted the friendship of top military officers. Due to the chaos that characterised the general election of 1964 and the Western Region election of 1965 it had already become obvious that Nigeria was overdue for a radical change.

By October 1965 rumours of an impending coup were circulating in the country and, as a result, once the coup was finally staged, not everybody was surprised.

War Planning Strategies: Mobilisation

The declaration of secession made war not inevitable, but imminent. At dawn on the morning of 6 July 1967 the first shots were fired – signalling the beginning of a 30-month civil war. Carnage followed, with brothers killing brothers.

Preparations for war had already been set in motion on the Federal Nigerian side by May 1967. All the soldiers of Northern, Western and Mid-Western origin had been withdrawn from the east and redeployed. Four of the regular infantry battalions of the army were placed under the command of 1 Brigade and re-designated 1 Area Command.

Mobilisation of ex-servicemen was ordered by the commander-in-chief. Of those 7,000 called up, four more battalions were created. Increased recruitment from the personnel of the Nigerian Police Force was initiated; that also led to civilians being trained in civil defence duties. In mobilising the people of Nigeria, the Federal Government had to make the war look a just cause in order to stop the disintegration of the country – and in doing this, a slogan was invented: 'To keep Nigeria one is a task that must be done'. Even the letters of the Head of the Federal Government, General Yakubu Gowon, was coined to read: 'Go On With One Nigeria' (GOWON). Clearly, this suggested powerful motives linked to propaganda.

Military

Delivery of arms and equipment for the Nigerian Army were hastened. The Nigerian Army Headquarters (NAHQ) operations plan envisaged a war that would be waged in four phases and, optimistically, would be over within a month. Ideally, they included the capture first of Nsukka; then Ogoja; Abakaliki; and finally, taking the eastern capital city of Enugu. The NAHQ assessment of the rebels in terms of men under arms and equipment did not allow much cause for concern – but the total mobilisation and the will of the people of Eastern Nigeria to fight against severe odds were radically underestimated.

Nigeria was aware that the survival of Biafra depended on the importation of materiel from abroad and, to sustain her war efforts, the only route was through the Atlantic Ocean. As part of strategic planning, the Nigerian Navy was tasked to blockade the region from the sea – thereby preventing the shipment of arms, equipment, food and other war materiel and services into the east. At the same time, all flights to the region were cancelled and the international community were informed that no flights into the region would be accepted without advanced clearance from Lagos.

The Nigerian High Command paid little particular attention to any kind of strategic intelligence coming through from the Eastern Region. In planning and concept, the war was intended to be fought by the troops located in the north and to be supplied mainly from Kaduna. Immediately, Biafra declared secession from the Federation; war was declared; and Nigeria sent in her warships to blockade and secure all sea routes in the region. For its part, the Nigerian Air Force was given the role of ensuring the control of the air space over the entire country.

The overall offensive was to be a two-pronged attack involving a combined mechanised infantry divisional attack from the north and an amphibious operation by another division from the south, with the aim of crushing the Biafran Army in-between (supported by both the air force and the navy). Two more fronts – a third and a fourth – were introduced later in the war.

Biafran Military

On the Biafran side, preparation for war was put into gear as soon as the troops of non-eastern origin withdrew from Enugu in August 1966. Thousands of people poured in for recruitment and comprehensive military training was established both for officers and soldiers, who were mainly lecturers and university students.

Before the outbreak of hostility, the Eastern Region had inadequate arms supplies because all soldiers who returned to their regions did so without their weapons. In contrast, troops redeployed out of Eastern Nigeria left with their weapons intact. All that remained of the Nigerian Army at Enugu Barracks were about 240 soldiers – the majority of them technicians and tradesmen (and not all of them were armed). However, it is also true that at the outbreak of the war, the Eastern Region had succeeded in securing some arms and ammunition from France, Spain and Portugal. When these arrived, two new battalions were created: the 9th and 14th Battalions.

A fair number of pilots and technicians – formerly attached to the Nigerian Air Force and of eastern origin – returned to the region to form the Biafran Air Force (BiAF). Two none-too-modern aircraft – a World War II vintage B-26 and an equally old B-25 – were acquired, together with new helicopters. The bombers were fitted with machine guns and locally-made rockets and bombs. As we have seen, the BiAF also acquired Minicon aircrafts.

A small navy was established in Calabar, with some patrol boats formerly used by the Nigerian Navy. More boats were later manufactured locally, and these were fitted with armoured plates and light machine guns. A People's Army – calling itself the Biafra Militia – was formed. Local leaders and ex-servicemen trained young men and women in the use of whatever weapons were available. These were mainly imported, together with some locally-made short guns.

The militia was tasked with providing a ready source of re-enforcement for the regular army and to assist with military administration immediately behind the front line. They were also required to garrison all areas captured or regained from the enemy, and to help educate the population on the reason why Biafra was fighting a war.

An establishment known as the Administration Support was formed. Before the declaration of hostility, the small Biafran Army was almost completely administered and maintained by donations from the civil populace. A Food Directorate –responsible for the purchase and distribution of all food, drink and cigarettes to the armed forces and the nation – was formed. A Transport Directorate was also established, as was a Petroleum Management Board for procurement, management and distribution of fuel. The board designed and built a sizeable and efficient fuel refinery which produced petrol, diesel and engine oil at a considerably fast rate.

Several other directorates such as Clothing, Housing, Propaganda, Requisition and Supply, and Medical were established. In particular, clothing was essential, as uniforms were unavailable in Biafra. Ultimately, a number of textile mills in the Eastern Region were reactivated to produce bales of uniforms.

A Research and Production Board was also established. This organisation researched and manufactured rockets, mines, tanks, grenades, launchers, bombs, flamethrowers, vaccines, biological and alcoholic beverages, and so forth.

Women also came into the scheme of things. They were trained in intelligence-gathering and how to infiltrate enemy defences. A Women's Voluntary Service was formed to assist in educating the females on the cause of the crisis and to keep them informed of developments, as well as the rehabilitation of war casualties; the setting up of nurseries and orphanages; the Civil Defence Corps; and the provision of cooks for the troops. An Advisory Committee was established to plan and execute the war and advise the head of state on political and military matters.

The Nigerian Army Offensive

Nigeria opened her offensive operations from the northern sector with 1 Area Command supported by an artillery brigade and armoured units equipped with British armoured vehicles, including both Ferret and Saladin armoured cars. Engineering units were issued operational orders for OPUNICORD – the codename for what was termed a 'police action' against the rebels.

The offence was launched on two fronts and the command was divided into two brigades, with three battalions each. 1 Brigade advanced on the axis of the Ogugu – Ogunga – Nsukka Roads, while 2 Brigade advanced on the axis of the Gakem – Obudu – Ogoja Roads. Ojukwu's rebels successfully repulsed the attack – however, with the many friends and acquaintances the command had cultivated since they concentrated on the border, they began to recruit a number of guides and informants. With these individuals came a good deal of intelligence on the disposition of the Biafran troops (their strength, together with their plans of a breakthrough).

By early July 1967 1 Brigade had captured all of its first objectives. Had they managed to acquire additional intelligence on the Biafran Army, there is no question that they would have pressed on and been able to take the Biafran capital of Enugu. By 12 July 2 Brigade had captured Obudu, Gakem and Ogoja. A second front was opened on the southern sector in late July, with an amphibious landing at Bonny by a division formed from men of the LGO. With the support of the navy, the division established a beachhead and exploited the north after a series of fierce sea and land battles; then the turnabout, with Biafra invading the former Mid-Western Region on 8 August with the view to relieving pressure on the northern sector and also to threaten Lagos.

While the LGO was making preparations for subsequent operations beyond Bonny, the news of the rebel infiltration into the mid-west was passed to the commander, who was then instructed to leave a battalion in Bonny; suspend all operations there; and move to Escravos with two battalions, with a view to dislodging the rebels and clearing the riverine area of the mid-west. These moves were carried out with the support of the Nigerian Navy and elements of Nigeria's mercantile marine.

Another division was formed to support the LGO clearing the mid-west of rebels: at this point, the formations were re-designated from 1 Area Command to 1 Infantry Division; the newly-formed division was designated 2 Infantry Division; and the LGO became 3 Infantry Division – and with this, the 'police action' turned into a full-scale military operation.

By the end of September 1969 a substantial part of the mid-west had been cleared of the rebels. The commander of 3 Infantry Division secured permission to change the designation of his formation to 3 Marine Commando because of the peculiarly riverine and creek operations already carried out by the division. This was the first time something bearing resemblance to a marine organisation was tried in the history of the Nigerian Army.

The division was not trained in amphibious operations; in fact, the troops were made up of the soldiers of the LGO. However, with some crash training, the division became the most feared and successful unit throughout the war. Enugu had already become Ojukwu's bastion of rebellion and the Federal Government of Nigeria expected that its capture would mean the end of secession.

The advance from Nsukka to Enugu began in earnest on 12 September 1967. The rebels counter-attacked and, for the first time, launched their 'Red Devil' tanks. These were modified pre-World War II armoured personnel carriers made in France. They were dangerous, slow, 'blind', cumbersome and not easily manoeuvrable. Also, it was acknowledged by those familiar with such things that they were easy prey for anti-tank recoilless rifles and bold infantry attack.

By early October, Enugu had fallen – and with this capture, 1 Infantry Division took time to refit and reorganise. The division maintained the erroneous belief that taking Enugu would automatically mean the collapse of the rebellion. The commander of 1 Infantry Division – in consultation with his superiors in Lagos – decided to give the rebel leader time to abandon his efforts at secession (not really appreciating the depth of resistance within Biafran ranks). It took the division another six months to resume the offence – thereby giving the rebels the necessary respite to also reorganise, as well as resupply and acquire more ammunition, weapons and equipment to continue the resistance.

Meanwhile, 3 Marine Commando opened another front on the south-eastern border. With the support of the navy, Calabar was captured on 13 October 1967. With Calabar, Warri, Escravos and Bonny under government control, the supremacy of the Federal authorities in Nigerian waters and international waters bordering the Nigerian coast was established. Biafra was sealed off – leaving Port Harcourt Airport as its only means of international communication and transportation with the outside world.

At this point, the Biafran leadership decided to seek alternative routes for the importation of everything needed to pursue the military campaign – including food, war materiel and medical aid. Three stretches of road were developed into airstrips at Awgu, Uga and Uli, which was just as well, as the Biafrans lost Port Harcourt not long afterwards.

On 10 January 1970 Lieutenant-Colonel Ojukwu – the self-proclaimed Head of State of Biafra – on realising the total chaotic and hopelessness of the situation, handed over to the commander of the Biafran Army – Major-General Philip Effiong – the administration of Biafra and flew out of the enclave with his immediate family members in search of peace. General Effiong consulted with the Biafra Strategic Committee on the situation, and the conclusion was reached that the only honourable way out was to surrender.

Ojukwu was offered sanctuary by several countries, but finally decided that his best option in exile would be the Ivory Coast, where he remained for many years, before being permitted to return to Eastern Nigeria as a civilian (as long as he played no political role). He died peacefully in 2013.[1]

Military

Morale and discipline were two of the most important factors that contributed to success in the Biafran War.

Olusegun Obasanjo – one of the Federal commanders who was involved in the war, and later became Nigeria's President on two separate occasions – commented on the effects of these factors thus:

> I observed amongst Nigerian troops during the war different aspects of human behaviour under the stress and strains of battle, and interaction between ordinary Nigerians, war or no war.

---

[1] Throughout Ojukwu's exile in the Ivory Coast, Frederick Forsyth regularly – and quite liberally – contributed towards his and his family's upkeep (including paying for the schooling of one or more of his children). When pressed for details by this author, Forsyth was not prepared to elaborate.

What I found amazing was the length to which soldiers would go when morale and discipline broke down, in order to avoid going to battle or, so to speak, facing death. In effect, while running away from death they inflicted death on themselves, as some of them died from their self-inflicted injuries. But towards the end of the war when everything was going right – the rebels were on the run, advance was fast and co-ordinated, morale was high – even our own wounded soldiers did not want to be evacuated to the rear for treatment and medical attention. Several times I heard such wounded soldiers saying to me, 'Oga, na you and me go end this war and capture Ojukwu.'

Motivation was another important factor. The Nigerian soldiers enjoyed rapid promotion and increase in pay throughout the war; this encouraged them to continue. It was also important to allow troops time to worship in their various religious faiths.

High standards of training can never be overemphasised. Most of the soldiers recruited during the war did not undergo enough depot training before being sent into battle – and this resulted in many casualties on both sides. Indeed, most of those who survived the war had to be retrained. Members of the military had to recognise that they depended more on the professional and technical competence and proficiency of their team members than on the formal authority structure.

The maintenance of highly sophisticated weapons and equipment procured during the war became a serious problem as hostilities progressed; most of the equipment lasted only a few months in combat. Weapons were imported from all over the world and this led to an element of non-standardisation after the war – and much of this equipment had to be phased out due to lack of spare parts.

The quality of initiative in the individual must be allowed to develop; it is the most valued of all leadership qualities and virtues in the military. In this period of tremendous technological change, military leaders are confronted with an almost perpetual change or crisis of organisation – especially in a fairly fluid combat situation. Whatever may be the technological achievement of our age and its impact on military science, improvisation is still the keynote of the individual fighter and combat group – as Major Atofarati observes: 'This aspect of military training must be emphasised in peacetime – and this is particularly important in the developing nation like ours'. Failures arising from a lack of adequate joint training became very obvious as a result of fratricide that occurred during the war. On many occasions, fire support requests made to the air force never came – and when it did come, it was sometimes on its own friendly positions; supply from the air (that became necessary at times) often fell on the enemy side.

It is commonly said that an army fights on its stomach. In the end, it was logistics that won the war for Nigeria. If the Biafrans had half of the resources Nigeria had, the story might be different. The rebels were better organised and managed the meagre resources available to them more effectively – and the Nigerian Army learnt a big lesson from this: the Army School of Logistics was upgraded and well-funded to train and produce high-quality logisticians for the army after the war.

Communication in the field was a big problem to both sides in the conflict. Radios were lacking – and when they were procured, trained manpower was not available. The importance of good and reliable communication and the gathering of adequate and up-to-date intelligence of the enemy was a big lesson.

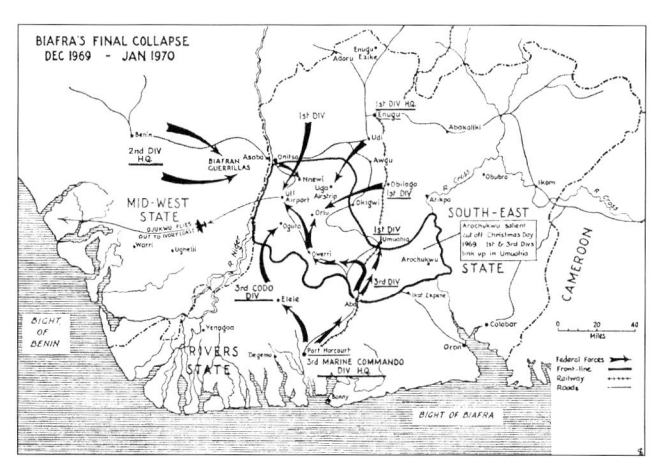

A graphic illustration of the final collapse of the State of Biafra.

Conclusion

The war had come and gone. The story of the war and what led to it has been told, is being told and will continue to be told. What seems to me a human tragedy all through the ages is the inability of man to learn a good lesson from the past so as to avoid the pitfall of those who had gone before.

There is also the innate and unconscious desire of man to remain oblivious of the lessons of the past. He hopes and believes that the past can be ignored; that the present is what matters; that no mistakes of the present can be as serious and grievous as the mistakes of the past. As a result, history tends to repeat itself. However, there are exceptions of nations and men who learnt from history to avoid collective and individual disasters, or a repetition of such disasters.

Major Abubakar Atofarati's closing words are: 'I feel confident that Nigeria must join the group of these happy exceptions if we are to have political stability, economic progress, integrated development, social justice, contentment and be the epicentre of African solidarity'. Since the end of the civil war, Nigeria has made considerable progress in all these areas.

18

Biafra's Mercenaries: A Diverse Bunch of Professionals

Employing 'hired guns' in Africa's wars was nothing new by the time Biafra reached the world stage. There had already been a thousand or more mercenaries fighting in the Congo. However, there was a notable difference between what went on in the Congo and this West African conflagration: Biafra's 'Soldiers of Fortune' – initially motivated by money – soon became totally (sometimes irrationally) committed to Biafra's humanitarian cause; some took no money for their efforts…

When Frederick Forsyth visited me in Washington to complete the research for his then forthcoming book *The Afghan*, we were able to discuss the mercenary role in Biafra at length. Being close to the Biafran leader, he had obviously been at hand when some of these things happened, which was clearly why he had such a remarkable insight into the way things developed in this peculiar West African environment (it was also why he went on to write his best-seller *The Dogs of War*). In a sense, Forsyth was the ultimate 'fly on the wall': unobtrusive, but always there when things happened. More salient, he was a good listener…

As he said, there was no question that a good deal of what appeared in his original novel came from time he spent in Biafra reporting on that dreadful conflict (first for the BBC and, after he had resigned, independently). There was a steady flow of mercenary hopefuls entering the enclave, though only a handful stayed the distance.

While mercenaries did become involved in the war with the rebels, French 'mercenaries' who were involved at the behest of President de Gaulle – as well as a South African Special Forces squad – were agents of their respective governments (something I deal with in the next chapter).

As it subsequently turned out – as intimated by Jan Breytenbach, who worked closely with the French – the departure of Denard and his boys was a ruse. The war was not going well for the rebel state and the last thing the Quai d'Orsay wanted was to be exposed as being Biafra's ultimate lifeline. Supplying weapons was one thing; that could always be denied – and security at Libreville was tight enough to keep the journalists at bay. Anyway, just about everybody was supplying one country or another with arms.

Manpower – in the shape of French 'volunteers', or as mercenaries – was another matter. Were that to be put onto the world stage, there was no saying what the outcome would be. The result was that this activity was kept secret; so was the South African military role, because Paris was picking up that tab – not that there were any 'big bucks' to be made by fighting freelance in this jungle country, where you had as good a chance of going down with an unspecified tropical disease as being shot by accident by one of your own men.

One of Breytenbach's key players, 'FC' van Zyl, only just survived a bout of typhoid after he was flown out of Biafra and put into an ICU unit at the best hospital in Gabon. There, acknowledging

Welsh-born and South African-based 'Taffy' Williams served several tours as a mercenary in Nigeria. After the war, author Frederick Forsyth would help him out when in need. (Author's collection)

that his life hung in the balance, one of the doctors stayed at his bedside for two days and nights until it became clear that he was over the worst; others were not so lucky.

There were actually more mercenaries active with the Biafran forces than are given credit for – in part because Ojukwu was reluctant to admit that these 'guns for hire', who earned $1,700 a month upwards, were a vital adjunct to his fighting capability. They were certainly a mixed bunch and included people like Major Taffy Williams (he turned 34 while serving in Biafra). *Time* magazine recorded at the time that he was a veteran of the 5th Commando mercenaries of the Congo:[1]

---
1 *Time* magazine, 25 October 1968.

Polish-born Jan Zumbach in Biafra, where he flew as a mercenary under the *nom de guerre* of John Brown. He organised and commanded the Biafran Air Force – flying the Douglas B-26 Invader. (Author's collection)

> He thinks he is bulletproof. By now, so do the Federals, who have reported him dead at least five times… Taffy came perilously close to being killed a few weeks ago, when a round smashed into his binoculars. Short-tempered, he curses his black troops constantly, threatening to kill them if they don't obey orders. 'You rotten bastards!' he would roar, when things went wrong, or 'you bloody, treacherous morons!…'

By the time hostilities in Biafra ended, Williams had made a name for himself among this elite band of freebooters. Having served two tours of duty with the Biafran Army, he was quickly recognised for his consistent bravery under fire – rising to the rank of Major. He was also the last white mercenary to leave the country as secession ended – by which time he had earned the deep respect of those who served under him. In fact, Williams later told a South African colleague they would have done anything for him, which made good sense, because he always led from the front. It is also notable that Williams found his Biafran troops to be completely different from those he had commanded in the Congo's southern province of Katanga. 'I've seen a lot of Africans at war,' he was quoted as saying, 'but there's nobody to touch these people. Give me 10,000 Biafrans for six months, and we'll build an army that would be invincible on this continent. I've seen men die in this war who would have won the Victoria Cross in another context.' In this regard (most of those who spent time), he was being loyal to his men – and not exactly truthful. The Biafrans were not fighters – nor had they ever been; they had been forced into this war.

Part of his allure stemmed from the fact that Williams liked to joke that he was 'half-mad'. He would personally lead his troops into battle – sometimes standing in a hail of Federal gunfire

Ares Klootwyk and one of his mercenary pals stand ahead of a Nigerian Air Force MiG-17 that they flew in the Biafran War. (Ares Klootwyk)

simply to prove to his troops that he was indeed 'bulletproof'. It worked – more by luck than design – and his resolve would often unnerve the more superstitious Nigerian soldiers and serve to rally his own.

Williams was initially assigned about 100 Biafran fighters and managed to effectively counter the presence of two battalions of mercenaries from the Chad Republic, who were serving with the Nigerian Federal Army for three months. The Muslim fighters were all armed with Modern AKs, while his men sported outdated World War II weapons.

Completing his first contract and having returned to Britain for a break, Williams went back to Biafra in July 1968 and was assigned to the 4th Commando Brigade, led by Rolf Steiner. The French Foreign Legion veteran had under his command a force of about 3,000 men and was assigned to the area around the critically-important Enugu/Onitsha Road (without which, the enclave would been split in two).

In August 1968 Williams was drawn into one of the most critical battles of the conflict: at this point, he had about 1,000 soldiers under him and was carrying out counter-offensives against two battalion-sized enemy units attempting to cross the Imo River Bridge. The fact that the Nigerian force had Soviet military advisers in its ranks did not go unnoticed. When Williams returned to the town of Aba for additional ammunition to continue the fight, he was told that there was none. The Nigerian Air Force by then had become successful in blocking supplies into the beleaguered

Rolf Steiner in Biafra. He left the rebel territory under a cloud – having been bundled onto a plane leaving Uli Airport with his hands bound. He was later taken prisoner by the Khartoum Government while fighting for Southern Sudan dissidents. (Author's collection)

French mercenary Bob Denard also served a while in Biafra – longer than it was thought at the time – because the Élysée Palace did not want to be seen to be involved in that civil war. (Fiona Capstick)

state – and some of Williams' men had only two rounds left for their rifles; many were forced to withdraw.

The so-called 'Captain Paddy' was one more Irishman who had spent 22 of his 54 years in Africa and had arrived independently from South Africa to be a master mechanic with one of the units. *Time* tells us that just before Port Harcourt fell, he scrounged up a convoy of trucks and 'liberated' – under fire – the entire workshop of the Shell-BP refinery there: 'When Aba had to be evacuated last for lack of ammo, Paddy was one of the last men out – a machine gun in one hand, a demijohn of wine in the other.'[2]

Another of these illustrious Europeans who were fighting this 'Black Man's War' was Captain Armand Ianarelli – a former French paratrooper and veteran of Algeria. He sported a Yul Brynner pate and fought on – despite bazooka fragments in one hand – and quickly made a name for himself by taking his men behind enemy lines and creating havoc. By the time he departed the enclave, people were referring to him as 'Armand the Brave'.

According to Forsyth, Armand was actually a Corsican from Paris 'who later secured a more comfortable assignment as bodyguard to Madame Claude in Paris; she was then the world's most famous procuress of top-class call girls,' he recalled. A *Vanity Fair* report – published in New York in September 2014 – had a lot to say about the Madame in an article headed 'Behind Claude's Doors' and certainly makes for some scintillating reading.

It would appear that the redoubtable Armand rubbed shoulders with quite a few of the most famous names of the day – including Charles de Gaulle (who was a regular), as well as Moshe

---

2 *Time*, Ibid.

One of the author's earlier books deals in great detail with mercenary activity in various African states.

Dayan and Muammar Gaddafi, which makes one wonder whether they ever shared the pleasures of the same girls. Other patrons included the Shah of Iran, Marlon Brando, Gianni Agnelli (who would take his post-orgy groups to Mass) and John F. Kennedy (the American President apparently requested a Jackie lookalike, 'but hot').

Interestingly, the magazine reports, Aristotle Onassis and Maria Callas would show up with depraved requests that made Madame Claude blush. There was even a story on how the CIA hired Madame Claude's charges to keep up morale during the Paris peace talks.

Another of Forsyth's mercenary friends in Biafra was Captain Alec (Alexander) Gay – a former British paratrooper. He used to walk around with a Madsen sub-machine gun, an FN rifle and a shotgun 'just in case I have to shoot my way out of this bloody place.' *Time* magazine said 'he believed in the 'little people', who, he would say in all seriousness, 'will jam your machine guns and cause your rockets to misfire." He was wounded four times in six days before he left Biafra.

Others who left their mark in the rebel enclave was 'Commandant' Kochanowsky – a middle-aged Pole who had served with British forces in North Africa and then spent some years in the Foreign Legion. There was also the unlikely-named Johnny Korea – a West Indian who claimed to have come from Barbados and who ran a bar in Eastern Nigeria before the war.

On Forsyth, I never did get around to asking him whether he used Taffy Williams as the basis for his character Carlo Shannon in *The Dogs of War*, but the similarities are striking. Freddie did

Quite a few of the mercenaries who saw action in the Congo ended up in Biafra
– including Ares Klootwyk and 'Taffy' Williams. (Leif Hellström)

maintain contact with Williams after the war ended, as he did with both Rolf Steiner and Alec Gay, but they lost touch after a while – even though he did help them financially when they were in need.

Alec Gay – a Glaswegian – was among the more interesting characters in the 'Soldier of Fortune' league. He had fought under Bob Denard at the final Battle of Bakavu (Congo) when the unit mutinied and ran circles around the Congolese Army and Air Force. After the town fell, Gay and the rest of the dissidents crossed into Rwanda, where they were all interned in a camp along with scores more mercenaries (both black and white). They remained in custody while the international community decided what to do with them, but security was lax. As a result, quite a few of the men escaped and made their way home.

One ended up adopting another identity (complete with false passport) and managed Rwanda's exclusive game lodge in the Kagera National Park and was never uncovered, but Gay stayed put and, with all the other mercenaries involved in that fracas, was flown out of Rwanda with their passports stamped 'Not Valid in Africa'. Later that year, he appeared in Biafra – fighting under the Frenchman Faulques, who he'd met up with in the Congo.

It was in Biafra that he made friends with Rolf Steiner and Frederick Forsyth – leaving the country in 1969. Not long afterwards, Gay spent a while in the Sudan with Steiner, but he had the gumption to leave that country when it became clear that Uganda's allegiances with its Arab neighbour had switched.

Interestingly, Colonel Mike Hoare – who had led Mobuto's 5th Commando in the Congo – flew into Biafra fairly early on and discussed the possibility of bringing several hundred South Africans to Biafra to 'fight for the cause'. In an interview with the BBC's '*24 Hours*', Hoare claimed that it would have been unethical to get involved, though Ojukwu later told Forsyth that he couldn't afford the kind of money that Hoare demanded.

It was also revealed that Alistair Wicks, who had served under John Peters in 5th Commando (after Hoare departed from his Congo command), left to start a business recruiting mercenaries for the Biafran leader. He supported Ojukwu while his former boss was hiring jet fighter pilots to fly Nigeria's Delfins and MiG-17s.

Mercenary aviators were required to fly all manner of aircraft, including helicopters both in Nigeria and Biafra. (Ares Klootwyk)

Rolf Steiner, Terry Aspinall tells us on his website 'Soldiers of Fortune: Mercenary Wars', was born in Munich in 1933 – a month before Hitler came to power. His father had been a flyer with the famous Richthofen Squadron during World War I and was credited with shooting down 26 enemy aircraft, for which he was highly decorated. He died before Rolf turned four. Young Rolf joined the *Hitlerjugend* at the age of 10 and was only 12 years old at the end of World War II. In his teens he signed on with the French Foreign Legion – doing so in the West German French zone – and went on to reach the rank of Sergeant. Steiner saw active service in Indochina, but did not take part in the Battle of Dien Bien Phu because his unit was stationed in Hanoi at the time.

Still with the Legion, he was parachuted into the Suez area in 1956 during the French, British and Israeli-attempted seizure of the canal from Egyptian control. Later he went on to fight in Algeria and, not long afterwards, was involved in the anti-de Gaulle OAS terrorist movement – becoming a member of the abortive 'Generals' Rebellion' against the French President.

Steiner was twice demoted in Indochina because of unruly behaviour – but nonetheless, was a first-class soldier. In 1959 he was found to be suffering from pulmonary tuberculosis and had a quarter of his lung removed – and for years afterwards, he would tell most of us who met him that his 'lung problem' was caused by a Viet Cong shrapnel blast. Having made a full recovery in 1961 – and not wishing to return to France in case of 'recriminations' – he went to the Congo (as a mercenary) as a member of Roger Faulques' 1st REP in Katanga. Later he became the personal bodyguard to Moise Tshombe – the former Katangese leader after the latter's exile to Spain, but he was not on board the plane when Tshombe was hijacked to Algeria, where the Congolese minister was imprisoned.

Steiner always liked to use the 'Skull and Crossbones' as his regimental symbol, which he thought would constantly remind his troops of the risks inherent to war, rather than any reference to his Nazi links. He admitted too that he found the Biafran troops with whom he came into contact to be quick learners and extremely highly motivated.

In May 1968 he led a successful mission against a Federal Nigerian airfield in the riverside city of Enugu and, in the process, destroyed six Soviet-built bombers and fighter aircraft. John de St Jorre tells us in *The Brothers War* that at one stage, Steiner was commanding the equivalent of a full division of Biafran troops – 3,000 men – and that initially, he worked hard (and sometimes quite brilliantly) for his newfound West African commitment: 'The 'Steiner Group', as it became known, specialised in training and leading the Biafrans in guerrilla-style operations. Even the best trained and most experienced Biafran officers had absolutely no conception of this kind of warfare – and Steiner's men gave good value for money'.[3]

Always controversial – and often at odds with his Biafran superiors – Lt-Col Steiner started displaying symptoms of a nervous breakdown, where he believed that all his friends were against him. His fall from grace came when he was ordered to present himself at the State House in Umuahia to answer questions on why he had commandeered three Swedish Red Cross Land Rovers. He arrived with a group of mercenaries – drunk and belligerent – and refused to hand over his weapon at the gate when asked to do so, and instead demanded a beer, but that was rejected when the glass he was offered was 'too warm'. Cursing and aggressive, he got into a confrontation with General Ojukwu's bodyguards – assaulting one and sparking off a free-for-all brawl. Hearing the commotion outside his headquarters, Ojukwu rushed out and personally saved Steiner from being put against a palm tree and shot. Far from being grateful, Steiner turned round and directed his insults against his saviour. Together with five other mercenaries, he was arrested and bundled out of the country the following night. Ojukwu admitted afterwards that he had been forced to expel him.

It is interesting that while designated a mercenary, Rolf Steiner fought a lengthy campaign in Biafra without pay – serving long after most of his European compatriots had abandoned the cause. He next turned up in the Sudan in November 1969 where he served what was termed 'The Conventional Army of the Anyanya' as a field commander. He stayed in that post for a year, was wounded in battle and evacuated to Kampala. There he was arrested, returned to the Sudan and put on trial for being a mercenary – having been involved in that country's southern war. At the conclusion of a series of court sessions (keenly followed from abroad), Steiner was sentenced to death – later commuted to 20 years in prison. After three years behind bars – and after a good deal of subtle pressure from the German Government, who threatened to withdraw all its aid personnel from the Sudan – the mercenary was released. Steiner retired to West Germany, where he wrote his memoirs, *The Last Adventurer*, which is well worth a read. Forsyth told me that he had fairly regular contact with him for a long time, but that it had lapsed.

It was notable, said one of the officers who served with him – and was subsequently also quoted in *Time* – that Steiner took his French Foreign Legion with him to Africa:

> Legion marches blared from a transistorized recorder that he carried almost everywhere, and the 4th Commando Standard bore the red and green of the Legion. At inspections, Steiner often got his troops' attention by firing off a few rounds from his Browning pistol and then

---

3 de St Jorre, *The Brothers War*.

lectured them – his walking stick under one arm: 'You are not Legionnaires' he would rant after a particularly bad showing. 'You are not men.'

Once he bust a captain to private's rank, but was also known to pick a good man from the ranks and make him an officer.

When he elevated a private to 2nd lieutenant, one of his officers complained: 'My dear chap, we can't have someone in the mess eating with his fingers.' Steiner, who spoke fluent French and German, replied that he did not care if the man ate with his feet, as long as he was a good soldier.

Steiner, said *Time*, liked beer, Benson & Hedges cigarettes, violence and very little else. Compulsively clean, he threw even slightly dusty plates at his mess waiters; then kicked them to drive the point home, but he also plucked a 21-year-old Ibo boy from the side of his dead parents, adopted him and named him Felix Chukwuemeka (after Ojukwu) Steiner.[4]

From the start of the military campaign (as we saw in previous chapters), the Biafran leader cultivated ties with several groups of freelance aircraft operators: some from Europe, one or two from the United States and several from Southern Africa (including Rhodesia's illustrious Jack Malloch).

---

4 *Time*, Ibid.

19

Colonel Jan Breytenbach Takes On the Biafran War

One of the unrecorded events of the Biafran War – until now – was the role of the South African Army in helping Colonel Ojukwu with the formation, training and deployment of his own Special Forces unit. Conducted in great secrecy, it was the brainchild of Jacques Foccart. It was also Foccart's job to maintain close links with Pretoria in order to persuade the South Africans to get involved in this distant, dirty West African conflict as part of his Operation 'Mabel'.

So secret was this relationship that almost half a century after the Biafran War ended, there has never been an official report released either in Africa or in Europe about exactly who was involved – nor anything relating to the nature of the roles played by serving South African soldiers.

This was a fairly modest bunch of professional soldiers and included Jan Breytenbach (then a serving major in the SADF), together with several more notable military personages who were to play their parts in the Southern African Border War that followed. Among this number was young Yogi Potgieter, who had been brought into the fighting group as a medic, though he had never received any formal medical training. In fact, Potgieter had taught himself and made his mark in the unit by being able to adapt to any position required of him.

It is worth mentioning that apart from the French, none of the non-Biafrans closest to Ojukwu – among them Frederick Forsyth who, as covered in these pages, went on to become a close confidante of the Biafran leader – had any knowledge of the South African role or were even aware that they were militarily active in the rebel enclave. It was on the insistence of Foccart himself that French involvement in the war be obscured to the extent that one mercenary group that entered Biafra (the same French squad commanded by the illustrious Colonel Bob Denard and mentioned in a subsequent chapter) were made to look as if they had arrived in the country, got cold feet after their first fire-fight with Nigerian troops and then demanded their immediate repatriation.

Ojukwu did his bit in this charade by telling Forsyth that that was the shortest mercenary contract in history. He complained (obviously with some success) that the French freebooters stayed only a couple of days and that he couldn't ask for his initial financial outlay back because he didn't want to annoy the French, who were his principal suppliers of weapons and ammunition. That bit of duplicity worked so well that French mercenaries – like the South Africans, and fighting on separate fronts from the rest of the Biafran military, or involved in cross-border raids – always remained in the shadows. It would have been a different matter had some of their number been killed or possibly taken prisoner by Nigerian forces. Lagos would have been quick to display either captured white live prisoners or their cadavers for the entire world to see, but that never happened either (though there were a few who were wounded – Breytenbach included).

An aerial view of modern-day Libreville. (Peter Wilkins)

Without Foccart, nothing like this would ever have taken place. For many years, this French senior civil servant was the chief advisor for the Paris Government on its African policies and, more crucially, Secretary-General of the Franco-African Community. He was also the co-founder (with Charles Pasqua in 1959) of the Gaullist *Service d'Action Civique* – a shadowy organisation that specialised in covert government operations. This, in the post-colonial epoch, was a vital adjunct to the politics of the *palais de l'Elysée*, considering that more than a dozen French colonies were granted their independence a short while before.

Foccart's devious roles – and there were many (to the extent that he was able to lift the phone and talk to almost any African leader whenever he wished to do so) – was worth a lot to the French. It helped too that he was his President's Chief of Staff for African Affairs from 1960 until 1974 – and it is common knowledge that he was involved in a number of African *coup d'états* (not all of which were successful).

Africa and its environs seem always to have been a happy hunting ground for military professionals (both legal and illegal). My old friend Bob Denard fought in half a dozen insurrections and wars in and around the continent – including several of his own making. A glance back at recent African history will produce a slew of foreign involvement in matters military. These days it is Boko Haram and AQIM (or, more formally, Al-Qaeda in the Maghreb). Before that it was Chad, Executive Outcomes in Sierra Leone and Angola (together with a host of others).

Most times it has been countries involved, but quite often (as with Biafra), individuals have crept into prominence. These are people like Denard, John Peters (the English mercenary of Congo notoriety), his friend Alistair Wicks or the Belgian adventurer Marc Goossens, who paid for his Biafran exploits with his life. Jan Breytenbach was there as well, for a lengthy six-month spell of duty under the auspices of the French Secret Service, but we'll come back to that. Like the South African, most of these soldiers would stay a while, do their thing and, more often than not, move on to other wars.

One such individual was the British SAS Colonel Jim Johnson, who I got to know quite well before he died in 2008. After World War II he left the regular army and joined Lloyds as an insurer. In his spare time, he continued playing at soldiers and went on to command 21 SAS – the Territorial Army Special Forces unit – before being appointed ADC to the Queen.

It was during this precarious post-war period that Gamal Abdel Nasser – who had taken over the Egyptian Government in a military coup – saw an option of gaining control of the Saudi Peninsula (if not all of it); then the Southern Region in and around Yemen. Strongly backed by the Soviets, Nasser engineered a *coup d'état* in Sana'a, the Yemeni capital, and promptly dispatched his army and air force across the Red Sea to consolidate his gains.

COLONEL JAY BREYTENBACH TAKES ON THE BIAFRAN WAR

Relations between Britain and Egypt had gone into something of a hiatus after the Suez debacle – and Nasser's actions immediately served as a warning to the British that the Protectorates of Aden and Oman were likely to be the next targets in Nasser's sights, which was when Whitehall decided to do something about it and Colonel Johnson was summoned. He was asked whether he was prepared to go into the Yemen and destroy Egyptian jets that were bombing local villages with phosgene poison gas. With typical British duplicity, he was warned by the General briefing him that his actions would be disavowed if he were ever to be caught. Undeterred, Jim accepted the challenge and set about recruiting a bunch of mercenaries, which was how Bob Denard landed up in what was otherwise an off-the-record SAS operation. Interestingly, the Saudis were as eager to rid their peninsula of the Egyptians as the Israelis were, so Riyadh paid all costs and the Israelis (in conjunction with Jordan's King Hussein) ended up co-ordinating the rest. It was left to Colonel Johnson to fight the war, which he did with alacrity.

After several dozen Egyptian MiGs had been destroyed in night raids on their bases, Nasser pulled the plug and everybody went home. The episode is not very satisfactorily recorded in a book by Duff Hart-Davis under the title *The War That Never Was* (previously referenced in Chapter 11).[1]

Two decades before, a still youthful British officer who had played a prominent role in training Jewish settlers in their 'Promised Land' the basics of insurgency was tasked by his London masters to counter the Italian military presence in Abyssinia (Ethiopia today); that man was Orde Wingate who, as a temporary Lieutenant-Colonel, created the legendary Gideon Force. With the aid of local resistance fighters, Wingate and his motley guerrilla fighters (having invited a number of his old buddies – all veterans of the Haganah SNS in Palestine – to join him) harassed Italian forts and their supply lines. In the meantime, British, South African and Indian armies took on the main forces of the Italian Army.

It was this modest Gideon Force – comprised of no more than 1,700 men – that accepted the surrender of about 20,000 Italians towards the end of the campaign. Modest by comparison with other campaigns of World War II, it powerfully underscored what a small, determined and committed group can achieve when they put their minds to it; Biafra was no different.

That brings us to the South African Army's involvement in the Biafran War – a relatively obscure episode neither as vast nor as illustrious as the two previous examples. The man in charge of training Ojukwu's Special Forces was a youthful Jan Breytenbach. It wasn't something that happened overnight: the future Colonel Jan Breytenbach – together with a bunch of hand-chosen counter-insurgency specialists – spent six months in one of the most remote corners of West Africa. Though still in the pay of the SADF, his role was at the behest of France's *Direction générale de la sécurité extérieure* (DGSE) and his role was secretly expanded to a carefully devised and meticulously-implemented programme. It was so secret that most of the regulars who were covering the Biafran War at the time had no knowledge of South African involvement. The Colonel subsequently told me that he was aware of my presence on the ground in the rebel territory, but his instructions were to steer well clear – and from what I subsequently heard from Frederick Forsyth, he was also never made aware of Pretoria's involvement in that war.

What took place in Biafra in the late 1960s ultimately led to the formation of a Special Forces group in South Africa that was to become the famous Reconnaissance Regiment. Tackle Colonel Jan Breytenbach on that half-year that he spent in Eastern Nigeria in the late 1960s and he will tend to talk of other things. Characteristically, he will probably switch the conversation to his beloved Fort Doppies, or possibly Operation '*Savannah*', where he led Combat Group Bravo in

---

[1] This work is, unfortunately, rather long on British and Arab politics and dismally short on most things military that took place.

Early days in South Africa's so called 'Border War' when a youthful Commandant Breytenbach was supported by Eland armoured cars. (Author's photo)

that unprecedented mobile land invasion of Angola that would lead him and his rag-tag group of fighters almost to a position that was within striking range of Luanda.

In fact, until we met at his home in Sedgefield along South Africa's Garden Route coast in October 2014 he'd never really discussed his experiences in that jungle war – nor that he had worked hand-in-glove with the French Secret Service for the duration. His group of operatives was never a large force (perhaps a dozen men in all), with a semi-permanent headquarters in Libreville – of which there was rarely more than a handful who were operational inside Biafra at any one time.

Jan Breytenbach tended to limit those inside the tiny beleaguered nation to perhaps four or five individuals – one of whom was a radio operator and another who doubled as a medic – with solid experience of battlefield trauma. Significantly, while he and his men were involved in many strikes against the Nigerian Army – the majority being a series of long-range penetrations behind enemy lines – none of his men were killed in action. There were a few wounds, including Breytenbach himself, who took a bullet in the gut, but here too, he was fortunate: 'It was a glancing shot in the stomach, in on the left and out under the skin on the right, without actually penetrating my body. A couple of Band Aids kept infection out… and yes, I suppose you could call it luck…' Interestingly, when Jan relayed this information to me at Sedgefield, he caught his wife Rosalind by surprise (he'd never ever told her that he'd almost 'copped it' in Biafra).

Of all the operators who went into Biafra during that civil war period, Breytenbach's military background offers a series of fascinating contrasts. Regarded by his contemporaries as a tough, but thinking fighter, he started his army career in tanks and then spent a year at the Army Gymnasium in Pretoria's Voortrekkerhoogte in 1950 before going on to study at the Military Academy in

COLONEL JAY BREYTENBACH TAKES ON THE BIAFRAN WAR

Saldanha Bay (north of Cape Town). The former head of South African Special Forces – Major-General Cornelius 'Borries' Bornman – made the point during a visit to his Irene home in 2014 that Jan Breytenbach was always streets ahead of his classmates in just about all departments, which is why he was awarded the Sword of Peace on passing out in 1953. It is worth mentioning too that he was among the first of a new generation of military specialists to complete their training at the academy, with most of his contemporaries (including Constand Viljoen) finishing their studies at the Faculty of Military Science at Stellenbosch.

Looking for a more invigorating challenge, the now commissioned Lieutenant Jan Breytenbach joined the Royal Navy Fleet Air Arm as a navigator. During the course of five years with the British, he served in several theatres of military activity – including the invasion of the Suez Canal while active on board the HMS *Ocean* in 1956, where he was involved in ground attack roles. While in the UK, he met and married his beloved Rosalind – the woman who has been pivotal to his life for more than half a century.

With South Africa leaving the Commonwealth in 1961 Royal Navy Lieutenant Breytenbach (his two rings made him the equivalent to an army captain) was given the option of rejecting his South African roots and remaining in Britain, or returning home. He made the obvious choice and rejoined the SADF the same year – almost immediately completing a course with 1 Parachute Battalion at Tempe, Bloemfontein. It was while in the Free State that Breytenbach was one of a dozen South African soldiers chosen to participate in the SAS selection course in Rhodesia with C Squadron 22 SAS; Jan was among only four that passed.

These were still early days and, at the time, the young Republic did not yet have its own Special Forces component. It also meant that when there was an opportunity to send a clandestine military squad to Biafra, Jan Breytenbach – with useful overseas military experience to hand – became the obvious choice as leader. The six-month West African posting was to have a significant influence both on Breytenbach's career and on subsequent developments in the South African Army… on his return to Pretoria, he was chosen in 1971 to found 1 Reconnaissance Commando. Even more significant is that while few soldiers anywhere have the privilege of forming a fighting military unit of their own, Jan Breytenbach created three.

Britain's SAS emerged from David Stirling's efforts in the Western Desert during World War II; General Orde Wingate founded the Chindits; Portuguese veteran Alves Cardoso was responsible for Portugal's *Comandos Africanos* (as well as the Flechas), while the irrepressibly innovative Ron Reid-Daly created Rhodesia's Selous Scouts. As a young soldier, Ron also served with the British SAS in Malaya and was awarded with an MBE for his efforts; some operator!

As for Breytenbach, apart from the so-called 'Recces', he was also tasked with taking in hand a large squad of recalcitrant Portuguese-speaking Angolan Army soldiers that had fallen out with the ruling Marxist clique in Luanda to form 32-Battalion (known colloquially as the 'Buffalo Battalion'). That unit was literally 'forged in battle' during the South African invasion of Angola in 1975; the creation of 44-Parachute Brigade followed. Another of Colonel Breytenbach's efforts was the formation of the South African Army's Guerrilla School, which he commanded until his retirement in 1987.

What is interesting about those mentioned above is that each one of them had rock-solid military backgrounds – and there was not one among them that had come through unscathed. Both Jim Johnson and 'Uncle Ron' were wounded several times – Jim critically, early on in his military career.

For Jan Breytenbach, he felt that Biafran involvement might almost have been preordained, because he was doing nothing useful at the time. Also, the consequences of that deployment would become seminal to his future career because he was thrust into something that, until then, had not been experienced by any other soldier then serving in the South African armed forces.

President Charles de Gaulle meets Gabon's President Leon M'Ba. Between them stands Jacques Foccart – chief advisor to his government on African Affairs. (Paris Match)

A portrait of Jacques Foccart – considered by many to be the French Government's *eminence grise* on the continent.

He was called into Military Headquarters by Fritz Loots (the General then in charge of South African Military Intelligence), given his orders and told to gather together his small body of men and get on with it. His orders were that the mission was 'top secret' and that he was to say nothing to anybody until they were on their way. Any evidence that the group was from 'down south' was *verboten* (to the extent that even the labels on their clothing were removed). No documentation and no letters from home would be permitted, should it fall into the wrong hands. Even library and club cards (for those who had them) fell into that category.

At the behest of the French, Jan Breytenbach and his group flew to Paris before taking a connection to Libreville. Paris (by then) was heavily involved in the Nigerian Civil War, with ammunition flights going into Biafra every night from the former French colony. Breytenbach recalls that although the journey to France and on to West Africa lasted several days, he was never required to present his passport or, for that matter, any form of identification: 'It was all very hush-hush, with us being met on arrival in France and taken straight from the plane to a safe house.' That process was repeated when the group got to Gabon.

Among these troops was Paul Els – detached from duties back home to handle communications between Libreville and Pretoria. Paul was tasked to maintain links with Breytenbach and his team while they were operational inside Biafra (using high-frequency French radio sets for the purpose). As a nucleus, a lovely old colonial house near the beach in the Gabonese capital – complete with all mod cons, which included servants – was made available for use by the South Africans.

For every one of the South Africans, the former French colony that, prior to independence in 1960, had been listed on the charts as one of four territories known as French Equatorial Africa,

Libreville was a revelation. Gabon was not exactly the 'Raw Africa' as depicted by Edgar Rice Burroughs in his *Tarzan* books; it was a thriving French colony where oil had recently been discovered. Also, its leader – President Leon M'Ba – remained impeccably pro-French towards his former imperial masters (in large part because he allowed Paris to maintain a large military force in his country). It went unsaid that one of their roles was that of bodyguard so that the newfound status quo would not be in any way disturbed.

Africa in the 1960s (it will be recalled) was being plagued by a succession of army mutinies and *coups d'état*, with one or two black states experiencing several in a year. The South Africans settled in almost immediately, but they weren't allowed to become too comfortable because within days, a call came for them to get ready; they would leave for Biafra that evening – thus, on their first night flight into the besieged Uli Airport, Breytenbach and his modest team went in with a French liaison officer. The following morning, they were driven through the jungle to Ojukwu's headquarters where, with a quiet and dignified formality, they were presented to their future commander.

Recalling the occasion, Jan Breytenbach says that his immediate impressions were that the Biafrans had a very British way of doing things: all very ordered and correct: 'I found Colonel Ojukwu to be a delightful fellow – the ultimate English gentleman – and the troops around him courteous and well-behaved. These people were not at all like I'd imagined they would be.' He'd already heard how officious Nigerian Army officers could be under similar circumstances, so it was a pleasant surprise. That same morning, Ojukwu took the group around to where they were to be billeted: a small posting not far from Biafran Military Headquarters.

Though offered a range of weapons, the South Africans preferred their own regular issue 7.62 mm NATO-style FN rifles with which to do the work entrusted to them, together with .45 ACP calibre pistols on their belts. 'The Tommy Gun wasn't ideal for my troops,' recalls Breytenbach, 'but with all the close-quarter fighting taking place in the jungle all around us, I suppose it made sense to somebody... and we didn't, or rather couldn't, argue.'

Initially, once they'd found their feet, the South Africans were deployed in an area close to Port Harcourt – Biafra's only remaining port in the south-west of the enclave. 'That was shortly before it was overrun by the Nigerians – and it was also the first time I saw the great Niger River; I thought it was the ocean, it was so vast.'

Once Port Harcourt was lost, they were diverted into the interior – but by then, these men were well into their prime role of creating (or, in Breytenbach's words, 'trying to create') a Biafran Special Forces group: 'We started with about 500 Biafran hopefuls – all keen to become elite soldiers. In the end, following a none-too-rigorous weeding-out process, we were left with about 100 reasonably competent and fit soldiers,' Breytenbach recalls – adding that Biafra was already in the grips of a serious famine, with people (children especially) starving and dying everywhere: 'Obviously we had to feed our men up, but the kind of food supplies needed to do that were limited for us. We'd radioed for South African Army ration packs, and these were flown in, as was lots of mealie meal (*pap*), as well as cans of bully beef – all of which became standard while it lasted.'

Local troops would do a bit of ferreting of their own and catch the occasional forest animal, which included cane rats, he recalled:

> Obviously with the Nigerian Army closing in, we didn't have all that much time, so we made do and turned out our first reasonably well-trained soldiers within about a month. Ojukwu demanded that we take them into action immediately, which we did – even though their weapons training was, to put it bluntly, shit.
>
> We had a really hard time getting the troops to properly aim their rifles in battle. Most of the time they would lift them above their heads and fire blindly into the jungle, exactly as the

Nigerian Army was also doing, which was fortunate for us… also, they'd sometimes empty an entire magazine in the air just for the hell of it.

A very large part of the problem, Breytenbach reckoned, was that many of the new recruits believed that it was the noise made by their firearms that killed: 'Our job was to persuade them otherwise – and to start with, that wasn't easy. We had to instil discipline, right from the start…' Essentially, the Biafran Special Forces concept evolved (as one of the French officers suggested) to give Colonel Ojukwu 'another string to his fragile bow'. The idea rested on the premise that it was essential for some Biafran troops to go where the Nigerians could not or would not go – and that was often deep in the jungle.

Breytenbach:

> I'd soon worked out a system whereby we'd penetrate enemy lines –sometimes 20 or 30 kilometres from our own people – and always on foot, because where we went, there were few roads. Anyway, we didn't have any vehicles – and then we'd attack their lines from the rear.
>
> Basically, the idea was to show the enemy that we were there, fighting them, so that they would have to reorganise their positions and possibly pull out of some strongpoints because they believed they might be cut off. It was a regular form of guerrilla warfare, and it actually worked very well – even if it took a while to get the men into that kind of mindset.
>
> To get them to that level was hell, because the average Biafran was really not a fighter. There were few who were actually belligerent – irrespective of the fact that it was the other Nigerians who had slaughtered thousands of their own people.
>
> One of the best examples of this was when they would bump into each other while moving through the bush; then they'd turn around and say sorry – often so everybody else in the group could hear. Quite a few times, I would trip on a log or something in the path, and half the squad would turn to me and, almost in unison, say: 'Sorry!'
>
> It was absurd, but that was the way these people were – and to get it out of them, me and the guys had to knock a few heads together and create a solid fighting force that could dish it out to the enemy. It took a while, but we got there in the end.

By then, Breytenbach admits, his men were much better fighters than any Nigerian soldiers they encountered in the jungle and could give much better than they got… all of it fire and movement – not fire and freeze!

'With time and good training (and the fact that we always led from the front and not from the rear, like they had been accustomed to until we arrived), this Biafran Special Forces unit proved they really could fight with the kind of dedicated determination that, until then, had had been missing within the ranks.'

As he goes on to comment, by the time Jan Breytenbach got his Biafran charges to charge when he ordered them to do so (usually with fixed bayonets), his men knew exactly what they had to do. It was also something the French observed on one of their visits which, Breytenbach suspects, was really only done to check on how the South Africans were shaping:

> One said something about our making 'stoics' of the troops we were training, which probably sums it all up – and on seeing it for themselves, they were astounded at our progress. They initially couldn't believe it, because we'd trained the unit up to battalion strength – and that was something that nobody had achieved until then… perhaps just as well, because we were dependent on the people in Paris for just about all our food and ammo…

A smiling Colonel Jan Breytenbach with his lovely wife Ros, taken some years after his Biafran adventure. It was only when being interviewed for this chapter at Sedgefield in 2015 that she discovered that Jan had been wounded in that deployment – almost half a century later …

While the newly-created Biafran Special Forces unit had its moments, it didn't take the South Africans very long to accept that they were fighting a losing war. They'd work an area where the bulk of the civilian population would be streaming north to escape the fighting; then, a few nights later, everybody (with their pathetic piles of goods and chattels) would be heading south after the war had swung in the other direction. As briefly mentioned in Chapter 8, there were never any animals in the long columns of starving humans because by then, every goat, dog or cat had been eaten (simply so that people could stay alive).

As the war started to draw to a close towards the end of 1969 most of the South Africans pulled back to their base in Libreville. They were all repatriated soon afterwards, but not before their leader was able to return to the troubled territory on one of the last flights into Uli. There was actually no need to go, but by then, the plight of so many thousands of starving children had got to him: 'I thought I could help, so I hitched a lift at Libreville Airport on one of the decrepit old DC-7s still doing nightly supply runs and flew across the Nigerian coast.'

At Uli Airport that last evening, he was surprised to see Colonel Ojukwu about to board his personal Super Constellation – the appropriately-dubbed 'Grey Ghost'. He realised then that it really was the end:

> I greeted him and he was his usually amiable self – saying something about having to go and look for support; then he was gone.
>
> Finally, it was our aircraft's turn to prepare for take-off, but then we were suddenly surrounded by scores of Biafran soldiers who could see what was happening around them (and were eager to get on board as well). They were a very determined bunch – and every one of them was trying to climb the ladder to the plane's rear door when, quite suddenly, it broke.
>
> Our crew quickly pulled it shut and we taxied towards the end of the runway before lifting off. Things could have worked out very differently had that ladder not fallen apart, because I think it was within the next day or two that the Nigerian Army overran Uli Airport.
>
> Certainly, with a hundred extra soldiers on the plane, we wouldn't even have been able to get off the ground…

Paul Els has written several books on South Africa's military efforts and has some interesting details of his own about his group's involvement in Biafra in a new full-colour edition of his classic on South Africa's Special Forces, *We Fear Naught But God*.[2] The unit's radio operator, Paul was

---

2 Els, Paul, *We Fear Naught But God* (49 Olive Road, Valhalla, Pretoria: Pelsa Books). Paul can be contacted by

The country has been subjected to a strong French influence for the past century. Many of the towns in the interior have French names. (Author's photo)

based in Libreville. He tells us that the Biafran connection came about after General Fritz Loots, while on a formal visit in Luanda (then still under Portuguese control), was approached in his hotel room by two black gentlemen. They were Biafran emissaries, they told him – adding that their country needed help in acting militarily against the Nigerian Government.

After meeting with P.W. Botha, it was decided to send a small team to train this African country's resistance group. Breytenbach was collared on Loots' return and that same night, he and Loots flew to Paris; it was the first time in his life that Jan flew first class. In Paris, they checked into one of the best hotels where, the following morning, they met with the French Secret Service (SDECE) to discuss an upcoming operation. South Africa was already helping Biafra, with weapons clandestinely being flown in on the DC-7C aircraft owned and piloted by Jack Malloch.

The French agent said that Breytenbach and his team would be working with the Biafran Organisation of Freedom Fighters (also known as BOFF). It was also decided that Major Breytenbach's team (still to be selected) would become instant French subjects – equipped with the necessary travel documents – despite the fact that none of them could speak a word of French.

Back in South Africa, Major Breytenbach set about the task of recruiting suitable instructors to make up his team. He naturally began his search in Bloemfontein at 1 Parachute Battalion, where they reluctantly obliged (no doubt because Pretoria had instructed the OC to co-operate fully).

---

email at paul@who-els.co.za; or phone +27.12-651-3188; or fax +27.866049967.

Staff Sergeants Trevor Floyd and 'FC' van Zyl were immediately recruited, while Yogi Potgieter (who had already resigned from the SADF) was located somewhere in the Orange Free State, where he was overseeing the tarring of roads. When Breytenbach put the proposition to Yogi, he promptly walked off the site – leaving the smelly macadam machine in the hands of an astonished crew. During preparations, they were sent to the Engineering School to attend a demolitions course, where emphasis was placed on the manufacture of home-made explosives –their instructor being Staff Sergeant Kenaas Conradie. Afterwards, they were sent to the CSIR for a further course under Dr Vernon Joynt and the late Dr Dan de Villiers.

Once in Paris, the team was joined by a man who General Loots said would be useful to the operation: his codename, in true British tradition, was 'Spuds'. From Paris to Libreville, the group spent time acquiring kit, which included three Chevoux kayaks. As one of them explained, 'these would come in very handy should they have to escape from a collapsing Biafran enclave… they would make their way through the extensive Niger Delta into Cameroon to the east.'

Breytenbach insisted that he and his team keep their FN rifles and .45 ACP Colt pistols, while the troops be given 7.9 mm MAS rifles and .45 ACP Tommy Guns. As for the MAS, the South Africans maintained, the less said the better. Staff Sergeants Potgieter, Floyd and van Zyl were all given field ranks of Captain.

Once in Biafra, they awaited the arrival of the first detachment of trainee guerrillas at a base still being built for them. This gave Major Breytenbach time to plan the training cycle with his team – and to get to know 'Spuds' better. 'Spuds' told them that he had served as a mortar platoon leader with the Royal Marine Commandos in Malaya; that he was a qualified paratrooper; and that he had served with Mike Hoare in the Congo as Hoare's adjutant – during which time he was wounded in a contact. They listened with amazement to 'Spuds'' incredible stories – especially about his 'airborne' exploits. He could apparently do things with a parachute that were out of this world, and kept on blathering about his experiences until Breytenbach curtly interrupted one day him by saying: 'Spuds, lay off the crap! All four of us are not just paratroopers… we are also jump instructors.' Apparently, General Loots had omitted to inform 'Spuds' about the military background of this crack team of specialists. After that, 'Spuds' made no more mention of things military to any of them –especially when it transpired that he could not even properly handle his FN rifle or his pistol; he could not even hit a target at 20 metres with either weapon. As far as the team was concerned, 'Spuds' had become a liability and was of absolutely no use as an instructor, so he was placed in charge of the daily 'War Diary', but after training began, the Englishman approached Major Breytenbach and asked to taken off the team. He said that he did not fit in with 'Boers' (the inference was that it was the team's fault, and not the other way around). He was returned to Libreville to run their logistics, which he proved to be no good at either.

Breytenbach had drawn up a roster whereby he sent two members of the team out to Libreville every two weeks for a long weekend break. This time, while Yogi and 'FC' were on R&R, he received a radio call informing him that the Frenchman – their back-up SDECE in Libreville – had told Yogi that 'Spuds' had been caught scratching around in the desk of the French Intelligence Commander (their link-man); then Yogi found a letter addressed to London in the Pom's backpack, in which it described in great detail to a certain 'John' what the South Africans were up to in Biafra. Yogi had already taken things into his own hands by beating 'Spuds' up in full view of an amazed SDECE audience. Evidently, the Frenchman's visit to the British Embassy in Libreville had confirmed that 'Spuds' was spying on the South Africans, as well as the French, who were (understandably) more than a little unsettled about the situation.

Breytenbach reacted immediately: he instructed Yogi to take one of the kayaks they had left behind in Libreville, truss up 'Spuds' and load him into it; he was then to row out into the middle of the wide estuary on which the city lies and dump the man overboard. It was important, he told

These days, modern Western hotels are the norm in the capital.

Yogi, to ensure that 'Spuds' had drowned before rowing back to shore. That done, he suggested that Yogi then return to the chalet and spin a yarn that the fellow had fallen overboard and had been swept away by the current.

The French, of course, were aware of what was about to happen and they informed their SDECE superiors in Paris, who immediately told Neels van Tonder (South Africa's Military Intelligence man in Paris). Alarmed, van Tonder contacted General Loots in South Africa, who wasted no time in mustering a special aircraft from Paris to Libreville to rescue his *protégé*. They only just made it in time – and 'Spuds' survived to bullshit another day.

It turned out that 'John' was the South African Military Intelligence handler of 'Spuds', who had been added to the team by General Loots to report back on whatever Breytenbach and his group were up to – this in spite of the fact that the Major was sending weekly hand-written progress report to Loots in Pretoria. Livid, Breytenbach wrote a lengthy letter to General Loots and complained bitterly that his Commanding General had posted his own spy on them – obviously because he trusted this English phoney more than he believed in his own soldiers. Breytenbach demanded to know why Loots had done this, and spelled out how useless 'Spuds' had been as regards his military experience and knowledge. He stressed too that 'Spuds' had been a liability – a dead weight – instead of an active contributor to the team. To the day he died, says Els today, Loots never gave Breytenbach a reason.

'FC' had just been through a serious bout of typhoid fever, which had nearly cost him his life. He had been rushed to the local hospital in Gabon, where an African doctor took charge, and even slept beside 'FC's' bed. It was later established that the doctor, upon hearing that 'FC' was a South African, was determined to make a good impression, as he was a great admirer of Dr Chris Barnard, who had performed the world's first successful heart transplant operation.

Paul Els provides us with an interesting insight into Breytenbach's last flight into Uli: the airport was already under extreme pressure from the Nigerians, who were closing in for the kill. Even the air traffic control staff had absconded, and there would be no lighting on the runway; thankfully, there was partial moonlight. The freighter ran the usual gauntlet of AAA fire – though this time, it was much closer than before. After landing, they taxied to an area where hundreds of Biafrans were trying to board the one and only aircraft still flying out of Biafra. Meanwhile, Major Breytenbach had written a letter to the rebel leader – urging him to get out of Biafra as, 'he who fights and runs away lives to fight another day'.

After getting off the aircraft, Breytenbach was escorted by a group of senior Biafran officers to a location in the bush alongside the runway. He gave his letter to Ojukwu who, after reading it (and showing some emotion), shook the South African's hand in a final farewell. Ojukwu's Super

Constellation took off as Breytenbach was making his way back to his aircraft – making his the last one to leave Uli – but the way was blocked by an unruly crowd trying to board Malloch's DC-7C. By now, the Nigerians were already shelling the runway and their ground troops were less than a mile off taking the airport. Fortunately, Trevor Floyd shouted that Breytenbach was the pilot – and that without him, the plane had no hope in hell of taking off. This got through to the mob, which (as luck would have it) made way for the 'pilot', who managed to scramble up a flimsy boarding ladder.

The South Africans then became spectators to a horrific display of panic from people who sensed that the end was near. The air crew had originally intended taking out a final bunch of kids from an orphanage, but the pressing mob made that impossible; the Caritas nun in charge of the children could not get near the ladder. A Biafran colonel scrambled on board and tried to help his family up the ladder, when it suddenly folded and collapsed – injuring some and pinning others under it. There was now no way to get anyone else on board unless a truck was brought forward, but then, some panic-stricken Biafran troops began shooting at the plane in a bid to keep it grounded; still more troops tried to scramble on board.

Since the aircraft's safety was paramount, Breytenbach advised the real pilot – Ed Davis, who had remained in the cockpit throughout this fracas – to taxi out and take off. Like everybody else on board, he feared that they might become just another body-filled wreck littering the outskirts of Uli. The pilot opened his throttles wide and, in the process, cleared the throng still trying to board with his prop wash. The DC-7 taxied fast to the end of the runway and took off. Throughout this process, there was artillery fire coming in from the approaching Nigerians, together with volleys of departing shots from an understandably desperate Biafran crowd, who watched their last hope lift off for Libreville. Says Els: 'Trevor Floyd was awarded a medal for that night's work, while Breytenbach just got one hell of a fright.'

An interesting sidelight to Jan Breytenbach's Biafran exploits was that on his return to the Republic, South Africa's Military Command realised that the country needed its own Special Forces. Following a lengthy briefing to Military Intelligence in Pretoria, General Fritz Loots put the proposal to his senior commanders, and the concept was given the go-ahead. Obviously, Jan Breytenbach would be a part of it:

> The trouble was that I had some very different ideas from Loots and wanted our main base to be at Oudtshoorn – and for several very good reasons. To be able to do their job properly, Special Forces personnel need to fire their guns every single day; it is all part of training and readiness.
>
> Additionally, Oudtshoorn was in the Eastern Cape, close to rows of mountains, a vast open Karoo terrain and some huge forests along the coast. For training, it was ideal. Also, we wouldn't be limited by space considerations, but the General had his own ideas – and it wasn't the only thing we differed on. He wanted what was to become known as the Reconnaissance Commando, and later, Reconnaissance Regiment, to be based at the Bluff in Durban, on the edge of one of South Africa's largest cities, which frankly, was plain stupid.
>
> I pointed out the shortcomings to him – including problems with weapons training – but my argument cut no ice, which underscored the fact that while General Fritz Loots headed an outstandingly elite and competent fighting force that, in its day, compared favourably with the SAS or America's Navy SEALS, he'd never actually experienced any real combat.

'… Fact is, the man had made up his mind and that was that,' added the Colonel, with undisguised disdain…

20

Keeping Biafra Alive: From the Air

There is no question that Biafra – having seceded from the Nigerian Federation in May 1968 – would have collapsed much sooner than it did were it not for the massive 'Air Bridge' that was launched by small groups of mercenaries, as well as religious and humanitarian aid and political groups. Some did so because they believed it was 'right'; others went into it for money. A handful – like the illustrious Jim Townsend – did so because he had a family to support. This is Jim's story.

A mercenary stalwart from the Biafra epoch, Jim Townsend was well known to both Mike Gibson and his father. He was much liked both personally and for his technical expertise in keeping aircraft that should never have left the ground operational. Clearly, covering similar African tracts, they were bound to cross paths from time to time – and by going in and out of Biafra, they did so often.

Townsend, helped by another aviator of the period (the late Peter Petter-Bowyer, who went on to distinguish himself in the Rhodesian War), wrote a brief autobiography. Some of his experiences are illuminating – especially where he explains how he managed to keep clapped-out old four-engine freighters airborne (some of them veterans of World War II), or where he deals with issues related to landing or taking off from African jungle airstrips better suited for Tiger Moths (or a contemporary Cessna-152).

Jim Townsend's autobiography – told in the first person – follows:

After six years' service in the Rhodesian Air Force, I returned to Britain in 1963 to obtain my civil aviation qualifications as a flight and maintenance engineer. Shortly afterwards, I was employed by Autair International, the company that assisted Jack Malloch in forming Air Trans Africa (ATA) in Rhodesia, a company restructured from what remained of Jack's old Rhodesian Air Services.

For most of 1968 I worked as a mercenary flying from Lisbon into Biafra for a private company owned and run by Hank Wharton, another successful aviator who spent years operating on the fringes of the legal world, sometimes for the CIA and other intelligence groups and quite often simply to make a buck.

It was a complex, competitive and cut-throat freelance environment, but Wharton seemed to manage very well. At the time he was operating a small fleet of L-1049 Constellation aircraft flying weapons into Biafra from a room in a Lisbon hotel that was his office.

The German-American arms dealer Hank Wharton had been flying in Czech and Israeli arms to Biafra via Spain and Portugal since October 1966. The military hardware they could not get, the rebels seized. For instance, a DC-3 and a Fokker F-27 were seized from the Nigerian Air Force in April. NNS *Ibadan*, a Nigerian Navy Seaward Defence Boat (SDB) that docked in Calabar Port, was quickly put under the Biafran flag.

But before that, it was all Jack Malloch…

Because the rebel enclave was completely surrounded by Nigerian forces and, starting in 1967, we flew in just about everything needed for Biafra to survive, sometimes from Gabon, other times from the Ivory Coast, South Africa and Portugal. For various reasons, including accessibility and price, most of our maintenance was handled by Woensdrecht, a Dutch concern that specialised in such things.

Mid-January 1968, I was scheduled to fly our Constellation VP-WAW into Woensdrecht for a maintenance check, at about the same time that Jack Malloch was ferrying a newly-purchased DC-7C aircraft from Europe to Biafra via the Togolese capital of Lome loaded with a cargo of newly-printed Biafran banknotes in the hold.

Somehow, the Nigerians had been tipped off and with the appropriate incentives, they were able to persuade a bunch of Togolese politicians to attach the plane and have Wharton and his crew arrested.

The first we heard about our boss being arrested was while we were with Woensdrecht in Holland and things got worse when an early report suggested that they might be executed on trumped-up charges of treason. Obviously, with Jack in jail and nobody to sign the cheques, it didn't take long for the money to dry up. Nor did it help that our ATA, DC-4 aircraft was still at Woensdrecht undergoing maintenance, which meant was that we had two full crews in a Dutch hotel in the middle of a bad winter with no money.

We sold anything of value to survive, even sending messages back to Rhodesia for financial assistance. Eventually after a variety of experiences – some good, others bad – it was decided that somehow we would abandon the aircraft in Holland and leave the country.

The two Captains and a flight engineer headed back to Rhodesia, while Bill Brown, the other flight engineer and me managed to get ourselves to Lisbon, the idea being to approach Hank Wharton for a job; he was flying Constellations at the time. We had heard that he was looking for reliable crews and it wasn't difficult to get the name of the Lisbon hotel.

As I was fully licensed and experienced on L-1049G aircraft, I was taken on, but Bill Brown had to fly as a second flight engineer until he was permitted to go alone on flights. There was good reason for this, including the fact that people who were familiar with the Constellation were aware that the 'Connie' was a flight engineer's aircraft and only as reliable and dependable as the technician in charge allowed it to be.

Early versions of the Constellations could present a mess of problems to somebody who hadn't done his time with these machines and understood the many idiosyncrasies that the plane could sometimes dish up. This was also accepted by Constellation flying crews that only professional flight engineers were qualified to operate this type of freighter.

Customarily, the flight engineer sat behind the pilot to allow him to operate any of the levers and buttons within reach, except, of course, the flight controls. The pilots did not even have a propeller-feathering button up front. Their only engine controls were the magneto switches, one master propeller lever and four throttle levers. Everything else was completely in the hands of us flight technicians, which was why there had to be absolute trust and understanding between the Captain and his engineer to safely operate the aircraft.

Significantly, the flight engineer was also in charge of the power levers or throttles during take-off, climb, cruise and landings. He was consequently a busy man once the engines started ticking over and the job was never boring.

Once I started to fly for Hank Wharton, all his crews were part-timers, spending time on relief flights into Africa when they could pull away from their regular airline jobs in the United States.

About 20 planes were lost at Biafra's Uli Airport during the course of the war – including many of their crews. (Björn Larsson-Ask)

The majority were pretty competent, but there was also a handful that was a bit rusty because they hadn't flown Constellations for a while.

Others found the stress of landing on a succession of Biafran airstrips that had been carved out of the jungle enormously engaging. This was often done in total darkness and sometimes in tropical thunderstorms that would thunder across the west coast of Africa, quite often with no more than three or four metres of tarmac on either side of their main wheels on touchdown.

To all of us, whatever our background, Biafra flights were always a challenge. Others called it dangerous, and there were quite a few pilots who did only one trip in and out of Biafra and headed home.

I was lucky in that I managed to team up with a former South African pilot, Captain Peitrie, from Johannesburg, who had been on some of the bigger Constellations – the L-1600 series. We formed a good team and flew together for about six months, which meant that we could trust each other's judgement without question. That is why, I am sure, we came away unscathed – most of the time – in spite of experiencing just about every type of emergency imaginable.

As a consequence, I became somewhat proficient in what the guys would refer to as 'hairy' situations, something that stood me in good stead later during the course of my flying career in the United States.

With the Hank Wharton set-up, we were always paid in American dollars – cash-in-hand from the man himself and nothing as mundane as cheques. That worked fine for many of the operators, the majority of whom didn't have bank accounts in any event. The truth was, that because there was not a lot of trust, we wouldn't consider going on another trip until we'd got paid for the last one. Hank Wharton had a German girlfriend called Ziggy living with him who seemed to run the financial side of things, together with a lot else besides.

The Constellations that Wharton had at Lisbon had mostly flown in Lufthansa's distinctive livery and initially all were in good shape, but although there was a skeleton crew of German mechanics at Lisbon Airport who were professional, they did very little of what we referred to as 'preventative' maintenance. They undertook only the rectification of flight defects and, sometimes, a sporadic 'pre-flight'.

I would always make a point of doing a thorough pre-flight inspection myself and it was worrying that I'd sometimes come across some hideous faults which would almost certainly have caused us problems during some of the long hauls to remote places in Africa that were required of us. Once, after take-off from Lisbon Airport, I had to shut down an engine because two spark plugs in one of the cylinders were shorted out by metal pieces from the valves. We were at or above our maximum take-off weight (or MTOW) and, even though I pulled power on all three engines, we were unable to maintain altitude; so I had to revert back to take-off power, which is fine for a few minutes, but terminal if you maintain that level of revs for too long.

After we'd put down again, I got Tom Flooney, the chief of the maintenance team and subsequently a Boeing rep, and told him that the engines were clearly all very tired and worn out and that I would like to see the engine log books, which he only eventually produced after a lot of pressure. After I'd checked them I found that every single engine on that aircraft were run-outs, which meant they were basically expired and sold with the airplanes. Naturally we refused to fly Wharton's planes until all the engines had been replaced.

This was done and, on the test flight, I found that the engines were again acting up. Again I checked the new engine logs and found them to be run-outs as well – all sold 'as is' by Lufthansa. Only then were we told by Hank Wharton that the only engines he had were run-outs.

Obviously I was not very popular with the mechanics, but I'd made my point about safety first – and even that didn't prevent us from flying with those same engines. From then on I tended those machines like a quartet of raucous teenagers.

Our average trip, with variations, was from Lisbon to Portuguese Guinea (today Guiné-Bissau) and on to Nigeria's Port Harcourt – Ihiala, a small but strategic town to the east of the great city of Onitsha on the Niger River in Biafra, followed by a return to the Portuguese island of São Tomé. Thereafter we would usually make our way back to Lisbon.

Normal flight time was about 31 hours from start to finish. Our 'full duty' time was approximately 35 hours and with normal time on the ground there would be an hour between each leg. After each one of these trips I would end up sleeping for at least 24 hours in order to get back to the normal world, but if we flew two trips a week I'd be completely shattered. The saving grace was the money, which was excellent.

Of course, there was no such thing as routine 'duty' or 'flight times'. We just kept going like automatons and, once settled down into something that resembled a cruise pattern, we'd take turns dozing off.

This kind of routine went on for several years, and in that time I did my share of experimentation and learned a lot about pushing limits, sometimes extraordinarily so, but I did get the best performances and range on these trips.

As an example, the return leg from São Tomé to Lisbon was a 14-hour flight (empty) and obviously fuel was critical. If we arrived back at Lisbon with, say 1,000 lbs (170 gallons), we'd be chuffed, because under normal circumstances we should still have had about 3,000 lbs in hand because the Constellations we were flying did not have the kind of tip tanks installed as with the longer-range models.

Once we had settled in the cruise I would 'lean out' the engines roughly 10 percent and set the power throttle (power levers) as near as possible wide open. Every hour I'd pull back the rev-per-minute pitch levers in 50 rpm increments.

After approximately seven hours into the flight I'd have full throttle on each engine with the rpm set at about 1,700 (which is clearly not in any instruction manual), but the airplane simply sailed along and you could just about see those paddle-prop blades rotating, with less frictional losses and much-reduced fuel consumption – and this was actually quite good for the machines.

It is worth going on record that our engines actually performed better, ran cooler and were a good deal more reliable that Constellations flown by other crews, some of whom suffered numerous engine failures.

It is worth noting that during all my time flying as a mercenary out of Portugal for Hank Wharton, I lost only three aircraft. One was due to landing gear problems going into Lisbon; one to a wing fire on take-off out of São Tomé; and the third was in Portuguese Guinea because a bomb had been secreted on the aircraft, but it detonated prematurely while we were still on the ground.

Wharton's people did lose a few other airplanes from landing mishaps at Nigeria's Port Harcourt and at Ihiala in Biafra, as well as others that simply disappeared, sometimes into the sea. We suspect that one or two of his aircraft crashed into the mountains in the Cameroons and Bill Brown, the other flight engineer from Rhodesia, was killed during a night-time go-around at Ihiala.

With regard to mishaps, I still have grey hair and very short fingernails as a legacy from our Lisbon to Biafra days.

Minor problems sometimes became major, such as the landing gear problem one of the crews experienced in São Tomé when they skidded their 'Connie' off the runway and ran its nose gear into mud. After the airplane had been towed off and offloaded, the gear was visually checked and everything seemed serviceable. However, our crew was then asked to ferry this machine back to Lisbon, which meant leaving our Constellation in São Tomé for another crew who would deliver our load into Biafra.

We would collect our plane when we again got back from Portugal. The plane we ferried to Lisbon was an L-1049-H with electric-operated propellers – a real dog of a machine.

After take-off from the island, the wheels gear would not lock up and we only succeeded after two or three attempts. From there on the flight was normal. However, 'normal' may be something of a misnomer because, when flying direct from São Tomé to Lisbon, I'd swear there was no need to navigate; we could just follow our oil slicks across the desert.

Then, on getting to Lisbon with 1,000 lbs of fuel after a 14-hour leg, the nose gear would not lock down. We tried several times more, unsuccessfully, before I started emergency nose gear extension procedures. Obviously, fuel now became a major consideration.

The L-1049-H 'Connie' is older and differs somewhat from the L-1049-G, which has an isolation selector valve in the cockpit to direct all hydraulic pressure to the nose gear down lines. This is used to lower the nose gear, which is at least eight ft long, and swings forward into the air flow which, in turn, naturally resists lowering of the gear. The main gear's lowering process, in contrast, was assisted by the air flow and that rarely presented any problems.

In the L-1049-H however I had to get myself into the lower forward baggage hold, remove the side panels and crimp certain hydraulic lines to ensure all pressure was directed to the nose gear actuator. Unfortunately, every time I crimped the line with pliers, it broke – probably because of old age – and then spewed hydraulic fluid all over the place, including over me.

I tried crimping, maybe three times, with no success except to lose more fluid, so the next step was to retrieve the fire axe from the cockpit and cut a hole in the forward cargo loading door of the front cargo compartment. This allowed me access to the front nose gear wheel well, where I could

A historic photo of the start of the airlift into Biafra. (Photo source unknown)

see the nose gear. Because I was covered in hydraulic fluid, I dared not try to open the door because I would almost certainly have been sucked out into the partially-open wheel well.

Through the hole that I had cut, I tried poking the downlock into a lock position with a broomstick, but that didn't work either because the broomstick wasn't long enough. What to do but go back up into the flight deck? There I decided to attempt to get to the downlock through the cockpit floor underneath the flight engineer's seat, but by now everybody on board had become anxious because we really were running out of fuel as we circled Lisbon Bay.

Again, with the use of the fire axe, I cut a large hole in the cockpit floor and managed to get to the uplock, where I managed to prod it into what I thought was the locked position.

Having now acquired three fuel 'greens', which told us that the fuel situation had become critical, we had no choice but to land. As we made final approach I feathered the number four engine – it had already started to 'cough' – and moments later, on finally touching down, number three engine quit altogether.

Having landed, we didn't have enough fuel on board to taxi, which was just as well because the nose gear would have folded up, as the uplock was holding by less than one-thirty second of an inch. The mechanics that came out to us had to chain the nose gear to prevent it from collapsing on the runway.

After that episode, it was finally decided that the aircraft was too costly to repair and was scrapped because of all the damage to the nose gear and structure I had caused with the fire axe. Nonetheless, as I was to discover later, the aircraft was eventually repaired.

Another serious emergency happened while we were operating out of São Tomé not long afterwards. We were flying into Biafra twice every night and that meant that instead of operating continuously from Lisbon, we would be based on the island for a week followed by a month in Lisbon. Though our trips were short, they were tough on the freighters because there were four take-offs every night.

Early on the evening of May 11th 1968, during a normal maximum heavy take-off from São Tomé on one of the 'Connies', I spotted from the corner of my eye immediately after gear up, clusters of sparks emerging from number three engine's power recovery turbines (PRT).

There are three PRTs in each of the four engines which are driven by engine exhaust and coupled directly to the engine crankshaft by oil clutches. Rotating at very high revs-per-minute, each delivers 150 horsepower to the crankshaft. Now, looking directly out of my window, I was alarmed to see that there were flames around the wing between the two starboard engines, yet we'd still had no fire warning.

The Captain was not yet aware of the situation, so I shouted urgently that we had a serious fire. He didn't hesitate, turned the airplane on a wing tip 180 degrees, lowered the landing gear and put the airplane right down back onto the runway. We quickly shut everything down and abandoned the plane on the runway burning fiercely.

Fortunately, we were only carrying Red Cross supplies, but the airplane was a write-off. But for the Captain's quick action and his not questioning my calling an emergency we would have probably have gone down. Another saving grace was the fact that we had to land south-to-north because there was a high mountain at the northern end of the runway. That would have made for a tricky landing and required more air time.

I later found that that our number three engine's top PRT had disintegrated. In the process, it shed white-hot turbine blades across into the adjacent engine and into the wing to which it was attached. Normally this occurrence would have been contained by the PRT exhaust hood ejecting debris out over the wing without causing further damage.

In September 1968, the Biafran War had reached crisis point. Clearly unable to cope with the volume of attrition that was dealt out by the Nigerian Air Force, Odumegwu Ojukwu and his planners desperately sought jet fighters with which to improve their situation. This was an extremely difficult situation because like the MiGs, the planes would have to come with some technical back-up. Still, a few new fighters were better than no fighters at all.

Consequently, the Biafrans approached the French and bought two French Mystere fighters. Getting them into Biafra was another matter.

Obviously the Lagos Government had an espionage network of its own and was aware of this situation. Because money solved most problems in this conflict, the word went out that the Nigerians were prepared to pay, either to prevent delivery or hijack the Mysteres. Even the delivery crews in Lisbon were approached and, as a consequence, none of the crews working for Hank Wharton would accept the contract.

I am not sure whether it was bravado, stupidity or greed that caused our crew to try to deliver the jets, but we did. Anyway, the decision was made as it seemed certain that none of the American crews could be trusted with the job. Jack thought the Americans might try to divert them to Lagos.

The result was that once the Mysteres had been disassembled, their wings were loaded into our Constellation early June 1968. During my pre-flight checks at Lisbon Airport, I found what appeared to be a bomb or a limpet mine inside a PRT exhaust hood. I quickly notified the airport police about the sabotage attempt, the airplane was unloaded and a search conducted for other devices. In the event, none were found. Because of this I slept in the plane that night and stayed with it while it was reloaded with the Mystere wings.

The following morning early, we were off. We had on board a French television camera crew of six to film a documentary on the war.

Our flight to Bissalanca Airport in Portuguese Bissau was uneventful until, on descent, our number three engine started losing oil. This was not uncommon with these planes, so after we'd landed I replaced the PRT. But on the subsequent engine run-up I spotted a cylinder with two shorted secondary patterns on the ignition analyser screen. That suggested cylinder failure.

We notified Lisbon and because of our load, they sent out two German mechanics to handle the problem. Throughout, the plane was securely guarded by the Portuguese military, as Bissalanca Airport was an operational base.

The next technicians arrived the next day, replaced the cylinder and called me from the hotel to run the engine. That was fine, but a hydraulic leak developed under the cabin floor in the centre section, meaning that half of our load had to be removed to get to the leak.

At that point, another of Hank Wharton's aircraft was scheduled to pass through Bissau and it was agreed that because we were lighter, we'd take some of the equipment the other freighter had on board. The second Constellation departed soon afterwards.

Once the mechanics found the leak and fixed it, they again called me to test the engines; that was after two more days of delays. Getting back to Bissalanca Airport by car, I was just coming around the terminal building when one of the mechanics almost rushed into me. He was hysterical, screaming in German that there was a fire.

At that moment a huge blast detonated nearby and I was knocked off my feet as our aircraft exploded on the tarmac. The explosion blew out every single window in the terminal, as well the air traffic control cupola, leaving just the frames.

When the dust and smoke had cleared, there were clouds of Biafran money floating out of the sky, blown from the cargo holds by the blast. Portuguese soldiers were running around grabbing fistfuls of banknotes, stuffing them into their tunics. They were not to know that the Biafran currency was worthless outside the rebel state.

We obviously examined the wreckage and found that the largest parts of the wrecked aircraft were the tripletail, which came to rest on the far side of the runway, together with the plane's landing gear struts. Everything else was gone, including our bags.

When I finally caught up with the terrified mechanics, they told me what had happened. Having put the flooring back in place, they were cleaning up when one of them noticed a column of yellowish smoke emerging from cargo that had been placed on board from the other 'Connie'. That was when they leaped off the airplane and ran.

Our crew got back to Lisbon by scheduled airline and we had to face the music there from Wharton and Biafran Embassy staff.

Much later I learned that one of the American flight captains (no names) who had been at the controls of the other Constellation had been nobbled by a Nigerian agent and 'persuaded' to stop our flight, 'at whatever the cost'.

He had taken it on himself to plant the bomb – and the way I understood it, the device should have exploded while we were in the air somewhere between Bissau and Nigeria. Truth is, we were damned lucky to have been delayed in Bissau.

I was to run into this same Captain sometime later in Miami. He nearly had a heart attack when he saw me; he probably thought I was after him.

During subsequent interviews in Lisbon after the sabotage, I was cleared of any wrongdoing and Wharton invited me back to fly with him. Unfortunately, my old friend Captain Peitrie remained under suspicion and was suspected of being involved. He disappeared afterwards and I have never seen or heard of him since.

While still in Lisbon, Jack Malloch arrived there after his release from prison in Lome. We met at his hotel, where he asked me to go back to Rhodesia with him and attempt to restart his company. I didn't hesitate and Jack also spoke to Bill Brown about returning to Rhodesia, but Bill wanted to do a few more trips with Wharton's people to get enough money to buy a smallholding and retire. 'Sod's Law' prevailed – and on his next trip, he crashed and was killed.

It took us a while to establish how and why Bill Brown was killed, which happened while he was trying to land at Ihiala in Biafra.

It was normal on short flights into Biafra to carry a fourth crew member to observe that all procedures and precautions were observed. This was necessary because things tended to happen pretty fast when under pressure in that primitive environment. Every crew member was relied

Years after the war ended, one of the original Super Constellations involved in the airlift was still deteriorating in the São Tomé heat at the edge of the capital's airport.

upon to be thorough with his checklists properly because there was rarely time for anybody else on the plane to double-check. Also, because it was dark, operational necessities demanded that we show no lights as a precaution against Nigerian aircraft that could drop bombs and outside ground threats.

As happens all too often, it was a sequence of events that led to the accident. For a start, the fourth crew member was not allowed onto the plane because he was drunk, and second, we always flew two airplanes for safety reasons. While the first was landing, the second would circle as a safety watch and then only come down after the first airplane was on the ground.

This system worked well, particularly when were targeted by the marauding Nigerian Dakota, but on this flight there was no second aircraft either.

During the descent of Bill's plane into Ilhalia – which, like Uli and Uga, was really only a road – it was pitch-black. There was no proper illumination alongside the runway as at the other strips, only automobile lights lighting up the runway. From experience, I know that it is exceptionally difficult to spatially orientate oneself under those circumstances with no reference to a visual horizon. It took a lot of judgement, which possibly explains why Bill's crowd must have misjudged the landing and overshoot, which was when they crashed.

I was called by the Red Cross and the local priest on behalf of Bill's wife Maureen to go back to both Biafra and Lisbon in a bid to find out what happened. Also, there was money due from Wharton and he proved a sticky customer with Bill's death. I did eventually get what money was owed to Bill, but I had to get help from some of the other crews, who threatened the American when they realised he did not want to fork up.

I then went onto Biafra in one of Wharton's aircraft and on inspecting the crash site, I found the downed plane's engine instruments, which indicated that on impact they had maximum power on numbers two and three engines but zero on one and four. So when Bill pulled max power for the go-around, he only gained full power on two and not four of his engines. It was an impossible situation!

We then looked around still further and found the fuel control selector pane that showed the levers to be in the wrong position – indicating that the outer engines were starved of fuel when full power was applied. This awful accident reinforced the reason why we carried a fourth crew member to back all crew members flying Constellation aircraft into a war zone.

There were many other incidents involving aircraft that emerged afterwards.

One occurred during landing at Port Harcourt when it was still in Biafran hands. A Wharton Constellation piloted by an American, Bob Majors, came in low and too slow. This situation, as we were all aware, was potentially fatal for this aircraft because tail elevator effectiveness became ineffective to prevent the aircraft nose from pitching sharply up when full power was applied for a go-around or missed approach. The speed would fall further and the nose would pitch up more rapidly. In those circumstances, there was only one option: cut power and accept a heavy landing – but Port Harcourt Airport had another problem. At one end of the runway there was a drop-off with a sharp edge of more than a metre. As the nose rose up under increased power, the wheels of the aircraft would clip in under this edge. In this case, both landing gears were torn away – causing the airplane to roll over and tearing off first one wing then the other in rapid succession.

As it was related to me by the flight engineer, the Constellation was tearing along the runway upside down, with the crew also hanging upside down in their safety belts. All they could hear was the metal above their heads being torn away.

Eventually, the sliding stopped and they all managed to crawl away without a scratch – but most amazing was that the plane had on board 12 Roman Catholic priests in the rear of the airplane. All of them got away without injury. As the flight engineer declared half-seriously, the priests must have had their joint prayers answered that day.

On another occasion, before my time with Wharton, there was a French Constellation called 'The Grey Ghost' operated by a French crew into Biafra out of Portugal. It eventually became Ojukwu's personal plane, though obviously, it did a lot of other work as well.

Their flight engineer quit because his flight companions would drink only wine on board. They always loaded two or three cases of wine for every trip. What then happened was that the two pilots decided that they could operate without a flight engineer – and because nobody would fly with them, this appeared to be fine for a couple of trips when nothing happened; then, early one morning on take-off from Lisbon, they had an engine overspeed – but because the airplane was so heavy and difficult to handle, with an abnormal amount of drag from the over-speeding engine, it took both pilots to fly the airplane. The result was that neither of them could get back to feather the engine. In the end they did manage to make an emergency landing at a military airport, but they never did another trip into Africa.

After flying with Wharton, I finally went back to working with my old friend Jack Malloch and continued flying into Biafra until the end of the war in January.[1]

---

[1] By kind permission of Terry Aspinall in Australia; also published on www.ourstory.com – 'The Changing Face of Aviation 1963 – 1980' (ORAFS – Old Rhodesian Air Force Sods).

DOUGLAS DC-7C «SEVEN SEAS»

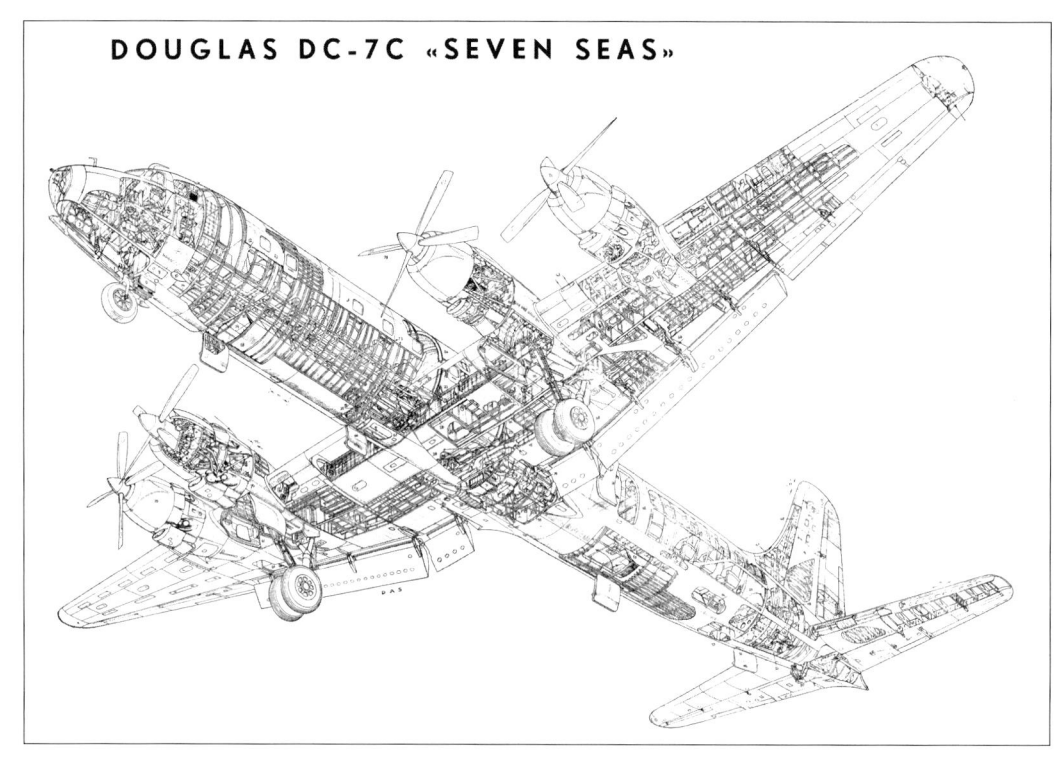

A diagram of a Douglas DC-7 by an unknown artist. (Wikipedia)

Aircraft Specifications

Type:	DC-4	L-049	DC-6B	L-749A
Wingspan	117 ft 6 in	123 ft	117 ft 6 in	123 ft
Length	93 ft 10 in	95 ft 3 in	100 ft 7 in	97 ft 4 in
Height	27 ft 6 in	23 ft 8 in	29 ft 1 in	22 ft 5 in
Empty Weight	43.300 lbs	39.392 lbs	55.357 lbs	56.590 lbs
Gross Weight	73.000 lbs	86.250 lbs	107.000 lbs	107.000 lbs
Cruise speed	227 mph	313 mph	315 mph	305 mph
Ceiling	-	25.300 ft	29.000 ft	24.100 ft
Range	2.500 miles	2.290 miles	3.005 miles	2.600 miles
Payload	11.400 lbs	18.423 lbs	19.200 lbs	20.276 lbs
Passengers	44-86	81	54/102	81
Remarks	non-pressurised	pressurised	pressurised	pressurised

21

A Portuguese Mercenary Aviator tells his Story

Decades after the Biafran War had ended, Artur Alves Pereira – a Portuguese pilot who flew for the rebels – told his remarkable story of adventure and intrigue on the rebel side. He spoke to Kenechukwu Okeke – an enterprising Nigerian journalist with the Lagos *Sunday Sun* who managed to track down this elusive aviator. The story, titled 'My Escapades as a Biafran Warplane Pilot', came as result of a series of lengthy internet exchanges.[1]

Artur Alves Pereira was apparently a most enterprising and innovative aviator who modified Biafra's B-26 plane to suit the purposes of his rebel masters – but, he told Okeke, even getting to Biafra was an adventure. After he had ended his commission with the Portuguese Air Force, he got a job working in Angola flying a Piper Aztec for a big coffee corporation. It was then that one of his Portuguese Air Force colleagues and good friend, Captain Gil Pinto de Sousa, invited him to help him organise a squadron of Harvard T-6Gs to take into Biafra. They would be used in combat missions, he said.

Pinto de Sousa had already been working in Biafra – contracted to fly a B-25 Mitchell, which was destroyed in an accident in Port Harcourt. As Alves recalls, this was not an easy task, because the rebel state was already landlocked (as it had been from early 1968). Also, as everybody by then was aware, the little country was fighting for its basic survival against starvation and an extremely well-armed adversary.

He goes on to explain that because of a variety of diplomatic reasons, they had to bring the aircraft into Bissau by ship:

> The Portuguese Air Force there did a great job mounting the aircraft very fast and it wasn't long before we had six of these Harvards ready to fly. The trouble was, there were only three pilots contracted for the job.
>
> The flight from Bissau to Abidjan was also very complicated. The British Foreign Office had a long and powerful arm and managed to convince Lisbon not to authorise Portuguese pilots to take the aircraft out of Bissau, but then we were a pretty experienced bunch, all veterans of the air force, and we formulated a plan.
>
> We convinced the Bissau Air Base Commander to let us hijack the planes one night and fly them onto Abidjan. Though the flight was within range, we still carried also an extra tank of fuel on the back seat, kind of 'just in case'. The result was that we were stuck with an almost

---

1 Okeke, Kenechukwu, 'My Escapades as a Biafran Warplane Pilot' – Lagos *Sunday Sun*, 8 December 2012.

American World War II vintage Harvards were also used by anti-Castro mercenary Cubans in the Congo against rebels in the east of the country. (Leif Hellström)

The terrain in Southern Nigeria – over which the air war was tropical, harsh and totally unforgiving if your plane happened to be forced down. Most times, there was little chance of survival. (Peter Wilkins)

overpowering smell of aviation the entire trip. It was so intense that I never dared light up a cigarette.

In the end, we put down at Sassandra – an Ivorian port to the west of our destination – and from there continued the flight to Abidjan.

We had our problems, of course. Already in Bissau, one of the pilots decided not to continue and then the same thing happened in Abidjan, but we were able to welcome a new pilot to our ranks, José Pignattely, also a veteran from the Portuguese Air Force. Meanwhile, Gil Pinto de Sousa returned to Bissau and flew out another of the Harvards to join us in Abidjan.

So now we had four of these aircraft in the Ivory Coast and three pilots to man them: Gil, Pignattely and me.

From Abidjan, we were required to tackle the final leg to Uli and it was decided that the most sensible option would be to get airborne and arrive in Biafra at last light; then, quite suddenly, we had problems, with Gil losing his radio and beacon system and getting lost in the dark. Of course he couldn't locate Uli and was forced to bail out over enemy territory. He was arrested after he had been captured and spent the next five years in Lagos.

I landed in Uli and a little later, Pignattely did the same. Next day, we took the planes to Uga, an airstrip in Akokwa.

Asked by Okeke what it was like being in Biafra during the war, Alves Pereira said that he and Pignattely – as well as two Portuguese engineers – were given a good house in Akokwa by the Biafrans and most of their needs provided for:

We had a chef and a guard, who was also the driver of our old Peugeot 403. Another man, Johnny Chukwukadibie, was our liaison officer with the headquarters. Everything around our house was very well camouflaged and we also had access to an underground bunker in the event of Nigerian air raids. There was very little variety in the food we got, usually chicken, cassava and sweet potatoes, which was not too bad, if you consider the situation.

Alves Pereira has numerous memories of his time in Biafra. He recalls the songs that were sung – usually war songs. It was almost Christmas 1969 and he was flying with the only T-6 that was still operational:

Pignattely had gone to Abidjan to fetch the other Harvard we had left behind; then I was sent for by Biafran General Godwin Ezeilo and he gave me the bad news. Apparently Federal troops

Former World War II RAF ace combat fighter pilot Jan Zumbach (13 'kills') with the surplus American bomber on arrival on Biafran soil. (Author's collection)

– more than a division-strong and heavily armed – were about to cross the Imo River. Were that to happen, said the officer, Owerri would be in serious danger and he said that I had to try to stop them; but then, as anybody knows, to attack a strong concentration of soldiers with a single airplane was not an easy task. I knew they were south of the river, but I hadn't been given their exact position, so what I did was to approach the area early in the morning with the river off my right wing. I came in [at] about 500 feet above the ground and nobody opened fire against me.

I swung towards the left, flew over our own positions and made another approach to the river. This time, the Nigerian troops reacted and started shooting from the south side of the river. There were thousands of tracers coming up at me, but now I could identify my target.

I just dived in towards the enemy, gained speed – and in the process, heard the plane taking some hits, but not enough to stop me – and by then I was so close to the ground that I was able to spot trucks and armoured cars sheltering below the trees. There were also plenty [of] soldiers running around, looking for cover.

I let go with everything I had and made my escape at a very low altitude towards the Biafran lines. I was even able to wave farewell to our soldiers.

On another day, at lunchtime, Johny Chukwukadibie arrived at our quarters place with a young Biafran Army captain who had been in the front line during my sortie at Imo River. He said the attack was terrific and a solid success. He told me that they subsequently heard Federal troops weeping a lot on the radio. The following day we went with him to front line to cheer up his men.

It was here, near the enemy line, in the Imo River that I heard war songs from the Biafran soldiers.

A PORTUGUESE MERCENARY AVIATOR TELLS HIS STORY

The Biafrans bought two British Gloster Meteor jets (like this one, still in RAF livery), but one was ditched at sea during its delivery flight and the other – with the words 'ENTERPRISE FILMS' emblazoned on its fuselage – was impounded by the Portuguese in Bissau, West Africa. (Wikipedia)

One of the highlights of Artur Alves Pereira's Biafran exploits was the attack on Port Harcourt – the same one that Ares Klootwyk witnessed from his hotel (see Chapter 10):

> It was my fifth mission – flying Harvards with Pignattely – and we'd been expecting information that Nigerian Air Force MiGs had landed and were parked at Port Harcourt Airport. Finally, the intelligence came in and we were ordered late afternoon to make the attack the following day.
>
> By sunrise the planes were fully armed with the usual four machine guns, as well as a dozen 68 mm Matra rockets. When we got to the strip, we found some light fog enveloping the jungle, but took off anyway. There were no reports of MiGs in the air, but we knew that we would face some of the strongest anti-aircraft fire once we got close to our target. What was essential was the surprise factor, which was very much in our favour: it would be a basic hit-and-run attack because each of the planes would only have time to make a single pass.
>
> Pignattely flew at treetop level and I remained a little higher during the course of the sortie. I felt that my position, above the other plane, would be a safer option once the Nigerian guns started shooting at us. Also, I had better visibility ahead and was able to gain a bit of speed during the final attack, which was the same strategy we'd used before.
>
> As Port Harcourt loomed up ahead, we came in with the sun at our backs, which meant that we approached from the east. Moments later the huge runway was within my sights, together with four MiG fighters parked near the airport terminal, which included hangars, the control tower and one other aircraft.

I shouted to Pignattely: 'MiGs on the tarmac' and started my attack dive in towards the enemy fighters.

By now there were tracers and explosions all around us – and following my instincts, I tried to curl into as small a ball in my cockpit as possible. Having given my engine full boost and with the nose down and the Harvard gathering speed, the four MiGs suddenly appeared ahead, well-centred in my sights. The moment I levelled my wing I started firing my rockets, coupled with several bursts from the Harvard's machine guns.

I could track my rockets in as they homed into the parked MIGs, but then, for a few moments, it seemed that nothing was happening. Suddenly, flames and black smoke erupted from the grounded aircraft. Satisfied, I wasted no time at all before I headed straight out towards the sea. Looking back, I could see that Port Harcourt was on fire with smoke everywhere. Also, Pignattely's T-6 – emerging from his attack – was surrounded by anti-aircraft explosions. He was obviously in deep trouble, but somehow he emerged from the fiery cauldron.

It was time to relax and return. I did a long turn over the water, all the time checking carefully to see whether there were any of the MiGs in the sky, and set an inbound course for home, guided by the Niger Delta. As was our custom, we followed the river northwards and finally landed in Uga. Pignattely's Harvard was already on the ground and camouflaged.

The result: three Nigerian Air Force MiGs destroyed and a four-engine aircraft also damaged. Also hit were a fuel station, the terminal building and Port Harcourt's control tower, which was quite a tally for two propeller-driven training aircraft making single passes.

As he tells us, many years later he was contacted on Facebook by a veteran Russian pilot who had served in Afghanistan. Included was an article in one of Moscow's magazines for veteran pilots which stated that during the course of the attack on the Nigerian MiG-17s at Port Harcourt Airport – which were being flown by British and South African mercenary pilots – two of the fighters were destroyed; one was badly damaged. The fourth aircraft in line was an Ilyushin bomber, which was also hit. After that onslaught, Lagos decided that the best policy would be to camouflage all its operational aircraft. Defensive bunkers would also be built at operational airports to protect any Nigerian aircraft parked there.

Commenting years later on flying in and out of primitive Biafran airstrips in the jungle, Alves Pereira made the point that this was not something new to him:

> Compared to the much smaller Minicons, I needed more length for take-off and landing the T-6s. Uga was little more than asphalt road in the bush, but in pretty good conditions. We had lights as well as goosenecks, for landing at night. There was also a lot of bush where we could secrete our planes.
>
> Essentially though, the flying bit was like David against Goliath. Our aircraft were old, but well-restored. We'd made all the necessary test flights in Portugal and again later in Bissau. Moreover, all our pilots came with good experience of flying on the African continent.
>
> Our biggest problems involved radio and navigation aids – and that started with the simple compass. When we began our Biafran operations, our primary targets were Federal troop concentrations along the Northern Front which lay to the north of Onitsha Road; then came the Southern Front, immediately south of Owerri and in support of the Biafran Army.
>
> Federal Nigerian air bases and oil installations also became the focus of several of our attacks, but we were always expecting information from our army intelligence people in order to be sure where the MiG17s were at any time. As we proved, we could hit them in some of

The remarkable Swedish Count Gustav von Rosen, who rushed to help the beleaguered Biafrans by buying - with his own money - a bunch of Minicon aircraft that were fitted with hard points and rocket pods and used quite effectively to harass the Nigerians in the war. Their sorties knocked out quite a few Nigerian Air Force planes, including several MiG-17s. He was later killed while flying in support of Ethiopia in the Horn of Africa. (Author's collection)

the airports like Port Harcourt, Benin and Enugu, but Lagos was out of range; so was Kano in Northern Nigeria.

Asked how it all ended for him, Artur Alves Pereira said that he had been visited by General Godwin Ezeilo after lunch on 8 January 1970:

> He told me that our Biafran leader, Odumegwu Ojukwu, was about to leave the country and perhaps this might be the right time for me to get out as well. There was a government flight going to São Tomé that night and a place on board had been arranged for my passage.
> I was with the other Ibo pilots when all this took place and though I accepted General Ezeilo's advice and tried to reach Uli, we gave up because the road was so overcrowded with

Port Harcourt Airport towards the end of the war. This Soviet Ilyushin-28 bomber came to rest just short of the runway and stayed there for more than a year. (Ares Klootwyk)

refugees. That was when we decided to prepare the last operational Harvard to fly to Libreville the next morning.

There was only two seats in the T-6 and the Biafran pilots decided that since Larry Obiechi was not an Ibo, it would not be safe for him to stay in what was left of the tiny country, by then almost totally overrun by Federal troops. The other pilots were willing to remain and take a chance on being captured by the Nigerian Army.

We were airborne very early the next day, with our tanks topped up, and made a fantastic flight to Libreville. Throughout, we kept the shoreline on our left always in sight. After we landed in Gabon, we were made very welcome, but I went with a deep sense of loss.

Which raises the question: What does Artur Alves Pereira think of Nigeria today? He is candid and says that not living in Africa, he is used only to bad news from Nigeria, about old politicians and corruption. They must bury their heads in shame and allow the younger generation to take the driver's seat…

I want to live to hug all my mates in the Biafran Air Force – wishing they are in good health – and I pray to God to take care of them. Rest in peace Ibi Brown and Alex Agbafuna, killed in combat fighting for their people.

Thanks too to Gil Pinto de Sousa for the five splendid years you gave me, for supporting a cause in which you so sincerely believed. My thanks also go to Sammy, Willy Bruce, August Opke and Larry Obiechi for the support you gave me in the last days of our dream.

22

Notes from the Diary of a Mercenary Fighter Pilot in Biafra

For some years, I have been in contact with Leif Hellström – one of Sweden's leading aviation authorities. There are few people anywhere who know as much about Africa's earlier air wars as he does. The Democratic Republic of the Congo was his specialty – and Biafra followed close. It is notable that Leif boasts the largest collection of historical photos from both those conflicts of anybody I know.

Leif was a good friend of the late Gunnar Haglund, who wrote the treatise on Biafra's Minicon operations – one of the few ever to appear in print – mentioned in Chapter 11: *Gerillapilot i Biafra* (*Guerrilla Pilot in Biafra*), which was published in 1988.

Leif sent me his translation of the work – and clearly, as the expression goes, it was 'a labour of love'. Sections of this remarkable work are detailed below.

Haglund said in his Foreword that because of his involvement in the Biafran War:

> I unexpectedly gained a fairly good insight into the political game going on behind the stage. I also got to experience the reality as it seems when the difference between life and death is a matter of seconds or only a small mistake, but I also got to observe another reality: that of the children of the war.
>
> Their fate moved me deeply and was a large part of my motivation to participate in attempts to eliminate at the very least the meaningless terror bombings.

This he tried to do by targeting Nigerian Air Force planes that were responsible for so much of the carnage. He kept a diary from the time he arrived in the rebel state – and that formed the basis of the book that followed. As he told us: '… as the years passed, I have in a strange and coincidental way met people who have given me additional facts about the war. This documentation has consequently become more bulky and more detailed'.

'Some of what you see here,' he wrote, 'is based on second-hand information, but most of it I saw with my own eyes'. Operation *'Biafra Babies'*, as it was called, became known to the world in May 1969 after the Swedish newspaper *Expressen* revealed the role of Minicon trainer/ground support aircraft that waged a rather one-sided war against Nigerian forces in the rebel state. As Haglund emphasises: 'After nearly two years of fighting, the Biafrans managed to hit back at Nigeria's Soviet jets, which had attacked civilian targets in Biafra and had tried stopping the air bridge from supplying food to the starving people'.

After the first year of the war, the hunger situation in Biafra had become critical – and the only way to get food in was by air. By mid-1968 various international relief organisations were flying into the rebel territory on a limited scale – most of them using the American airlines that also brought in weapons from Europe to Port Harcourt (and later to the remote Uli jungle airstrip).

The Air War[1]

Early in the war, Egypt sent some 15 MiG fighters to Nigeria. Later, six Ilyushin Il-28s were supplied by Egypt and Algeria.

Attacks on schools, hospitals and marketplaces started in 1967 and continued unabated for the rest of the war. Virtually every hospital in Biafra was attacked at least once, with several totally destroyed. In retrospect, one came to accept that these terror bombings had no real military value; indeed, indiscriminate bombings only served to strengthen the Biafran will to resist.

During the first few months of the war, Biafra had a certain upper hand in the air war, since they had pilots fighting with greater motivation. Most BiAF pilots and mechanics had previously served with Nigerian Airways or the Nigerian Air Force.

An important contribution was also made by Friedrich 'Freddy' Herz, an old friend of most of the Biafran pilots, who had spent time in training in West Germany. Herz received several letters from his Biafran friends asking him to come to Africa and help. After some deliberation, he went first to the Cameroons where, in September 1967, he was permitted to enter the rebel state.

Nigeria's Pilots[2]

The MiGs and Iluyshins were initially flown by Egyptians. They were not very skilled, however, and many aircraft crashed on landing. The number of operational aircraft steadily decreased. The aircraft flew at day and kept away from the diminutive Biafran anti-aircraft artillery. They were based at Enugu, Calabar and Port Harcourt.

The Ilyushins attacked using anti-personnel shrapnel rockets. 20 kg HE bombs and 100 kg HE bombs were also used, particularly against Uli. The most serious threat was the bombing of Uli. In most cases, DC-3s based at Benin were used for these strikes. They circled Uli at 3,500 metres – waiting for the lights to come on when a relief plane was approaching.

The DC-3 also homed in on the two radio beacons near Uli – even though these only transmitted when requested and often changed frequencies.

Bonzo was one of the mercenary pilots flying DC-3s for Nigeria. He was an eccentric around 60 years old, almost always under the influence of whisky. He often wore a knitted cap, one of those used by the Hausa men of Northern Nigeria. Bonzo was an Englishman and returned to England in the summer of 1969, before the end of the war. A leg injury, inflicted during one of the Biafran Air Force's attacks, forced him into a long convalescence. After being injured, he stayed in a village near Escravos and consumed even greater quantities of whisky than before. For a while, his injury became critical and there was a risk of his leg having to be amputated.

Jimmy was another pilot in Nigeria, a South African and considerably younger than Bonzo. Jimmy was powerfully built and had a large red beard. He was high-spirited and very talkative. After drinking a few beers he would tell with delight of his raids against Biafra.

Ares, Jimmy's good friend and countryman, was much more silent and never talked about what he had accomplished during his raids. Ares was almost timid. He was relatively young

---

1 Haglund, *Gerillapilot i Biafra,* pp.16-20.
2 Haglund, Ibid., pp. 21-24.

and small in stature, behaved well and went easy on the liquor. He flew MiG-17 aircraft and participated in the chase of Minicon planes in Biafra and also succeeded in finding two of them on one occasion.

Another MiG pilot was **Mike**, a dark Englishman around 30 and a former Royal Air Force pilot. His wife and three-year-old daughter were with him in Nigeria. At the beginning Mike served in Kaduna as instructor on the Jet Provost aircraft. However, these were soon destroyed in training flights and as the need for MiG pilots increased, the more well-paid terror flights against Biafra became increasingly attractive to Mike. Despite a certain resistance from the wife, Mike began making raids on Biafran villages and roads anyway – but fate did not give Mike much time to shoot at the Biafran civilian population. During a flight home to Benin it had become dark and when Mike was about to land, the airport personnel made the mistake of not handling the runway lights correctly. The runway lights were turned off too soon; Mike tried to land anyway with the help of the MiG aircraft's own landing light, but he misjudged at the end of the landing, crashed and was killed.

Francis was another mercenary pilot. A French national and a man of the world in his behaviour, he was dark and good-looking. Francis flew DC-3s and, like Bonzo and Jimmy, had a permanent runny nose because they spent so much time operating in the cold and dark at 3,500 metres over Uli Airfield, where they lay waiting for approaching relief aircraft.

Marian Kosobsky was originally Polish but had become an English citizen. During the Second World War he served with the Royal Air Force as a night fighter pilot, on Mosquito aircraft. After the war he started a succession of air transport companies, which were not successful. An unusual fellow, Kosobsky had a pointed grey beard, was a Bohemian and had experienced many adventures.

He tended to radiate a strong presence and his enthusiasm rubbed off on people around him. Presumably he flew DC-3s. The information on his flights in Nigeria is somewhat uncertain and he did not stay there for long. Also, Kosobsky was old and he really wanted to take it easy: he said once that he intended to go home to England, buy himself a house and spend his time on his big hobby, fishing.

The mercenary pilots in Nigeria was thus a motley bunch of people. The main motive for their involvement seems to have been the very good salary – around £800 (roughly $1,500 at the time) a month plus bonuses for every successful attack, which meant, in effect, after they had got rid of their ammunition or bombs. In addition, there were other benefits like free board, liquor and women.

There was also a Nigerian pilot, Captain **Alfa**, who flew MiG fighters. He was probably the only Nigerian aviator flying actively and most of his raids against Biafra he carried out with Ares.

Benin[3]

On the Friday, von Rosen went to the BiAF Headquarters while the others stayed by the base. There had initially been talk of making three attacks the first day, but von Rosen wanted to plan properly to assure success.

Haglund spent the day walking around in the neighbourhood, taking photos and talking to people. Any remaining doubts he had about the just cause of the Biafrans disappeared during these walks. Von Rosen returned in the afternoon – and during the evening, they planned for a new

---
[3] Haglund, Ibid., pp.58-65.

attack the next day. The airport at Benin was chosen, since it was known to be used by the NAF (including those aircraft used for night-time bombings of Uli):

> At three o'clock I was woken by a Biafran, who shook me to life. There was warm water for the morning coffee. Scattered sounds were heard from the other parts of the bungalow, as the others began to wake up. Willy would pass on this one. The other four of us went along the narrow path to the aircraft. We were all rather tired and a little peeved, but despite this it felt good to take off at a time of day when the Nigerians definitely would not expect an attack.
>
> The camouflage had been removed and the aircraft stood parked along the runway with the rocket pods loaded. It was very dark. Each of us prepared for flight – checking the lights, sight, fuel level, instruments and everything else that belongs to the pre-flight procedure.
>
> The Warrant Officer could be glimpsed out in the dark. 'There was no torch in your plane, so I put one behind your seat,' he said. 'You may need it.'
>
> I closed the canopy, started up the engine and waited.
>
> CG took off first. He would lead this time as well, with me as Number Two and Martin and August bringing up the rear. CG wanted to lead the group during every strike – considered it his duty, since he had the responsibility. The rest of us thought we could take turns, but CG got his way.
>
> My aircraft stood furthest up at the end of the runway and I did my engine check in the middle of the bushes. As soon as CG had disappeared, I turned directly out on the runway, guided by a soldier with a torch; then it was my turn and I open up the throttle. The aircraft accelerated very slowly. It was bumping across the uneven runway. I picked up speed, faster and faster – the aircraft must be very heavy, I thought and looked at the airspeed indicator, which showed an ever-increasing speed. The flaps were down one-and-a-half notches. That was exactly the position we should use. If we had less flaps we would not be able to climb at all. If we had more flaps, like two notches, air resistance would become too much and we would not get off the ground.
>
> When the speed had finally reached take-off speed, I pulled the stick slowly and felt the wheels come off the ground. With high nose and low speed I began flying by instruments. At the very end of the runway there was a bush, which we had nagged and begged the ground crew to cut down, but it had not been done. I now saw CG's white rear light turn to the left – strange that the bush could not be cut down. After all, it was not a holy tree…
>
> At that very moment the fuse for the lights in my aircraft blew and everything turned black. I could not see anything. All lights, both position and instrument lights had the same fuse. I held the stick completely still with one hand and with the other frantically groped for the torch which the Warrant Officer had put in the cabin. To my indescribable relief, I found it quickly and could put it between my knees, with the beam on the instruments.

Lacking position lights, Haglund positioned his aircraft 500 feet above the agreed 2,000-feet altitude to avoid the risk of collisions. He lost the others for a while, but picked them up again at dawn when the formation dropped down to lower altitude. The last 15 minutes of the approach was made in daylight, although the sun had not yet come up over the horizon:

> We came from the east and the last buildings we passed before the Benin Airfield proved to be a number of military barracks. No children or women came out and looked up, only semi-dressed officers and privates. CG climbed, turned left and went into a long dive. I followed him and during the climb the city of Benin was visible to the right. In front of me

lay the airport with the runways, control tower and a MiG fighter, half-hidden by the terminal building. Only the tail section was visible.

CG's task was to put an anti-aircraft battery out of action which, from the direction we attacked, lay to the right of the terminal building. He now dived towards his target. I saw white puffs of smoke blossom up and clearly heard the ack-ack start shooting with – as I later found out – Swedish-made 40 mm Bofors guns. I fired my first rocket at the MiG aircraft, which was half-hidden by the side of the house. To my surprise I saw one of the rockets hit just at the wing root.

At the same moment, the aircraft was turned into a large ball of fire and black smoke poured out. I fired my remaining rockets straight into the buildings and against the centre of the runway, thereby hoping to destroy the runway lights. The whole thing was done very quickly.

I was still in a slight left-hand turn, went directly over into a right-hand turn and passed over the burning MiG aircraft. The heat cushion from the burning aircraft gave me a strong push upwards. All this time the guns on the ground were firing. The two soldiers I had time to see, who were manning the ack-ack, were cranking away furiously to aim the gun at me. But, as I said before, everything happened very quickly and surprisingly and they simply could not keep up. They were shooting all the time, however, and a weak knocking sound could be heard through the Plexiglass canopy at each burst.

CG had perhaps been hit. The gun was going full bore and he was not to be seen. After flying through the black smoke from the burning MiG aircraft, I went down over the field, flew at a very low altitude and then climbed a little. I turned right to enable the wing tip to clear the ground and then headed for the cover of the bush.

At the last moment I spotted some telephone wires, which was when I pulled the plane up and over them. By then I was then out of range of anti-aircraft fire.

When I once again passed the barracks to the east of the airfield, a lot more people had come out – they had presumably heard the explosions and wondered what was going on. I asked over the radio if everybody was with us and CG answered that he did not yet know. Apparently he had survived, anyway, despite the bold dive towards the anti-aircraft guns.

The time was now 06.35 and our attack had taken two minutes. The sun was now over the horizon. I soon found the other three and we headed for home. It became a very difficult flight home. During the night and the dawn the Plexiglass canopy had become full of insects which we had collided with.

During the return flight we had the sun straight in our eyes and saw almost nothing through the canopy. We had to open a small hatch in the canopy next to the pilot seat to be able to see forwards, or at least at an angle forwards.

The pilots all kept low over the treetops on the flight back. Smoke from the burning MiG was visible from far away when Haglund looked back. Along the way, he aimed at some power pylons (in case he had any rockets left), but his launchers were empty. They crossed the border river south of Onitsha. After a while, von Rosen started circling and talking to Martin Lang over the radio. To Haglund, it seemed like they were unsure of where to find their own field – and fuel was starting to get a bit low:

We circled for nearly 20 minutes. By now we were annoyed at not being allowed to return to base. Just when I was in a turn over a small village, the engine quit. I shifted back to the reserve tank and at the same time tried to turn towards a small meadow, while preparing for an emergency landing. Then, when I had only a few metres before I hit the ground, the engine started again. There was plenty of people down there and, startled, they looked up at me, much too close it seemed.

Haglund then prepared to land on one of the wide, black-top roads which were plentiful in Central Biafra: 'At that moment I spotted Martin, who was turning and descending towards a small road. It was always easy to recognise his aircraft, since it had a canopy of green Plexiglass, while the others were colourless'.

As it transpired, they landed at an airbase after all – though not the one they took off from. When they did their checks, they found that Haglund had only three litres of fuel left, which was enough for about five more minutes' flight:

> At first the aircraft were parked under some bread-fruit trees, until it was realised that one of those fruits falling from 20-30 metres up would probably go straight through the aircraft, so the MFIs were quickly shifted to a safer place.
>
> All of von Rosen's rockets were still in the launchers. For some reason, they would not launch during his dive on the Nigerian anti-aircraft position. The fault was never traced and was put down to a temporary electrical problem.
>
> It turned out afterwards that August had fired three or four rockets straight through a night bomber, which stood on the runway's apron. He and Martin had approached the target from the west and August had immediately spotted the machine, which was out of sight from the direction I approached. He saw all [of the] rockets go into the bomber and we could therefore report his bomber, if not destroyed, then badly damaged.
>
> Martin attacked an anti-aircraft gun in the western part of the airbase and, in addition, had had time to fire a couple of rockets on the control tower.
>
> After an hour or so, Willy turned up to congratulate them. August disappeared to get some fuel, since there was none at the base. The others relaxed under the trees, once spotting an Ilyushin passing over them at high altitude, before turning towards the east.

Enugu[4]

They took it easy on Sunday, 25 May – the day after the Benin attack. By then, both the BBC and Radio Lagos (for the first time) had reported their strikes. Later, it turned out that the BBC had had a reporter in Benin during their attack.

After some discussion, Enugu was selected as the next target and the time set for the afternoon the following day. They would use four aircraft and approach from the west – having made a detour to avoid flying over the heavy fighting at the Northern Front. Afterwards, they would land back at Camp II:

> Again, an Ilyushin was spotted at high altitude, escorted by two MiGs which were seen attacking some target far away.
>
> At roughly 16.00 hours on the Monday the pilots took off from a field they now called Camp III. Once more they flew at treetop level.
>
> In front of us I saw the pylons for a power line and I immediately thought of CG, who was in front. We used to warn each other by quickly pressing the transmit button a couple of times. I did so and got an immediate reply. I was now sure that CG was aware of the danger ahead. When we got nearer and the cables themselves were visible, I expected him to climb a little and pass above. To my consternation he continued in his stubborn way directly towards

---
4 Haglund, Ibid., pp. 66-75.

the power lines, which were drooping treacherously, only a metre or so over the treetops. It was now too late to try and warn a second time and I expected to see the aircraft trip over the lines and disappear into the greenery.

To my surprise and great relief, the aircraft instead continued on, apparently through the power lines. I could hardly believe my eyes. I had to climb about five metres to get clear and so did Martin and August. I could not understand how CG had not been able to collide with the drooping wires. He must have flown right between them, or possibly he had passed over them with his wheels almost touching the cables.

He has luck, too, I thought.

The tiny aircraft flew over the road west of Onitsha. There was a lot of evidence of the fighting that had taken place on the ground below – and some shots could still be heard – but there were no troops visible. Haglund again lost sight of the others for 20 minutes or so and was preparing to attack on his own:

During my final approach I suddenly spotted the other aircraft. They were to the left of me, slightly behind. I did not have to think anymore about this, since suddenly – just above the low trees in front of me – I caught sight of a MiG aircraft taxiing on the ground. It was about half a mile away.

I made my lowest attack so far. In fact, unlike previous times, I did not climb at all but fired almost all my rockets just above the bushes in a long stream towards the Soviet jet. No rocket hit the aircraft directly but went in just beside it and exploded. The MiG – engulfed in smoke and shrapnel – stopped, rocked and then came to a complete halt.

When I turned sharp-left shortly afterwards as we'd agreed to do earlier, the other MFI aircraft came in on a line, diagonally behind me. In order not to hinder them in their attack, I dived down as low as I could so as to get out of the paths of their rockets. A few seconds later, just above me, I could see a bunch of white trails as their rockets headed in towards their targets with a hissing sound.

At that moment, my right wing hit the top of a bush. Although it was only a small bush, the cascade of leaves and the jolt to the aircraft came as a shock. For a moment I thought I'd crash, but moments later I'd regained control of my plane again. I continued flying in a series of zig-zag patterns over the forest and decided that perhaps I should keep a better lookout next time…

My flight path took me over a part of the airport that revealed a Canberra bomber at [*sic*] had obviously been hit by one of our guys and was emanating great volumes of smoke. I didn't linger [and] continued to move away from the airport. Only then did I realise how silent it had suddenly become: We had apparently been subjected to some really intensive ground fire!

How had the others fared? I had no idea, though I could hear someone talking over the radio, but couldn't tell who it was. The humidity and heat were tough on our communications equipment and sometimes we picked up only static and crackling.

When I was safely over bush country, I tried to work out how many rockets I had left. I felt that I couldn't have fired all of them during the attack, so I circled around once more until everything appeared to be quiet over at the airport and made back there. Once it came clearly into view, I lifted my nose and fired a long shot towards the terminal building. The rocket left me in a wide curve and ended up going straight into the building. It was 18.40 when I turned away and began the return flight.

It was turning dark very quickly. Haglund decided to take a more northerly route than originally planned: to go around some of the mountains his group had crossed on the way in. It was pure coincidence that he suddenly crossed the paths of von Rosen and Okpe – themselves an hour or so into the flight (and despite the fact that they had taken a different route). He lost them again a while later, however.

At their base, there was a radio beacon transmitting for 30 seconds every 15 minutes – and the little fighters would home in on this. When close (and ground crews could hear them approach), they would ignite oil-filled tin cans that served as runway lights. By then, Haglund was unsure of his position and, due to his detour, was starting to run very short of fuel. Worse, he had another 15 minutes to go until the next beacon transmission. He therefore asked the Uga Airstrip to turn on their lights for a few moments so he could get his bearings on Camp II. Shortly afterwards, he landed safely. Once back in the bungalow with the others – and beer in hand – he was told about Lang's adventures during the mission.

Haglund:

> Martin Lang – an excellent pilot – had followed me to begin with, but due to my turn to the left, was prevented from going into the attack. Consequently, he held his fire for a few moments and then aimed and fired at what looked like a petrol dump to the immediate south of the terminal building. At the end of this firing sequence, and still at the edge of the jungle at the south-western edge of the airfield, his aircraft was hit towards the rear fuselage by ground fire.

When Martin recounted this experience, he said that he immediately dived, but got so low that his nose hit the uppermost branches of one of the last trees on the perimeter of the airfield. Leaves and foliage whirled around his plane and some of it got stuck in the engine air intake.

Lang:

> That decreased the air flow into the engine and my revs went down from 2,400 revs to about 1,700. After my collision with the jungle I continued the dive down until I was almost level with the ground and then flew straight and across the runway, turned right and passed just beside the MiG aircraft which had just been shot at a short while before. Still, my speed decreased steadily and I no longer got any power from the engine.
>
> With my decreasing speed and at this low altitude, which almost put me on the deck, I made a slow turn around the entire airport complex desperately trying to pick up knots. By now, my stall warning was sounding almost constantly.
>
> My wide circle took me around a large terminal building, where I passed some high radio aerials – after which I found myself over the runway again. I caught sight of another jet fighter in front of the terminal, but though I tried, I couldn't make a tight enough turn to fire upon it.
>
> In the distance I spotted another of our MFI aircraft disappearing over the treetops, heading north-west. For a moment or two I hesitated between trying to escape and possibly continuing to find a target – all the while continuing along the runway at the lowest possible altitude. My stall warning was still making noises…

The runway at Enugu Airport stretches east to west and is more than a thousand metres long. Martin flew its length with half his rockets left. At the far, western end stood four or five Canberra bombers with their noses pointed towards the same jungle into which both Martin and Haglund had almost disappeared. A little further away stood another aircraft: a parked Heron. 'What did surprise me was that nobody on the ground was firing at me,' Martin recalls. As he reckons, it might have been because he was flying so low – most of the time little more than a metre above the asphalt of runway 09-27; it is possible that the Nigerians feared hitting each other if they shot at his aircraft.

DIARY NOTES OF A MERCENARY FIGHTER PILOT IN BIAFRA

About 500 metres from the row of camouflage-painted aircraft he had spotted earlier, he fired the rest of his rockets and believed that he might have hit a couple of the Canberras and certainly the Heron. As he stated, his aircraft suddenly became much lighter after he'd released the rockets – and he barely managed to clear the bush at the far end of the runway and disappear over the horizon.

Lang had a bit of trouble gaining enough altitude to clear the high ground on the way back to base, which was why he turned south earlier than planned; his engine was now in a very poor condition. He crossed directly over the front between Akwa and Onitsha at dusk – and it was there that his stabiliser was hit by ground fire. Again he dived to treetop level and (eventually) made it back home.

Following every mission, the pilots involved in strikes were required to compile a report which was forwarded to the BiAF Commander. These were used for detail compilation and comparison with what their colleagues had seen and experienced.

That night, the Biafrans arranged a dance in an empty school building. Von Rosen (the BiAF Commander), along with several army officers – as well as just about everybody at the base –came, together with a large part of the local population. The next day, the pilots slept late – and when they eventually surfaced, Haglund and Lang went for a long walk in the countryside and talked with many of the locals. They could see that the community was much relieved, because three nights had passed without any attacks by the Nigerians on the Uli Airfield; daytime attacks had also been sparse.

Not long afterwards, they visited the Biafran Army Headquarters, where they were told of an incident at the Owerri Front about a week earlier – and it amused the Biafrans who were present immensely. What had happened was that a fairly large force of Biafran troops had encircled a small Nigerian force. After a while, a Nigerian Air Force DC-3 appeared and dropped supplies to their men below. To mark the spot, the Nigerians fired green signal flares. The next time that plane appeared – also to drop supplies – it was the Biafrans who fired green flares (and all the supplies came down behind Biafran lines).

The general impression at that stage, recorded Haglund, was that morale in the rebel army was very high. All the Biafran personnel at Camp II did everything they could to make things work – despite the majority of them lacking any kind of proper military training.

MiG Attack[5]

Gunnar Haglund continues with his report – this time recording a Nigerian Air Force MiG attack:

> One of the consequences of our first three attacks was that for the first time in a long while, there were no Nigerian aircraft in Biafra's airspace.
> The Red Cross and church relief flights could, reportedly, also be carried out undisturbed. On one of those attack-free nights, 50 relief flights crossed the Nigerian coast with food and armaments and landed at Uli – a record for a single night – but one day, while CG, Martin and I were sitting drinking coffee, we heard the sound of a jet overhead. We went out in the open and looked up at the sky – and there, high above us, was an Ilyushin bomber   ame a surprise: two MiG fighters at a much lower altitude turned in towards the b
> into a shallow dive. Seconds later, shrapnel exploded all around us. We threw

---

5 Haglund, Ibid., pp. 76-79.

one of the bunkers and stayed there for several minutes – all the time aware of more rounds exploding in and around our base.

Another sound could be distinguished from the dull thuds, and that came from the automatic cannons with smaller calibre – a little harsher and faster. After each dive the MiG aircraft made, it took a few seconds while they went around to come back and give a new shower of bullets. The bomber remained at high altitude, as if to keep [an eye] on developments during the course of the onslaught.

As suddenly as the attack had come, it was over – and then everything went quiet; then shouts were heard and people started to run out from their cover.

At any rate, it seemed as if Nigeria now had a new type of pilot flying. Normally, only places without anti-aircraft guns were attacked, but this time they had attacked a military position – and had done it very professionally.

One of our people had been killed and there were nine injured. Even the camp doctor was hit: he took a small wound in the forehead. Like the rest, our ground crews were very unhappy at the prospect of becoming targets.

Haglund set of for his bungalow and sat down with a beer (brought in to him by one of the gun runners); then the MiGs reappeared again – about 20 minutes after the first attack – and hit the base once more. This time, the MiG pilots knew exactly were to strike: they came in a bit lower, used some flap and throttled back, which was why he had heard them so late, he recalled afterwards:

The first burst hit the bungalow where I was sitting and a 37 mm rocket went straight through the wall, passed right by my face and landed in front of me, smoking on the floor. I sat looking at it where it lay smouldering, incapable of doing anything, but it did not explode; then I really got going. I put down the beer and threw myself under the bed in the adjoining room. There I lay for the remainder of the attack – counting myself lucky to be alive. The others had also been surprised by the second attack – and at least one more person was killed.

On another occasion afterwards, Haglund and Lang were out walking when they saw a MiG attack another military target about half a mile away. They got a lift to the area, where they found two boys in their late teens, who had returned from the balcony of a house with a heavy machine gun. The walls of the building from which they had retaliated were pock-marked with hits from the MiG's guns – and what became clear afterwards was that they had apparently hit it. Witnesses in the area said they had seen something fall from the fighter, which then broke off the attack; it had obviously been hit by ground fire.

23

The Air Attacks Continue

A good part of this war of attrition centred on how much the respective air forces could pummel each other's ground positions. While the Ilyushins – flown by Arab pilots – rarely took chances and were regarded as almost superfluous to the war effort by most of those involved, the Minicons did a lot, but they were hardly a match for the Egyptian-supplied Soviet MiG-17s flown by European mercenaries.

Ughelli[1]

The fourth MFI strike was made on the same day that their base had been attacked by the MiGs. The target was the power station at Ughelli, which supplied power to large parts of the Mid-West Region, as well as Benin Airport. One MFI would take off from the base which had been attacked, while the other three were to start slightly later from another field. They were all rather nervous when taxiing out and kept an extra-sharp lookout for MiGs.

Okpe was supposed to meet up with the Swedes over a small village near the river, but did not turn up. Due to a technical problem, he had not been able to take off. The other three reached the giant, grey power station at around 1845 hours. The original plan was that Okpe and Haglund would attack from the east, but Haglund now chose to join the others, attacking from the west, where a number of transformers stood next to the building:

> CG was now very close to the building – too close it seemed, but the building was big and in the twilight I was probably the victim of an optical delusion. CG's machine climbed a little and then descended again. His rockets streaked away against the lower part of the building, where the transformers stood. Blue and white flashes shot out from the transformers in a mix of explosions and short-circuits.
>
> When CG had fired all his rockets, Martin became irritated – he was at a suitable firing distance and thought that CG remained in his shallow dive too long. 'Move over, damn you,' he said.
>
> CG turned left and Martin's rockets streaked away in pairs, with continued explosions in the building as a result. As soon as Martin turned away after firing all [of] his 12 rockets, it was my turn. The target was now engulfed in white smoke. I started shooting and the rockets went straight into the same part of the building as the others had fired upon. The slight tug could be felt each time I pressed the trigger and the rockets left their capsules, but one rocket streaked diagonally upwards and disappeared over the roof of the building. I did not have

---
1 Haglund, *Gerillapilot i Biafra*, pp. 80-83.

Egyptian Air Force Ilyushin Il-28 bombers (such as this one) were sent to Biafra on Moscow's insistence to help the Federal Nigerians in their war against the rebels. (Wikipedia)

time to consider where it might end up; then a left turn and up over the low bush. Right then it struck me that I had not counted the number of launches. Six launches, two rockets at a time; then all rockets are away – but I was unsure whether I had in fact fired all of them. At a very close distance to the building, perhaps 100 m, and level with its roof, I kicked right rudder and skidded the aircraft in the air while at the same time lowering the nose and aiming for what looked like long windows in the upper part of the building. When I pressed the trigger, two rockets streaked away: one in through the window, the other one passing the roof; then I turned left and went down to minimum altitude, over the protective bush.

By coincidence, several years later I met an engineer who had helped repair the power station after our attack. He told me that the transformers naturally had been shot to pieces and had to be replaced or repaired, but this only took two-three weeks. However, one rocket had hit the vital oil cooler situated at the highest point of the building. To make it work, parts had to be ordered from England with great delays, which meant that the power station was out of action for half a year.

He also said that he had been impressed by the penetration power of the rockets. One rocket which had hit beside the transformers had gone through the half-metre-thick concrete wall, continued a few metres in a stairwell and finally passed through the next wall inside the building.

Once again, they returned to base after dark. The landing drill had been carefully rehearsed and the approach and landing did not take more than three minutes for the three aircraft – whereupon the runway lights were immediately extinguished.

Uli's historical jungle airstrip was bulldozed immediately after the war. Without it, Biafra wouldn't have survived more than a few months. (Courtesy of Björn Larsson-Ask)

They went to bed late that night. An hour or so later, a poisonous snake got into Haglund's and Lang's room, but was spotted by Lang in time. It was beaten to death with sticks by the Biafrans, who came rushing in to see what the commotion was all about.

Owerri[2]

The fifth mission was flown on 30 May: the Biafran Independence Day. The Biafran forces had been advancing southwards, but had been stopped west of Owerri. At that moment, they had a well-supplied Nigerian force surrounded, but needed to dislodge them before advancing further. The mission of the MFIs was to attack the surrounded force, just south of the village of Obigwe. The target would be difficult to identify and also heavily armed.

It was decided that they would fly in two pairs and within sight of each other – attacking from the north at 1700 hours. About half of the rockets would be fired at the village itself, and the rest at any vehicles or other targets on the roads within 500 metres of the village:

> We passed Owerri and went down to very low altitude. CG and Martin were slightly ahead of August and me; then I saw CG climb a bit like he always did before attacking, but he did not lower the nose to shoot, but instead continued to climb. Now he was up to about 100 feet and he began talking to Martin: 'I cannot see any village, Martin,' he said.

---

2 Haglund, Ibid., pp. 84-87.

Michael Robson provided this grainy shot of one of the Biafran bombers in a rather dilapidated condition.

While CG continued to climb, Martin also started to climb. They were now talking constantly.

When both of them were circling at at least 300 feet during a lively discussion on where the target might be, I told August: 'We stay here.' Thus August and I were circling over a deserted field – and very low. I thought: 'Descend CG, for God's sake.' And he did so.

All four aircraft flew home by way of Obigwe – the same way we came – and without firing a single rocket.

They were later told that the Nigerians had been firing away with machine guns, rifles, bazookas – everything. Although the mission had been a failure, at least the Nigerians now knew that it was no longer entirely safe to move on the roads. Von Rosen, Haglund and Lang had to leave Biafra the next day to return home to their civilian jobs. They met the BiAF Commander a last time – and it was obvious that he now believed in his air force. On the wall of his office was a photo showing him and some other officers with a MiG canopy between them.

The Swedes wanted to leave Biafra as discreetly as possible, since August was now the only one in the country trained on the MFIs (a fact they did not want the Nigerians to know about). On the way to the airport, their car had a puncture and they nearly missed their flight.

During their trip home to Sweden, they were told that a Red Cross aircraft had been shot down. The co-pilot, Stig Karlsson, had been a friend of Haglund's. They expected this act to have severe repercussions on the Nigerians, but this was not to be.

The Attacks Continue[3]

The five Swedes (von Rosen, Lang, Haglund, 'The Doctor' and the mechanic) had gone home, but the five MFIs were still in Biafra. During July 1969 the BiAF had only two pilots available: August Okpe and the Swede Rune Norgren. During his month in Biafra, Norgren carried out a total of 21 attacks – sometimes in co-operation with Okpe, but in most cases on his own.

Norgren made several attacks along the front line in co-operation with the army, both north of Onitsha and south of Owerri. After von Rosen's aborted attack on 1 June [*sic* - in the Owerri chapter, the date is given as 30 May] the Biafran Army had devised a system where they put out

---
3 Haglund, Ibid., pp. 92-101.

THE AIR ATTACKS CONTINUE

A close-up of one of the Nigerian Air Force's Czech-built Delfin jet fighter/trainers. (Wikipedia)

metal plates to show the position of their own positions; they also shot signal flares to guide the pilot:

> The first mission carried out by Rune and August was to attack the target at the front where we had been before without shooting, due to CG's and Martin's vain attempts to find the position. Rune and August took off from a base near the Niger River at lunchtime and flew south. They followed the road between Orlu and Owerri, located the village of Obigwe and found the plates put out by the Biafran soldiers. The forest still hid the small village held by Nigerian troops.
>
> They did not climb, but flew just next to the treetops. Just before the edge of the forest, each one turned in a different direction. August attacked from the west, [and] Rune from the east against the village held by Nigerian soldiers. This was Rune's first attack. He saw the rockets go into a lower trajectory than he had expected. He saw soldiers run in the village when he aimed for the buildings. It was difficult to estimate the effect of the strikes. It all went very fast. Rune concentrated on the flying and to handle the rocket launching correctly. This was his first ever shooting with rockets. He did not have time to see much of August during the attack, but he too attacked and fired all his rockets at the village.

During the flight to the target, Okpe's aircraft had been fired upon by Biafran anti-aircraft guns north of Owerri – and the person responsible for this mistake was later arrested. The next morning, Okpe and Norgren took off again for a new attack on the same target, but they ran into heavy rain and had to turn back. Back on the ground, Norgren had a talk with von Rosen, who was visiting Biafra for a few days, and later took off on his own:

> He found the target and now came in from the south against the same village they had attacked the day before, and started looking for a 'green house'. The Biafrans had found out that in this green house in the village, there was an ammunition dump. When Rune passed the front line from the south, he spotted the green house. Since he was then too close to shoot at it, he turned sharply to the left and pulled the aircraft through a complete turn. Now he was in a better position to fire.

Count Gustav von Rosen in a casual moment near his Biafran headquarters. He was the man who provided Ojukwu with his Minicon strike wing. (Author's collection)

When the house was visible in the sight, he pushed the trigger on the stick. The first rockets launched went straight into the house. The result was a terrible explosion. Parts of the house flew into the air and above the aircraft. Rune did not have time to turn away, but passed close by and was very close to being hit by the roof of the building, when this was on its way down after the explosion.

The army took advantage of the situation and managed to take half of the village moments later. Norgren then carried out a reconnaissance flight for the navy – against the small tributaries of the Niger – looking for Nigerian gunboats. He did not find any during his two-hour flight.

The next mission (a couple of days later) was aimed at the Nigerian ferrying near the destroyed Onitsha Bridge. No boats were spotted by Norgren or Okpe, but a couple of buildings and a truck were destroyed. They were met by very heavy fire from the town on Onitsha. Norgren later made a point of always ascending slightly when passing this area to keep the Nigerians on edge. They always fired anyway, but never hit him.

The same day, Norgren made two more attacks against buildings in Onitsha, with the first target thought to be used by Nigerian officers; the rockets went straight into the houses. The Nigerians later claimed that a hospital had been hit, with one pregnant woman killed and 10 civilians wounded. This was probably untrue, since Biafran Intelligence was usually very accurate. He went back to the base, and five minutes later took off in another aircraft – attacking three buildings thought to be Nigerian barracks; all three buildings were hit.

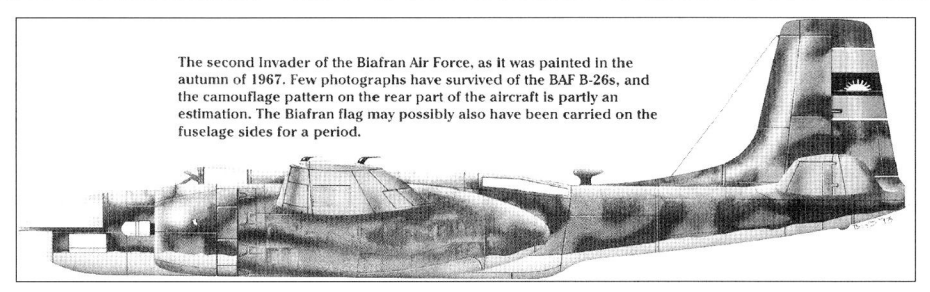

A beautiful depiction of one of the Biafran Air Force B-26 Invader bombers. (Source unknown, but believed to have been painted by 'Boyd' in 1973)

At the BiAF base, a warning system against NAF aircraft had been worked out: if there was a sentry at a crossroads near the field, it was OK to land, but if he was gone, this was a danger signal. Norgren could see no sentry when he returned from Onitsha and made an extra turn around the field. Since all looked quiet, he went in and landed. Just as he touched down, he got a warning over the radio, but by then he was already down, and hurriedly taxied into cover. He was later told that two NAF MiGs had been circling the field for five minutes – disappearing at the same moment Norgren approached.

The next attack was scheduled against a gunboat yard at Warri – and the flight would take 48 minutes. Okpe was to lead the attack, but was apparently not too keen on the mission (he had been flying for months by now and was getting tired out). Forty-three minutes into the flight –when they were approaching the coast – they met with a rain shower, turned around and headed for home. On the way back, Norgren recalled that they had passed close to a steel pipe sticking out of the jungle, with a flame burning at the top. He guessed that this must be some kind of oil installation and decided to attack it on the way back:

> Rune climbed slightly and spotted the flame again. He went down to minimum altitude again and flew towards this improvised target. He passed just next to the plant. If there were any workers there, they would be warned. There was a large pressure tank. On both sides of this rose pipes, with flames emitting from their top ends. Next to the tank there was also a building. A multitude of pipelines followed the ground in different directions from the plant. When he had passed the position, Rune climbed, made a wide turn and came back in a long shallow dive.
>
> He fired two rockets: no explosion, when they hit the building. Two more rockets: still without visible effect. At the third salvo, a large fire broke out next to the pressure tank. The fire spread quickly and became increasingly violent. Rune fired the remaining rockets in quick succession, since he was now close to the large pressure tank. He was afraid that the whole tank would explode.

Back at the base, Norgren wrote the usual report on the mission. Later that evening, the Chief of the Intelligence Service arrived and asked Norgren to point out the exact location. He then stated that Norgren must have hit one of the main pumping stations. After this strike, Nigerian oil production decreased significantly and the oil export figures soon became classified.

Other attacks were made west of the Niger during this period to disrupt the Nigerian lines of supply. Norgren describes one of these:

There are very few of the aircraft that saw service in the Nigerian Civil War still around. This former Egyptian Air Force Ilyushin bomber sits in a museum.

I followed the road westwards towards Benin. A few kilometres from the Niger, a Land Rover was driving behind a large military truck. I went out over the bush and attacked from the rear quarter. The first thing hit was the top of a palm tree which stood in the way. It was transformed into a flame of fire. I missed the target with two more rockets, but then hit the Land Rover, which had speeded up. It went burning into the ditch; then I caught sight of one more Land Rover, behind the first one. This too had speeded up, but on seeing the fate of the first one, the driver of this car apparently decided to stop. This was done so abruptly that it turned over and rolled into the ditch. The line of sight was now masked by trees and, in addition, I had passed the target, and I therefore returned homewards.

Okpe participated in some of the attacks (e.g. in one against a Nigerian HQ building in Asaba, opposite Onitsha, which was completely destroyed). For a week, they carried out strikes against roads and also particular buildings – and then they too took a few days off. Okpe went to his wife in Urlu and Norgren went for walks near the base. The Biafrans wanted to allocate a bodyguard to Norgren, since they were afraid of Nigerian assassination attempts, although it was very difficult for strangers to move about unnoticed inside Biafra.

A few nights later, the BiAF Commander visited the base. By this time, Norgren had made 12 attacks and Okpe four or five. The BiAF Commander told them that several DC-8s had recently unloaded troops and equipment at Enugu at night, and he seemed very angry that the BiAF had not been told about this in time, so they could attack the aircraft on the ground.

The Nigerians were now advancing from Abagana towards Okigwe – and the next day, Norgren and Okpe destroyed a truck, an artillery piece and a couple of Jeeps north of Abagana. As soon as he got back, Norgren took off in a new aircraft to attack a village recently captured by the Nigerians. A building apparently used by Nigerian troops was completely destroyed with six hits. The following day, Norgren made a recce flight in the area and shot at some Nigerian cars. He also made an attack on the Eastern Front at a railway station between Port Harcourt and Enugu. Several Nigerian Saladin and Ferret armoured cars had been reported, but Norgren was unable to locate these. Instead, he attacked two trucks – destroying at least one of them.

The above strikes were all made during July and the first half of August. The rest of the Biafran pilots had not yet been trained on the MFI and, with only two available pilots, the BiAF Command preferred to let the army decide what targets to attack. If nothing else, it was calculated to force

A trio of Nigerian Air Force Czech-built Delfin fighters (foreground), with several more modern jets behind. (Wikipedia)

the Nigerians to be more careful – thereby slowing down their advance. However, it was decided to attack the oil installations in Escravos before Norgren left the country – and Okpe was to lead the mission. The first attempt failed due to strong winds, which made them drift off-course. A renewed attempt was made a couple of days later – and this was Norgren's last mission before he went back home.

The flying time to the target was about an hour. The weather became increasingly bad and when they got to the coast, it was raining constantly (with the visibility down to less than a kilometre). After some problems they found the oil tanks, but decided to try to locate the drilling platform first. However, the bad visibility made this rather risky and they soon gave up (they went for the oil tanks instead):

> We found the bay for the second time. Followed the beach and there they lay. Large grey silhouettes in the mist. At very close range I fired two rockets. They disappeared into the tank. In the left-hand turn I then had to make I saw how oil was spurting out of the holes from the rockets. The oil coloured the ground black. The next moment it started to burn. August lay close behind me and we turned in over the bush. I do not know if he had time to shoot. We then turned back again. Then we spotted a landing field. At the far end, the end nearest to the tanks, stood three helicopters and we both fired at them as soon as we spotted them. The rockets did not hit directly, but we still calculated on having damaged them with shrapnel, which must have enveloped them on the ground. The impacts were only the odd metre or so from them.

24

Fault Lines: Nature of the War

As with all human enterprises – conflict included – things do not always go to plan. The Biafran War was no exception, with some enormous history-altering blunders creeping into the scenario on both sides of the front. Had the Nigerian Military Government not been as arrogant as it was – and its generals so utterly ruthless while hostilities progressed – the war might have ended much sooner.

Jan Breytenbach's efforts in the Biafran War went unreported, but with his characteristically unconventional approach, he'd succeeded in making an impact – yet his group of specially-trained fighters was tiny compared to the bulk of the forces on both fronts (which, at best, on the Lagos side alone, numbered close to six figures).

Clearly, to have matched this effort, Colonel Ojukwu – later elevating himself to full General – managed to pull a few tricks of his own out of the hat. He continued doing so for more than two years, which tells you a lot about this genocidal tribal struggle, for basically, that is what it was: the tiny Ibo nation – or as some prefer, the Igbos – raggedly ranged against the rest of Africa's most populous state.

As we saw in Chapter 3, Biafra's failure to go in for the kill when Ojukwu's forces had taken the city of Benin and the mid-west – and were clearly within striking distance of Lagos – was arguably the single biggest blunder of the rebel campaign. Frederick Forsyth accompanied the attacking force as an observer and, as he told me, he couldn't understand the reticence. Only afterwards, when it became obvious that Victor Banjo – a senior Yoruba army officer and close associate of Ojukwu – had betrayed his command within the Biafran forces, did any of it make sense: 'Had they gone right on in – the road to Lagos was wide open because any deployable Federal troops had already been sent north – they would have walked into the capital,' he stated; then there was the inability of Lt-Col Benjamin 'Black Scorpion' Adekunle's 3rd Marine Commando Division to summon a larger force than anything the Biafran Army could muster at the time to cross the Niger and take Owerri – especially since he had, for support, two full battalions of black mercenaries from the Chad Republic; that lapse was nothing short of culpable.

He went on (in a single day) to lose 1,500 of his men in a stupid onslaught across the Niger – exposing him for the brutal, unthinking charlatan that he was. The man was relieved of his command shortly afterwards – and none too soon either – but then Adekunle had always been something of a loose cannon within the ranks of the Nigerian Army (and there are many instances on record of him executing his men with his pistol for real or imagined infringements of discipline). That would very rarely happen within Biafran ranks – and then only if there was treachery or a charge of cowardice in the face of the enemy involved. Still, to give him his due, Adekunle was tasked with knocking into shape a unit composed of regular soldiers, as well as a surfeit of criminals and brigands.

In an interview with Michael Gould in September 2008 he made the point that he was given the task of recruiting from public sources what amounted to a full division of troops. Most of those taken into his ranks – often shanghaied or brought there under duress – were taken off the streets of Lagos and other cities.

As he told Gould:

> … I selected men from all walks of life, but found that some of my best soldiers, after training, came from the dregs of society. Many of my men had formerly been in prison, and were released to serve in my division. The 3rd Marine Commando Division was created from scratch by me from such dubious sources as street thugs, outlaws and renegades – mainly from Yoruba [Western Nigerian] ethnic groups. I then had the task of moulding them into a credible fighting unit.[1]

The Yorubas always seemed to have played a devious role in this war, both in the ranks of the military and along its fringes. Indeed, it was Lt-Col Victor Banjo who had originally switched sides to serve in the Biafran Army. His betrayal of the Benin invasion (by making contact with his former Federal bosses in Lagos through the British High Commission) in the hopes that he could end up leading the war against the rebels didn't work – and when he returned to Biafra, Ojukwu put him up against the wall with the other plotters and had them all shot. This is something I deal with in detail in my earlier interview with Forsyth (Chapter 3).

Considering the number of innocents who died during the course of the war – a figure of one million (mainly children) is constantly mentioned – Britain's role, according to Forsyth, was sometimes culpably duplicitous. It also included some military help, though Whitehall has consistently denied this. He told me that early on in the war a large number of British Army NCOs arrived in Lagos to help with Nigeria's war effort. From corroborating evidence that came to him from London, these men were referred to in official documentation as 'on attachment for training purposes' – but, as Forsyth said, their effect on the war effort was immediate.

In his book *The Biafra Story*, he states that following their arrival, there were many new developments. For instance: 'Nigerian radio communications became infinitely better and the Biafran monitors heard clipped British voices issuing instructions across the ether'.

He goes on:

> Complex co-ordinated manoeuvres previously beyond the scope of the Nigerians became the order of the day. Vehicle maintenance on the Nigerian side increased at the same time and their shortage of transport a few weeks previously was solved. More notable, by April [1968] these specialists were constructing Bailey bridges which were used to cross rivers that had previously baffled them for months. The Engineering Corps of the Nigerian Army had originally been composed almost entirely of easterners and the Biafrans were aware that building Bailey bridges at that speed was beyond the capabilities of the Nigerians alone.[2]

What also emerged afterwards was that in one of his key assaults south of Afikpo, Adekunle used the expertise of British amphibious experts to stage two landings across the strategic Cross River. The river (at that point) was almost a mile wide, so it was a significant breakthrough because it was not expected. His forces first captured the market town of Oron and, with his fast-moving

---

1 Gould, *The Biafran War*.
2 Forsyth, *The Biafra Story*.

Leif Hellström provided this photo of one of Biafra's 'home-made' tanks.

mercenary-led columns, they went on (in quick succession) to take Ikot Ekpene, Ooyo, Abak, Eket and Opobo.

His glittering prize at the end of it all that April was Port Harcourt, which the Nigerian Army (in conjunction with its navy) took soon afterwards. The city, with its modern airport, was to become a forward staging post for Nigeria's Soviet-supplied MiG-17 jets flown by South African, British, Australian and other mercenary pilots.

As we have seen in previous chapters, mercenaries played a prominent role in the Biafran Army. Rolf Steiner helped to create a brigade of shock troops that were pushed into desperate frontline positions at short notice – and his closest associate, 'Taffy' Williams, helped him to put together the Biafran Fourth Brigade. 'Taffy' always claimed that the Biafran troops under his command were the best fighting men in Africa – and there was nobody around who would argue with him. In truth, while their spirit was hugely willing, starvation played a debilitating role throughout the Biafran Army and they were no match physically when it came to matching strength with the average Nigerian soldier.

By July 1968 Steiner had managed to train a very substantial force of 3,000 men, which he split into six battalions (or as he preferred to call them, 'Strike Forces'). Forsyth goes into a lot of detail about these mercenaries in 'Thirty Months of Fighting', which forms Chapter 9 of his book *The Biafra Story* – still rated as the best and most detailed work to emerge from that war (if only because from the start, Forsyth's friendship with Ojukwu was close to the heart of it). He also tells us of Johnny Erasmus – another unusual young character from Rhodesia who prided himself (and the Biafrans) as being a wizard with explosives. At one stage, south of Owerri (one of the most important rebel centres), Erasmus was put to work building a ring of explosive-charged obstacles to stop the Nigerians advancing. He dug pits, laid mines, arranged arcs of fire and planted booby-trapped grenades at every vantage point imaginable. When the Nigerians did eventually arrive, they were unable to breach these defences (which were eventually dismantled by the Biafrans themselves).

One of the most important battles of this early stage of the conflict is reported in detail by Forsyth and involves the Nigerian attack on the city of Aba – the only large Biafran city left to the rebels and overflowing with refugees. It became the prime target for Lagos' forces – now bolstered by Soviet technicians on the logistical and engineering side. This series of battles was seminal to both sides – and I quote Forsyth in detail with regard to some of the action around Aba:[3]

> Aba, shielded from the south and west by the curve of the Imo River, was presumed to be safe from attack. It was the biggest city left – now overflowing not only with its original refugees, but many of those from Port Harcourt. It was also the administrative centre of Biafra. Across the Imo there had been two bridges: one at Imo River Town on the main road from Aba to Port Harcourt; the other at Awaza, further towards the west.
>
> The first bridge had been blown up; the second was intact, but mined. It was the Awaza Bridge the Nigerians chose. When they appeared on the far bank, the Biafrans blew the charges, but they had been badly placed. It was one of the most serious errors of the war. The bridge went down, but a gas pipeline a few yards to one side escaped the blast. Along the top of this pipe ran a catwalk, and the Biafrans, out of ammunition, watched helplessly as the Nigerians started to cross on foot in single file. This was on 17 August. Williams was sent for with 700 men, but he could not get there until the morning of the 19th. By this time the Nigerians had put across three battalions.
>
> The Commandos fought for two days to try to get the bridgehead back, but while two Federal battalions held them a mile from the water, the third marched south and captured the northern bank of the other, bigger bridge. Seeing that it was useless, Williams pulled back to the main Aba-Port Harcourt Road.
>
> For six days the Biafran 12th Division, assisted by Williams' men (now made up to 1,000), fought back as a tide of Nigerians crossed the Imo on foot. Feverish work was in progress, reportedly with Russian engineers, to rebuild the Imo River Bridge to bring over the heavy equipment.
>
> Williams, holding the main axis, did not rate the Nigerians very dangerous so long as they lacked their armour and artillery, although they still outnumbered the Biafrans many times in guns, bullets and mortars.
>
> On the 24th [of] August the bridge was completed and the attack column rolled across. The ensuing battle was the bloodiest of the war. Williams threw in his 1,000 Commandos in attack rather than wait in defence. The impertinence caught the Nigerians off-guard. They had a reported three brigades in the main column up the main road, and the intention was to march easily to Aba, brush aside the resistance and move on to Umuahia.
>
> For three days Williams and Erasmus led less than 1,000 young Biafrans clutching bolt-action rifles against the pride of the Nigerian Army. They had no bazooka rockets. Their machine guns and repeater rifles did not stop for seventy-two hours. The backbone of the defence was the 'Ogbunigwe' – a weird mine invented by the Biafrans. It looked like a square cone with dynamite packed into the narrow end and the rest stuffed with ball bearings, nails, stones, scrap iron and metal chips. The base is placed against a tree to absorb the shock;

---

3   Forsyth, Ibid., pp. 134-136.

the trumpet-shaped opening, covered over with plywood, faces down the road towards the oncoming forces. It is detonated by a wire and experts advise the firer to stand well back.

On exploding, the 'Ogbunigwe' sweeps clear a 90-degree arc in front of it, with a maximum killing range of over 200 yards. Such a device let off at short range will normally destroy a company and stop an attack in its tracks.

The Nigerians came up the road standing upright with no attempt at taking cover, chanting their war cry: '*Oshe-bey*'. They were swaying oddly from side to side. Williams, who had done time in the Congo, took one look and said: 'They're doped [up] to the eyeballs.'

Erasmus started to let off the 'Ogbunigwes' at point-blank range. The Nigerians were cut down like corn. The survivors swayed, moved on. On the first day, Erasmus triggered over 40 'Ogbunigwes'. One of the Saladin armoured cars had its tyres shredded and withdrew. Biafran ammunition ran out, but the leading Nigerian Brigade had been ruined. Impeded by anti-tank ditches, they had filled them in with shovels – one relay team taking over from the previous one as the teams were cut down. Faced with fallen trees weighing many tonnes, they lifted them bodily out of the way – the team doing the work being blown to fragments as the mine beneath the tree went off automatically.

As the leading Nigerian brigade was changed, Williams urged his exhausted men to take advantage of the disorder in front of them and charge. They won back the three miles they had lost during the day and returned to their original positions. Waiting for the next day, the troops slept while Erasmus started preparing more booby-traps and Williams returned to Aba for ammunition – but the ammunition planes were not arriving.

Steiner, promoted to Lieutenant-Colonel, who had moved his headquarters to Aba, appealed to the Army Commander; then to Colonel Ojukwu. There was no ammunition. Williams returned to the front. For Sunday, 25th August his men had two bullets each.

That Sunday was a repeat performance of Saturday, and Monday followed suit – then for six days there was calm. Later it was reported that Adekunle had filled the hospitals of Calabar, Port Harcourt, Benin and even Lagos with his wounded from the Aba column. How many dead [who] never got off that road was not counted, but Williams put the number at close to 2,500.

There were many anomalies in this war. One of these was the use of landmines – of which roughly 50,000 were laid (mainly by the Nigerian Army). Decades later, according to Dr Emeka Uhiegby (who subsequently worked with an international demining organisation), these bombs were still being lifted – and it is only in recent years that most had been cleared.

Another interesting series of reports (almost a dozen in all and headed 'Nigerian Civil War Files') was published a few years ago by Nowa Omoigui – a historian. He has many other essays (quite a few detailing events that took place in Nigeria after the civil war), but those involving Biafra provide a fascinating and reasonably objective view of some of the battles and related issues that took place in the 30-month conflict. He referred to them as 'Blunders', which is appropriate considering the range of subjects covered.

As he declared: '[In any war] numerous factors at strategic, operational and tactical levels can lead to disaster – including inept decision-making, poor intelligence, mediocre command and lack of detailed staff work, not to mention ill-trained and equipped troops, weather and bad luck.' He reckoned that Biafra was no different – and in this regard, one factor frequently stood out: and that was when an army or a military unit had its supply chain cut or threatened. That was precisely what befell the beleaguered 16th Brigade under the valiant Lt-Col E.A. Etuk of the 3rd Marine Commando Division, under Colonel Benjamin A.M. Adekunle of the Nigerian Army at Owerri from January to April 1969 (CUT during the civil war). More than any other event, this single disastrous development directly led to its change of command.

Crack Biafran troops of the 60th, 52nd and 63rd Brigades – along with the 68th Commando Battalion detachment of the 'S' Division (all under the 14th Infantry Division, led by Colonel Ogbugo Kalu) – carried out what was subsequently referred to as the 'Owerri Pincer Operation'. It proved to be a huge boost to Biafran morale. However, remnants of the badly-mauled 16th Brigade of Adekunle's 3rd Marine Commando Division later miraculously slipped out of encirclement under the command and leadership in crisis of Colonel Etuk – widely regarded by former Biafran commanders as the best Nigerian field commander of the war.

It was also at Owerri that Major Ted Hamman, Etuk's Second-in-Command, lost his life – a man still feted as a hero of the war on the Nigerian side.

Elsewhere, Noma Omoigui tells us that as the war raged – and I quote this writer very extensively below – various external actors sought ways to resolve a number of elements of the crisis in favour of one or the other of the contending forces. These included the Commonwealth, World Council of Churches, Organisation of African Unity and various nations (among other state and non-state actors). Both Nigeria and Biafra conducted a furious war to influence international opinion by various means… they sent entities and delegations abroad for this purpose, as well as to shop for weapons and ammunition.

For example, former Eastern Region Premier Michael Okpara and former Nigerian President Nnamdi Azikiwe were roving Biafran Ambassadors to several East African and Francophonic countries. In the wake of Azikiwe's diplomatic offensive, Tanzania, Gabon, the Ivory Coast, Mauretania and Zambia recognised Biafra. Importantly, General de Gaulle of France openly acknowledged already the ongoing support for Biafran self-determination, but there were other pro-Biafran forces in the background: Biafra sought and got support (of varying quantity and quality) from Israel, Portugal, Rhodesia, South Africa, the Vatican and non-state actors like Joint Church Aid, Holy Ghost Fathers of Ireland, the Roman Catholic Caritas International, Mark Press of Geneva, US Catholic Relief Services and the rest.

Meanwhile, Federal delegations visited many other African countries to stem this tide of Biafran recognition and obtain official OAU backing – considerably enhanced by the sympathy of the OAU Consultative Committee on the Nigerian crisis.[4] At the same time, Nigeria was negotiating with countries like Belgium, the United Kingdom, the Netherlands, Italy, West Germany, Spain, Poland, the USSR and the United States for weapons and other items of military ordnance. In August, for example, Dr Okoi Arikpo was dispatched to the USSR on what was described as a 'goodwill visit' – coming exactly one year after a 'cultural pact' between both countries (negotiated by Soviet Ambassador Alexandr Romanov) had resulted in the supply of Mig-17 fighter aircraft to Nigeria.

The Nigerian international shopping list in 1968 included some of the most modern artillery available on international arms markets: armoured, as well as infantry, fighting vehicles; shells; rifles; ammunition; machine guns; side arms; landmines; mortars and their bombs, as well as a proliferation of ancillary that went with it all (including Eastern Bloc military specialists). In the background, peace talks were stuttering in London, Kampala, Niamey, and Addis Ababa, as international concern increased about relief for civilians caught in the fighting.

Nowa Omoigui goes on:

---

4 The members of this committee – led by Emperor Haile Selassie of Ethiopia – were the Cameroons, the Congo, Ghana, Liberia and Niger.

On the battlefield, facts were being created and recreated on the ground and in what developed into one of the most vigorous propaganda campaigns since the end of World War 2.

In March 1969, Onitsha finally fell after many bloody unsuccessful attempts. A month later, Abakaliki – another important eastern town – was captured, followed in May by the collapse of Biafran authority in Port Harcourt to troops of the 3rd Marine Commando Division. At the end of July, an increasingly confident Colonel Benjamin Adekunle – Commander of the 3rd Marine Commando Division – announced to the press that he would capture Owerri, Aba and Umuahia within a fortnight. Nevertheless, it was not until August 15th, 1968 that Major-General Gowon announced that the 'final offensive' which would bring the war to an end would begin on August 25th. Following this announcement, Aba fell to Federal forces on September 4th – followed by Owerri on September 16th – but by the time Okigwe was taken on October 1st, it was evident that all was not well with the so-called 'final offensive'. Biafra had its own sources of supply, and the Biafran nation – having the year before observed the slaughter of so many of their people in other parts of Nigeria (the north especially) – feared that the same could happen in the east were they to let their guard down.

Yet it would be simplistic to think that it was all about French weapons and ammunition. Long before General de Gaulle publicly declared support for Biafra and began sending in large consignments of weapons, the Federal Army had already begun betraying bad habits that would eventually be brilliantly exploited by Biafran commanders who would spot a gap and exploit it – especially since determined Biafran troops were so thoroughly familiar with their own ground.

There were formidable obstacles facing the Nigerian Army. First was the sheer size of the area of responsibility allocated to the 3rd Marine Commando [Division]. They were stretched across a vast area of jungle and riverine creeks that seemed to go on forever – and called the 'Southern Front'. These extended more than 200 kilometres from the Orashi River through Owerri, Aba and Ikot Ekpene to Itu along the Cross River.

The second factor was the Federal Army ['s] tendency to rely almost solely on main roads for advance, which made them the delight of any soldier skilled in the arcane delights of ambush.

The third was the notorious tendency (particularly among units of the 2nd and 3rd Nigerian Army Divisions) to rush in to seize objectives without securing and vigorously patrolling lines of communication and flanks – particularly behind their own lines.

The 2nd Division took Onitsha in that matter [*sic*] with absolutely no contingency plan in hand for securing control of the Onitsha-Enugu Road. A lot of Nigerian soldiers travelling in convoys died there as a result; then, during the 3rd CDO Division dash to Umuahia, no effort was made to secure lines of communication either. To amplify this dangerous tendency, a fourth element crept into the mix: Federal battalions, brigades and divisions rarely acted in co-ordination and GOCs often disobeyed orders coming from [a] higher command from Lagos.

Then came the imponderables – and Nowa Omoigui phrases it well:

Many hastily-recruited and trained Federal soldiers, though initially enthusiastic and eager to kill Biafrans, were totally unfamiliar with the kind of bush country in which they were required to operate, for the simple reason that the majority were city boys. It was also no secret that many were superstitious about the dark hours – making night-time operations highly unattractive, for fear of 'juju'.

Last, such daytime operations as were carried out, particularly by the 2nd and 3rd Divisions, were characterised by heavy expenditure of ammunition and poor fire discipline. The sheer volume of fire they could deliver 'at anything that moved' was the basic source of motivation for the average Federal soldier as he carried out what were termed in the argot, 'clearing operations'.

Junior tactical level leadership was seriously lacking outside the Nigerian Army ['s] 1st Division, which had the benefit of retaining the core of the old Nigerian Army.

Military planners in Lagos, for example, projected five million rounds of ammunition for the 3rd Marine Commando Division alone at the beginning of the operation which was to take Owerri, Aba and Umuahia in 1968 – but even more startling, in planning for offensives after May 1969, Nigerian Army Headquarters projected a minimum of about 15 million rounds of 7.62 mm rifle ammunition for each division. That would be supplemented by another 15 million rounds held in reserve in Lagos – never mind all the mortar and artillery shells and a lot else that would be needed for an ongoing war.

All of this (to the delight of a number of international arms merchants) was to be purchased from the Soviet Union and Spain, as well as the United Kingdom in other words, declares Nowa Omoigui: '… enough ammunition to kill all 60 million people living within the geographical boundaries of Federal Nigeria at that time…'

This so-called 'Ammunition Mentality' was amplified by regular public reassurances that the war would end soon; that Biafran soldiers either had no weapons or were poorly armed – but, as Federal casualties mounted and it became apparent that the rebels could account pretty well for themselves (and also sport a range of excellent firepower – albeit only from time to time), government soldiers became increasingly reluctant to take risks whenever they went out on patrol.

Nobody has yet focused on the role of the handful of mercenaries who fought with the Biafran Army and were, unquestionably, responsible for a significant slice of their basic and operational training. Without the likes of people like 'Taffy' Williams, Steiner, Goossens, Bob Denard, Jan Breytenbach and a handful more, Biafra's jungle war would probably have been over in half the time…

Nowa Omoigui again:

> To the 'Bad Federal Habits' must be added certain 'Good Habits' and some of the advantages enjoyed by the Biafran soldier.
>
> The first was that, as we have observed, they were very highly motivated and determined – fighting as they were on home ground. To Federal troops, the battlefields might have been little more than places on maps and abstract names of hamlets, villages and towns populated by a raving bunch of misguided civilians. To the Biafrans, they represented the safe haven of ancestral lands held by generations of their own people. These were the homes, farms, burial grounds [and] places of enormous ritual and tribal significance.
>
> The role that such motivation increasingly played as the war progressed became apparent as Federal divisions crossed from the usually pro-Federal or neutral minority areas of the Eastern Region into the core Igbo (or Ibo) areas, where the fear of 'genocide' was not only a horrible realty that dated back to the events of July – September 1966, but was constantly reinforced by Biafran radio. In this regard, Ojukwu clearly had the edge in psychological warfare.
>
> The second was the enterprising and recurrent ability of Biafran units and sub-units to actually penetrate Federal lines – sometimes even operating far in the rear of supposedly captured Federal areas – where they could rely on a sympathetic population.

A weapons check at a Biafran ordnance base near Uli Airport. (Author's collection)

Third came the ability of some Biafran commanders to resourcefully exploit the natural terrain in defensive positions (including concrete bunkers) well connected by all-weather communication trenches. Such defensive positions were often set up to cover strategic roads and demolished bridges, as well as any lines of Federal retreat from pre-positioned Biafran home-made minefields.[5]

The problem was that these defensive positions were often not deployed in depth. Also, Biafran troops were almost always chronically short of weapons and ammunition (in spite of some heroic scientific efforts to produce their own).

One of the more interesting comments came not long after the war ended from no less a person than the British Prime Minister Harold Wilson in his book *The Labour Government 1964-1970*. He refers specifically to the propaganda campaign and the effect it had on the British people. There is no question that other countries were similarly affected. Wilson's words were:

---

5   Omoigui, Dr Nowa, 'Nigerian Civil War Files' No.1-10 (Nowa_o@yahoo.com).

That whether inspired by European financial interests or directly controlled by Colonel Ojukwu himself, the public relations campaign carried out on behalf of Biafra was one of the outstanding features of the [civil] war.

If Biafra's military prowess had been one-tenth as efficient, the war would have ended in weeks. The purveyors of Biafran propaganda [Mark Press of Geneva] flooded the Western press and Western legislatures with literature and secured a degree of moral control over Western broadcasting systems with a success unparalleled in the history of communications in modern democratic societies.

Their switch of line was remarkable: as soon as Col Ojukwu's forces were pressed back out of the western areas – and indeed out of Enugu and other Ibo heartland areas – the cry was 'genocide'. They suggested, in the strongest terms, that should Biafra fall, there would be mass extermination. When food shortages developed, as a result of deliberate military decisions by Ojukwu to close supply lines, the propaganda cry was 'starvation'… starvation by all who failed to support the Biafran military cause – and especially by the 'arch-criminal', Britain.

No language was spared in distortion of the truth, nor subtlety left unexercised in the supply of filmed 'evidence' avidly snapped up by gullible producers, bringing home to every fireside the responsibility of the Federal Government – and therefore Britain – for every death from malnutrition.

These campaigns had their effect in the Western World and I have never doubted the sincerity of those affected by them… for my colleagues and me in Parliament, there were bitter sessions at Question Time and in Debates. As we travelled through the country, demonstrations were increasingly hard to bear… every single death was laid at our door… The easiest route for food and relief supplies would have been… along the road from Enugu to Biafra-held territories…

Later, when the relief organisations sought to fly the food in, [the Biafran leader] rejected day flights: because, under cover of night relief flights, he could fly in the French arms he so sorely needed to carry on the war… What I did resent was the suggestion that it was our [British] obstinacy and not Colonel Ojukwu's deliberate military policy which caused the starvation.[6]

This book must close with some thoughts about somebody who was never a public figure when it came to defending Nigeria, but who – from the start – played a seminal role in the war: Major-General Philip Effiong, who I got to know only cursorily because he was never one for the media. I'd met him several times before and during the war and always found him to be quietly-spoken and, when the occasion was warranted, self-effacing.

Chief Effiong held the chieftaincy title of *Akakang Ibimo Ibom* (The People's Sword) and was 78 when he died in November 2003. It was then the Nigerian people were publicly told for the first time that apart from taking over as Administrator of Biafra after the then Head of State of Biafra, Chief Chukwuemeka Odumegwu Ojukwu, had fled to the Ivory Coast on 12 January 1970 it was also declared in a broadcast on Radio Nigeria that 'I am convinced now that a stop must be put to the bloodshed which is going on as a result of the war. I am also convinced that the suffering of our people must be brought to an immediate end'.

It was also General Effiong who signed the surrender document with the Nigerian Army's Colonel Olusegun Obasanjo – the man who, by then, was also elevated to the rank of General

---

[6] Wilson, Sir Harold, *The Labour Government 1964-1970: A Personal Record* (London: Weidenfeld & Nicolson, 1971).

Everyday life in Nigeria as the war dragged on was marred by such images which appeared in the newspapers of the world and generated enormous sympathy for the starving nation. (Author's collection)

Even with all the troubles, life seemed to go on - and there was even the occasional marriage, though this tended to happen more among those who had the resources to feed themselves. (Wikipedia)

and who was to overthrow more of his erstwhile colleagues in a military putsch and take over the government (by then relocated to a new capital city at Abuja).

A day after Effiong died on 9 November 2003 John Nwokocha, a journalist with the Lagos newspaper *Vanguard*, posted details of his death on the web – adding that:

> Major-General Philip Effiong had joined the Nigerian Army on July 28, 1945 and rose to the position of ordnance corps member in the Colonial Army before teaming up with the rebels.
>
> After the war, he was thrown into detention by the then military government of General Yakubu Gowon.
>
> Recounting his experience during the war to *Vanguard* in a June 1996 interview, he said: 'I have no regrets whatsoever of my involvement in Biafra or the role I played. The war deprived me of my property, dignity, my name – yet, I saved so many souls on both sides and by this, I mean Biafra and Nigeria. I'm denied everything; no gratuity, no pension. Nothing!
>
> 'I felt that I played a role which has kept this country united till today. I never shot anybody; all I did was as a military [man] and officer. I trained soldiers who went to the bush to fight.

'At the end of it all, when I saw they (my Biafran soldiers) could no longer continue and Ojukwu had fled, I did what was ideal, after wide consultation, that today Ojukwu is a hero in this country.

'I'm not envious, but why am I being persecuted by the country in which I played a significant role in is [sic] unity?'

Hostilities ended abruptly in early 1970 after the Biafran people, literally, had been starved into submission. What was notable was that the slaughter of the Ibo nation – something we all expected after Federal forces had overrun the rebel territory – never happened. All credit here must go to General Yakubu Gowon. More's the pity too that he was ousted in a military putsch after the war ended. It was interesting that he ended up attending a British university as a student and, till now, is the only former African Head of State to have pushed back his personal clock.

In the interim, not a great deal has changed in Africa's most populous nation. Almost half a century on, there are disturbing trends that could very well be the precursor for another civil war. Once more, the imbroglio is Christian against Muslim – and again, there have been internecine clashes that have been mindless, bitter and ruthless. In early 2005 the Nigerian Government admitted that in the previous three years, there had been 50,000 deaths in religious and sectarian violence – and sadly, there's barely a region of the country hasn't been affected.

Now, with Boko Haram *Jihadis* achieving brutal prominence in the north of the country, conditions have deteriorated ever further – something I deal with at length in the chapter that follows.

Things aren't much better in the old Biafra either. After spending decades in exile in the Ivory Coast, Odumegwu Ojukwu – no longer a military man – returned home to Nigeria after 13 years of exile. On occasion, he could be remarkably outspoken about the plight of his people in the modern era.

On several notable occasions, he pointed to the reality that these same easterners – his people – were today more distressed about the country's oil industry than ever before: all those hundreds of billions of dollars earned in fuel exports in the past half-century and almost nothing to show for it. As he also said, so much of it ended up in the foreign bank accounts of his country's leaders. The deposed Nigerian leader, President Sonny Abacha, siphoned off a billion or three – only a small proportion of it ever having been returned by the Swiss banks, where it was lodged before he died.

It was actually Ojukwu that publicly warned before he died that if things did not improve, the region could very easily find itself embroiled in 'another Biafran war'. Harsh words – or, as somebody else was heard to say, 'war talk – and not to be ignored'.

What he said though, made good sense – especially to those of us who have kept our fingers on the pulse of a nation that seems to be eternally in transition.

25

The Next Great African War – Christian against Muslim – and the Role of Boko Haram

One of the most significant news reports to emerge from Africa for a long time almost slipped by unnoticed in late 2015. The BBC reported on 14 October that President Obama had announced that the United States' armed forces had been deployed in West Africa 'to help fight against the Islamic militants Boko Haram'. It was a sizeable force, the report said, and would begin its work in the Cameroons. The American President added that his troops would remain in Cameroon 'until no longer needed'.

The statement was purposely vague – especially since Boko Haram and its *Jihadist* associates are now waging war in half a dozen West African countries. In the process, tens of thousands of people have been murdered.

What we do know is that the radical Islamic group had started its machinations in Northern Nigeria almost a decade before and that if the American President was as good as his word, American troops will be fighting that threat for a very long time.

Boko Haram is not alone in its quest for martyrs. AQIM (or more colloquially, Al-Qaeda in the Islamic Maghreb – a prominent Boko Haram fundamentalist affiliate) started its insurgency in Mali in early 2012. This required France to step in smartly in order to stop the rot before the Bamako Government fell. Since then there has been AQIM-sponsored violence in several other West African countries including Chad, the Niger Republic, Burkina Faso and, of course, the Cameroons.

The terror group Al-Shabaab, which has been killing people in Somalia for more than a decade, is another Islamic organisation with ties to both AQIM and Boko Haram… What does surprise many independent observers, as well as government and intelligence agencies that have made the effort to investigate this threat, is that almost without exception, the violence that is perpetrated by all these zealots is directed almost solely by one group of Muslims on other people of the Islamic faith.

Should there be an occasional Christian in the firing line, then well and good – but the reality of this carnage rests with both Boko Haram and AQIM's declared objective to mutilate, maim and kill Muslim people (men, women and children) who do not conform to what their Imams believe are the 'absolutely correct' teachings of the Holy Koran. That this unspeakable level of barbarism compares with the kind of Salafist 'Islamic revivalism' that the world witnessed not long ago in Algeria – then also battling for survival – there is no question. Figures are vague, as they usually are in the Arab world, but a conservative estimate of deaths in Algeria during the troubles exceeded a quarter of a million souls – 99 percent of them civilian…

Nigeria's National Mosque in Abuja, the nation's capital. (Dan Gore)

It is well worth mentioning that the tenets of these diverse revolutionary groups are almost identical to that of Islamic State (or ISIL), currently waging war in Syria and Iraq. Consequently, it comes as no surprise that the African and Middle Eastern combatants – Islamic State, Boko Haram and Al-Shabaab, as well as AQIM – have forged an alliance to create (in the long term) the largest revolutionary Islamic caliphate the world has seen. By their own exhortations, they proclaim that it will eventually encompass all of Africa, the Middle East and Central Asia – as well as Europe. Parts of Western China, where there is a strong Islamic presence, are also included in the equation.

Of the little we have been allowed to observe of Islamic State methodology in the field, this is an extremely brutal business – and so too with AQIM and Boko Haram… Illustrating this trend was Terrence McCoy's story in the *Washington Post* on 9 January 2015 where he disclosed that 2,000 civilians had been slaughtered in the Northern Nigerian town of Baga. His report made a significant play of the fact that the killings of civilians had been on a monumental scale – and, as in other attacks, many of the victims had their eyes gouged out; still more had been burned alive.

The reports were horrific. One man who escaped with his family told *Agence France Presse* that he had to navigate through 'many dead bodies on the ground and that the whole town was on fire'. Another told Reuters that he'd escaped with his family in the car after seeing how Boko Haram was killing people: 'I saw bodies in the street. Children and women, some were crying for help… Bodies were littered everywhere on the streets and surrounding bushes'.

What made Baga different from similar attacks in Northern Nigeria was the fact that the town was a military strongpoint manned by soldiers of the Nigerian Army and backed by troops from

A Boko Haram press picture which was released after 2,000 civilians were slaughtered in the northern town of Baga in early January 2015. Cruelly, almost everybody killed was Islamic.

both the Chad Republic and Niger. Not long after the first shots had sounded – shortly after dawn on that momentous day – the entire multinational garrison jumped into their vehicles and fled.

Boko Haram apart, there is a disturbing trend that some students of Africa acknowledge is manifesting itself throughout much of the continent. It includes a series of 'battle lines' drawn between militant Christian and Muslim influences all the way across Africa. The majority of these occur in a broad east-west axis from the Atlantic to the Indian Ocean. In Khartoum – the Sudanese capital, where some of this activity is co-ordinated – it is referred to as 'The Most Holy Crescent'.

Still more zealots are busy recruiting in South Africa under the banner of a group that calls itself PAGAD – an acronym for People Against Gangsterism and Drugs. In other parts of Africa, there have been powerful Islamic inroads in countries such as the Ivory Coast, which emerged recently from a north/south – largely Christian/Muslim – conflict of its own; Ghana; the Central African Republic; Chad; Kenya; Somalia; the northern parts of Uganda; Tanzania; Mozambique; and even normally passive Senegal, which has been battling a Christian-led insurgency in this predominantly Muslim country for decades. This hallowed sword is clearly double-edged.

The limited civil war in Senegal's Casamance Region has been a factor for almost three decades – making it (after the Sudan) Africa's longest ongoing guerrilla conflict. London's Chatham House produced an excellent paper on the subject in 2004. Written by Martin Evans, it is titled *Senegal: Mouvement des Forces Démocratiques de la Casamance (MFDC)* and appeared under the auspices of its Armed Non State Actors Project.

Low-key and barely reported abroad, the struggle has had some bloody moments –including the ambush of a Senegalese Army patrol in which 24 government troops were killed. That was preceded on 18 December 1983 – known colloquially as 'Red Sunday' – when demonstrators entered Ziguinchor (the largest town in the region) and marched on the *gouvernance* (seat of regional administration) and the local office of the *gendarmerie*, as well as the radio station. The Dakar Government claimed afterwards that there had been several dozen dissidents killed, but the real figure – according to independent observers (and recorded by Martin) – was nearer 200. Over the years, an estimated 3,000 to 5,000 people have died in the war and tens of thousands more displaced.

The *Maquis* involved in the struggle sometimes call themselves *Attika* (which is 'warrior' in the Diola tribal tradition) and were fully mobilised in 1990. Additionally, parts of the disputed region

A Nigerian armoured vehicle patrolling the streets of a northern town. (Wikipedia)

have been seeded by landmines – both anti-tank and anti-personnel – and have included former Soviet TM-46 anti-tank mines, as well as TM-57s (and curiously, some mines of Spanish origin), with numbers coming from the colonial war in what was formerly known as Portuguese Guinea (today Guiné-Bissau). As an indication of the large numbers planted, the Senegalese Army between October 1995 and May 1998 dealt with 845 anti-vehicle mines and 2,053 anti-personnel mines, while a total of 1,150 mines were either lifted or destroyed in the first year of de-mining activities.

While Martin Evans maintains in his report that the perception of Christian/Muslim hostility may have been overrated, I visited the region several times from the mid-1960s onwards. The last time, I was filming in Senegal in the mid-1980s and spent time in Ziguinchor. I stayed with my crew in a delightful little hotel in the heart of the settlement, which resembled a miniature Beau Geste fort, and I went out of my way to make contact with some of the older *Maquisards*. They presented a very different picture to what Dakar would have liked us believe: some of these veterans were Christians and they maintained that much of the hostility originally centred on Christian communities living in this southern region being targeted by Muslims – including local sects of the Mourides.

A more recent development has been the emergence of a burgeoning Iranian influence in parts of the continent: Tehran's *mullahs* have been inordinately active in several East African countries on the Indian Ocean, which Tehran today regards as within its sphere of influence. To a lesser extent, these Shi'ite clerics have also been working in Burkina Faso, Mauritania, Nigeria, Chad, the Congo, Algeria and elsewhere. Somalia is subject to special interest by Tehran because of its unusual revolutionary prospects, but like the West, the *mullahs* have made little headway because Shi'ites are in the minority.

In several confidential briefings before Congress, Washington has acknowledged that there is not one Islamic country where Iran's Pasdaran – its secret religious intelligence, as well as its military *mujahadeen* – have not been active. This effort is largely clandestine (as it is in Egypt, where the banned Muslim Brotherhood keeps an extremely discreet undercover grip on its activities – as well as in the Philippines, Jordan, Morocco, Algeria, Indonesia, Malaysia and elsewhere), or it sometimes comes with the unofficial blessing of the incumbent government, as with Syria, Sudan, Pakistan and Somalia. Overseeing all these efforts is Iran's supreme religious leader – a post first held by the Ayatollah Khomeini until he died. I detail much of this in my book *Iran's Nuclear Option*, including the role of the Islamic Revolutionary Guards Corps, which is otherwise known as Pasdaran (the paramilitary organisation that originally created Hizbollah).[1]

---

1 More comprehensive details of these events can be found in Venter, Al J., *Iran's Nuclear Option* (USA: Casemate, 2005) pp. 173-174.

After Boko Haram had overrun several Nigerian Army military establishments, they deployed some of the armour captured. (*Agence France-Presse*)

With time, the Muslim/Christian confrontation in Africa has become more militant and, in some countries, it has transmogrified into open conflict. The on-off festering civil war in the Ivory Coast, with the nation split between the Muslim north and a predominantly Christian/animist south, is symptomatic – so too with some of the differences between Eritrea and Ethiopia (with one militantly Islamic and totally opposed to an Amharic Ethiopia, whose Christian traditions go back a millennium-and-a-half). Both nations fought a series of bitter conflicts that claimed almost 300,000 casualties a decade ago. Looking back, today's historians are aghast at the utterly senseless carnage that erupted between two bankrupt countries. Violence was totally driven by faith, and Ethiopia's misguided claim to what it considered was part of the original Empire but, in fact, was not.

In at least a dozen more African states, there are other insurrections or insurgencies. These include Chad, Congo (Brazza), North Mali, Uganda, Rwanda, Burundi, Somalia, Angola (Cabinda separatists) Zimbabwe and others. The Central African Republic was invaded out of neighbouring Chad by a mainly *Jihadi* force that included nationals from half a dozen Islamic states – and once across the border, they set about killing every Christian encountered. Again, it was France that had to rush to the rescue, though a modest South African Army contingent also offered strong resistance.

Much of the turmoil has been 'imported'. Libya, while the dictator Muammar Gadaffi was still around, is on record as having supplied rebels with arms in half a dozen sub-Saharan rebellions. For instance, almost all the weapons initially used by rebel forces in Sierra Leone in their 1997 uprising came (at the behest of Libya) from Iran, trans-shipped initially through (Muslim)

> There are powerful Islamic undercurrents at play in this insurrection, including strong anti-Israel sentiments, which might be expected since Boko Haram is partially funded by several Arab states.

Ouagadougou's international airport in Burkina Faso before being sent south to Liberia. This hardware was then taken overland into the neighbouring territory on the backs of local people – usually at gunpoint.

What is unsettling to some of the major powers is that African political differences have become much more entrenched in recent years. This development suggests that with time, there will not only be more conflicts involving Christians and Muslims, but that the conflicts will be a good deal more expansive and certainly more intense. Child soldiers became a feature of hostilities of several of them when Sierra Leone's Revolutionary United Front fomented revolt (and before that, in the Congo) – and that trend continues – and then there is Nigeria, where today there are Christians battling Muslims in a series of low-key insurgencies that stretch all the way across the country. Not a week goes by without more reports emerging of groups – and sometimes entire communities, both rural and in many of the towns in the interior – being slaughtered either by Christian militants, or in reprisal raids by those of Islamic persuasion. Clearly, much of this bloodshed has become polarised. Instead of traditional factional, political or regional differences, religion entered the equation following the murder by southern army officers of groups of northern religious leaders in 1965 – something I deal with at length in the opening chapters. These differences have cut like a swathe across entire societies that include Ibo/Ibibio (and other Eastern Nigerian tribes) and Yoruba in the south, as well as Hausa and Fulani in the north of Africa's most populous nation.

For the west, such developments herald long periods of instability that could ultimately affect basic issues, such as the supply of oil from the nations at present producing most of it. Among these are Nigeria, Gabon, Angola, the Cameroons, Ghana, the Ivory Coast and Equatorial Guinea. The Sudan has also recently entered the ranks of oil-producing countries.

For the developed world – which includes China – such dislocation might ultimately affect other natural resources such as diamonds, aluminium, cobalt, manganese, copper, gold and a variety of rare earth minerals such as tantalum, yttrium, neodymium and lanthanum (many of which are needed in modern electronic devices such as electric motors, iPods and batteries). In some countries (such as the Congo), attempts have been made to halt production in certain areas because of ongoing hostilities – and Coltan (short for Columbite-tantalite) is now being classified in some quarters as a 'conflict mineral'. Without Coltan, we would be deprived of our computers, tablets, mobile phones and the rest...

All of this raises the question: how serious are these disturbances? History long ago taught us that political instability has often enough been a precursor of war. What is notable is that Islam has scored some striking successes in Africa in recent years – and the Muslim world, as well people of all religions in the west, are asking why. This was highlighted by a comment made by the former BBC Reith Lecturer Ali Mazrui – a professor of African history at the New York State University – that Islam 'is far outstripping the number of Christian converts'. So it is too. That was followed by a series of Voice of America broadcasts titled 'Islam and Africa', where it was declared that no other religion had seen such growth in the past century.[2] Of Africa's one billion souls, it declared: 'More than half the population was already Muslim'.

This is all the more sobering when it is considered that there were perhaps a hundred million Islamic people in Africa at the end of World War II – most of them settled comfortably in several Arab countries that fringed the Mediterranean, as well as Iraq, Iran and others in the Former Soviet Union (FSU) and along Indian Ocean shores. Others were found in scattered communities in East and West Africa – a condition that still holds today. The only difference is that their numbers have burgeoned.

Even more compelling is a recent American study that indicated that roughly 14 of Africa's 52 states are more than 75 percent Islamic. Another eight count those who read the Koran – among more than half of their populations. Countries like the two Congo Republics, Kenya, Uganda, Tanzania, the Central African Republic, Sierra Leone, the Ivory Coast and others formerly had tiny Islamic communities and are now nudging up towards the 50 percent mark. That also applies to Ethiopia – a Christian nation where, in recent years, Islam has made big inroads in a hardscrabble society that formerly owed its allegiance to the church. Even South Africa – until recently a staunchly Christian state – is now acknowledged to have a powerful fundamentalist core group within its extensive Asian and 'Coloured' (mixed blood) communities. Many of these adherents have identified closely with religious-based conflicts in Afghanistan, Kosovo, Chechnya, Iraq, Syria and, more directly, Palestine. Some South African militant Muslims have seen action for the Islamic cause in all these countries, as well as with Al-Qaeda.

The question now being asked in both secular and Christian circles – as well as by Muslim clerics in the Middle East (specifically with a view to possibly expanding Islamic influences towards Asia) – is how has this phenomenon managed to develop in the way that it has? The answer, in part, stresses the activism and creativity of Africa's new generation of Islamists. Also, Africa's Muslim 'reformers' are in the process of constructing new types of Islamic societies in their invocation of divine mandates from the Koran and Sunna. It is notable that this emergence moves beyond presumptions of economic and political discontent. Similarly, it underlines remarkable 'self-denying' efforts taken by Islamists to attract followers to their cause – and since most African Muslims are mainstreamers, encounters between Islamists and other Islamic leaders are producing new configurations that not only disturb traditionalists, but will ultimately shape relations with the rest of the Muslim world (possibly for generations to come). Here, both traditional Saudi Wahabbism, as well as Salafism, has come into play.

The question consequently begs: why is Islam on the ascendancy on the African continent? To those who believe they know Africa and understand its history, its culture and colonial background, and its manifold allegiances – as well as the convoluted role of African politics – the reasons are clear:

---

2 Hilletwork, Mathias, 'Islam and Africa' Voice of America broadcast – 1 April 1997.

THE NEXT GREAT AFRICAN WAR AND THE ROLE OF BOKO HARAM

Radical Islamic-fuelled insurgency has spread to several other West African states. France stepped in to rescue Mali after its government had almost been toppled by AQIM (Al-Qaeda in the Islamic Maghreb). (Yann Peducasse)

The first centres on economic factors that simply cannot be ignored. In the rough and tumble of the impoverished African environment, Islam offers hardscrabble succour to the masses. It starts with those who have *nothing* being given *something* – a fundamental tenet of everyday Islam. Additionally, it replicates many of the disciplines and traditions of the continent's early traditional leaders. In this regard, it is worth recalling that more than a century ago, political or tribal power was always vested in a paramount central authority – usually a chief. Uganda's historical Kabaka or a Zulu Chaka, while not Islamic, were prime examples of this tradition – so too, for instance, is the Sultan of Sokoto today, as well as many of Northern Nigeria's Imams who count Arabs among their earliest ancestors. Their edicts, based solely on Muslim precepts, are inviolable.

This earlier period was also an age when influences such as colonialism and organised European-style religion was rigorously opposed by the mosques – something that started after Europe embarked on its territorial scramble in the last quarter of the 19th century. The British, French, Belgians, Germans and Italians of the period believed – sincerely, no doubt, as did Iberian proselytisers of an early period in Central and South America – that they had a God-given mission to go forth not only to govern, but also to convert benighted blacks in their respective fiefs to Christianity. At the same time, legions of British and French colonial district commissioners had to deal with large Islamic communities during the course of their daily duties.

While new 'enlightened' systems propagated by the so-called 'Imperialists' established fanciful governing systems (that were totally alien to the majority of black people), Islam quietly and almost imperceptibly returned to old and trusted values of subservience before the Divine Allah. What many Africans see in the Word of the Prophet – whether it is Shi'ite, Sunni and Sufi (or, for that matter, Senegal's Mouride Islamic sect) – is Islam's powerful emphasis on communal living. The majority appreciate its tolerance for polygamy, as well as its clearly demarcated roles for men and for women, which though regarded as harsh in the so-called 'civilised' world, make good common sense to people not yet tainted by Western mores.

In Nigeria for instance, a popular argument in Kano's *Saban Gari* (the traditionally-named Stranger's Quarter) is that Christianity has always been alien to the African psyche – and for several reasons: they propound the fact that Islam embraces the poor, while manifestly the Imams proclaim that Christianity does not. Though this thesis might be regarded as spurious by some observers, it is not altogether incorrect. Consequently, such sentiments have a strong following in societies where a dollar or two will buy you somebody to do your bidding for a day. So too with the Islamic no-nonsense style of jurisprudence that makes good sense to the African mind, which (in tribally-based societies) is hardly as sophisticated as it might be in places like San Francisco, Cape Town or London. As Professor Ali Mazrui observed, Islam has an elaborate (and sometimes understated) system of laws that are easily implemented in the daily lives of its adherents – the majority of whom are unsophisticated, ordinary tribal folk.

'Places like Timbuktu were famous long ago, partly because there was a lot of studying that combined investigation into jurisprudence and into legal theory partly derived from Islamic culture,' he declared.

Then there is language, where Islam has played a major role not only on the continent of Africa, but also in large parts of Asia and beyond. The most widely-spoken languages in East and West Africa are Swahili and Hausa – and both have borrowed extensively from the Arabic. Suleiman Nyang – a professor of African studies at Howard University in the United States – maintains that Islam has penetrated a number of African languages and cultures because of a thousand years of cohabitation. This does matter, he declared, because such cultural influences must have an effect on these societies – nor can one ignore that Islam has helped to facilitate co-operation between Africans and Arabs, irrespective of whether or not the Arabs were abducting black people to work as slaves (and they did so quite often, wherever victims could be found).

The fact that Europe and America extricated themselves from a responsible role on the continent following the end of the Cold War also had a part to play. Politicians on both sides of the Atlantic long observed that the Organisation of African Unity (now the African Union) consistently maintained close relations with the Arab League. Countries such as Algeria, Tunisia, Egypt and Libya maintained membership with both groupings.

What is relevant here is that Christian/Western values, like democracy, have failed almost throughout the continent in almost all instances. It has done so dismally, said Norimitsu Onishi – an American journalist with the *New York Times*[3] a while back – that the kind of democracy put into effect by the colonial powers in the 1960s 'have often produced sham elections, misrule and deep poverty.' Corruption is a significant part of it.

Also, these shortcomings have been ruthlessly exploited by tens of thousands of wandering Islamic proselytisers (or *griots*, as they are termed among believers in West Africa). They depict so-called 'civilised' Western values as being a culture of selfishness – linked almost solely to exploiting the poor (as well as their national mineral resources) and half-naked women.

One of the most pertinent points raised by British Arabist Stephen Ulph was the fact that Muslim leaders everywhere are appalled by the kind of rampant sexual freedoms that are integral to everyday society in the West today. For some – whether they surreptitiously view pornography

---

3   Onishi, Norimitsu, 'Rising Muslim Power Causes Unrest in Nigeria and Elsewhere' – *New York Times* (New York: 1 November 2001), p. A12.

The Bible and the Koran both compete with increasing vigour and violence for hearts, minds and souls in much of Africa. Most often, the consequences are disastrous.

on their computers or not – opposition to this kind of licentiousness is the cornerstone on which some of them base their teachings[4] – and why not? In historical terms, this kind of demonstrative sexual freedom (on the part of both sexes) is a relatively new phenomenon.

---

4 A personal interview with Stephen Ulph at his London home.

The Cameroon Army has had to counter bands of Boko Haram insurgents that have crossed over from Nigeria. Both Chad and the Niger Republic are now also dragged into this series of religious conflicts. (Wikipedia)

'Muslims have become an angry, organised force in several important African states, and it often comes with a wariness of the West – especially the United States,' explained Onishi, which could be a reason why former French Premier Jacques Chirac – originally sensing a gap towards the end of his tenure – launched what he termed was an 'African Summit' (something that hadn't been achieved in almost half a century of African independence).

This tradition will persist under France's new leaders because it involves all 52 African heads of state. Part of the original reason for taking this step – something that Westminster has never even contemplated with its own former African colonies – was to counter an increasingly militant Islamic political trend by taking a more pliable European stance towards France's former *protégés*. It is also possibly why, for a long time, Paris was not prepared to become directly involved in any of the more recent African civil wars – including hostilities in the Ivory Coast, where the main adversaries were Christian and Muslim. With hostilities in the Sahel ongoing, that approach has changed – and there is quite a large French Reaction Force based permanently in West Africa today; and then, in everyday African society, there are the basics of life itself. To the majority of followers, Islam is an egalitarian religion underscored by five daily rituals and a commitment to caring for the disadvantaged – all of which makes for good common sense. Arguably, Islam is the most visible of all religions; you can hardly miss the chants at regular intervals from the minarets, as I was reminded during a recent visit to Egypt, where the Imams start their first calls well before dawn. The first chants sounded, I observed from my notes, at 4:47 a.m.

Travel eastwards out of the countries that fringe the Red Sea, across Africa and towards the Atlantic, and there is barely a village without its mosque. Many millions of dollars – much of it Saudi, but a fair proportion of it Iranian – is being spent annually for this purpose in just about every country in the continent. In KwaZulu/Natal in South Africa, for instance, striking new mosques have been built in just about every town where there were none before. The transition is

THE NEXT GREAT AFRICAN WAR AND THE ROLE OF BOKO HARAM

The most active European state in this African region at present is France, with a French Foreign Legion temporary base seen here in Mali. More recently, the Americans and the British have followed, but not nearly as intensively. These conflicts will soon escalate. (Yann Peducasse)

all the more remarkable because it comes at a time when the rest of the country is troubled by an economic recession.

Here too, politics sometimes comes into play. In Vryheid – a large South Africa town with a huge Christian cross atop one of the nearby hills, and usually brilliantly lit after dark – local Muslim leaders offered to totally revamp the police force if this 'utterly offensive' Christian symbol was removed. No small gesture, because they would have had to rebuild the police station and equip the force – already stretched in an over-consuming budget – with a dozen new vehicles, as well as modern radio equipment. The offer was disregarded by a majority of town folk – and significantly, one of the most striking buildings in town was a recently completed three-tier mosque (complete with minarets) and regarded by many as one of the finest in this Southern African province.

In a report back to his American church some years ago, evangelist Geoff Stamp[5] said he found a remarkable Islamic vitality during his visit to West Africa: 'Anyone doubting this rising power should research the numerous projects including clinics, madrasas, village wells and farming assistance that have been funded by Middle Eastern states – almost throughout sub-Saharan Africa,' he declared. It was impossible to travel west from Khartoum to Mauritania without encountering evidence of a vigorously resurgent Islam, added Stamp.

In Chad, on the road between N'djamena to Moundou, he recalled:

---

5 Geoffrey Stamp of United Bible Societies recently spent some time in Northern Nigeria and recorded much of what he saw – quite a lot of it extremely disturbing – on film.

One visitor lost count of the new mosques that had sprung up, village after village, some with fewer than 50 houses. These were well-built, not far from the road and brilliantly painted… meant to be a visible sign that the community had embraced Islam.

At the same time, poverty is obvious and on the increase – but Islam offers hope in a world where quality of life is rarely considered. Men are given the opportunity to start a business in Mali or Niger with a loan from a Muslim bank (they charge no interest). And when an individual cannot repay the loan, he is simply given the option: if Christian, you must convert to Islam and reject your former faith.

Stamp observed that almost all religious instruction throughout this broad African swathe was in Arabic and that promising students were being sent to Muslim universities in the Gulf. Similarly, Arabic was being promoted in many northern African states as the language that every Muslim should speak. In Chad recently, the University of N'djamena offered 50 first-year teaching positions to anybody who could speak Arabic and French – 10 times the number normally reserved for scientists, mathematicians and other specialised subjects.

The trend is widespread to the extent that in some countries such as Sierra Leone, parts of Nigeria, Northern Cameroon and Senegal, there are many Western-style schools that have yielded to Islamic instruction – and while the system might not produce a surfeit of academics, one consequence is basic functional societies in which almost everybody is literate. The majority in these disparate (and sometimes far-flung) societies are able to read their Koran, even though Arabic is very different from Hausa, Bamelike or Yoruba.

Politics is another factor that predominates… Osama bin Laden's picture – even though the man is dead – is everywhere in the Sahara and sub-Saharan Region. There is good reason for all these developments – not least a powerful groundswell of anti-American sentiment among the rank and file of most Muslims – and this applies equally to Nigeria as it does to countries like the Sudan and Mali.

Onishi asked a Kano cleric, Dr Ibrahim D. Ahmad – president of a militant group that called itself 'Hisbah' (which deploys hundreds of young men in green uniforms to enforce Sharia laws in this Northern Nigerian city) – why Islam had managed to emerge so powerfully in the country's politics. 'It is the failure of every (political) system we have known,' the Muslim cleric replied. 'We had colonialism, which was exploitative; we had a brief period of happiness after independence. Then the military came in and since then, everything has been going downhill – but before all that, we had an Islamic system that worked. We had Sharia… we are Muslims and we are returning to ourselves.'

It is an attitude that is of concern to many Africans who are Christian. In Africa, declared The Rev Benjamin Kwashi – Anglican Bishop of Jos (a large tin-mining Nigerian complex perched precariously between Christian and Islamic homelands in Central Nigeria: 'Muslims are winning the religious war. They have already won.' Jos is also a city where thousands of people have died in religious clashes in the past few years.

These ethno/religious confrontations are nothing new. Nigeria has experienced one tribal and religious killing after the other in past decades, dating all the way back to the time of the Biafran War in the 1960s.

Wole Soyinka – Nigeria's distinguished Nobel Prize recipient – also entered the fray by making an impassioned plea to his people against implementing Sharia law in his own country:[6] 'A cobbled-

---

6 Soyinka, Wole, 'Thoughts of a Favourite Son' – FRONTLINE/World: Nigeria – The Road North (January 2003).

A Nigerian soldier in front of a captured 105 mm artillery piece after the northern village of Damboa had been retaken from Boko Haram. (Wikipedia)

together nation like Nigeria can only withstand so much stress,' he wrote in Lagos' *The News* and went on: 'There is no longer even a *façade* of unity – Nigeria is, today, a nation polarized as never before.' It was also worth noting, he declared, that along the northern borders of Nigeria 'there are three vast, independent Islamic nations – Chad, Niger and Mali – and none of them has tried to impose Sharia governance on their nations, although the Sharia exists for adjudication in civil cases.'

Mr Soyinka was unequivocal in equating the imposition of Sharia to Nazi-like tactics. 'We are speaking of a minority – and when that minority leads their captive masses to intone *Allahu Aqbar*, they are in reality screaming '*Sieg Heil*!"' His appeal followed the attempt to impose Sharia law in Nigeria's northern Kaduna State, which triggered demonstrations and counter-demonstrations and resulted in a two-day rampage – leaving 3,000 people dead. Since then, Soyinka disclosed (with characteristic aplomb) that quite a few more states had 'joined the Sharia trail'. Effectively, Nigeria's Sharia issue, which now involves the majority of Nigeria's 36 federated states (or roughly a fifth of the world's black people), has split the nation of 180 million as never before – and while sectarian violence in Nigeria between Christian and Muslim is nothing new, recent events have reminded some observers of the run-up to the Biafran War of the late 1960s.

Today there is a real fear in the streets of Lagos, Kano and Abuja – almost half a century later – that a similar civil war (this time, Muslim ranged against Christian and vice-versa) could ravage the country as never before.

One of the less-publicised developments about recent Nigerian unrest in the east of the nation was a succession of comments that came from former leaders of breakaway Biafra. As we saw earlier, the rebels were led by the charismatic Colonel Ojukwu, who died unexpectedly in 2011.

Though he went into exile to the Ivory Coast for several years, he'd returned to his Nigerian birthplace to warn the nation that the portents for another civil war were already in place. 'This country is on the boil,' were his words – adding that 'if we don't do something about it, we are all doomed.'

Ojukwu dealt with a question about whether the Nigerian Government was being deliberately sabotaged 'by all this violence' which, he declared, had resulted in 'thousands of people being murdered in Christian/Islam violence that stretches across much of the central and northern parts of the country.' Ojukwu stated that as things stood, Nigeria simply could not afford another civil war. If the violence continued and more of his people were murdered, neither he nor the Ibo people 'would idly stand by'. His words had impact: 'Our inalienable rights as Nigerian citizens continue to be ignored.'

Interestingly, while Ojukwu is gone, his sentiments remain and are being regularly quoted by Eastern Nigerian leaders each time Christians are slaughtered by Muslims. The fact that the country is involved in a low-intensity insurgency because of disputes over oil – and has resulted in weapons entering the region in increasing quantities – tends to play into their hands.

It is not only easterners that are affected by Muslims propagating *Jihad* against the 'unbelievers' in Nigeria today. The multi-million strong Yoruba community that remains entrenched in the Muslim-Hausa-dominated north – a huge region, bigger than France –has also come under attack. Moreover, the killings have escalated. Recent reports tell of thousands of people having died in religious clashes in Nigeria's Central Highlands, Cross River and Akwa Ibom states, as well as almost all the northern cities (including Kano, Katsina and Maiduigari). Meanwhile, the massacres go on and, more ominously, all have the makings of a never-ending cycle of killings. One Lagos newspaper referred to it as a 'saturnalia of blood' – except that there are many more Muslims than Christians in these areas. The situation was bad enough during an earlier phase to have necessitated sending in the 7th Amphibious Battalion of the Nigerian Army in a bid to settle matters. Not that that was of much help, because most of the country's military is Muslim anyway.

Prior to that, seven Nigerian Air Force helicopter gunships were dispatched to the oil-rich south-east at the request of the Mobil Oil company after youths had seized a helicopter and some weapons. In doing so, the dissidents succeeded in closing down a large number of oil pumping stations – cutting Nigeria's oil production by a third.

One Western diplomat to whom I spoke in Abuja – and who declined to be identified in print – equated the level of violence in Nigeria to 'a steadily escalating civil war'. What was interesting, he added, was that militant civilians were now more active than ever before. He was also of the opinion that if there were to be another army mutiny (such as the one that ultimately led to the Biafran debacle), many more Nigerian civilians were more than likely to react with force – 'and make no mistake,' he declared, 'Nigeria's more militant (south-eastern) communities have displayed a level of aggression that was underrated before.' If they are to be roused in a (Christian) holy war against the Islamic north, 'there will be so much bloodshed that the nation would simply disintegrate' – and would the nations of the world be prepared to stop it? The consensus is clear, he declared: 'It would most certainly be not an American interventionist force – not after the Somalia debacle.' Nor the United Nations, which most observers now accept has become the most bureaucratic (and ineffectual) international organisation on the planet. One only needs to look at the UN's totally ineffectual role in the civil war in Sierra Leone to see that: it took a British intervention force under the then Brigadier David Richards – and afterwards, Britain's Chief of the Defence Staff – to bring an end to that carnage.[7]

---

7   Venter, *War Dog*; Chapter 6 – 'The United Nations Debacle in West Africa', pp. 131-154.

THE NEXT GREAT AFRICAN WAR AND THE ROLE OF BOKO HARAM

Nigerians cram into a bus fleeing the town of Mubi after the attacks. (EPA)

An indication of the extent of bloodletting in Nigeria was provided to this author personally by Danny O'Brien – a director of the Oregon firm International Charter Incorporated (ICI). ICI has done sterling work over the years in many of the world's trouble spots – including Pakistan, the Balkans, Sierra Leone, Liberia, Haiti and elsewhere. One of its contracts involved providing logistical support for American military training elements involved with the Nigerian Army. O'Brien told me that he'd spent many hours flying over a vast area towards the east of the country:[8] 'We'd be operating immediately north of a region that formerly called itself Biafra,' he explained – indicating that much of it lay on either side of the great Niger River. 'I'd traverse a region that had been entirely depopulated by the Nigerian Army in my helicopter – entire areas where villages had been torched – and those local residents who hadn't been murdered or maimed had fled into the bush.' It didn't take a great stretch of imagination to appreciate that since the army was preponderantly Islamic, their victims were certainly not, was his view. O'Brien admitted that it was the most graphic example of ethnic cleansing that he had witnessed and, as he observed, while Washington had been made aware of these massacres, the American Government never voiced disapproval – basically because of Nigeria's oil exports to the States.

What makes the present Nigerian situation notably different from past insurrections – and the country has had almost half a century of this kind of upheaval – is that many civilian paramilitary groups involved in these disturbances (or on the fringe of them) are now much better organised and armed than before. Some elements within dissident groups such as the Ijaw and Ogoni people appear to have received military training – crudely elementary in some respects, but remarkably effective in others.

Another report mentions foreign money and 'a lot of arms' having entered Nigeria's oil-rich delta from abroad. It failed to provide details or any kind of corroborating evidence, but judging from the number of attacks by dissidents, it must be substantial. Also, the reality that a group of armed militants that likes to call itself 'MEND' is managing to keep the Nigerian Army on the back foot tends to substantiate this argument.

---

8   Communications by email and a visit to O'Brien's home in Washington State.

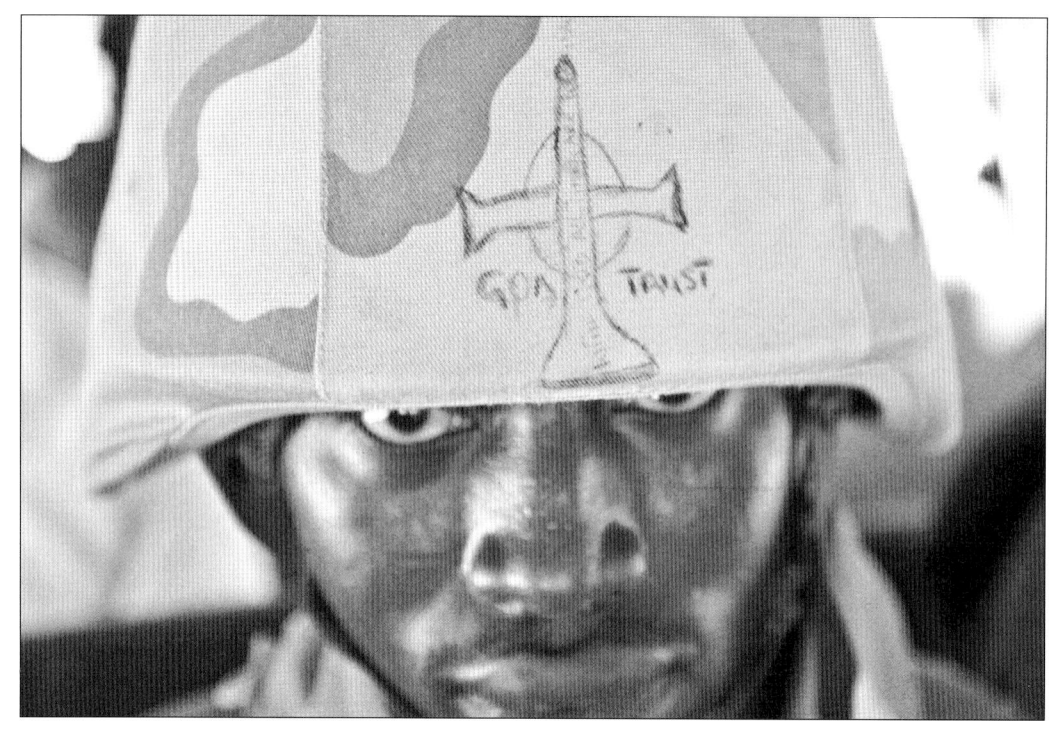

The cross on the helmet of this Nigerian soldier waging war against Boko Haram says it all.

One of several sources close to the oil industry in Lagos with whom this author has been in contact maintains that some insurgent groups were 'remarkably well-equipped' with modern weapons. Their leaders certainly had a lot of money – enough to travel abroad to lobby causes that have lain dormant for a generation or more. None of this will surprise the most knowledgeable of 'Africa Watchers'. Nigeria's relations with its neighbours are at an all-time low. There are running disputes with just about all of them – including serious differences with Yaoundé over title to the oil-rich Bakassi Peninsula and enough to prompt troop movements along both borders. At one stage, all the traditional leaders in Bakassi were escorted out of the territory by the military and forced to take refuge in Calabar.

In recent years, several *Jihadist* movements (including Al-Qaeda and Boko Haram) have made pronouncements with regard to both Nigeria's oil and its long-term security –all of them menacing. This was especially evident prior to 2011 when the name of Libyan leader Muammar Gadaffi had been consistently linked to Nigeria's troubles. Indeed, some pundits declared that even with Gadaffi dead and buried, these developments remain unsettling – and for a variety of reasons:

- The first is that Nigeria – with oil reserves of between 20 and 30 billion barrels – is the fifth biggest supplier of oil to the United States. Nigeria also has the 10th largest natural gas reserves in the world. Because of insurrections, Nigeria's oil production has fallen markedly in recent years.
- Some sceptics have declared that it is certainly in the interests of Al-Qaeda to cripple Nigerian oil production. Should this happen, it is axiomatic that international oil prices would escalate and hurt Western economies.

THE NEXT GREAT AFRICAN WAR AND THE ROLE OF BOKO HARAM

French Special Forces preparing for an operational dispatch to rebel positions near Timbuktu, Mali. Such events will become more regular in the future as Boko Haram and its affiliates expand their operations. (Yann Peducasse)

- Osama bin Laden, in one of his early keynote speeches, declared that one sure way to damage Washington would be to cripple Nigerian oil supplies. It has not been lost on the West that Islamic subversives have been at the root of many of the anti-Christian pogroms in the past few years.
- There is a great deal of money from the Persian Gulf and Middle East entering the region: US officials maintain that private Saudi donors have funnelled money to Sunni Muslim schools and mosques not only in Nigeria, but throughout West Africa. One intelligence official noted that much of it was intended to counter the influence of Iran, which tended to focus on Shi'ite interests in the region.
- A sizable population of potentially impressionable young people come into play if conditions deteriorate further: West Africa is roughly half-Muslim (some authorities maintain two-thirds), with higher concentrations in the Sahel. With its extensive links to the Middle East, the region is fertile ground for radical ideas.

With all these factors in mind, it is significant that the three arms of the Nigerian military – army, navy and air force – recently reached a consensus that 'there are both internal and external forces seriously threatening the country.'

There have been other developments – equally unsettling. Cameron Duodu, one of Nigeria's most famous literary figures (who tends to use his multitude of contacts within that society as litmus tests for future happenstances), has suggested that Nigeria's problems were serious enough for one of the former presidents – in a meeting with Nigeria's 36 governors – to have warned that the brutal killings in the north of the country had brought equally serious revenge killings in the south. Quoted by the Johannesburg *Mail & Guardian*, he declared that the situation 'had created a security nightmare that could easily snowball across the country and make it ungovernable'.

There has been much speculation as to whether there might be another army *coup d'état* like the two that preceded the civil war of the late 1960s. If one is to go by the country's track record, this is long overdue. Nigeria's *Post Express* reported in early 2009 that the country's Chief of Army Staff had warned officers and men of the Third Armoured Division in Jos to 'avoid the temptation of a military takeover.'

A more recent Washington report suggested that Nigeria's experiment in democracy might be at an end. This is not exactly true – even if recently, elections were powerfully flawed – though a succession of oil riots have dented the country's social and political credibility.

The final (and certainly the most interesting) issue raised by those who keep tabs on Nigeria is how the West is likely to react should violence became so widespread throughout the country that it threatens the stability of the Abuja Government and ends up forcing the closure of its oil wells. Nigeria, it should be noted, is not only a significant source of crude oil and a solid supplier to the West, but is also the most logical alternative to fuel supplies should the Near East become involved in a regional war. This could easily happen if Iran were to blockade the Straits of Hormuz, which it has repeatedly threatened to do. Of all the large Western oil cartels active in West Africa, the majority are either American or British – though France and Italy have significant holdings.

Over decades, billions of dollars have been invested in exploiting oil resources in West Africa, with the bulk of it going to Nigeria. Should Western oil interests now be threatened with closure or driven out of the region, Washington and London are hardly likely to stand idly by; the issue would then become strategic rather than economic. Indeed, the survival of societies, economies and even countries would be threatened, which is why events in Nigeria are being so closely monitored. Clearly, with ongoing intrareligious riots, factional killings and oil sabotage by tribal dissidents in the east, the region is clearly neither safe nor secure. Should Al-Qaeda succeed in destabilising it further, the entire infrastructure might collapse – and if that happens, there is no question that a military option to rectify matters might be mooted not only by Washington and London, but by other Western capitals as well – which raises the ultimate question: what would happen should Western forces invade Nigeria to protect their oil interests? It has already become a regular subject for discussion at military establishments like West Point, Sandhurst, *École Spéciale Militaire de Saint-Cyr* and others – and the question most often raised as a consequence is how would the rest of Africa react? Certainly, any Western invading force – for whatever reason it gives for taking action – would be regarded as a serious long-term military threat by the majority of African states. South Africa was extremely vocal in its criticism of NATO's role at dislodging Muammar Gadaffi – claiming it was an affront to African sensibilities – and then, since Nelson Mandela took over power from the whites (who were always pro-West), Pretoria has been demonstrably pro-Palestine, pro-Hamas and virulently anti-Israel.

In Nigeria itself – today preponderantly Muslim – the reaction would be immediate. Without question, a call would go out for the invading infidel to be repulsed – and while no match for the kind of sophistication that is likely to be fielded by a joint military operation launched by Britain and/or the United States, the West is currently experiencing the consequences of a similar kind of debilitating guerrilla war in Afghanistan.

The situation in Nigeria is likely to be no different and, in fact, it could be a lot worse. Immediately such an invasion takes place, Muslim leaders in Nigeria are likely to make a worldwide appeal to the international Islamic Brotherhood to fight the invading unbeliever. As in Iraq, Afghanistan,

Chechnya, Bosnia and elsewhere, volunteer fighters would come from all over – nor would they be restricted by geography, for the simple reason that Africa's frontiers are more porous than anywhere else on the globe. Worse, Nigeria is among the least developed of countries that provides the international community with its fuel. The entire oil-rich Delta Region is largely triple-tiered rainforest. Roads are reasonable, but few – as are bridges across thousands of rivers and streams in the south of the country, where most of the oil deposits are found.

I travelled this country extensively while living there and fighting any kind of guerrilla war in the tropical south would be problematical – nor would Nigeria's basic infrastructure be of much use to either side. Railroad facilities, for instance, are minimal – and while main roads are in good condition, the blowing of a single bridge across any one of the larger rivers could isolate an entire region until it was repaired (*if* it is ever repaired…).

There are other issues – and no less momentous. Disease is a perpetual issue (as we observed with Ebola further towards the west), which is one of the reasons why the colonial administrators of an earlier generation dubbed it 'White Man's Grave'. Even today, malaria is rife – and a range of tropical ailments like typhoid, yellow fever, hepatitis and the rest would make the place a medical nightmare. Marburg – a fast-mutating cousin of Ebola – is only one of several hemorrhagic viruses that might be encountered in Nigeria's tropical regions. Certainly, this would be a grim environment in which to fight a war, or as one commentator phrased it: 'It would be a bit like Burma during World War Two, only ten times worse.'

There would be additional (but vital) issues like protecting isolated drilling installations in West Africa's jungles, as well as their pipelines – all spread out onshore and offshore over an area half the size of Texas. Even without hostilities, Nigeria's oil lines are being regularly sabotaged by dissidents – and one can only ponder what it would be like in wartime.

In brief, this would almost certainly become a nightmare of a conflict for any military commander when it comes to tactical support and logistics. Historically, what is taking place in Syria, Iraq and Afghanistan today would be modest by comparison – and essentially, the implications of any such military action would be horrendous. The worst part is that if things continue to deteriorate in West Africa, this is exactly the scenario that might take place in the medium-term future.

Bibliography

A Selected List of Titles of Contemporary Interest:

Achebe, Chinua, *The Trouble with Nigeria* (London, 1983)
——, *There was a Country* (London, 2012)
——, *No Longer at Ease* (London, 2013)
Achuzia, Joseph, *Requiem Biafra* (Enugu, Nigeria, 1986)
Adebayo, Major-General Robert, *Onward Soldier Marches On* (Ibadan, 1998)
Adewusi, Richie, Biafra: *Lest We Forget* (Bloomington, Indiana, 2011)
Adichie, Chimamanda, *Half of a Yellow Sun* (London, 2007)
——, *Purple Hibiscus* (London, 2005)
Alabi-Isama, Godwin, *The Tragedy of Victory: On-the-spot Account of the Nigeria-Biafra War in the Atlantic Theatre* (Ibadan, Nigeria, 2013)
Aneke, Luke Nnaemeka, *The Untold Story of the Nigeria-Biafra War* (London, 2008)
Armand, Captain, *Biafra vaincra* (Paris, 1969)
Baxter, Peter, *Biafra: The Nigerian Civil War 1967-1970* (London, 2014)
Birch, Geoffrey and Dominic St George; *Biafra: The Case for Independence* (London, 1968)
Black, Maggie, *A Cause for our Time: Oxfam – The First Fifty Years* (Oxford, 1992)
Boutet, Remy, *L'effroyable guerre du Biafra* (Paris, 2004)
Cagnoni, Romano; *Romano Cagnoni: Il mondo a fuoco* – Italian Ed. (Rome, 2000)
Cervenka, Z., *The Nigerian Civil War* (Frankfurt, 1971)
Clergerie, Jean-Louis, *La crise du Biafra* (Paris, 1985)
Collis, Robert, *Nigeria in Conflict* (London, 1970)
Cronje, Suzanne, *The World and Nigeria* (London, 1972)
Crowder, Michael, *The Story of Nigeria* (London, 1978)
Draper, Michael and Forsyth, Frederick, *Shadows: Airlift and Airwar in Biafra and Nigeria 1967-1970* (Crowborough, Sussex, 1999)
Ebba, Obi, *Broken Back Axle: Unspeakable Events in Biafra* (Bloomington, Indiana, 2010)
Effiong, Philip, *Nigeria and Biafra: My Story* (New York, 2011)
——, *The Caged Bird Sang no More* (Solihull, 2015)
Egbujor, Virginia, *As the Sky Darkened: The Untold Story of Biafra the Homeland* (Bloomington, Indiana, 2014)
Ekwe-Ekwe, Herbert, *Biafra Revisited* (London, 2006)
Elaigwu, J. Isawa, *Gowon: The Biography of a Soldier Statesman* (Ibadan, Nigeria, 1986)
Els, Paul, *We Fear Naught But God* (Pretoria, 2015)
Emefiena, Ezeani, *In Biafra Africa Died* (London, 2012)
Erner, Guillaume, *La société des victimes* (Paris, 2006)
Fage, John, *A History of Africa* (London, 2002)
Falola, Toyin, *A History of Nigeria* (Cambridge, 2008)
Forsyth, Frederick, The *Biafra Story* (London, 1969)
——, *Biafra: The Making of an African Legend* (London, 1983)

―――, *The Outsider: My Life in Intrigue* (London, 2015)
Forsyth, Frederick and Byrne, Tony, *Airlift to Biafra: Breaching the Blockade* (New York, 1997)
Gbulie, Ben, *Nigeria's Five Majors: Coup d'état of 1966* (Onitsha, Nigeria, 1981)
―――, *The Fall of Nigeria* (Enugu, Nigeria, 1989)
Gilles Caron, Bonneville, F., *La mort au biafra !* (Paris, 1967)
Gould, Michael, *The Biafran War: The Struggle for Modern Nigeria* (London, 2012)
Graham-Douglas, Nabo, *Ojukwu's Rebellion and World Opinion* (London, 1970)
Herskovits Jean, *Nigeria: Power and Democracy in Africa* (New York, 1982)
Hunt, Sir David, *Memoirs Military and Diplomatic* (London, 1990)
Ike, Chukwuemeka, *Sunset at Dawn* (Ibadan, Nigeria, 1976)
Ikpe, Samuel, *Red Belt: Biafra Rising* (London, 2013)
Imoh, Chima, *Biafra: Conflicts, Principles, and Death of the General* (Houston, Texas, 2012)
Kirk-Greene, Anthony, *Crisis and Conflict in Nigeria* (Oxford, 1975)
Koren, David L., *Far Away in the Sky: A Memoir of the Biafran Airlift* (US, 2012)
Kwarteng, Kwasi, *Ghosts of Empire: Britain's Legacies in the Modern World* (London, 2012)
Lewis Stephen, *Journey to Biafra* (Ontario, Canada, 1968)
McCullin, Don, *Unreasonable Behaviour: An Autobiography* (London, 1990)
―――, *Don McCullin* (Photo portfolio) (London, 2003)
Meredith, Martin, *The State of Africa: A History of Fifty Years of Independence* (London, 2005)
Mezu, Dr Sebastian Okechukwu, *Nigeria Ojukwu Azikiwe Beyond the Rising Sun* (Baltimore, Maryland, 2012)
Nicholson, Mike, *A Measure of Danger: The Memoirs of Legendary War Correspondent Michael Nicholson* (Long Beach, California, 2014)
Niven, Rex, *The War of Nigerian Unity* (Ibadan, Nigeria, 1970)
Nkwocha, Dr Onyema, *The Republic of Biafra: Once Upon a Time – My Story of the Biafra-Nigerian Civil War* (Bloomington, Indiana, 2012)
Nwanko, Arthur Agwuncha, *Nigeria: The Challenge of Biafra* (London, 1972)
Nwanko, Arthur Agwuncha and Ifejika, Samuel, *The Making of a Nation* (London, 1969)
Obasanjo, Olusegun, *My Watch: Volumes 1, 2 and 3* (Lagos, Nigeria, 2013/2015)
Odu P.J., *The Future that Vanished: A Biafra Story* (Bloomington, Indiana, 2009)
Ogunsheye, F. Adetowun, *A Break in the Silence: Lt. Col. Adebukunola Victor Banjo* (Ibadan, Nigeria, 2001)
Okeke, Godfrey, *The Biafra-Nigeria War – A Human Tragedy* (Self-published, 1968)
Okotcha, E., *Blood on the Niger – The Untold Story of the Nigerian Civil War* (Port Harcourt, Nigeria, 1994)
Okpe, Captain August, *The Last Flight: A Pilot Remembers the Air Force and the Biafran Air Attacks* (Nigeria, 2011)
Ojukwu, C. Odumegwu, *Biafra: Random Thoughts of C. Odumegwu Ojukwu* (New York, 1969)
Oyeweso, Siyan, *Perspectives on the Nigerian Civil War* (Lagos, Nigeria, 1982)
Packenham, Thomas, *The Scramble for Africa* (London, 1991)
Saro-Wiwa, Kenneth, *On Darkling Plain; An Account of the Nigerian Civil War* (Port Harcourt, Nigeria, 1989)
Schwarz, Walter, *Nigeria* (London, 1968)
Schittly, Louis, *L'homme qui voulait voir la guerre de près: Médecin au Biafra, Vietnam, Afghanistan, Sud-Soudan* (Paris, 2011)
Sherman, John, *War Stories: A Memoir of Nigeria and Biafra* (Indianapolis, Indiana, 2012)
Sidos, François-Xavier, *Les soldats libres : La grande aventure des mercenaires* (Paris, 2008)
Siollun, Max, *Soldiers of Fortune: A History of Nigeria* (Abuja, Nigeria, 2013)

Soyinka, Wole, *The Man Died: Prison Notes of Wole Soyinka* (London, 1994)
———, *Ake: The Years of Childhood* (London, 2000)
———, *You must Set Forth at Dawn* (London, 2015)
St Jorre, John de, *The Brothers' War: Biafra and Nigeria* (New York, 1973)
Steiner, Rolf and Cox, S., *Last Adventurer: From Biafra to the Sudan* (Littlehampton, 1978)
Stremlau, John, *The International Politics of the Nigerian Civil War* (Princeton, New Jersey, 1977)
Ugochukwu, Françoise, *Biafra, la déchirure : Sur les traces de la guerre civile niégériane de 1967-1970*
Umweni, Samuel, *888 Days in Biafra* (Lincoln, Nebraska, 2007)
Uwechuwe, Raph, *Reflections on the Nigerian Civil War: Facing the Future* (London, 2006)
Uzokwe, Alfred, *Surviving in Biafra: The Story of the Nigerian Civil War* ((Lincoln, Nebraska, 2003)
Venter Al J., *Africa at War* (Old Greenwich, Connecticut, 1974)
———, *Africa Today* (Johannesburg, 1975)
———, *Iran's Nuclear Option* (US, 2005)
———, *War Dog: Fighting Other People's Wars* (US and UK, 2006)
———, *Barrel of a Gun: Misspent Moments in Combat* (US and UK, 2010)
———, *War Stories by Al Venter and Friends* (Pretoria, 2011)
———, *African Stories by Al Venter and Friends* (Pretoria, 2013)
———, *Mercenaries: Putting the World to Rights with Hired Guns* (US and UK, 2014)
Waugh, Auberon and Cronje, Suzanne, *Biafra: Britain's Shame* (London, 1969)
Whiteman, Kaye, *A Last Look at Biafra* (London, 1970)

Index

Aba 105, 134, 188, 191, 199, 215, 217, 277-278, 280-281
Abakaliki 84, 206, 280
Abidjan 166, 247, 249
Atofarati, Major Abubakar A. xvi, 204, 210, 211
Achuzia, Colonel J.O. 'Hannibal' 104 105, 306
Addis Ababa 45, 102, 192, 279
Adekunle, Colonel Benjamin 54, 80, 98, 104-105, 188-189, 274-275, 278-280
Aero L-29 Delfin 38, 124, 126, 128, 139, 147
Afghanistan 38, 100, 102, 252, 292, 304-305
Aguiyi-Ironsi, Major General Johnson 23, 31, 33, 48, 67, 174-177, 205
Air Bridge xii, 134, 137, 195, 236, 255
Air Rhodesia 159, 164, 172
Air Trans Africa (ATA) 149, 172, 236-237
Algeria 94, 103, 137, 139, 217, 220-221, 256, 286, 289, 294
Al-Qaeda xiii, 99, 224, 286, 292-293, 302, 304
   AQIM xiii, 224, 286-287, 293
Angola xiii, 58, 73, 224, 226-227, 247, 290-291
Annabelle 57-58, 134, 167, 169
Anti-aircraft xvii, 58, 60, 66, 94, 101, 130, 140, 153-154, 164, 167, 199, 234, 251-252, 256, 259-260, 264
Anusiem, Silas xv, 34-35, 37
Apapa viii, 25-26, 28-32, 34-35, 55
Atlantic Ocean 193, 206, 288, 294, 296, 306
Australia 66, 202, 245

Balewa, Sir Abubakar Tafawa ix, 20, 173
Banjo, Victor 51, 73, 274-275
BBC xvii, 29, 40-41, 70, 81, 102, 104, 145, 191-192, 212, 219, 260, 286, 292
Benin 19, 51, 72-73, 93, 126, 128-129, 140, 143, 155, 253, 256-258, 260, 265, 272, 274-275, 278
Biafra i, iii, vii-ix, xi, xiv-xvii, 23-24, 26, 34, 38, 40-42, 44, 47-48, 50-51, 53-54, 56-60, 65-72, 74-76, 80-83, 86-87, 89, 91-93, 95, 98-105, 107, 109-111, 113-115, 117, 119, 122-123, 126, 129, 131, 134-137, 139-140, 142, 145, 147-150, 153-156, 158-166, 169, 172, 178, 180, 183-187, 190-199, 201-203, 206-209, 211-221, 223-229, 231-234, 236-245, 247, 249, 255-257, 260, 263, 265-269, 272, 274-281, 283-285, 299, 301, 306
Biafran Air Force (BiAF) 135, 137, 139, 155-157, 184, 207, 214, 254, 256-257, 263, 268, 271-272
Biafran Army 41-42, 51, 63, 70, 72, 83, 98, 101, 113, 169, 202, 207-209, 214, 250, 252, 263, 268, 274-276, 281
Biafran Headquarters 78-80, 83, 97, 153, 193, 221, 229, 249, 263, 270
Biafran Special Forces 229-231
Bissau 150, 184, 239, 242-243, 247, 249, 251-252, 289
Boeing C-97 Globemaster 63, 75, 171
Boko Haram xii-xiii, 99, 101, 198, 224, 285-288, 290-291, 296, 299, 302-303
Bonny 154, 208-209
Border War xi, 223, 226
Breytenbach, Colonel Jan xiv, 91-92, 98, 212, 223-235, 274, 281
Britain viii, 22, 26-28, 34, 38, 40, 44, 52, 60, 66-67, 69-70, 99, 104, 139, 157-159, 163, 175, 179, 193, 201-202, 215, 225, 227, 236, 275, 283, 300, 304
   British Army xvi, 24, 104, 119, 158, 193, 275
   British Government 41, 67, 178, 190, 197, 200, 205
   British High Commission ix, 29, 52, 73, 99, 177, 192, 275
   British Intelligence 46, 120, 159, 197
   British Special Air Service (SAS) 139, 160, 224-225, 235
Brown, Bill 237, 240, 243
Bruce, Willy 135, 142-143, 145, 150, 254, 258, 260
Burkina Faso xiii, 286, 289, 291

Cagnoni, Romano xv, 106-108, 194
Calabar 19, 24, 40, 74, 136, 140-142, 167, 207, 209, 237, 256, 278, 302
Cameroon xiii, 19, 38, 40, 55, 74, 139, 174, 233, 240, 256, 286, 291, 296, 298
Camp II 145, 260, 262-263
Canada 66, 166, 307
Cape Town ix, 34, 56, 119, 128, 140, 192, 227, 294
Caritas xii, 48, 75, 137, 190, 198, 235, 279

Catholic Church 45, 48, 63, 75, 94, 166, 192, 198, 201, 203, 245, 279
Central African Republic xiii, 288, 290, 292
CG 142-145, 258-261, 263, 265, 267-269
Chad xiii, 66, 215, 224, 274, 286, 288-290, 296-299
Chechnya 38, 292, 305
China 91, 287, 291
Christianity vii, xii-xiii, xvi, 19, 21, 23, 33, 42, 44, 93, 173-174, 186, 196, 201, 285-286, 288-292, 294, 296-300, 303
Central Intelligence Agency (CIA) 54, 66, 160, 162, 180, 183, 218, 236
Claymore mines xi, xiii, 66, 84
Cold War 69, 124, 159, 294
Commonwealth 22, 70, 89, 191, 201, 227, 279
Congo xiv, xvi, 32, 44, 54, 64, 66, 78, 85, 88-89, 91-92, 118-120, 124, 128, 147, 159-160, 174, 212-214, 219-220, 224, 233, 248, 255, 278, 289-292
Cotonou 137-138, 186
Coups viii-ix, 21, 23-27, 29, 31, 33, 35, 40, 42, 67, 155, 173-174, 178-179, 185, 192, 204-206, 224, 304, 307
Cross River 275, 280, 300

Dahomey 137, 160, 174, 186
Daily Express 54, 63, 65, 71, 191
Dakar 150, 288-289
Douglas A-26 Invader 147-148, 150, 153-155
Douglas B-26 Invader 88, 137, 139-141, 147-149, 153-155, 157, 207, 214, 247, 271
Douglas Dakota C-47/DC-3 xii, 60, 62, 128-129, 136, 140-141, 153-154, 158-159, 164, 170, 236, 244, 256
Douglas DC-4 132, 158, 169, 171-172, 237, 246
Douglas DC-6 xv, 116, 138
Douglas DC-7 74, 138, 164, 169, 235, 246
Douglas DC-8 158, 160, 172
de Gaulle, President Charles 87, 91, 163, 187, 212, 217, 220, 228, 279-280
de Havilland Dove 137, 153-154
Denard, Bob 55, 139, 160, 212, 217, 219, 223-225, 281
Dogs of War, The 87, 197, 212, 218
Douala 55-57

Effiong, Philip xv-xvi, 78-80, 97, 105, 193, 209, 283-284
Egypt 53, 139, 225, 256, 289, 294, 296
  Egyptian Air Force 66, 93, 123, 134, 145, 266, 272

Egyptian pilots 39, 54, 66, 89, 93-94, 124, 126, 131, 134, 191, 199, 256
Els, Paul xiv, 91, 228, 231, 234-235
Enugu 24, 42-43, 49, 96, 105, 128, 139-140, 147, 149-150, 153-155, 175, 199, 205-209, 215, 221, 253, 256, 260, 262, 272, 280, 283
Equatorial Guinea xiii, 38, 66, 291
Erasmus, Johnny 276-278
Escravos 208-209, 256, 273
Ethiopia 107, 225, 253, 279, 290, 292
Ezeilo, General Godwin 153, 249, 253

Famine xvii, 117, 166, 194-195, 229
Faulques, Roger 87, 92, 220
Fernando Pó xii, 66, 74, 137, 166, 186
Ferret armoured car 199-200, 208, 272
Foccart, Jacques 91-92, 223-224, 228
Fokker F-27 153, 155, 236
Forsyth, Frederick viii, xii, xiv-xv, xvii, 23, 40-46, 49, 51, 58-59, 62, 66-70, 73-74, 81, 87-90, 92-94, 96, 102, 104-106, 134, 191-195, 197, 209, 212-213, 217-219, 221, 223, 225, 274-277
France 38, 44, 52, 91, 102, 115, 134, 148, 157, 163-164, 207-208, 220, 225, 228, 279, 286, 293, 296-297, 300, 304
  French Foreign Legion 66, 87, 94, 215, 218, 220-221, 297
  French Government 115, 161, 228
  French Secret Service 160, 162, 224, 226, 232
Freetown ix, 100-101, 116-117, 180, 190
Fulani 20, 24, 68, 81, 90, 188, 196, 291

Gabon xii, 53-57, 63, 65, 71, 93, 106-107, 136, 148, 162-164, 169, 187, 190, 212, 228-229, 234, 237, 254, 279, 291
Gadaffi, Muammar 290, 302, 304
Gay, Alec 88, 218-219
Geneva 50, 63, 107, 114, 116, 197, 279, 283
Genocide 70, 161, 185-186, 195, 198, 201, 281, 283
'Genocide' (Nigerian Airforce bomber/pilot) 61-62, 136
Ghana 54-55, 64, 89, 174, 204, 279, 288, 291
Gibson, John 158-159, 171
Gibson, Mike xv, 158-161, 164-165, 167, 169, 172, 236
Goossens, Marc 88, 224, 281
Gould, Michael 41, 45-46, 90, 105, 275
Gowon, Colonel Yakubu vii, 33, 42, 45, 70, 72-73, 86, 89-90, 99, 106, 173-179, 185, 206, 280, 284-285

INDEX

Haglund, Gunnar xv, 135, 140-145, 255-265, 267-268
Hausa 20, 24, 26, 37, 68-70, 81, 90, 177, 188, 196, 201, 256, 291, 294, 298, 300
Hellström, Leif xv, 61, 84-85, 219, 248, 255, 276
'Herman the German' 60-61, 63
Herz, Friedrich 'Freddy' 139-142, 153, 155, 256
Hoare, Colonel Mike 66, 119, 219, 233
Holland 91, 157, 237, 279
Holt Shipping Services, John viii-ix, xv, 22, 25, 32, 34, 40, 52, 54, 139
Hunt, Sir David 42, 45-46, 90

Ibadan 44, 176-177, 205
Ibibio 49, 109, 291
Ibo/Igbo viii-ix, xv, 20-21, 23-24, 26, 30-31, 33-34, 38, 40, 42-46, 48-49, 51, 63, 66-70, 72, 75, 78, 81, 86, 92, 101-102, 104, 136-137, 173-174, 177-178, 185-186, 194, 196, 201, 222, 253-254, 274, 281, 283, 285, 291, 300
Ihiala 58, 105-106, 167, 239-240, 243
Ikeja viii, 26, 29, 32, 42, 52, 67, 74, 133, 179
Ikeja Airport viii, 21, 24-25, 27, 38-39, 42, 54, 123, 133, 175, 179, 205
Ikot-Ekpene 48, 96, 276, 280
Ilyushin IL-28 bomber 62, 89, 93, 124, 131, 134, 136, 139, 145, 147, 191, 252, 256, 260, 263, 266, 272
Imo River 69, 88, 105, 215, 250, 277
Indian Ocean 160, 288-289, 292
Indochina 87, 94, 220
'Intruder' aircraft 60, 62, 128, 136-137
Iran 218, 289-290, 292, 303-304
Iraq 38, 102, 287, 292, 304-305
Islam viii, xii-xiii, 19-21, 27, 39, 44, 51, 67, 95, 102-103, 173, 196, 286-294, 296-301, 303-304
Israel 102, 134, 279, 291, 304
Ivory Coast xiii, 53-54, 162, 187, 197, 209, 237, 249, 279, 283, 285, 288, 290-292, 296, 300

Jihad 19, 285-286, 300, 302
Johannesburg 29, 38, 52, 56, 161-162, 192, 238, 304
Johnson, Colonel Jim 160, 224, 227
Joint Church Aid 63, 66, 75, 83, 89, 138, 172, 279
Jordan 102, 225, 289
Jos 40, 298, 304

Kadidal, Akhil xiv, 172, 174
Kaduna 24, 106, 128, 155, 205-206, 257, 299
Kano 21, 24, 27, 40, 49, 67, 125-126, 128, 153, 155, 205, 253, 294, 298-300

Katanga 44, 78, 119, 157, 160, 214, 220
Kennedy, John F. 177, 180, 218
Kenya xiii, 56, 81, 288, 292
Khartoum 103, 216, 288, 297
Kilometre Onze xii, 63, 106, 190
Klootwyk, Ares xiv, 53, 56, 85, 118-129, 131-133, 140, 143, 194, 215, 219-220, 251, 256-257
Koran xiii, 286, 292, 295, 298
Korea 104, 137, 159, 218
Kouchner, Bernard 109, 114-117
Kwashiorkor 106, 179, 197

Lagos viii-ix, xv-xvi, 19, 22, 24-29, 31-32, 34-35, 38-40, 44-45, 49, 51-52, 54-55, 60, 62, 66-68, 70, 72-74, 77-78, 80, 87-88, 90, 96, 99, 104-105, 116, 120, 123-126, 128-9, 131-132, 139, 145, 153-155, 166, 173, 175, 177-179, 184, 187-189, 191-192, 197, 200-201, 205-206, 208-209, 223, 242, 247, 249, 252-253, 260, 274-275, 277-278, 280-281, 284, 299-300, 302
  Lagos Airport 120, 122, 127, 179
  Lagos Garrison Organisation (LGO) 175, 205, 208
  Lagos Government 26, 38, 83, 136, 198, 242
  Lagos Harbour 30, 34, 92
Lang, Martin 142, 144-145, 258-263, 265, 267-269
Liberia 103, 279, 291, 301
Libreville xii, xiv, 54-56, 60, 66, 71, 88, 91, 107, 135, 137, 161-166, 169, 190, 212, 224, 226, 228-229, 231-235, 254
Lisbon 54, 136, 147, 149-150, 166, 199, 202-203, 236-237, 239-245, 247
Lockheed Constellation/Super Constellation 60, 116, 138, 162, 164, 166-167, 169-170, 172, 231, 234-237, 240, 242-243, 245
London viii, xv, xvii, 19, 22, 33-34, 41, 45-46, 52, 65-67, 69-71, 74, 81, 83-84, 90, 99, 106, 120, 133, 158-159, 173, 192, 198, 225, 233, 275, 279, 288, 294, 304
Loots, General Fritz 91, 228, 232-235
Luanda 164, 171, 226-227, 232
Lykes Lines 30-32

Makurdi 123-124, 128-129, 153
Malaria xii, 19, 134, 193, 305
Mali xiii, 286, 290, 293, 297-299, 303
Malloch, Jack 91, 159-161, 164, 166, 169, 171-172, 222, 232, 235-237, 243, 245
Mark Press of Geneva 63, 107, 197, 203, 279, 283
Martin B-57 Canberra 136, 261-262
McCullin, Don xv, 106, 194, 20

Médecins Sans Frontières (MSF) vii, 109-111, 113, 115, 117
Mercenaries ii, vii, x, xiv, xvi, 32, 38, 44, 54, 56-57, 59, 61-62, 64, 66, 74, 85, 87, 89, 92-94, 100, 116, 118-119, 123-125, 127-131, 136, 139, 143-144, 147, 155, 157, 160, 163, 166-167, 180, 183, 191, 193, 197-198, 203, 212-215, 217-219, 220-221, 223-225, 236, 240, 247-248, 252, 255-257, 265, 274, 276, 281
MFI-9B Minicon xv, 47, 64-66, 73, 75, 93, 118, 130-132, 135-137, 146, 148, 154, 156, 184, 207, 252-253, 255, 257, 260-262, 265, 267-268, 270, 272
Middle East 102, 157, 172, 287, 292, 303
MiG aircraft x, xiv, 39, 47, 53-54, 59, 74, 78, 85, 89, 93, 106, 109, 118-120, 125-126, 128-132, 136-137, 139-140, 143, 145, 147, 155, 193, 199, 215, 219, 251-253, 256-257, 259, 261-265, 268, 276, 279
Mines 34, 40, 66, 84, 158, 200, 207, 277, 289
Mitchell, Alex 202-203, 247
Moscow xvii, 53, 125, 128, 180, 252, 266
Mozambique 53, 160, 183, 288
Muhammed, Murtala viii, 25, 90, 179
Muslim vii, xii-xiii, xvi, 21, 33, 42, 44, 49, 67, 173, 194, 215, 285-286, 288-290, 292-294, 296-300, 303-304

Nairobi 54, 65, 74, 102, 108, 192
Nasser, Gamel Abdel 134, 139, 224-225
NATO 38, 111, 118, 229, 304
NDB 167-168, 171
New York 38, 57, 123, 217
New York Times 180, 197, 294
New Zealand 138, 158-159
Niger xiii, 24, 35, 64-65, 69-70, 72, 86, 91, 95, 140, 155, 164, 174, 188, 229, 233, 239, 252, 269-272, 274, 279, 286, 288, 296, 298-299, 301
  Niger Delta 65, 91, 95, 164, 233, 252
  Niger Republic xiii, 174, 286, 296
  Niger River 35, 69-70, 72, 95, 140, 155, 188, 229, 239, 269, 301
Nigeria i, iii, vii-ix, xii-xvi, 19-20, 22-27, 29-30, 32-36, 38, 40-42, 44-46, 48-49, 51-52, 54-55, 58, 60, 66-70, 72-73, 78, 87, 89, 91, 98-100, 102, 104, 106, 114, 116, 118, 120, 122, 124, 128-129, 133-134, 136, 139, 144, 147, 153-155, 161, 163-164, 166-167, 173-175, 177-180, 182-187, 189, 191, 193-199, 201, 204-211, 213, 218-220, 225, 239-240, 243, 249, 253-257, 264, 275-276, 278-281, 283-287, 289, 291, 293-294, 296-306

Eastern Nigeria 24, 44, 60, 68, 78, 91, 98, 134, 185, 196-197, 205-207, 209, 218, 225
Eastern Region 21, 23-24, 35, 38, 40, 42-44, 48, 68, 70, 78, 86, 98, 105, 206-207, 279, 281
Middle Belt 33, 42, 174-175
Mid-Western State 51, 67, 72, 96, 140, 178, 188, 205-206, 208, 265, 274
Northern Nigeria viii-ix, 69, 173, 186, 198, 205, 253, 256, 286-287, 293, 297
Northern Region 20, 27, 51, 106
Southern Nigeria 114, 204, 249, 289
Western Nigeria 20, 70, 72, 197, 205-206, 275
Nigerian Air Force (NAF) xii, xiv, xvii, 38-39, 47, 52-53, 56, 59, 61, 85, 93, 100, 107, 119, 122-123, 125-126, 128-130, 133, 136, 139, 141, 143, 147, 155-156, 167, 170, 184, 191, 195, 205-207, 215, 236, 242, 251-253, 255-256, 258, 263, 269, 271, 273, 300
Nigerian Airways 139, 155, 256
Nigerian Army (Federal Army) 19, 23, 25, 29, 37, 42-43, 51, 54, 58, 60, 67-69, 72, 74, 80-81, 85, 89, 92, 96-99, 101, 103-104, 136, 139, 142, 153, 161-162, 186-187, 189, 193, 195, 197, 204-208, 210, 215, 226, 229-231, 254, 274-278, 280-281, 283-284, 287, 290, 300-301
  1st Division 99, 187, 208-209, 281
  2nd Division 187-188, 208, 280
  3rd Marine Commando Division 54, 167, 187 188, 208 209, 274 275, 278 281
  16th Brigade 188-189, 278-279
  Nigerian Army Headquarters 67, 155, 174, 188-189, 206, 281
Nigerian Civil War xvi, 64, 66, 74, 96, 103, 134, 149, 167, 174, 192, 204, 228, 272, 278, 282, 306
Nigerian Federation 19-21, 23-24, 43, 48, 51, 68, 95, 174, 178, 185, 201, 204, 206, 236
Nigerian Government viii, 62, 64-65, 74, 90, 115-116, 119, 139, 163, 205, 232, 285, 300
  Federal Government 20, 42, 53-54, 65, 104, 179, 196-197, 206, 208, 283
  Federal Military Government 46, 184-185
  Nigerian High Command 60, 188, 206
Nigerian Navy 29, 32, 34, 142, 153, 155, 175, 206-209, 237, 276, 303
Norgren, Rune 268-273
North American B-25 Mitchell 139-141, 155, 207, 247
North American Harvard T-6 xiv, 118, 130, 132-133, 136-137, 180, 184, 247-249, 251-252, 254
Nsukka 196, 206, 208
Nussey, Wilf 29, 36, 52
Nwakanma, Obi xvi, 46, 49

INDEX

Obasanjo, Colonel Olusegun 188-189, 209, 283
Obigwe 267-269
Ogbunigwe 84-85, 277-278
Oil industry xiii, 20-21, 23-24, 26, 38, 43-44, 55, 64-65, 69, 72, 81, 83, 90, 148, 153-154, 161, 163-164, 174, 179-180, 184, 187, 193, 201, 207, 229, 252, 271, 273, 285, 291, 300-305
Ojukwu, Colonel Odumegwu "Emeka" xi-xiii, xvi, 23-24, 40, 42-46, 48-51, 54, 62, 66-70, 72-76, 78-79, 81-82, 84-85, 87-91, 94-95, 97-98, 101, 105-107, 134, 147, 150, 153-154, 156, 163, 175-177, 180, 185, 189-190, 192-193, 197-198, 200-202, 208-210, 213, 219, 221-223, 225, 229-231, 234, 242, 245, 253, 270, 274-276, 278, 281, 283, 285, 299-300
Ojukwu, Sir Louis 45-46, 48-51, 67
'Ojukwu Buckets' xi, xiii, 66, 84-85
Okeke, Kenechukwu xvi, 247, 249
Okpe, August 135, 142-143, 145, 155, 258, 260-262, 265, 267-273
Omoigui, Noma 278-281
Onishi, Norimitsu 294, 296, 298
Onitsha 19, 24, 34-35, 43, 49, 70, 72, 86, 96, 134, 140, 154, 215, 239, 252, 259, 261, 263, 268, 270-272, 280
Opobo 48, 125, 276
Organisation of African Unity (OAU) 45, 96, 179, 187, 192, 279, 294
Owerri x, 35, 58, 76-78, 80, 96, 98, 106-109, 111, 145, 167, 188-189, 250, 252, 263, 267-269, 274, 276, 278-281
Oxfam xvii, 89, 200
Oxford 43-45, 49-51, 106

Pakistan 102, 117, 289, 301
Palestine 225, 292, 304
Pan American Airways 38, 52, 123
Paris 39-40, 44, 57, 87, 91-92, 94, 115, 149, 160-161, 164, 172, 212, 217-218, 224, 228-230, 232-234, 296, 306-307
Peace Corps xvi, 28, 36, 40
Peace talks 58, 183-184, 218, 279
Pereira, Artur Alves 136, 247, 249, 251-254
Peters, Colonel John 119-120, 219, 224
Pignattely, José 249, 251-252
Port Harcourt 19, 24, 27, 35, 37, 43, 49, 58, 60, 69, 74, 87-88, 91, 93, 95, 122-123, 128, 132-133, 137, 140-144, 147, 153-154, 156, 167, 184, 198, 200-201, 209, 217, 229, 239-240, 245, 247, 251-253, 256, 272, 276-278, 280
Portugal 54, 91, 136, 166, 207, 227, 236-237, 240, 245, 252, 279

Portuguese Air Force 136, 150, 247, 249
Portuguese Guinea 184, 239-240, 289
Potgieter, Yogi 223, 233-234
Pretoria 74, 91-92, 223, 225-228, 231-232, 234-235, 304
Prisoners of War 80, 95, 103, 157, 180, 195
Propaganda 62, 70, 78, 101, 103, 179, 192, 195, 197, 199, 201, 206-207, 280, 282-283

Ramrakha, Priya 74, 82, 102, 192
Red Cross (ICRC) xvi, 54, 59, 74-75, 78, 83, 109, 114-117, 137-138, 161, 166, 186, 195, 199, 201, 221, 242, 244, 263, 268
Red Sea 102, 224, 296
Reuters 29, 40, 287
Revolutionary United Front 100, 180, 291
Rhodesia 44, 66, 69, 91, 158-161, 164, 172, 183, 222, 227, 236-237, 240, 243, 276, 279
  Rhodesian Air Force 159, 164, 171, 236
  Rhodesian Special Air Service (SAS) 160, 183, 227
Robson, Michael xiv, 147, 268
von Rosen, Count Gustav 75, 93, 118, 135-137, 143, 145-146, 156, 253, 257, 259-260, 262-263, 268-270
Royal Air Force (RAF) x, xiv, 40, 66, 118-119, 124, 126, 132, 143, 148, 157-159, 163, 250-251, 257
Royal Navy 123, 153, 227
Revolutionary United Front (RUF) 100-101, 180

Sahara xiii, 66, 298
Sahel xiii, 296, 303
Saladin armoured car 199-200, 208, 272, 278
Salisbury 158-159, 161, 163-164, 171
Sandhurst 23, 26, 78, 89, 105, 174, 304
Sankoh, Foday 100, 180, 190
São Tomé xii, 54, 60, 63, 66, 74-75, 89, 115, 137-138, 143, 166, 186, 190, 198, 239-241, 244, 253
Saudi 160, 224, 292, 296, 303
SDECE 232-234
Senegal 150, 288-289, 294, 298
Shi'ite 289, 293, 303
Shuwa, Colonel Muhammed 187-189
Sierra Leone ix, xvi, 97, 100-101, 103, 116, 174, 180, 183, 190, 204, 224, 290-292, 298, 300-301
Smith, Ian 44, 69, 159
Sokoto 27, 67, 293
Somalia 107, 135, 286, 288-290, 300
Sousa, Gil Pinto de 155, 247, 249, 254

South Africa ix, 19, 34, 52, 55, 66, 91-92, 158-159, 161, 172, 175, 217, 225-227, 231-232, 234-235, 237, 279, 288, 292, 296-297, 304
   South African Air Force 58, 100, 118
   South African Army 91, 223, 225, 227, 229, 290
   South African Defence Force (SADF) 91, 223, 225, 227, 233
   South African Military Intelligence 228, 234-235
   South African Reconnaissance Regiment 91, 225, 235
   South African Special Forces 66, 212, 227, 231
South America 140, 172, 293
South East Asia 69, 118, 193-194
Soviet Union/Russia 38, 52, 104, 193, 279, 281
Spain 91, 207, 220, 236, 279, 281
St Jorre, John de xv, 58, 191, 202, 221
Starvation ix, xii, 50, 57-58, 62-63, 65, 70, 77, 85, 99, 106-107, 109, 116, 133, 137, 161, 165-166, 180, 185, 190, 195, 197-198, 201-202, 229, 231, 247, 255, 276, 283-284
State House viii, 42, 78, 105, 221
Steiner, Rolf 55, 88, 93-95, 163, 215-216, 219-222, 276, 278, 281
Sudan xiii, 93, 103, 139, 159, 216, 219, 221, 288-289, 291, 298
Suez xiii, 220, 225, 227
Sunday Times 81, 106, 202-203
Sweden 146, 200, 255, 268
Switzerland 53, 76, 134, 137, 153
Syria 102, 194, 287, 289, 292, 305

Tanzania 53-54, 160, 187, 279, 288, 292
Times, The 83, 180, 191-192
Time magazine 80, 162, 191, 213, 218
Titania 55-56, 64-65, 73
Tshombe, Moïse 78, 160, 220-221
Typhoid 193, 212, 234, 305

Uga 128, 166-167, 169-171, 209, 244, 249, 252, 262
Uganda 58, 89, 179, 219, 288, 290, 292-293
Uli xii, xiv, xvii, 56-62, 77, 79, 81, 83-86, 105-106, 128-129, 134, 137-139, 164, 166-167, 169, 171, 184, 193, 203, 209, 216, 229, 231, 234-235, 238, 244, 249, 253, 256-258, 263, 267, 282

Umuahia 76, 82, 94, 96, 98, 188, 199-200, 221, 277, 280-281
United Africa Company 49, 78, 155
United Nations 100, 174, 300
United States (US) xiii, 53, 69, 84, 132, 134, 137, 139, 147, 149, 159-161, 174-175, 180, 182, 186, 191-192, 194-195, 197, 204, 222, 237-238, 279, 286, 294, 296, 302-303, 304

Vanguard xvi, 46, 49, 284
Victoria Island 19, 27-28, 66
Vietnam 53, 102, 118, 131, 135, 180, 193

Warri 55, 64-65, 73, 75, 209, 271
Washington DC viii, xvi, 31, 69, 74, 148, 159, 173, 183, 289, 301, 303-304
Webb, Jimmy 126, 128, 132
West Africa xvi, 22, 26, 33, 38, 40, 45, 52, 54, 57, 64, 69, 79, 86, 94, 99, 105, 109, 120, 130, 134, 154, 161, 163, 166, 175, 183, 187, 190-191, 193-194, 204, 225, 228, 251, 286, 292, 294, 296-297, 300, 303-305
West Germany 139, 193, 221, 256, 279
Westminster 54, 198, 296
Wharton, Hank 74, 91, 198-199, 202, 236-240, 242-245
Whirlwind 124, 128-129
Whitehall 44, 69, 120, 159, 177, 190, 225, 275
Wicks, Alastair 119, 219, 224
Wilde, James 80, 162, 191
Williams, 'Taffy' 88-89, 213-215, 217-219, 276-278, 281
Wilson, Harold xii, xvii, 26, 161, 163, 186, 198, 201, 282
World War II xiv, 24, 47-48, 61, 101, 135-137, 147, 159, 174, 180, 184, 207-208, 215, 220, 224-225, 227, 236, 248, 250, 292
Wragg, Bill 159, 171-172

Yellow fever 56, 199, 305
Yemen 114, 139, 160, 224-225
Yoruba 20, 23, 34, 44, 70, 73, 81, 109, 174, 188, 274-275, 291, 298, 300

Zambia 53, 81, 160, 164, 183, 187, 279
Zaria 21, 174, 205
Zimbabwe 158-159, 172, 290
Zumbach, Jan 148-150, 153-157, 214, 250